写|作|论|坛

长三角研究生学术写作论坛优秀论文

主 编 肖福寿

副主编 毛建华 张建琴 张 颖

上海大学出版社

图书在版编目(CIP)数据

长三角研究生学术写作论坛优秀论文. 第一辑 / 肖福寿主编;毛建华,张建琴,张颖副主编. —上海:上海大学出版社,2022.11
ISBN 978-7-5671-4554-2

Ⅰ.①长… Ⅱ.①肖… ②毛… ③张… ④张… Ⅲ.①学术研究—写作—研究生—教学参考资料 Ⅳ.①H052

中国版本图书馆CIP数据核字(2022)第196741号

责任编辑　贾素慧
封面设计　缪炎栩
技术编辑　金　鑫　钱宇坤

长三角研究生学术写作论坛优秀论文　第一辑
肖福寿　主编
上海大学出版社出版发行
(上海市上大路99号　邮政编码200444)
(https://www.shupress.cn　发行热线021-66135112)
出版人　戴骏豪

＊

南京展望文化发展有限公司排版
江苏凤凰数码印务有限公司印刷　各地新华书店经销
开本710mm×1000mm　1/16　插页1　印张18.75　字数316千
2022年11月第1版　2022年11月第1次印刷
ISBN 978-7-5671-4554-2/H·407　定价　58.00元

版权所有　侵权必究
如发现本书有印装质量问题请与印刷厂质量科联系
联系电话: 025-57718474

2020年度长三角区域研究生写作能力培养论坛

2020年10月31日 · 上海大学

序

根据《教育部办公厅关于进一步规范和加强研究生培养管理的通知》(教研厅〔2019〕1号)要求,高等院校要"加强学术规范和学术道德教育,把论文写作指导课程作为必修课纳入研究生培养环节"。习近平总书记在上海考察中强调,必须完善长三角地区合作协调机制,加强合作专题,拓展合作内容,要树立"一体化"意识和"一盘棋"思想。在此背景下,为了加强研究生写作能力培养和促进长三角区域高等院校的交流、合作与创新,我们举办了2020年度长三角区域研究生写作能力培养论坛。

论坛由上海市教育委员会主办,上海大学承办,苏州大学、安徽大学、南京师范大学、东华大学、上海理工大学、浙江中医药大学、温州医科大学、中国知网协办,于2020年10月30日至11月1日在上海大学举行。中国科学技术协会原副主席冯长根、上海大学党委副书记欧阳华、上海大学研究生院副院长张之江、上海大学研究生院培养管理处处长毛建华和来自长三角区域20多所高校的10余名专家学者及200余名研究生参加了线上与线下论坛。

在论坛上,上海大学党委副书记欧阳华发表了热情洋溢的开幕词,中国科学技术协会冯长根就"研究生如何撰写学位论文"做了主旨报告,厦门大学胡兆云教授、上海大学牟成博教授、中国知网运行总监朱宁先生就"读写译三位一体论""科技英语写作的基本规范"及"基于知网研学的研究生培养质量提升方案"做了学术报告,南京师范大学王永祥教授、东华大学乔雪瑛教授、上海理工大学韩戈玲教授、苏州大学袁影教授分别就"语言学方向论文写作学术规范""经典文学研究空间""学术思维创新与论文写作"及"学术创新三部曲"主题作了主题报告,从不同角度对研究生写作能力培养加以阐发和探讨。

本论坛征集到了来自香港浸会大学、北京大学、南京大学等27所高校的46

篇研究生论文,其中包括语言学方面的论文,如《专名等于限定摹状词吗?》;文学方面的论文,如《论萨拉·沃特斯〈轻舔丝绒〉中的女性亚文化风格》;医学方面的论文,如《覆盆子总黄酮降尿酸及抗痛风性关节炎作用研究》。诸如此类,涉及众多学科。

细读这些莘莘学子的论文,不禁想起王国维先生在《人间词话》中提到的做学问、做人的三个境界。王国维曰:"古今之成大事业、大学问者,必经过三种之境界:'昨夜西风凋碧树,独上西楼,望尽天涯路',此第一境也。'衣带渐宽终不悔,为伊消得人憔悴',此第二境也。'众里寻他千百度,蓦然回首,那人却在,灯火阑珊处',此第三境也。"我以为,这些莘莘学子已经大致能够体悟出前两种境界。面对生活中"昨夜西风凋碧树"的烦躁,他们却向往着"独上西楼",希望尽早摆脱平庸,超脱于那些平凡生活的琐屑,使自己的人生树立起更高、更大的目标,进而能够"望尽天涯路"。不仅如此,他们似乎已经做到了"衣带渐宽终不悔",为了自己的人生目标,从脆弱迷茫中坚强、坚定起来,无怨无悔,更是做到了"为伊消得人憔悴",为了自己的人生目标而憔悴,不顾一切执着追求自己的人生目标。执着诚可贵,执着再执着更为可敬可佩。我坚信,通过他们的执着及执着之付出,应该能够在不远的将来悟出"众里寻他千百度,蓦然回首,那人却在,灯火阑珊处"的学术研究最高境界。

品读这些论文,也不禁想起英国散文家、哲学家培根说过的一句话:"Some books are to be tasted, others to be swallowed, and some few to be chewed and digested.",意思是说"一些书可以浅尝辄止;一些书可以狼吞虎咽;而有些书则需要细嚼慢咽,好好消化"。我以为,本论坛征集到的论文绝非是可以浅尝辄止或狼吞虎咽的,而是应该细嚼慢咽的,值得你我去好好消化。纵然论文可能存在这样或那样的问题,学子们孜孜不倦追求知识的精神却是令人鼓舞的,让我们看到了未来学者的风范。

从这些莘莘学子的论文中,本论坛的专家组经过严格评审,共评出了一等奖 10 名,二等奖 15 名,其中浙江中医药大学的史悦悦、上海大学的麻小晶、河南中医药大学的李鑫涛、南京大学的高仁刚、西安外国语大学的王星皓 5 位一等奖获得者登台发表了获奖感言。他们表示在本次论坛中学习到很多论文写作的新知识,希望在接下来的学术生涯中能再接再厉,不断提高自己的学术素养。

本辑收录的部分获奖论文均尊重作者原文,略有修改,且每篇都配之以点评,更有利于学习者参考,可资借鉴,可资鉴戒,"他山之石,可以攻玉"。面对这些获奖论文,难免让人跃跃欲试,欲先睹为快。用美国前总统里根的话来说,"If not us, who? And if not now, when?"(如果我们不做,更待何人?如果不是现在做,更待何时?)让我们现在就采取行动吧,踏上佳作共赏之旅,从中得到启发,得到鼓舞,得到灵感。

愿本论文集能成为您学术写作之路的好伙伴、好帮手。

肖福寿
上海大学教授、博士生导师
2021 年 10 月 30 日

目　录

序 ··· 肖福寿　1

上　编

解毒祛瘀滋阴方对 MRL/lpr 狼疮小鼠肾脏 CDK6 分子表达的影响 ············ 3
专名等于限定摹状词吗? ·· 14
College Students' Positive Psychology in English Learning ············ 23
脑梗死住院期患者中成药应用特征的真实世界研究 ························· 47
多模态隐转喻视角下的图文语篇分析
　　——以《经济学人》封面为例 ··· 56
覆盆子总黄酮降尿酸及抗痛风性关节炎作用研究 ···························· 67
社交媒体报道对女性医护人员印象的固化
　　——以《人民日报》与"央视新闻"微博为例 ························· 78
汉语道歉话语策略性别差异实证研究
　　——以工龄 10 年内的当代青年为例 ···································· 87
长三角一体化发展背景下基于长三角中心区的城市规模结构和经济
　　地理格局分析 ·· 107

下　编

中国服饰企业的供应链柔性研究
　　——以森马电商为例 ··· 125

浅析系统性红斑狼疮与巨噬细胞的联系 …………………………………… 138
学术创新三部曲：研典、追踪、交汇
　　——袁影教授访谈录 ………………………………………………… 147
品牌道歉声明中的权势与亲密关系构建
　　——基于级差系统视角的分析 ……………………………………… 157
俄罗斯电影《八次初遇》局部会话结构分析 ……………………………… 168
"战争与儿童"主题小说中"孩子"形象对比分析
　　——以《团的儿子》和《小兵张嘎》为例 ………………………… 177
The Effects of Word Exposure Frequency and Second Language Proficiency
　　on Second Language Incidental Vocabulary Learning in the High
　　Constraint Context ………………………………………………… 188
酒店网络关注热度时空特征及影响因素
　　——以西安市三星级以上酒店为例 ………………………………… 209
On the Application and Translation Strategies of Economic and Trade
　　Contract from the Perspective of Cooperative Principles ………… 221
《中国日报》和《纽约时报》态度资源运用对比研究
　　——以2020年意大利新冠肺炎疫情暴发后对政府行为的新闻
　　报道为例 …………………………………………………………… 243
问卷调查法在外语教育研究中的应用 ……………………………………… 253
论萨拉·沃特斯《轻舔丝绒》中的女性亚文化风格 …………………… 266
山本鼎的"自由画"美术教育运动及其儿童个性观 …………………… 279

上 编

解毒祛瘀滋阴方对 MRL/lpr 狼疮小鼠肾脏 CDK6 分子表达的影响

范雪敏　嵇丽娜　陈可玥　李荣群*

摘要：目的　研究解毒祛瘀滋阴方对 MRL/lpr 狼疮小鼠肾脏 CDK6 分子表达的影响,探讨解毒祛瘀滋阴方对 CDK6/NF－κB 炎症相关信号通路的影响,为临床用药提供理论支持。**方法**　30 只 SPF 级 6 周龄 MRL/lpr 雌性小鼠随机分为模型组、中药组和西药组,每组 10 只;10 只 SPF 级 6 周龄 MRL/Mp 雌性小鼠作为空白对照组。连续给药 10 周后,取小鼠肾脏,HE 染色观察小鼠肾脏组织病理学变化情况;ELISA 法检测血清中抗 ANA 抗体和抗 dsDNA 抗体的含量,尿液中白蛋白含量;Western blot 法检测肾脏 CDK6 和 NF－κB 蛋白表达水平;RT－PCR 法检测肾脏 CDK6 和 NF－κB mRNA 表达水平。**结果**　解毒祛瘀滋阴方能够有效缓解 MRL/lpr 狼疮小鼠肾脏病变,有效降低小鼠血清中抗 ANA 抗体和抗 dsDNA 抗体的含量,尿液白蛋白的含量;中药组肾脏 CDK6 和 NF－κB 蛋白和 mRNA 表达水平与模型组比较显著降低;西药组肾脏 CDK6 和 NF－κB 蛋白和 mRNA 表达水平与模型组比较显著较低。**结论**　解毒祛瘀滋阴方能够降低 MRL/lpr 狼疮小鼠肾脏中 CDK6 蛋白和 mRNA 的表达水平,提示解毒祛瘀滋阴方通过 CDK6 分子调控炎症反应可能是其治疗 SLE 的靶点之一。

关键词：系统性红斑狼疮;解毒祛瘀滋阴方;CDK6;NF－κB

系统性红斑狼疮(systemic lupus erythematosus，SLE)是一种全身性的自身

---

*　范雪敏,嵇丽娜,陈可玥:浙江中医药大学基础医学院 2018 级硕士研究生。
　　李荣群:医学博士,浙江中医药大学副教授,硕士生导师。

免疫性结缔组织病[1],其特征是自身免疫性抗原-抗体复合物沉积在组织中,包括皮肤、肾脏和大脑,随后诱发的炎症反应可导致无法修复的组织损伤[2-4]。全球 SLE 的发病率和死亡率存在明显差异[5],我国 SLE 患病率为 30.13～70.41/10 万,位居全世界种族发病率的第二[1]。

目前,SLE 的发病机制已被进行广泛研究,其中 B 细胞和 T 淋巴细胞异常、细胞凋亡失调、凋亡物质清除缺陷和表观遗传等因素被认为有助于 SLE 的发生和发展。已有研究指出 CDK6 分子的异常表达与 SLE 的炎症反应之间存在联系[6,7],这提示 CDK6 可能参与 SLE 的发生发展,但其机制还需进一步研究。

SLE 的临床治疗以皮质类固醇、免疫抑制剂等西药为主,这些药物短期治疗效果明显,但长期服用会带来严重的不良反应[8,9],如组织损伤、药物毒性等。解毒祛瘀滋阴方是全国名中医范永升教授治疗 SLE 的经验方[10],在临床治疗上已取得良好的治疗效果,同时可以缓解西药带来的不良反应,但其作用机制需要进一步研究。本研究探讨解毒祛瘀滋阴方给药干预 MRL/lpr 雌性狼疮小鼠后,其体内的 CDK6 分子水平以及炎症指标的变化,从而为解毒祛瘀滋阴方临床治疗 SLE 提供科学的理论依据。

1. 材料

1.1 动物

30 只雌性 MRL/lpr 小鼠,SPF 级,6 周龄,体重(25±2.5)g;10 只雌性 MRL/Mp 小鼠,SPF 级,6 周龄,体重(25±2.5)g,饲养于浙江中医药大学动物实验中心,实验动物生产许可证号:SCXK(沪)2013 - 0016,实验动物使用许可证号:SYXK(浙)2013 - 0184。

1.2 药物制备

解毒祛瘀滋阴方药物组成:生地黄 15 g、炙鳖甲 12 g、青蒿 12 g、白花蛇舌草 15 g、积雪草 15 g、赤芍 12 g、丹皮 12 g、佛手 9 g、升麻 9 g、生甘草 6 g,由浙江中医药大学中药饮片厂提供。上述 10 味中药加入单蒸水 800 mL 浸泡 20 min 后,炙鳖甲先煎 30 min,再加入剩余 9 味中药煎煮 1 h,共煎 2 次,将两次的滤液混合后再浓缩至 1.56 g/mL。把 5 mg 甲泼尼龙溶于 10 mL 双蒸水中,配制成混悬液。

1.3 主要试剂与仪器

PrimeScript™ RT Master Mix(TaKaRa 公司,RR036A);Trizol 试剂

(TaKaRa 公司,9108);iQ™ SYBR ® Green Supermix(BIORAD 公司,1708882);小鼠内参 GAPDH(上海生工公司,B662304-0001);RIPA 蛋白裂解液(碧云天生物技术公司,P0013B);BCA 蛋白浓度测定试剂盒(碧云天生物技术公司,P0012);鼠抗 NF-κB(Cell Signaling Technology 公司,6956)、鼠抗 CDK6(Cell Signaling Technology 公司,3136)、鼠抗 β-actin(Santa Cruz Biotechnology 公司,sc47778)、二抗马抗小鼠 IgG(Cell Signaling Technology 公司,7076)、二抗山羊抗兔 IgG(Cell Signaling Technology 公司,7074)、MM-0210M1 小鼠抗双链 DNA 抗体(dsDNA)ELISA 试剂盒(酶免公司,MM-0210M1)、小鼠抗核抗体(ANA)ELISA 试剂盒(酶免公司,MM-1042M1)。

酶标仪(Thermo Scientific 公司,Varioskan Flash);LightCycler 96 SW 1.1 型定量 PCR 仪(美国 Roche 罗氏公司);微量核酸蛋白分析仪(Thermo Fisher Scientific 公司);PCR 扩增仪(BIORAD 公司);蛋白扫膜仪(FluorChem Q 公司);冷冻高速离心机(Thermo Fisher Scientific 公司)。

2. 方法

2.1 动物分组及给药

将 30 只 MRL/lpr 雌性小鼠随机分为模型组、中药组和西药组,每组 10 只。其中模型组小鼠予蒸馏水灌胃,中药组予解毒祛瘀滋阴方水煎剂灌胃,西药组予甲泼尼龙混悬液灌胃(5 mg/kg),每日一次;10 只 MRL/Mp 小鼠作为空白组,予蒸馏水灌胃,每日 1 次。灌胃量按成人等效量换算为 10 mL/kg,根据小鼠体重计算得出灌胃量,持续给药 10 周。

2.2 一般情况

小鼠给药期间,主要观察小鼠皮肤毛发、活动度及颈部、腋下、腹股沟淋巴结肿大情况。

2.3 小鼠肾脏组织病理切片观察

小鼠脱颈处死后取左侧肾脏 1/2 固定在 4% 多聚甲醛溶液中,用于病理切片 HE 染色,光镜观察各组小鼠肾脏病理学情况。

2.4 小鼠尿液白蛋白含量的测定

小鼠眼球取血,室温静置 2 h 后离心,3 000 rpm,15 min,缓慢吸取上层淡黄色血清,用于ELISA检测小鼠抗ANA抗体和抗dsDNA抗体的含量;小鼠处死前一天利用代谢笼收集小鼠24 h尿液,4℃离心,5 000 rpm,15 min,缓慢吸取上层淡黄色尿液,用于ELISA检测小鼠尿液白蛋白含量。

2.5 小鼠肾脏CDK6和NF-κB mRNA水平的测定

应用RT-PCR检测小鼠肾脏组织中CDK6和NF-κB mRNA的表达。采用Trizol提取总RNA,取500 mg RNA进行逆转录。逆转录条件:37℃ 15 min;85℃ 5 s,采用实时荧光定量PCR仪对CDK6和NF-κB mRNA表达水平进行检测,以GAPDH为内参。引物根据Primer5.0引物设计软件自行设计,再由生工生物工程(上海)有限公司合成,小鼠内参GAPDH由生工公司提供,引物序列详见表1。

表1 各基因引物序列

基因		引物(5'-3')
CDK6	上游	5'- GGCGTACCCACAGAAACCATA -3'
	下游	5'- AGGTAAGGGCCATCTGAAAACT -3'
NF-κB	上游	5'- GCCGTGGAGTACGACAA -3'
	下游	5'- CGGTTTCCCATTTAGTATGT -3'

2.6 小鼠肾脏CDK6和NF-κB蛋白表达水平的测定

应用Western-blot方法检测小鼠肾脏组织CDK6和NF-κB的蛋白表达水平。取30 mg肾脏皮质加入裂解液,收集组织蛋白,应用BCA法测定组织总蛋白含量。样品总蛋白80 μg进行12% SDS-PAGE凝胶电泳,转移至PVDF膜上,5%脱脂奶粉室温封闭1 h,4℃孵育一抗过夜,二抗羊抗鼠/羊抗兔室温孵育1 h,将膜置于蛋白成像分析仪中,进行化学发光扫膜,扫膜后用FluorChem FC3软件对图像进行分析,以β-actin为内参,以目的蛋白的相对表达量为参数进行半定量统计分析。

2.7 统计学方法

采用SPSS软件进行统计分析,Graph PadPrism5.0软件对结果进分析和作图,采用单因素方差分析及独立样本t检验,结果采用$\bar{X}\pm s$表示,以$P<0.05$表示差异有统计学意义。

3. 结果

3.1 一般情况

空白组小鼠皮毛及活动情况正常,未见明显浅表淋巴结肿大;模型组小鼠皮毛晦暗枯槁、缺乏光泽,背部皮肤毛发缺损,浅表淋巴结数量明显增多;中药组和西药组小鼠皮毛、皮损明显优于模型组,尤其是面部皮损明显减轻,中药组和西药组小鼠相较模型组浅表淋巴结的数量明显减少。

3.2 各组小鼠肾脏组织病理切片比较

空白组小鼠肾小球、肾小囊、肾小管等形态结构基本正常,未见明显异常。模型组见肾小球系膜细胞和内皮细胞弥漫性增生,白细胞浸润,肾小管上皮细胞空泡及颗粒状变性,毛细血管周围炎性细胞大量渗出,聚集于相邻肾小球周围,远曲小管水肿等病变情况均较为严重。中药组和西药组肾小球、肾小囊轻微融合,欠清晰。与模型组比较,中药组与西药组小鼠毛细血管内皮细胞增生减轻。见图1。

3.3 各组小鼠尿液白蛋白含量的比较

与空白组比较,模型组抗ANA抗体含量升高($P<0.01$),经解毒祛瘀滋阴方治疗后,与模型组比较,中药组抗ANA抗体含量降低($P<0.01$),与模型组比较,西药组抗ANA抗体含量降低($P<0.01$)见图2-A;与空白组比较,模型组抗dsDNA抗体含量升高($P<0.01$),经解毒祛瘀滋阴方治疗后,与模型组比较,中药组抗dsDNA抗体含量降低($P<0.01$),与模型组比较,西药组抗dsDNA抗体含量降低($P<0.01$)见图2-B;与空白组比较,模型组尿液白蛋白含量升高($P<0.01$);经解毒祛瘀滋阴方治疗后,与模型组比较,中药组尿液白蛋白含量降低($P<0.01$),与模型组比较,西药组尿液白蛋白含量降低($P<0.01$),见图2-C。

3.4 各组肾脏CDK6和NF-κB mRNA表达水平比较

与空白组比较,模型组NF-κB mRNA表达升高($P<0.05$),CDK6 mRNA表达升高($P<0.05$);经解毒祛瘀滋阴方治疗后,中药组NF-κB和CDK6 mRNA表达较模型组降低($P<0.05$),西药组NF-κB和CDK6 mRNA表达较模型组降低($P<0.05$);西药组与中药组NF-κB和CDK6 mRNA表达无统计学差异($P>0.05$)。见图3。

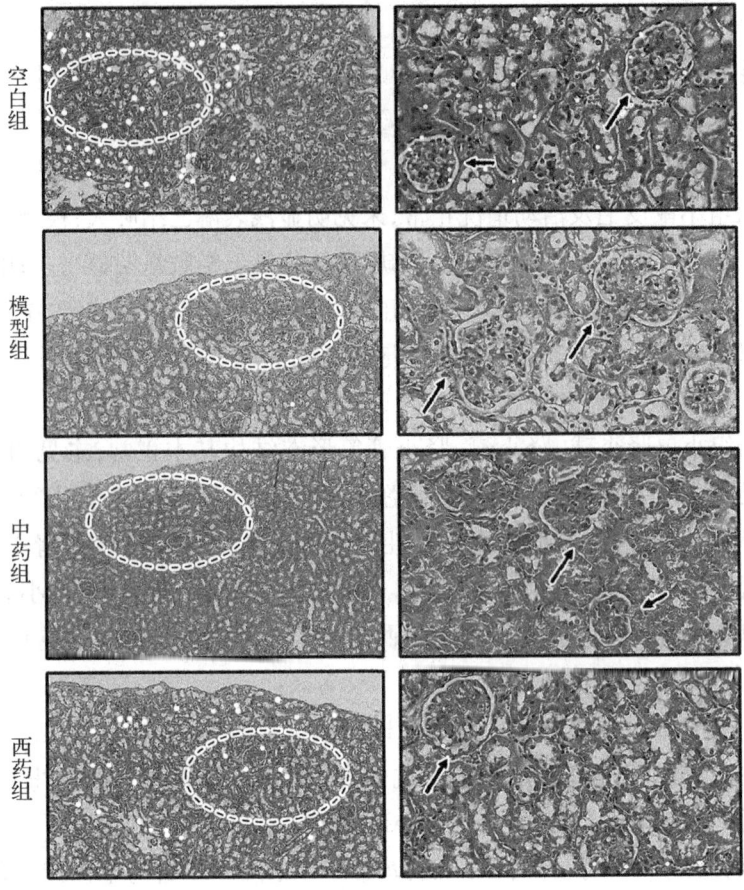

图 1　各组小鼠肾组织病理 HE 染色结果

注：左列 5×，比例尺为 100 μm；右列 20×，比例尺为 20 μm

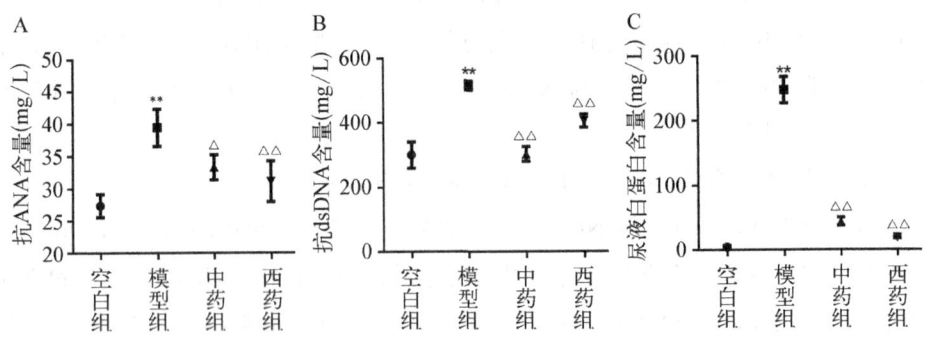

图 2　小鼠血清抗 ANA 抗体、抗 dsDNA 抗体和尿液白蛋白含量

注：与空白组比较，**$P<0.01$；与模型组比较，△△$P<0.01$。

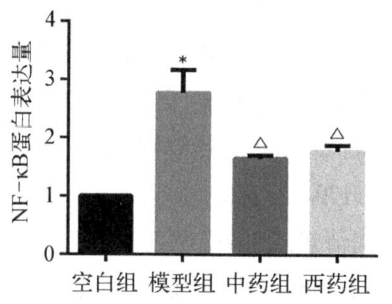 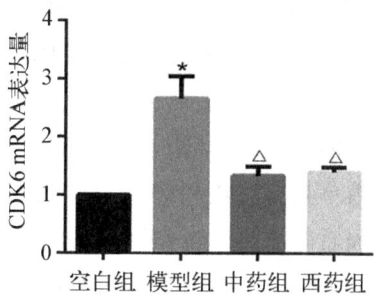

图3 各组小鼠的NF-κB、CDK6 mRNA表达

注：与空白组比较，*P<0.05；与模型组比较，△P<0.05。

3.5 各组肾脏CDK6和NF-κB蛋白表达水平检测的结果

与空白组比较，模型组NF-κB蛋白表达升高（$P<0.01$）、CDK6蛋白表达升高（$P<0.01$）；经解毒祛瘀滋阴方治疗后，中药组NF-κB蛋白表达较模型组降低（$P<0.01$）、CDK6蛋白表达较模型组降低（$P<0.01$）；西药组NF-κB和CDK6蛋白表达较模型组降低（$P<0.01$）；与中药组比较，西药组NF-κB和CDK6蛋白表达降低（$P<0.05$），见图4。

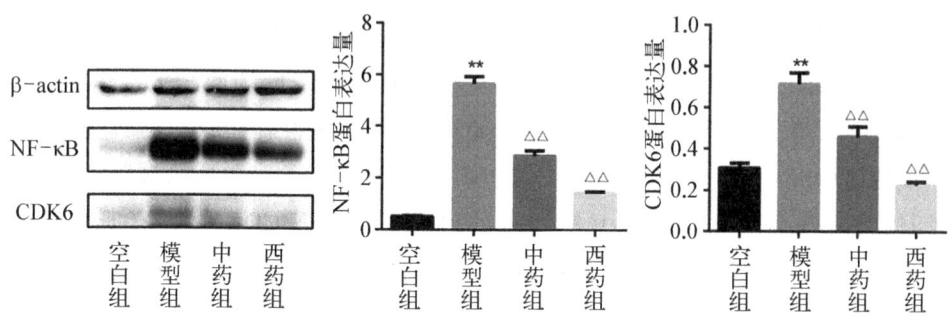

图4 解毒祛瘀滋阴方对小鼠肾脏NF-κB、CDK6蛋白表达量的影响

注：与空白组比较，**$P<0.01$；与模型组比较，△△$P<0.01$。

4. 讨论

根据临床症状及体征把SLE归纳为中医学的"阴阳毒""蝴蝶斑"等病症范畴，其病因错综复杂，主要以先天不足、肝肾亏虚为本，外感热毒、瘀血阻滞为标，治疗应标本兼顾。临床研究表明解毒祛瘀滋阴方结合糖皮质激素治疗SLE能够减少糖皮质激素的用量,同时减少糖皮质激素、免疫抑制剂等药物带来的毒副作用[1,11]。解毒祛瘀滋阴方是全国名中医范永升教授治疗 SLE 的经验方[10],解毒祛瘀滋阴方中以生地黄为君药,具有清热凉血、养阴生津的功效。升麻具有发表透疹,清热解毒,升阳举陷的功效;白花蛇舌草具有清热解毒,利湿通淋的功效;积雪草具有清热利湿,解毒消肿的功效,升麻、白花蛇舌草和积雪草共为臣药,增强君药清热解毒作用。炙鳖甲具有滋阴清热、潜阳熄风、软坚散结的功效;赤芍具有清热凉血、散瘀止痛的功效;丹皮具有清热凉血、活血化瘀的功效;佛手具有疏肝理气、和胃止痛、燥湿化痰的功效;生甘草具有益气补中、缓急止痛、润肺止咳、泻火解毒的功效,以上 5 味中药共为佐药,配合君药、臣药起到滋阴益肾、清热凉血之效。青蒿具有清透虚热,凉血除蒸,祛风止痒之效,可缓解阴虚发热等症状,以为使药。全方诸药共用,起到滋阴益肾、清热解毒、活血化瘀之效,起到标本兼顾的效果。

周期蛋白依赖性激酶(cyclin-dependent kinases,CDKs)是一类参与调控细胞周期、转录调节和 DNA 损伤修复等多个生理过程的蛋白质[12]。其中 CDK6 是调控细胞周期进程的重要组成蛋白质,在很多肿瘤细胞中都发现了 CDK6 的异常表达[13-15]。有研究发现 CDKs 和 CDK 抑制剂(CDKI)可以通过调节细胞周期从而影响自身免疫反应 T 细胞和 B 细胞的活化和增殖[16]。SLE 是一种自身免疫性疾病,Toll 样受体和 I 型干扰素是影响 SLE 发展的两个关键途径[17]。Handschick 等[18]的研究表明 CDK6 与 p65 共定位并相互作用,通过染色质免疫沉淀测序(chip-seq)显示 CDK6 和 p65 NF－κB 在特定的染色质区域存在重叠,并且在许多转录活性 NF－κB 靶基因的启动子处发现 CDK6。另有研究发现 SLE 患者骨髓间充质干细胞(MSCs)的衰老可能是其发病的一个促成因素,同时 MSCs 的衰老由 p16INK4a、CDK4 和 CDK6 等表达的影响[19]。

研究证明核 CDKs 与炎症介质表达的分子机制相关,许多促炎基因的诱导转录在细胞周期的 G1 期以 CDKs 依赖的方式增加[6]。有研究证实了在 IgA 肾病中 CDK6 的表达受 miR－29b－3p 的调控,同时 miR－29b－3p 下调引起的 CDK6 过度表达是通过磷酸化 p65 来活化 NF－κB 信号,其结果可能促进炎症反应[7]。此外,CDK6 基因扩增或过度的表达主要被证明与肿瘤相关[20],发现 miR－320c 过表达和 CDK6 的抑制可以减少炎症因子 IL－1β 的表达和调节 NF－κB 信号分子[21]。目前尚没有关于 CDK6 在 MRL/lpr 狼疮小鼠体内实验的研究,本实验通过使用 MRL/lpr 狼疮小鼠研究解毒祛瘀滋阴方对 CDK6 分子表达的影响,探讨CDK6分子对SLE疾病的影响。本实验结果初步表明,未经解毒祛瘀滋阴方干预的MRL/lpr狼疮小鼠肾脏中炎症信号分子NF-κB和CDK6表达明显升高,我们猜测CDK6可能通过影响自身免疫反应,从而影响NF-κB炎症信号通路,诱发相关炎症反应,导致MRL/lpr狼疮小鼠的发病,同时解毒祛瘀滋阴方可以抑制这种反应的发生。

课题组前期研究证明解毒祛瘀滋阴方可以通过抑制NF-κB炎症信号通路,减少炎症因子分泌从而抑制LPS诱导的小鼠单核巨噬细胞的炎症反应[22]。本研究发现解毒祛瘀滋阴方可以同时抑制小鼠肾脏中NF-κB、CDK6蛋白质和mRNA的表达($P<0.01$),说明解毒祛瘀滋阴方可能是通过抑制CDK6表达从而抑制炎症反应然后影响NF-κB炎症信号通路,以上结果均证实了我们的猜想。

综上所述,解毒祛瘀滋阴方可明显缓解狼疮小鼠皮损和肾脏损害,其作用机制可能是通过下调MRL/lpr狼疮小鼠肾脏CDK6蛋白质和mRNA的表达调控NF-κB转录因子抑制炎症反应的发生,进而延缓SLE的发病。由此可见,本实验的研究意义在于通过试验探讨解毒祛瘀滋阴方对CDK6/NF-κB炎症相关信号通路的影响,为今后小鼠炎症模型的进一步试验奠定基础,也为其抗炎临床用药提供良好的理论支持。

参考文献

[1] 范永升.系统性红斑狼疮的中医临床探索与实践[J].浙江中医药大学学报,2019,43(10):1030-1035.

[2] GOTTSCHALK T A, TSANTIKOS E, HIBBS M L. Pathogenic Inflammation and Its therapeutic Targeting in Systemic Lupus Erythematosus[J]. Front Immunol, 2015, 6:550.

[3] 丛珊,高翠荣,李潭,等.系统性红斑狼疮心脏受累患者临床特征及免疫抑制干预对并发全心脏扩大者的效果[J].中国现代医学杂志,2019,29(15):87-92.

[4] 高蔼萍,袁维.血清sUA、sCys-c、Um-ABL/Cr在系统性红斑狼疮早期肾损伤患者中的诊断价值[J].临床医学研究与实践,2019,4(22):127-129.

[5] O'NEILL S, CERVERA R. Systemic lupus erythematosus[J]. Best Pract Res Clin Rheumatol, 2010, 24(6):841-855.

[6] SCHMITZ M L, KRACHT M. Cyclin-Dependent Kinases as Coregulators of Inflammatory Gene Expression[J]. Trends Pharmacol Sci, 2016, 37(2):101-113.

[7] XING L N, WANG H, YIN P H, et al. Reduced mir–29b–3p expression up-regulate CDK6 and contributes to IgA nephropathy[J]. Int J Clin Exp Med, 2014, 7(12): 5275–5281.

[8] DURCAN L, PETRI M. Immunomodulators in SLE: Clinical evidence and immunologic actions[J]. J Autoimmun, 2016, 74: 73–84.

[9] DORIA A, GATTO M, ZEN M, et al. Optimizing outcome in SLE: treating-to-target and definition of treatment goals[J]. Autoimmun Rev, 2014, 13(7): 770–777.

[10] 李荣群,刘文洪,侯晓丽,等.解毒祛瘀滋阴方对MRL/lpr狼疮小鼠CD4 T细胞MeCP2信号通路的影响[J].中医杂志,2018,59(04): 321–324+338.

[11] 范永升,温成平,吴国琳,等.解毒祛瘀滋阴法对系统性红斑狼疮类固醇性骨质疏松症的防治作用研究[J].中华中医药杂志,2005(11): 28–30+5.

[12] 陈星.以CDK6为靶点的小分子抑制剂的设计、合成、活性评价及构效关系研究[D].安徽医科大学,2019.

[13] 刘静,江叶,闵敏,等.P21及CDK6与宫颈鳞状细胞癌的关系[J].重庆医学,2017,46(23): 3231–3233.

[14] 邱丽湞,吴共发,姚金科,等.CDK4和CDK6在甲状腺乳头状癌中的表达及其临床意义[J].中国组织化学与细胞化学杂志,2018,27(03): 251–255.

[15] 王海林.CDK6在鼻咽癌中的表达及临床意义分析[J].心理月刊,2019,14(04): 110–111.

[16] GOULVESTRE C, CHEREAU C, NICCO C, et al. A mimic of P21WAF1/CIP1 ameliorates murine lupus[J]. J Immunol, 2005, 175(10): 6959–6967.

[17] LESSARD C J, ICE J A, ADRIANTO I, et al. The genomics of autoimmune disease in the era of genome-wide association studies and beyond[J]. Autoimmunity Reviews, 2012, 11(4): 267–275.

[18] HANDSCHICK K, BEUERLEIN K, JURIDA L, et al. Cyclin-dependent kinase 6 is a chromatin-bound cofactor for nf-kappab-dependent gene expression[J]. Mol Cell, 2014, 53(2): 193–208.

[19] GU Z, CAO X, JIANG J, et al. Upregulation of P16INK4A promotes cellular senescence of bone marrow-derived mesenchymal stem cells from systemic lupus erythematosus patients[J]. Cell Signal, 2012, 24(12): 2307–2314.

[20] 陈彦洁,柳传毅,吕满霞,等.鱼藤素诱导肺癌细胞凋亡和细胞周期阻滞的分子机制[J].中国药理学通报,2019,35(08): 1109–1114.

[21] SUN H, HUANG Z, Wu P, et al. CDK6 and miR–320c Co-Regulate Chondrocyte

Catabolism Through NF-kappab Signaling Pathways [J]. Cell Physiol Biochem, 2018, 51(2): 909-923.
[22] 嵇丽娜,侯晓丽,庄爱文,等.解毒祛瘀滋阴方含药血清对小鼠单核巨噬细胞IRAK1信号通路表达的影响[J].中国药学杂志,2019,54(3):189-192.

 点评

论文通过研究解毒祛瘀滋阴方对MRL/lpr狼疮小鼠肾脏CDK6分子表达的影响,较为深入探讨了解毒祛瘀滋阴方对CDK6/NF-κB炎症相关信号通路的影响,可为临床用药提供一定的理论支持。全文结构完整,研究目标具体,研究方法科学,所得结果具有一定说服力。有关解毒祛瘀滋阴方作用机制的阐述还不够具体、鲜明,希望文献综述能作进一步完善。

专名等于限定摹状词吗?

高仁刚*

摘要：专名与摹状词二者发生关联的关键在于指称,但专名不等于摹状词,二者根本不同。专名与摹状词之间的关系在描述论与直接指称理论两派中的情况截然不同：一方面,描述论中"简单的"相等关系和维特根斯坦意义上的"复杂的"相等关系均无法成立,只有塞尔意义上的"复杂的"相等关系才能成立；另一方面,在直接指称论者那里,专名与摹状词之间的关系表现为全异与交叉关系。彻底澄清专名与摹状词二者之间的关系,需要回到亚里士多德的"实体-属性"范畴理论。专名的指称对象,对应的是实体范畴；而摹状词则是对其所指对象的属性的表达,对应于性质范畴。正是在这个意义上说专名不等于摹状词,二者根本不同。

关键词：专名；摹状词；指称；范畴

引言

　　自穆勒(J. S. Mill)以来,名称意义理论中的一个极富争议的焦点问题是：专名是否具有涵义(sense)。围绕这一问题,描述论与直接指称理论两派进行了数十年的激烈争论。其中,以弗雷格(Frege)为代表的描述论认为专名具有涵义,其涵义由与之关联的一个(或一簇)限定摹状词[1]给出,且专名必须通过涵义进入指称。然而直接指称理论与此相反,认为专名直接指称对象,因而专名不具有涵义[2],且专

---

* 高仁刚：南京大学哲学系2019级硕士研究生。

[1] 由于本文不涉及对"非限定摹状词"的讨论,加上学界用语习惯,本文将"限定摹状词"(英文中是指形如"the""that"的一类表达式)简称为"摹状词"。

[2] 详细地说,直接指称理论者认为：专名是其所命名对象的标签,专名的意义等同于专名所指称的对象(或者用穆勒的话来说,专名的意义被其所指对象全部占据)。也正是因为这一点,空名的存在对直接指称理论构成了极大挑战。当然,本文不讨论空名问题。

名根本不需要通过涵义进入到指称。需要指出的是,两派争论中有两个基本预设:一是摹状词具有涵义①;二是专名可以指称对象(不论专名是否具有涵义)②。

不难发现,两派聚焦的对象是两类看似发挥同样功能的指称性表达式:专名与摹状词。与此同时,二者发生关联的关键在于指称(reference)。那么专名等于摹状词吗?确切地说,在什么意义上专名等于(或者不等于)摹状词?比如专名"亚里士多德"(Aristotle)与摹状词"亚历山大大帝的老师",二者相等(equal)③吗?本文就此问题进行探讨,以期澄清、阐明专名与摹状词二者之间的关系,有助于扫除两派之争出现的障碍与"盲区",也有利于准确理解和把握名称意义理论的核心问题。

1. 两派争论中专名与摹状词的三种相等关系

专名与摹状词之间发生关联的关键在于指称。但从语言学意义上来讲,专名与限定摹状词本身均属于语言域④。从集合论的角度来说,可以将专名、摹状词所表达概念的外延分别视为一个集合⑤。采用《普通逻辑》教科书中对概念间的外延关系的划分,结合对两派争论中出现的核心观点的分析,专名与摹状词(所表达概念的外延)二者之间的关系,大致分为三种不同的情况:(1)"简单的"相等关系;(2)"复杂的"相等关系;(3)全异与交叉关系。

(1)"简单的"相等关系

"简单的"相等关系,"专名=摹状词",即专名与其关联的某一摹状词之间具有相等关系。假设这种相等关系成立,经过简单推理,将会出现高度反直觉的荒谬结论。描述论的代表罗素(Russell)认为(普通)专名是缩略的、伪装的摹状词⑥,因而在这个意义上说"专名=摹状词"似乎没有问题。但是,按照如下示例

---

① 关于这一点,鲜有学者发起质疑,弗雷格的意义组合原则可以合理地说明摹状词具有涵义。
② 关于专名如何具有指称功能以及在什么意义上专名具有指称,斯特劳森(Strawson)在"On Referring"(1950)做了澄清与区分,专名涵义的分析也由此前的语义学扩展到语用学领域。
③ 本文对"相等(关系)"、"等于"和等号"="三者不加区分,将三者视为同义关系。
④ 参考借鉴张建军教授在他的逻辑行动主义方法论中三域的划分。
⑤ 诚如弗雷格所言,"专名"是饱和的,"概念"是不饱和的,因而专名与概念二者根本不同。本文出现的诸如"专名与摹状词所表达概念的外延"中的"概念"一词,具有一定的特设性,与弗雷格这一观点并不矛盾。
⑥ 罗素作为一个经验论者,在其亲知理论基础上,将名称分为普通专名和逻辑专名("这""那")两类。

深入考究"专名=摹状词"这一简单的相等关系的正确性(不考虑模态语境),运用等值替换律,将产生高度反直觉的荒谬结论。

　　(a) 亚里士多德是亚历山大大帝的老师。
　　(b) 亚里士多德是古代世界最后一位伟大的哲学家。
　　(c) 亚里士多德是《形而上学》的作者。

若承认"专名与其关联的一个摹状词相等",那么(a)—(c)这三个命题,在运用等值替换律后,都将变为逻辑形式为"a 是 a"的永真命题,似乎也成了无意义的命题。即:在不考虑模态语境的情况下,诸如(a)—(c)这类经验到的传统意义上的主谓式命题,要么是永真命题,要么为永假命题(相应的否定命题自然也就会成为永假命题)①。也就是说:经验到的包含专名的主谓式命题要么永假,要么永真。这也就意味着:接受"专名与其关联的一个摹状词相等"的观点,将"扼杀"经验的偶然性。毫无疑问,这是一个高度反直觉的荒谬结论,难以让人信服、接受。因此,该现象的出现是对"专名=摹状词"这一假设正确性的严峻挑战。由此观之,专名与摹状词的关系不应是、也不能是这般"简单的相等关系"。

(2)"复杂的"相等关系

"复杂的"相等关系是指,专名和与之关联的若干摹状词的逻辑合取(或析取)之间具有相等关系。描述论的另一代表维特根斯坦(Wittgenstein)主张,专名的涵义是由与之相关联的一定数量的摹状词的合取给出的②。由此可知,专名"亚里士多德"与相关摹状词之间满足如下关系:

　　(d)"亚里士多德 = 亚历山大大帝的老师∃古代世界最后一位伟大的哲学家∃……"。

运用等值替换律,将(d)式分别代入上述(a)—(c)三个命题并替换三个命题中的主项(即专名"亚里士多德"),容易发现这些经验命题真值始终是"真",

---

① 本文不严格区分"陈述"与"命题"这两个概念,二者交替混合使用。
② 参见:Ludwig Wittgenstein. *Philosophical Investigations*. London:Blackwell, 1953.

即这类命题成了永真命题(相应的否定命题自然也就会成为永假命题)。依旧出现了前述的高度反直觉结论。

直至塞尔(J. R. Searle)提出簇摹状词理论①,才较好地阻止了上述高度反直觉的结论,也恰当地解释了日常语言中的诸多现象。塞尔所持观点是:专名的涵义是由与之相关联的足够多的摹状词析取式给出的。(只要我们掌握了与专名相关的一定数量的摹状词[析取支],我们便能识别出相应的专名及所指。)此时,按照塞尔的理论,专名"亚里士多德"与相关摹状词之间将满足如下关系:

(e)"亚里士多德 = 亚历山大大帝的老师∪古代世界最后一位伟大的哲学家∪……"。

类似地,运用等值替换律,将(e)分别代入前述(a)—(c)三个命题中,然后对命题的真值进行一一判断,不难发现这些经验命题或真或假,并没有成为永真(或永假)命题。上述高度反直觉的奇异现象不再出现,这说明塞尔的簇摹状词理论的具有很好的解释性。由此看来,"复杂的"相等关系中,仅在塞尔那里可以成立(即专名与若干摹状词的逻辑析取相等)。

(3) 全异与交叉关系

专名与摹状词所表达概念的外延之间,具有交叉关系,这一点可以在直接指称理论当中得到论证。直接指称理论发端于穆勒,他认为:名称是对象之名,名称是用来命名对象的,因而名称的所有意义都被指称所占据②。

而在克里普克(Saul Kripke)③的著作《命名与必然性》(1980年版)(*Naming and Necessity*)中,他提出了著名的严格指示词(rigid designator)理论。通过区分严格性(rigidity)与非严格性(non-rigidity),他将包含专名与摹状词在内的指示词划分为严格指示词与非严格指示词(non-rigid designator)。严格指示词在所有可能世界(possible worlds)中都指示同一对象④;并非在所有可能世界中都指

---

① 参见:Searle J. R. *Intentionality: An Essay in the Philosophy of Mind*. New York: Cambridge University Press,1983.
② 参见:穆勒.逻辑体系(一)[M].上海:上海交通大学出版社,2014.
③ 本文按照学界习惯,将克里普克归为直接指称理论者(尽管克里普克不承认自己是直接指称理论者)。
④ 克里普克进一步指出:不要求所指示的对象必须存在,如果所指对象在所有可能世界中都存在,那么这种被称为"强严格指示词"(strong rigid designators)。

示同一对象,称为非严格指示词。基于这一区分,克里普克将专名(如"亚里士多德")归入前者,而将摹状词(如"亚历山大大帝的老师")归于后者①。这导致的哲学后果是,先验地将专名与摹状词严格地区分开来②。因此,从基于严格性的区分而产生的严格指示词理论上来说,专名与摹状词所表达的概念外延,属于全异关系(因为严格与非严格指示词所表达的概念外延是全异关系)。从集合的角度上来说,专名所表达的概念外延(用集合↓表示)与摹状词所表达的概念外延(用集合≦表示)二者之间满足如下关系:

$$↓ \cap ≦]\quad\cdots\cdots\cdots\cdots\cdots\cdots\cdots\cdots(*)$$

值得注意的是,正如克里普克在《命名与必然性》的前言(preface)部分最后一个脚注(footnote 21)指出的那样,严格性本身还可以进一步区分为"根据法则的"严格性和纯粹"根据事实"严格性(尽管被他本人故意避开了,他在全书主张的是较弱的严格性)。由此,他举例说诸如"最小的素数"(摹状词)严格地指示数字"2"(专名)。因此根据他的严格指示词理论,陈述"最小的素数=2"不仅为真,同时还表达了一个(数学)真理。从这个意义上来讲,专名与摹状词二者存在相等的情形③。在此种情形下,集合↓与集合≦之间满足如下关系:

$$↓ \cap ≦ A]\quad\cdots\cdots\cdots\cdots\cdots\cdots\cdots(**)$$

但是更多情形下,专名(如"亚里士多德")和摹状词(如"亚历山大大帝的老师"、"古代世界最后一位伟大的哲学家")二者之间的关系,基本符合前述的全异关系——因为尽管二者在某一可能状态(possible state)指示同一对象④,但是这是认识论意义上的"偶然",不能用等号"="将专名与摹状词联接起来——因为在克里普克那里,由等号联接起来的为真的等式(陈述或命题)表达的是一个

---

① 此外,他还提出了关于名称的历史因果命名理论,创造性地从社会交往的角度阐释了专名指称对象的过程与机制——通过回溯一根传递名称所指的因果链条(casual chain)直至最初对该对象的命名仪式(baptism)。
② 概括来说,克里普克意义上摹状词与其指示对象的关系是:摹状词可以 fix 对象,但是无法 determine 对象。克里普克认为能 determine 对象的是与专名唯一对应的那根传递因果的链条。此外,克里普克基于严格性区分而产生的严格指示词理论,也遭到了国内外一些学者的质疑、反驳乃至批评。
③ 其实这也暴露了克里普克严格指示词理论的不足,招致部分学者(诸如 Baumann、陈波)对"严格性"概念的反驳。
④ 例如在现实世界中,"亚里士多德是亚历山大大帝的老师"是一个真陈述,但不必然为真。该陈述中摹状词"亚历山大大帝的老师"是非严格指示词,因此按照克里普克的说法,我们完全可以设想某一反事实情形,其中"亚历山大大帝的老师"不指称亚里士多德,而指其他人。此时,不能将该命题写成等式"亚里士多德=亚历山大大帝的老师"。

形而上学意义上的必然真理①。

2. 彻底澄清二者关系：回到亚里士多德

在我们看来，想要彻底澄清专名与摹状词之间的关系，必须回到亚里士多德的"十范畴理论"。亚里士多德曾在《范畴篇》里提出了十个哲学基本范畴：实体、性质、地点、时间、数量、关系、姿态、状况、主动、被动。我们援引张建军教授提出的"实体-实体关联"（entity-entity connection）与"实体-属性关联"（entity-attribute connection）②，结合其在逻辑行动主义方法论中三域的划分，不仅能清晰地将专名与摹状词之间的关系厘清、阐明，还有助于更准确把握、理解名称的意义理论的核心问题。

首先应当明确的是，专名与摹状词本身均处于语言域③。其次，专名的指称所对应的应当是实体范畴；摹状词是对其所指称对象的属性的表达，对应的是性质范畴。

请看如下四个例句（陈述），分别展示的是"专名与摹状词相等"的四种可能的组合形式。陈述（1）展示的是两个相同专名的相等关系的一个示例；陈述（2）展示的是专名和与之关联的某一摹状词的相等关系的一个示例；陈述（3）展示的是两个不同摹状词的相等关系的一个示例；陈述（4）展示的是两个不同专名的相等关系的一个示例。并且依据文学与历史学知识来判定，四个陈述全部为真，都表达了真命题。

（1）"亚里士多德是亚里士多德"。
（2）"亚里士多德是亚历山大大帝的老师"。
（3）"古代世界最后一位伟大的哲学家是亚历山大大帝的老师"。
（4）"鲁迅是周树人"。

---

① 用克里普克的话说，若"a""b"均为严格指示词，那么若 a=b 为真，则必然 a=b；认识论意义上的偶然不能掩盖形而上学意义上的必然。张建军（2017）认为，如果我们像克里普克所强调的那样时刻注意本体论与认识论的区分，当 a=b 为真时，a=b 所表征事态是 a 与 b 所共同指称的那个个体的自身等同。用亚里士多德的实体（entity）概念来讲，就是实体-实体关联（实体与自身同一是必然的），后文将会引入张建军教授的这一主张，结合本文进行讨论。
② 参见：张建军.正规模态集合论悖论及相关问题[J].逻辑学研究,2017,10(3)：43.
③ 在张建军（2008）提出的逻辑行动主义方法论中，"三域"分别指：语言域、思想域和实在域。按照他的这一划分，专名和摹状词均应划入语言域。

倘若此时结合模态语境加以考虑,在上述(1)—(4)四个陈述前都加上"必然地"(必然模态算子),得到相应的必然命题(1)*—(4)*,这四个必然命题的真值情况会是怎样呢?

(1)* "必然地,亚里士多德是亚里士多德"。
(2)* "必然地,亚里士多德是亚历山大大帝的老师"。
(3)* "必然地,古代世界最后一位伟大的哲学家是亚历山大大帝的老师"。
(4)* "必然地,鲁迅是周树人"。

若将专名("亚里士多德"、"鲁迅"和"周树人")所指对象视为实体,而将摹状词("亚历山大大帝的老师"、"古代世界最后一位伟大的哲学家")视为对其所指对象的属性的表达,容易发现,只有陈述(1)*和(4)*为真。因为陈述(1)和(4)所表征的是"实体-实体关联"的事态,陈述(2)表征的则是"实体-属性关联"的事态,陈述(3)所表征的是"属性-属性关联"的事态。而依据亚里士多德的理论,我们可以得知:实体必然与自身同一,即实体与自身同一是必然的①;而关于同一实体的所有属性中,除了表达其本质属性外,其他属性之间的等同不具有必然性。由此,结合模态逻辑中的必然化规则,可以作出如下判定:命题(1)*和(4)*为真,(2)*和(3)*为假。

与此同时,在克里普克意义上来判断上述四个必然命题的真值情况,结论恰巧也是:只有陈述(1)*和(4)*为真,(2)*和(3)*为假,只是相应的解释有所不同而已。因为"亚里士多德"、"鲁迅"和"周树人"都是克里普克意义上的严格指示词,且陈述(1)"亚里士多德是亚里士多德"表示的是个体自身同一,所以(1)不仅为真,而且必然为真(表达的是形而上学意义上的必然性,即实体必然与自身同一)②,因此相应的必然命题(1)*也为真;陈述(4)实质上表征的也是对象(周树人)自身同一,只不过后验真命题的形式来呈现,因此(4)*也为真。但陈述(2)*和(3)*都为假,因为"亚历山大大帝的老师"和"古代世界最后一位

---

① 正如奎因所言:"没有同一性就没有实体。"
② 当然,陈述(1)也可以从语言域层次上来分析,它显然是一个分析性陈述,因此它不仅为真而且永真。但正如克里普克极力强调的那般:分析与必然(以及先验)这是不同层次的概念,必须时刻作出区分,不能混为一谈。

伟大的哲学家"两个摹状词都是非严格指示词,从"反事实"理论角度来说,它们这两个摹状词可以不指"亚里士多德",而指其他任意两个不同的人(比如在某一反事实情形中,这两个摹状词可以分别指 A 与 B)。

如此看来,无论从亚里士多德的范畴理论、还是从克里普克的严格指示词理论进行分析研判(1)*—(4)*四个必然命题的真值情况,都是相同的结论:陈述(1)*和(4)*为真,而(2)*和(3)*为假。

仔细考究亚里士多德与克里普克两种理论之间的关联,陈述(1)*和(4)*中的专名,不仅可以理解为克里普克意义上的严格指示词,还可以理解为亚里士多德意义上"实体"的表达。陈述(2)*和(3)*中的摹状词,不仅可以理解为克里普克意义上的非严格指示词,也可以理解为亚里士多德意义上的"(偶然)属性/性质"的表达。因此,我们可以认为克里普克严格遵循了亚里士多德的"实体-属性"区分。而恰恰是这一区分,使得在"描述论-直接指称理论"两派论争中模糊不清的专名与摹状词关系"泾渭分明"。

探究分析表明了专名与摹状词二者根本差异之所在:专名的指称所对应的是实体范畴;摹状词是对其所指称对象的属性的表达,对应的是性质范畴,因而专名与摹状词二者根本不同。

3. 结论

通过以上论述探究,我们可以得出如下结论:首先,专名与摹状词二者发生关联的关键在于指称,但专名不等于摹状词,二者根本不同。其次,专名与摹状词二者之间的关系在描述论与直接指称理论两派中的情况是截然不同的:一方面,描述论中"简单的"相等关系和维特根斯坦意义上的"复杂的"相等关系均无法成立,只有塞尔意义上的"复杂的"相等关系才能成立;另一方面,在直接指称论者那里,专名与摹状词二者之间的关系表现为全异与交叉关系。最后,彻底澄清专名与摹状词二者之间的关系,需要追溯到亚里士多德的"实体-属性"范畴理论:专名的指称对象,对应的是实体范畴;而摹状词则是对其所指对象的属性的表达,对应于性质范畴。也正是在这个意义上,专名与摹状词二者根本不同。

参考文献

[1] 余俊伟.理解弗雷格的专名涵义[J].逻辑学研究,2014(4):69-86.

[2] 张建军.摹状、规范与半描述论——"金岳霖—冯契论题"与当代指称理论的"第三条道路"[J].清华大学学报(哲学社会科学版),2016(1):158-164.

[3] 王振."严格性"问题和专名的意义[J].湖北大学学报(哲学社会科学版),2018,45(05):113-119.

[4] 张建军,等.当代逻辑哲学前沿问题研究[M].北京:人民出版社,2014.

[5] 张建军.正规模态集合论悖论及相关问题[J].逻辑学研究,2017,10(3):35-57.

[6] 张建军.逻辑行动主义方法论构图[J].学术月刊,2008(8):55-64.

[7] 弗雷格,王路.弗雷格哲学论著选辑[M].北京:商务印书馆,2006.

[8] 张力锋.专名的摹状词理论初探[J].重庆师范大学学报(社会科学版),1999(2):52-58.

[9] 张力锋.专名指称理论:历史、现状及反思[J].重庆师范大学学报(哲学社会科学版),2002(3):62-68.

[10] 刘叶涛,马领弟,高峰.现代名称理论的两个基本问题[J].河北学刊,2006(5).

[11] 刘叶涛,白玮.专名的严格性与指称的转移[J].燕山大学学报(哲学社会科学版),2009(4).

[12] 穆勒.逻辑体系(一)[M].上海:上海交通大学出版社,2014.

[13] 塞尔.意向性:论心灵哲学[M].上海:上海人民出版社,2007.

[14] GOTTLOB FREGE. Sense and Reference[J]. The Philosophical Review, 1948, 57(3): 209-230.

[15] PIERRE BAUMANN. Are Proper Names Rigid Designators? [J]. Axiomathes, 2010, 20(2-3): 333-346.

[16] SAUL A. KRIPKE. Naming and Necessity[M]. Cambridge, MA: Harvard University Press, 1980.

点评

论文对专名与摹状词二者之间的关系从逻辑学和语义学角度进行了较为深入的探讨。论文结构完整清晰,研究问题明确,论述逻辑较强,说理较为透彻,结论合理,分析和解释较有逻辑性与说服力。语言流畅,层次清晰,格式基本规范。

College Students' Positive Psychology in English Learning

Wei Jin[*]

Abstract: Starting from the perspective of positive psychology, and combining with second language acquisition, this paper takes advantage of questionnaire to research 101 college students' positive psychologies in English learning, who are of different provinces in some University. Through factors' analysis, the writer puts forward four positive psychologies, namely, happiness, transcendence, Optimism and attachment. Independent sample test indicates that college students don't have sex and family background difference in four dimensions. Variance test suggests students of different grades just show diversity in three dimensions, happiness, optimism and attachment. Multiple regression analysis reflects that transcendental psychology has a positive prediction on College Students' English level, that is, the stronger the student's transcendental psychology is, the better his English is. The results will have an important implication to English teaching and students' learning itself as well as their physical and mental health.

Keywords: college students; English learning; positive psychology; positive prediction

---

[*] Wei Jin: School of Foreign Languages, Shanghai University, master's degree candidate of the class of 2019.

Introduction

As we all know that psychology has three objectives: first, to help people eliminate their suffering; second, to help people pursue happiness; third, to identify and cultivate talents. However, a great number of past researches on psychologists have paid much more attention to the negative emotions, while those on positive psychology such as happiness, gratitude, superior characters and so on are numbered.

Regarding that, the well-known American Psychologist Martin Seligman and Laura King established positive psychology at the end of 20th century, which has soon become a new trend of research. Marked by the publication *Positive Psychology: An Introduction* by Seligman and Csikszentmihalyi in January 2000, more and more psychologists devoted themselves to this new-rising field. The premise of positive psychology is that man is an self-managed, inner-directed, and adaptive individual. It devoted to studying the vitality and virtue of ordinary people, encouraging the full exploitation of human beings' inherent, potential and constructive forces, and calling for the individuals' and social coordinated development, so as to guide people towards happiness.

By far, positive psychology has been a maniac trend. Therefore, many foreign and domestic scholars are trying to apply the theory of positive psychology in SLA. Foreign scholars in SLA have gradually introduced positive psychology to research and practice, while in China, the studies of "positive psychology" in SLA is still in its infancy. Accordingly, in order to further study, the writer wrote this paper to explore the positive psychologies of college students in English learning. What's more, the writer analyzed their individual differences including gender, grade and family background as well as the predication effect of positive psychology on English learners' performance. At the end of this thesis, the writer proposed some significant enlightenment for teachers and students, making a great influence on the quality of English teaching and student's learning effect as well as their sound mind.

The whole text includes seven chapters. In chapter one, the writer described the latest foreign and domestic research results of positive psychology in SLA. Besides, the writer pointed out the its developmental insufficiency. In chapter two, the writer introduced the three phrases of emotions rescarches in SLA concluded by J.M Dewaele and li Chengchen (2020). In chapter three, the writer explained two important theoretical models of positive psychology, that is, PERMER and EMPATHICS. In chapter four, the writer introduced research design, specifically, research questions, participants, data collection and data analysis. In chapter five, the writer elaborated three research results about the component of the positive psychology, individual differences, and prediction of the positive psychology. In chapter six, the writer made a in-depth discussion on results, analyzing the potential reasons behind the results and looking into the future prospect of positive psychology in SLA. In chapter seven, the writer concluded the whole thesis.

1. literature Review

1.1 Theoretical Research

At abroad, there are many theoretical researches on positive psychology in SLA. (Seligman and Csikszentmihalyi, 2000: 5) "positive psychology was established on three pillars: positive experiences, positive character traits and positive institutions." (Fredrickson, 2001) "Broaden and Build theory" pointed out that positive emotions (such as happiness, interest, satisfaction, pride, and love) had at least five positive functions: 1) to expand attention and thinking mode, helping broaden horizon and pursue new knowledge; 2) to eliminate the residual effect of negative emotions after awakening, improving mental (or even physical) health; 3) to enhance psychological resilience; 4) to create individual resources; 5) an important component of spiral rising to higher happiness. MacIntyre and Gregergsen (2012) believed positive emotions were good to enhance learners' ability to pay attention to new things and enable them to take in more language input information.

Pekrun and his collaborators (2006) put forward a conceptual framework of Academic Emotion, which pointed out that various academic emotions has different impacts on learning and affirmed positive emotions' role. Pekrun and Linnenbrink-Garcia (2012) defined academic emotion as the emotion aroused in academic context and divided it into three dimensions: potency (positive and negative emotions), activity (arousal of emotions), and goal (specific objects of arousal of emotions). Pekrun (2006) proposed the Control-Value theory for academic achievement, and thought that academic achievement emotion was influenced by two factors: one was learners' cognition of past, current and future academic activities or results degree, named control appraisal; the other was learners' value judgment of academic activities or results, named value appraisal. (Salovey et al., 2011: 238) "Emotional intelligence is the ability to understand feelings in the self and others and to use these feelings as informational guides for thinking and action" Dewale (2013) claimed for a multilingual learner, the higher emotional intelligence he had, the less foreign language anxiety he would feel.

(Jean Marc and Li, 2020: 38) "Aligning with the tradition in psychology, in terms of the underlying theories to conceptualize emotions in L2 learning, there are two main approaches: the basic approach and the dimensional approach." Traditionally, based on the basic emotion theory, it has labeled six basic emotions, happiness, surprise, fear, disgust, anger and sadness. Based on the dimensional theory, emotions are individual constructions of three independent and bipolar dimensions: pleasure/valence arousal/activation, and dominance. (Mehrabian and Russell, 1974). (Dewael et al., 2018; Jiang and Dewaele, 2019; Li, 2019) Foreign language pleasure is positively correlated to most of the individual differences including foreign language level, personal learning attitude, personality characteristics, emotional intelligence, etc.

At home, although there are fewer theories about positive psychology in SLA field than that in foreign countries, there are also some positive psychology variables, such as positive emotion and positive individual characteristics entering domestic SLA scholars' vision. Jiang Guiying and Li Chengchen (2017) concluded that positive psychological role to positive turn of SLA research, namely, from negative emotion to positive emotion, from negative emotion to emotional intelligence, from PERMA to EMPHATHICS. Zeng Guang, Zhao Yukun and others (2018) thought that positive education is the result of positive psychology's application in the field of education. Positive education aims to cultivate students' positive character and the ability to create a happy life. Wang Fushun (2018: 161) thought "Moderate emotional excitement can make individual's mind and body in the best state of activity, and then promote the individual to effectively complete the task." Yu Weihua et al. (2015) pointed out that emotional intelligence, as an individual trait, can regulate anxiety, thus indirectly and positively affect foreign language performance.

1.2 Empirical Research

At abroad, Tin's research (2013) verified interest as a combination of positive emotion and cognition, which stimulated in-depth learning in various educational environments. Through empirical research, Lake (2013) pointed out that the positive self variable may play an intermediary role between the overall positive self variable and motivation variable, such as effort, self-efficacy. The empirical research of Dewaele and MacIntyre (2016) showed that the relationship between foreign language pleasure and foreign language anxiety was not binary opposition. They coexist in different levels of foreign language learners, and the anxiety and pleasure level of female students are higher than that of male students, but Jiang and Dewaele (2019) suggested students didn't show gender differences in Chinese universities.

At home, Han Ye and Xu Yueting (2020) took written corrective feedback (WCF) as an example, and used case study method to explore four Chinese college students' academic emotions and their adjustment strategies in the process of second language writing learning. They found that WCF awoke different academic emotions across positive, neutral, negative valence and high, medium and low levels, and there were individual differences in dynamic changes in emotions. Li Chengchen (2020), taking advantage of a questionnaire survey and combining English assessment, studied 1307 Chinese senior high school students to explore emotional intelligence, emotion (pleasure, anxiety and burnout) and English performance's relationship. He found three emotions played multiple parallel mediating roles between emotional intelligence and English performance. Jiang Yan (2020) adopted the focus-writing research method to investigate 646 freshmen of non-English majors in some university in Beijing to study teachers' factors influencing Chinese college students' foreign language pleasure.

Compared with foreign researches, positive psychological development in SLA at home is relatively slow, which is still in its infancy. The inadequacy includes: 1) The term of positive psychology is very rare in Second Language Acquisition at home and the systematic research of relevant theories is far from enough; 2) A large number of positive psychology researches on SLA researches mainly focus on pleasure and anxiety, and fewer researches on other psychological variables; 3) Effective empirical researches show great deficiency, for example, much attention of the researches is paid on middle and primary school students, while the sample of college students are few.

In view of this, the writer selected 101 college students to study their positive psychology, aiming to solve three problems: 1) To identify the positive psychological factors of college students during the process of English learning. 2) To analyse individual differences including gender, grade and family background. 3) To explore positive psychology's predictive effect on students' English achievement.

2. Three Phases of Emotion Research in SLA

According to J.M Dewaele and Li Chengchen (2020), there are three broad phases of development of emotions' research in SLA. The first is Emotion-Avoidance phases during the early 1960s and the mid-1980s. At that time, researches focused on the cognitive effect in language learning while the affective factors were just the marginal effect. (Scovel, 1978) What's more, the word "emotions" was also very scant and even not absent. There were only some traces of it such as "desire" "attitudes" and so on. This phase was characterized by sparse and confusing foreign language anxiety studies in the so-called "Confounded Approach" (MacIntyre, 2017: 11). More specifically, there was confusion surrounding the construct of "anxiety" and its measurement, which were not necessarily or consistently related to the specific domain of L2 learning. This further led to "mixed and confusing results" (Scovel, 1978: 132) in the correlations between anxiety and foreign language learning, supporting the "facilitating and debilitating anxiety" distinction (Scovel, 1978). In the paper, Scovel (1978) reviewed the anxiety research and highlighted the need to define and measure both anxiety and anxiety-related language learning dimensions, sowing seeds for the next phase, namely the Anxiety-Prevailing Phase." (J.M Dewaele. and li Chengchen, 2020)

The second is Anxiety-Prevailing phase between the mid-1980s and early 2010s. In this period, researches put heavy focus on the single anxiety factor, which was originated from the Krashen's Affective Filter Hypothesis (Krashen, 1985) and the work of Foreign Language Classroom Anxiety. Anxiety-Prevailing phase admitted that affective emotions played a role in SLA and the anxiety had been studied extensively.

The third is Positive and negative emotions phase. Since the PP was introduced in SLA in 2012, it has soon strengthened the affective turn in SLA. Various emotions that were overlooked in the past has attracted linguistics' eye to research them including negative emotions and positive emotions. "The growing number of studies on FLE and FLCA have catalyzed the emotional turning applied linguistics and inspired researchers to consider diverse emotions using a variety of theories and methods. However, greater diversity is encouraged as well as closer integration of emotion theories in SLA research designs. Shao et al. (2019: 3) pointed out that "The past three decades has witnessed important development in research on emotion and SLA". Indeed, a considerable number of empirical studies have highlighted the causes, effects and correlates of emotions experienced in L2 learning, while insufficient attention has been paid to the underpinning theories at work for the conceptualization of L2 emotions and their associations with other factors." (J.M Dewaele and Li Chengchen, 2020)

3. Theoretical Model

3.1 PERMA

PERMA model of Seligman (2012) is one of the important achievements of positive psychology. Seligman believed that happiness and prosperity are two different concepts. Prosperity is an independent component of subjective well-being with life satisfaction as the main indicator. Prosperity means living in an ideal human society, which means kindness, reproduction, growth and flexibility. Thus, Seligman further put forward his famous PERMA theory.

The term PERMA is the acronym of five factors including Positive emotions, Engagement, Relationships, Meaning and Accomplishment. 1) Positive emotions: including pleasure and subjective well-being. Positive emotions make us more successful in friendship, love and cooperation, and can generate more comprehensive attention, more creative and comprehensive thinking. 2) Engagement: the feeling of Engagement is a flow. In this state, people forget the time flying and the external things, putting his heart and soul into their current activities. The reliable way to let a person enter the state of flow is to give full play to strength and apply them in life and work. 3) Relationships. Researchers have found that helping others is the most reliable way to improve happiness. Loneliness has a great negative effect on life and positive relationships can effectively improve people's health and life span. 4) Meaning: to belong to and commit to something that you think is beyond yourself. 5) Accomplishment. This can be an ultimate pursuit, regardless of any positive emotions. Some people only regard wining as the purpose of life, in order to win to win.

3.2 EMPATHICS

Oxford (2016: 24 – 25) pointed out that there were four problems in PERMA model: 1) Positive psychology only focuses on positive emotions and ignores the prevailing negative emotions; 2) Participation and meaning separate; 3) lack of consideration of background factors; 4) the concept of "Accomplishment" is vague. In view of these, Oxford modified PERMA model and proposed the EMPATHICS model, namely, Emotion and Empathy, Meaning and Motivation, Perseverance, Agency, Time, Hardiness and Habits of mind, Intelligence, Character strengths and Self factors. (MacIntyre, Gregersen and Mercer, 2016: 10)

EMPATHICS has greatly promoted the development of positive psychology in SLA. It takes negative emotions into account and points out that negative emotions may also play a positive role. Besides, it promotes the social turn of SLA research and opens up a new vistas for theory and research, for language teaching practice and of course, for language learning itself.

Focusing positive psychology mainly on Emotion and Empathy in EMPATHICS, the writer studied four positive emotions further.

3.2.1 Happiness

Firstly, Happiness. Happiness refers to a series of emotions of joy and pleasure that human beings subjectively produce based on their satisfaction and security, which is used mainly for philosophers of the modern era of speculation and people's choices of individual lifestyle. Until the modern time, it came into social movements and the system construction, which embodied a kind of historic progress to human. An important achievement brought by modernization is the continuous improvement of living conditions and quality. However, modernization is also a process full of paradoxes. Compared with the improvement of objective well-being, subjective happiness does not show a corresponding increase, which undoubtedly constitutes a dilemma of modernization. The measurement of people's subjective well-being became a hot research in psychological field from the late 1960s to the mid-1980s.

In addition, the understanding of subjective happiness involves many analytical levels, mainly including cognition and emotion, horizontal and vertical, time points and periods, individuals and groups, and so on. Among the close connections between subjective happiness and many factors and levels of social psychological system, there is one point that is very unique and important: Achievement motive level. The achievements needs people to determine their level of achievement motivation and their expected goal. Of the people, their achievement level of consciousness is an important link, because if they realize their achievement level is higher than their ambitious goal, then, they will have an intense feeling of happiness; Conversely, there is no sense of happiness if people are aware that their level of achievement is below their desired level of ambition.

(MacIntyre, Gregersen and Mercer, 2016: 34) "Positive psychology often view happiness as a prime positive emotion, and some detractors of positive psychology and even some proponents used to call the field 'Happiology'." Seligman (2002) believed, "happiness originates from one's own advantages and virtues. Only when he makes his own efforts can he gains a real sense of happiness." That is to say, satisfaction of happiness will be obtained when one achieved something by his effort.

3.2.2 Transcendence

Secondly, Transcendence. Transcendence is a process of knowing oneself, daring to challenge oneself, conquering oneself, transcending oneself and others and going to success. (Adler, 2016: 34) "Everyone can find such a clue in their lives, that is, from bottom to top, from failure to success, from humble position to superior position. Such a line of action starts from childhood and spread to the end of life." Maslow (1987), a famous humanistic psychologist, pinpointed that self-transcendence and self-realization were human nature. And this personality power doesn't vary by nationality, culture, gender or age, which is possessed by everyone. Maslow called this power of personality as transcendental motivation. He also put forward the concept of "peak experience" by studying many successful people, which is a kind of emotional experience of satisfaction, transcendence and happiness from the heart. Everyone will feel the peak experience in life, but the frequency of experience varies. The difference between individuals who are called self-realization and ordinary people is that the peak time is far more frequent, intense and pure in self-realization people than that in ordinary people.

3.2.3 Optimism

Thirdly, Optimism. (MacIntyre, Gregersen and Mercer, 2016: 34) "Optimism is particularly linked to expectancy-value theories of motivation, which assume that the behaviour reflects the pursuit of goals. Compared with pessimists, it's easier for optimists to believe they can achieve a valued goal and they confidently persevere, even when facing adversity."

(Carver et al., 2011) Optimism and pessimism are broad versions of confidence or doubt pertaining to most situations in life; a key definition of optimism is a pattern of generalized positive expectations for the future dispositional optimism. People attempt to fit their behaviour to attain the goal, and they have a certain expectancy or degree of confidence that the goal can be attained. Optimists are more likely than pessimists to believe they can achieve a valued goal, and they confidently persevere, even when facing adversity. In this way, Optimists look much like resilient people. (Carver et al., 2011) Conversely, pessimists doubt that the goal can be reached and are therefore hesitant or reluctant when dealing with adversity.

For a pessimist, defeat seems permanent, destroys everything and appears to have been caused by the person himself or herself. For an optimist, defeat is viewed as temporary, restricted to a specific case and not his or her fault. For instance, a pessimist might say, self-disparagingly, "I don't have an ear for languages", while an optimist might leave the door open for improvement and say "I haven't yet developed my ear for languages."

3.2.4 Attachment

Fourthly, Attachment. (Wang, 2018: 94) "Attachment means a strong feeling of affection for somebody or something. In language learning, this attachment relationship between mother and child can be compared to the relationship between students and other people or things."

"① Student-teacher relationships and classroom are significantly related to students' achievement and attitude towards learning. ② Certain teacher behaviors, e.g., teacher leadership, Being understanding, helpful and friendly are positive teacher behaviors that teachers should demonstrate liberally in class-more of such teacher behaviors will result in better/supportive classroom environment. ③ A classroom environment is conductive to learning environment affects both the cognitive and affective developments of students. ④ Most of the students worldwide revealed that the learning environment affects both the cognitive and affective developments of students. ⑤ The evidence is clear-the learning or classroom environment can promote or hinder students' learning; the more conductive the environment, the better the students' achievement and attitude towards learning. ⑥ A close teacher-student relationship will further enhance and maintain this conductive classroom environment."

4. Research Design

4.1 Research Questions

This paper aims to solve the following three problems: First, what kind of positive psychology do college students have in English learning? Second, is there a significant difference in sex, grade, and family background among students? Third, is there a predictive effect of positive psychology on students' English levels?

4.2 Participants

In total, there are 101 college students participating in survey including 27 male students and 74 female students, who come from different provinces and different family backgrounds.

4.3 Data Collection

For data collection, firstly, the writer interviewed some students around this subject. Secondly, the writer compiled 25 questions about positive psychological factors and made three tests and modifications. Each time, the number of people in test was more than 5 times of the number of questions. After each test, the writer analyzed the reliability and validity of the questionnaire until it met writer's expectation. The final questionnaire comprises two parts, students' personal information needed filling out including the sex, grade, province, family background and self-rated English level and 16 questions left for research. About 9 questions are deleted which are tested as non-sense questions. Each question has five Likert scale, from total agreement to total disagreement. The scores are 5, 4, 3, 2 and 1.

The questionnaire was issued in April 2020. After requesting for students' consent, the writer disputed 113 questionnaire to students and promised that all information would be absolutely confidential. At last, the writer adopted 101 valid questionnaires used for statistical analysis after removing some invalid questionnaire.

4.4 Data Analysis

After collecting data, the writer input all the scores of the questionnaire and other information into the computer, and takes advantage of social science statistics software SPSS 25 for processing. The statistical procedures were: 1) using factor analysis to extract common factors in 16 questions. 2) using independent sample t-test to analyse students' sex and family backgrounds difference in positive psychology. using variance test to analyse students' grades' difference in positive psychology. 3) Using multiple regression analysis to observe students' positive psychological prediction on English levels.

5. Results

5.1 Components of Positive Psychology

In order to have a better understanding of college students' positive psychology, this study adopts the method of factor analysis. The priority is to ensure whether the original observation variables are suitable for factor analysis (See Table 1). We can see the KMO value is 0.854, and the companion rate in the spherical test is 0.000 less than 0.05. As a result, it is suitable for factor analysis.

Table 1 KMO and Bartlett's Test

Kaiser-Meyer-Olkin Measure of Sampling Adequacy		.854
Bartlett's Test of Sphericity	Approx.Chi-Square	1 031.296
	df	120
	Sig.	.000

As can be seen from Table 2, four factors are extracted by Principal Component Analysis. The naming principle of factor is the size of factor load coefficient. The principle of arrangement, analysis and interpretation is the size of its variance contribution rate. The factor load after orthogonal rotation is shown in Table 2.

Table 2　Rotated Component Matrixa

Question	Component			
	1	2	3	4
5	.811			
6	.761			
7	.752			
4	.598			
9		.801		
8		.754		
10		.693		
12		.662		
11		.552		
14			.821	
13			.815	
15			.581	
16			.569	
2				.765
1				.723
3				.650

According to the factor load matrix after orthogonal rotation, there are four factors were extracted. The specific correspondence is as follows:

1) Happiness (Question 1. Teachers' commendation makes me feel happy to study. Question 2. When I can apply what I have learned to practice, I have a sense of achievement. Question 3. English learning not only enables me to acquire new knowledge, but also broadens my horizon.)

2) Transcendence (Question 4. I expect my better performance in English class. Question 5. I often compare with excellent students and try to surpass them. Question 6. I aspire transcendence in learning. Question 7. By contrast, I work harder than others in my class.)

3) Optimism (Question 8. I encourage myself to relax and play normally in the exam. Question 9. There are more ways than difficulties. Question 10. Facing challenges, I encourage myself to overcome difficulties and forge ahead. Question 11. The occasional test failure will not reduce my confidence. Question 12. It's common to make mistakes in English learning.)

4) Attachment (Question 13. I hope to have more native English speaking foreign friends. Question 14. Cooperative learning can improve my English learning ability. Question 15. The profession of English teachers makes a great difference on me. Question 16. My oral English training mainly depends on vivid class teaching.)

5.2 Individual Differences

5.2.1 T-Test of Sex and Family Background

This research adopts Independent Sample T-Test to observe whether there are sex and and family background differences in college students' positive psychology in English learning. (See Table 3 and Table 4)

Table 3 Independent Sample T-Test of Sex

Dimensions	Sex	Number	Average	Standard Deviation	df	t	p
Happiness	Male	27	4.135 9	.828 84	99	−1.219	.226
	Female	74	4.320 0	.605 64			
Transcendence	Male	27	3.601 9	1.058 98	34.113	.080	.937
	Female	74	3.584 5	.679 04			
Optimism	Male	27	4.029 6	.814 68	33.393	.517	.609
	Female	74	3.943 2	.499 34			

续表

Dimensions	Sex	Number	Average	Standard Deviation	df	t	p
Attachment	Male	27	3.787 0	.987 19	34.777	−.594	.556
	Female	74	3.908 8	.657 64			

1) (See Table 3) Independent Sample T-Test of sex suggests the P values of four positive psychologies are larger than 0.05. Thus, there is no sex difference in college students' positive psychologies in English learning.

2) (See Table 4) Independent Sample T-Test of Family background shows the P values of four positive psychologies are larger than 0.05. Consequently, there is no family background difference in college students' positive psychologies in English learning.

Table 4　Independent Sample T-Test of Family Background

Dimensions	Family Background	Number	Average	Standard Deviation	df	t	p
Happiness	Town	59	4.293 7	.695 29	99	.404	.687
	Countryside	42	4.238 6	.647 59			
Transcendence	Town	59	3.516 9	.872 06	99	−1.085	.280
	Countryside	42	3.690 5	.662 15			
Optimism	Town	59	4.010 2	.619 70	99	.874	.384
	Countryside	42	3.904 8	.564 37			
Attachment	Town	59	3.839 0	.761 07	99	.585	.560
	Countryside	42	3.928 6	.755 64			

5.2.2　Variance Test of Grade

This survey takes variance test to observe whether there are grade differences in college students' positive psychology. (See Table 5)

Table 5 Variance Test of Grade

Dimensions	Grade	Number	Average	Standard Deviation	F	Sig.(2-tailed)
Happiness	Sophomores/Freshmen	23/2	4.188 7/2.830 0	.649 83/.707 11	3.794	.005
	Juniors/Freshmen	31/2	4.279 7/2.830 0	.639 67/.707 11		.003
	Seniors/Freshmen	45/2	4.370 7/2.830 0	.648 15/.707 11		.001
Optimism	Sophomores/Freshmen	23/2	4.052 2/2.800 0	.464 04/1.414 21	3.432	.004
	Juniors/Freshmen	31/2	3.871 0/2.800 0	.547 84/1.414 21		.012
	Seniors/Freshmen	45/2	4.040 0/2.800 0	.611 41/1.414 21		.004
Attachment	Sophomores/Freshmen	23/2	3.956 5/1.875 0	.601 38/1.237 44	5.548	.000
	Juniors/Freshmen	31/2	3.959 7/1.875 0	.544 28/1.237 44		.000
	Seniors/Freshmen	45/2	3.866 7/1.875 0	.831 89/1.237 44		.000

$P<0.05$

1) Freshmen and the other three senior students show significant differences in three positive psychologies, that is, happiness, optimism and attachment.

2) In detail, first of all, in happiness, freshmen (Likert average score is 2.830 0) don't support this test score, while the other three senior students (Likert average score is more than 4.1) are sure of learning well-being. And the gap between Freshmen and seniors is the biggest. Secondly, in terms of learning optimism, freshmen (Likert average score is 2.800 0) lack of optimism about

difficulties in learning. Compared with freshmen, sophomores and seniors (the average score of Likert is more than 4) are more hopeful. One point worthy noting is that juniors (Likert is 3.871 0) are more optimistic than freshmen, but the degree is not high. 3) In terms of attachment psychology, freshmen (Likert average score is 1.875 0) don't recognized attachment emotion, while sophomores, juniors and seniors (Likert average score is more than 3.8 but less than 4) have stronger attachment, though the degree is not high.

5.3 The Prediction of Positive Psychology on English Levels.

Table 6 Results of Multiple Regression Analysis

	Positive Psychology	R	R2	F	β	T	Sig
1	Transcendence	.332	0.101	12.343	.332	−3.499	.001
							$P<0.01$

To identify learners' positive psychological prediction on their English scores, the writer takes four Positive Psychology extracted as independent variables and self-assessment English levels as dependent variables, and uses stepwise method to conduct multiple regression analysis. The results are shown in Table 6.

According to Table 6, only one factor, transcendence, enters the regression equation model. The R complex correlation coefficient of model 1 is 0.332, and the R2 determination coefficient is 0.101. That is to say, transcendence psychology can explain the variance of 10.1% of English achievement. The significance level is small, which indicates that the regression coefficient is significant. In a word, transcendence can positively predict students' English levels.

6. Discussion

In a word, by investigation and research, this paper holds that 1) students have four positive psychologies of English learning, happiness, transcendence, optimism and attachment. 2) In individual difference, college students does not show differences in gender and family background, but exhibits grade diversity in happiness, optimism and attachment. 3) Transcendental psychology has a positive predict on students' English scores.

Through discussing this outcome, the writer explained as follows: firstly, the writer found different from her conclusion of no gender difference in positive psychology, Dewaele and MacIntyre (2006) believed that female students obtains more pleasure from foreign language than male students. Jiang and Dewaele (2019) embraced the same view as writer. All of them denied sex difference. About this, the author added the reason causing difference may because the proportion of female students (73%) in the survey is too large, it's difficult to tell sex differences.

Secondly, the research negated family background influence on students' positive psychology. The writer inferred it's closely related to government's great efforts to narrow urban and rural areas' gap to advance education equity. Besides, the role of online education is inevitable. It is said that online education has greatly reduced the education gap between urban and rural areas.

Thirdly, as for grade differences, as the Table 5 shows, in terms of happiness, optimism and attachment, freshmen show great uncertainty and neglect. We can infer that it may because of some freshmen's unfamiliarity and inadaptability to surrounding environment, when they came into a totally strange school, it's difficult for them to develop significant positive emotions. Adding that if they are faced with more free space but low self-disciplinary, more trifles but weak-resist pressure and more social open occasions but the poor psychological defense mechanism, they easily develop in the unhappier and more depressed way. Nevertheless, with the increase of grade, we can observe that there are remarkable increase in three emotions. That's because that college students have gradually established good interpersonal relationship, more self-discipline and strong psychological defense mechanism through the adaptation to the surrounding environment and rich experience during four years. Therefore, in English learning, they will feel more sense of well-being, establish intimate attachment relationship with teachers, classmates and other things, and take an optimistic attitude when facing difficulties. At last, the writer had to mention that the cause of big grade difference may also be the lack of freshmen sample.

Fourthly, as for transcendence's positive prediction, Maslow (2003: 31) believed the happiness of life is not the sum of the number of satisfaction generated by individual needs in the long distance of life. The establishment of happiness of life is not based on the cascade connection of successive satisfaction, but a satisfaction formed by constantly updating and expanding their own influence in their value world. This kind of satisfaction makes human nature in the state of full and uninterrupted pursuit, which is the spiritual state that can be possessed by people who are constantly developing their potential and pursuing self transcendence. The people who pursue self realization are not motivated by basic needs, but by transcendental needs — existence value. In addition, the self-determination theory proposed by American psychologists Deci and Ryan (2017) held that the individual had original driving force and potential for growth and the tendency of active development. This point has been verified in the practice of transcendental teaching method. Both of these two important theories verified the inner power of transcendence, which can explained its positive prediction on students' English levels.

The above conclusions brings much light to the future development of Positive Psychology in SLA. It's crucial to look ahead the prospects of positive psychology in SLA.

First of all, more space are supposed to the further study of conception and empirical research of Positive Psychology in SLA. Despite the large number of studies in positive psychology in L2 language learning, the concepts were drawn from the neighbouring disciplines, especially in educational psychology and social psychology, thus they cannot be well-adapted in L2 learning. (J.M Dewaele and Li Chengchen, 2020)

Second, a wider range of emotions can be taken into account to enrich present fruits, helping students' all sound development. That is to say, the further studies should extend the range and emotions in order to give a full play to examine the role of other language emotions, which is conductive to language teaching and learning.

Third, more efforts should be made for teachers to strengthen the practical application of psychological intervention in teaching. For example, based on this paper's conclusion, teachers can formulate different teaching plans according to students' grade difference in positive psychology, and make full use of students' transcendental psychology to help improve students' English grades, which is conductive to students' learning effect as well as their physical and mental health. It's urgent for L2 teachers to draw on their emotional competence to perceive and moderate freshman's negative emotions. In happiness of learning, it's advisable to conduct a plan of achievement appraisal for students to lead them have a happier learning experience and produce a kind of self-fulfillment. In optimism, teachers could pay attention to encourage freshmen to challenge themselves and try to overcome adversity of language learning. In attachment, more activities and interactions about language learning could be considered by higher educational institutes to enhance their language attachment.

Fourth, students should also utilize the positive psychology to improve their English level. According to the research results that the transcendence psychology has a positive prediction on English achievements, students who want to improve their language level should attach more importance to develop their competent emotions. Only in such a way that their language level can have a significant improvement.

7. Conclusion

With an eye on positive psychology and second language acquisition, by means of interview and survey questionnaire, this paper researches 101 college students' positive psychologies in English learning, who are of different provinces in some University. By factors' analysis, the writer puts forward four positive psychologies, namely, happiness, transcendence, optimism and attachment. By independent sample test, it indicates that college students don't have sex and family background difference in four dimensions. By variance test, it suggests that students of different grades just show diversity in three dimensions, happiness, optimism and attachment. By multiple regression analysis, it reflects that transcendental psychology has a positive prediction on College Students' English grades, that is, the stronger the student's transcendental psychology is, the better his English is. The results of this study will be of great significance to foreign language teaching and learning as well as students' health in China.

Last but not at least, about this passage, the writer thought there are still much space to improve, such as more data collecting, more emotions researched, more deep analysis from different angles and so on. Next, the writer spare no effort to further studying in positive psychology in SLA.

References

[1] CARVER C S, SCHEIER M F, MILLER C J, and FULFORD D. Optimism. In Lopez, S.J. and Snyder, C.R. (eds) Snyder The Oxford Handbook of Positive Psychology [C]. New York: Oxford University Press, 2011: 303-311.

[2] DEWAELE J M. Emotions and language learning. In Byram, M. and Hu, A. (eds) Routledge Encyclopedia of Language Teaching and Learning [J]. London: Routledge, 2013, (2): 217-220.

[3] DEWAELE J M, ALFAWZAN M. Does the effect of enjoyment outweigh that of anxiety in foreign language performance? [J]. Studies in Second Language Learning and Teaching, 2018, 8 (1): 21-45.

[4] DEWAELE J M, CHENGCHEN L. Emotions in second language acquisition: critical review and research agenda [J]. Foreign Language World, 2020, (1): 34-49.

[5] DEWAELE J M, MACINTYRE, P D. Foreign language enjoyment and foreign language classroom anxiety: The right and left foot of FL learning? [A]. In MacIntyre, P.D., Gregersen, T. and Mercer, S. (eds) Positive Psychology in SLA [C]. Bristol: Multilingual Matters, 2016: 215-236.

[6] FREDRICKSON B L. The role of positive emotions in Positive Psychology: The broaden-and-build theory of positive emotions [J]. American Psychologist, 2001, 56 (3): 218-226.

[7] JIANG Y, DEWAELE J M. How unique is the foreign language classroom enjoyment and anxiety of Chinese EFL learners? [J]. System, 2019, 82: 13-25.

[8] KRASHEN S D. The Input Hypothesis: Issues and Implications[M]. London: Longman, 1985.

[9] LAKE J. Positive L2 self: Linking positive psychology with L2 motivation[A]. In Apple, M.T., Da Silva, D. and Fellner, T.(eds). Language Learning Motivation in Japan[C]. Bristol: Multilingual Matters, 2013: 225-244.

[10] LI C A. Positive Psychology perspective on Chinese EFL students' trait emotional intelligence, foreign language enjoyment and EFL learning achievement[J]. Journal of Multilingual and Multicultural Development, 2019.李成陈老师2019年科研成果。

[11] MACINTYRE P D, GREGERSEN T M. Emotions that facilitate language learning: The positive-broadening power of the imagination[J]. Studies in Second Language Learning and Teaching, 2012, 2(2): 193-213.

[12] MACINTYRE P D, GREGERSEN T M, MERCER S. Positive Psychology in SLA[M]. UK: Short Run Press Ltd, 2016.

[13] MEHRABIAN A, RUSSELL J. An Approach to Environmental Psychology[M]. Cambridge, MA: The MIT Press, 1974.

[14] PEKRUN R. The control-value theory of achievement emotions: Assumptions, corollaries, and implications for educational research and practice[J]. Educational Psychology Review, 2006, 18(4): 315-341.

[15] PEKRUN R, LINNENBRINK-GARCIA L. Academic emotions and student engagement[C]. In Christenson, S.L., Reschly, A.L. and Wylie, C.(eds) Handbook of Research on Student Engagement[C]. New York: Springer, 2012: 259-282.

[16] RYAN R M, DECI E L. Self-determination theory: Basic psychological needs in motivation, development and wellness[M]. New York: Guilford Press, 2017: 86.

[17] SALOVEY P, MAYER J D, CARUSO D, YOO S H. The positive psychology of emotional intelligence[A]. In S.J. Lopez and C.R. Snyder (eds). The Oxford Handbook of positive Psychology[C]. New York: Oxford University Press, 2011: 237-248.

[18] SCOVEL T. The effect of affect on foreign language learning: A review of the anxiety research[J]. Language Learning, 1978, 28(1): 129-142.

[19] SELIGMAN M E P. Authentic Happiness[M]. New York: Free Press, 2002.

[20] SELIGMAN M E P. Flourish: A visionary new understanding of happiness and well-being[M]. New York: Simon and Schuster, 2012.

[21] SELIGMAN M E P, CSIKSZENTMIHALYI M. Positive psychology: An introduction[J]. American psychologist, 2000, 55(1): 5-14.

[22] TIN T B. Exploring the development of "interest" in learning English as a foreign/second language[J]. RELC Journal, 2013, 44(2): 129-146.

[23] 阿德勒.自卑与超越[M].徐珊,译.北京:民主与建设出版社,2016.

[24] 韩晔,许悦婷.积极心理学视角下二语写作学习的情绪体验及情绪调节策略研究:以书面纠正性反馈为例[J].外语界,2020,(1):50-59.

[25] 江桂英,李成陈.积极心理学视角下的二语习得研究述评与展望[J].外语界,2017,(5):32-39.

[26] 姜艳.影响中国大学生外语愉悦的教师因素研究[J].外语界,2020,(1):60-68.

[27] 李成陈.情绪智力与英语学业成绩的关系探究:愉悦、焦虑及倦怠的多重中介作用[J].外语界,2020,(1):69-78.

[28] 马斯洛.自我实现的人[M].许金声,刘锋,译.北京:生活·读书·新知三联书店,1987.

[29] 马斯洛.马斯洛人本哲学[M].成明,编译.北京:九州出版社,2003.

[30] 王福顺.情绪心理学[M].北京:人民卫生出版社,2018.

[31] 余卫华,邵凯祺,项易珍.情商、外语学习焦虑与英语学习成绩的关系[J].现代外语,2015,(5):656-666.

[32] 曾光,赵昱鲲,等.幸福的科学:积极心理学在教育中的应用[M].上海:人民邮电出版社,2018.

点评

论文采用积极心理学的模型对大学生二语习得进行问卷调查,分析了不同年级学生的积极心理因素对外语学习的作用。分析论证过程层次清晰、论证比较充分,研究结果对于外语教学和学习具有一定的参考价值。论文用英语写成,语言表达顺畅达意,可进一步学术化。文献综述和理论介绍部分可进一步凝练。

脑梗死住院期患者中成药应用特征的真实世界研究

李鑫涛 崔伟锋 范军铭*

摘要：**目的** 本研究旨在发掘脑梗死住院期的中成药应用规律，为脑梗死住院期的中成药应用提供科学可靠的证据。**方法** 本研究选择自2014年1月至2015年12月期间在各研究中心住院的脑梗死患者病例数据，分析诊断信息，并运用关联规则分析方法分析其中成药联合用药特征。**结果** 796例脑梗死住院期患者常合并有高血压病、贫血、冠心病等，高血压病最多（555例，占69.7%），其次为糖尿病（246例，占30.9%），TIA病史（234例，占29.4%），冠心病（223例，占28%），高脂血症（198例，占24.9%）。脑梗死住院期患者，常联合应用复方丹参片、血塞通软胶囊、血塞通片、通心络胶囊、黄竹定眩丸、天智颗粒等中成药。**结论** 真实世界中脑梗死住院期患者活血化瘀类、益气活血类和理气活血类中成药联合应用较为常见，其药理作用适合脑梗死住院期患者的合并疾病，且常用联合用药关联规则组合呈特定规律，为后续研究和临床合理用药提供了参考和依据。

关键词：脑梗死住院期；中成药；联合应用；真实世界；关联规则

脑梗死又称缺血性脑卒中，是指由于脑部血液供应障碍，缺血、缺氧引起的局限性脑组织的缺血性坏死或脑软化[1]，在中国传统医学中属于"中风"一类。脑梗死（Cerebral Infarction，CI），包括现代医学的脑栓塞、腔隙性脑梗死、脑血栓

---

* 李鑫涛：河南中医药大学2018级硕士研究生。
  崔伟锋：医学硕士，河南中医药研究院副主任医师。
  范军铭：医学硕士，河南中医药研究院主任医师。
① 原载《时珍国医国药》2020年第8期，本书收录时略有修改。

形成、短暂性脑缺血发作等病,是目前最为常见的一种脑血管病。在《柳叶刀》杂志上发表的全球疾病负担研究中,在2010年和2013年,在中国脑血管病都是排名第一的死因。《中国脑卒中防治报告2015》的数据显示年龄超过40岁的人群患脑血管病的概率为2%;流行病学相关资料显示,我国人口死因第一位为恶性肿瘤,而恶性肿瘤之后就是脑血管病,每年患脑血管病人口超过150万人并且趋向年轻化,发病率更是逐年上升。脑梗死的发病率占据了脑血管病的80%,脑梗死的高发病率、致死率、致残率及复发率严重危害着人类生存质量。脑梗死常引起肢体功能丧失及大脑损伤,导致患者生活不能自理,不仅危害健康而且给家庭和社会造成巨大的经济负担,防控形势已经十分严峻[2]。

鉴于脑梗死的发病率和死亡率都较高,对人们健康造成严重威胁,对于其真实世界临床用药特征的研究必不可少。本研究采用多所中心大样本队列研究方法,选择自2014年1月至2015年12月期间在河南省中医药研究院附属医院、郑州大学第一附属医院、河南省人民医院、河南中医药大学第一附属医院、河南省中医院住院的脑梗死患者病例数据进行描述分析,并运用关联规则分析方法分析其中成药联合用药特征,为后续中医药研究和临床用药提供参考依据。

1. 资料与方法

1.1 数据来源

自2014年6月至2016年6月期间在河南省中医药研究院附属医院、郑州大学第一附属医院、河南省人民医院、河南中医药大学第一附属医院、河南省中医院住院的第一诊断为脑梗死的796例住院患者病例数据。

1.2 分析内容与方法

分析内容主要包括脑梗死住院期患者的合并西医诊断信息、中成药应用信息。基于诊断信息表对脑梗死住院期患者合并疾病分布情况进行频数分析;基于用药信息表对脑梗死住院期患者的治疗结局和中成药联合应用分布情况进行频数分析;依据医嘱记录,利用关联分析算法对脑梗死住院期患者的中成药联合应用特征进行分析。

1.3 统计分析

统计软件采用SAS 9.4,SPSS 25.0和R3.5.1软件arules、arulesViz包进行频次统计和关联规则分析。对患者入院一般信息(合并诊断、联合用药等)进行基于频数与率的描述性分析,采用数据挖掘中的关联规则对中成药应用情况进行分析。

2. 结果

2.1 脑梗死住院期患者的合并西医诊断

合并西医诊断合并西医诊断频数前5名:高血压病最多(555例,占69.7%),其次为糖尿病(246例,占30.9%),TIA病史(234例,占29.4%),冠心病(223例,占28%),高脂血症(198例,占24.9%)。合并西医诊断涉及疾病说明脑梗死住院期患者合并疾病主要涉及心脑血管系统、内分泌系统等。

2.2 脑梗死住院期患者的治疗结局

治疗结局中,796例住院脑梗死患者的治疗结局频数分布:治愈230例,占28.89%;显效364例,占45.73%;有效137例,占17.21%;无效56例,占7.04%;恶化9例,占1.13%。

2.3 中成药应用的名称频数分布

在全部796例脑梗死住院期患者医嘱记录中,应用的中成药共12种,主要为复方丹参片、银杏叶制剂、血塞通片、逐瘀通脉胶囊、芎竹定眩丸、血塞通软胶囊、天智颗粒等。中成药应用的名称频数分布特征见表1。

表1 中成药应用的名称频数分布

序号	中成药	频数/例	百分比/%	序号	中成药	频数/例	百分比/%
1	复方丹参片	242	30.40	7	天智颗粒	174	21.86
2	银杏叶制剂	236	29.64	8	通心络胶囊	170	21.36
3	血塞通片	228	28.64	9	中风胶囊	162	20.35
4	逐瘀通脉胶囊	201	25.25	10	脑心通胶囊	131	16.46
5	芎竹定眩丸	187	23.49	11	脑栓康复胶囊	114	14.32
6	血塞通软胶囊	180	22.61	12	消栓肠溶片	73	9.17

2.4 中成药应用的药理作用频数分布

从药理作用看,脑梗死住院期最常应用的是活血化瘀类、益气活血类和理气活血类中成药,见表2。

表2 中成药应用的药理作用频数分布

序号	药理作用	频数/例	百分比/%
1	活血化瘀	625	78.52
2	益气活血	327	41.08
3	理气活血	196	24.62
4	化痰补虚	104	13.07
5	平肝潜阳补肝肾	87	10.93

2.5 中成药应用的名称关联规则分析

脑梗死住院期患者,常联合应用复方丹参片、银杏叶制剂、血塞通片、血塞通软胶囊、茰竹定眩丸等中成药,见表3 表4。

表3 两种中成药联合应用关联规则

序号	关联规则	支持度/%	置信度/%	提升度/%
1	血塞通片=>复方丹参片	24.75	86.42	2.84
2	复方丹参片=>血塞通片	24.75	81.41	2.84
3	银杏叶制剂=>复方丹参片	24.27	81.88	2.69
4	复方丹参片=>银杏叶制剂	24.27	79.84	2.69
5	血塞通片=>银杏叶制剂	22.35	78.04	2.63
6	银杏叶制剂=>血塞通片	22.35	75.40	2.63
7	茰竹定眩丸=>逐瘀通脉胶囊	19.87	84.59	3.35
8	逐瘀通脉胶囊=>茰竹定眩丸	19.87	78.69	3.35
9	血塞通软胶囊=>复方丹参片	17.38	76.87	2.53
10	复方丹参片=>血塞通软胶囊	17.38	57.17	2.53

注:按支持度排序,节选前10位(表4同)。

表 4 三种中成药联合关联规则

序号	关联规则	支持度/%	置信度/%	提升度/%
1	血塞通片+银杏叶制剂=>复方丹参片	17.75	75.78	2.49
2	复方丹参片+血塞通片=>银杏叶制剂	17.75	69.15	2.33
3	银杏叶制剂+复方丹参片=>血塞通片	17.75	65.02	2.27
4	血塞通片+荭竹定眩丸=>逐瘀通脉胶囊	16.27	83.74	3.32
5	荭竹定眩丸+逐瘀通脉胶囊=>血塞通片	16.27	87.95	3.07
6	血塞通片+逐瘀通脉胶囊=>荭竹定眩丸	16.27	79.37	3.38
7	脑心通胶囊+血塞通软胶囊=>复方丹参片	12.38	86.14	2.83
8	复方丹参片+血塞通软胶囊=>脑心通胶囊	12.38	64.28	3.9
9	脑心通胶囊+复方丹参片=>血塞通软胶囊	12.38	75.72	3.35
10	通心络胶囊+脑心通胶囊=>血塞通软胶囊	9.98	58.70	2.60

总体来说,复方丹参片、银杏叶制剂、血塞通片、血塞通软胶囊、荭竹定眩丸联合应用较为常见,如图1。

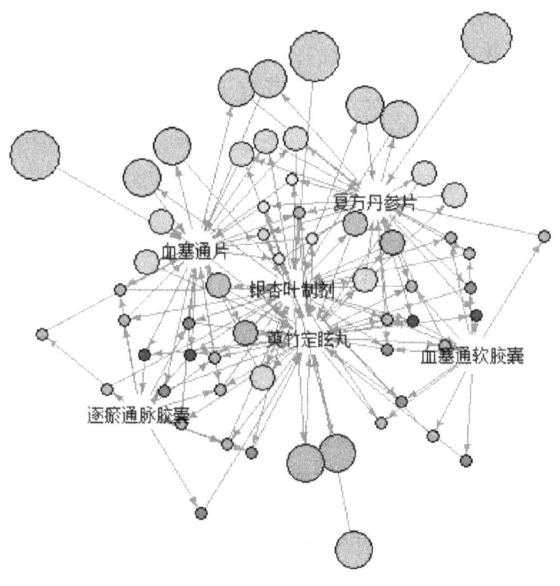

图 1 中成药应用的名称关联规则分析

2.6 中成药联合用药的药理作用关联规则分析

从药理作用看,脑梗死住院期患者主要联合应用中成药的药理作用是活血化瘀类、益气活血类和理气活血类,见表5、表6。

表5 两种中成药联合应用药理作用关联规则

序号	关联规则	支持度/%	置信度/%	提升度/%
1	活血化瘀=>益气活血	26.79	34.12	1.61
2	益气活血=>活血化瘀	26.79	65.21	1.34
3	活血化瘀=>理气活血	20.48	26.08	2.13
4	理气活血=>活血化瘀	20.48	83.18	1.71
5	化痰补虚=>活血化瘀	8.85	67.1	1.39

注：按支持度排序,节选前5位(表6同)。

表6 三种中成药联合应用关联规则

序号	关联规则	支持度/%	置信度/%	提升度/%
1	益气活血+理气活血=>活血化瘀	18.47	90.10	1.15
2	益气活血+活血化瘀=>理气活血	18.47	54.48	2.21
3	活血化瘀+理气活血=>益气活血	18.47	74.29	1.81
4	化痰补虚+理气活血=>活血化瘀	10.84	90.38	1.15
5	化痰补虚+活血化瘀=>理气活血	10.84	86.03	3.49

总而言之,脑梗死住院期患者活血化瘀类、理气活血类和益气活血类中成药联合应用较为常见,如图2。

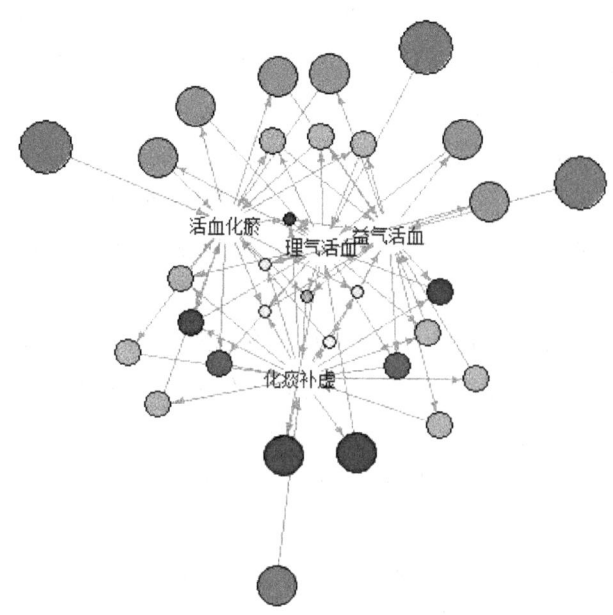

图 2 中成药联合用药药理作用关联规则分析

3. 讨论

依靠关联规则来进行数据挖掘,能够在临床药物应用数据中挖掘频繁项目集,比如药物频数分布特征等,进而能够发掘联合用药深层次相关特征规律[3-4]。支持度、置信度和提升度是不同的量化标准,能够量化关联规则的强度。支持度主要反映关联规则的重要性,也就是 A 与 B 同时出现的概率;置信度主要反映关联规则的可靠性,指的是在使用 A 的基础上再使用 B 的概率。提升度表示在含有 A 的条件下同时含有 B 的可能性与没有 A 这个条件下项集中含有 B 的可能性之比;该指标与置信度同样衡量规则的可靠性,是置信度的一种互补指标。因此,该算法能够探索复杂数据集变量间的内部隐藏联系[5]。

关联规则分析结果显示,脑梗死住院期患者联合应用 2 种中成药时,最常见的组合为复方丹参片+血塞通片,其次是银杏叶制剂+复方丹参片,血塞通片+银杏叶制剂,苋竹定眩丸+逐瘀通脉胶囊以及血塞通软胶囊+复方丹参片;联合应用 3 种中成药时,最常见的组合为血塞通片+银杏叶制剂+复方丹参片,其次为血塞通片+苋竹定眩丸+逐瘀通脉胶囊,脑心通胶囊+血塞通软胶囊+复方丹参片,以及通心络胶囊+脑心通胶囊+血塞通软胶囊。分析以上结果后可以得知,临床上脑梗死住院期患者常常联合应用复方丹参片、银杏叶制剂、血塞通片、血塞通软胶囊、黄竹定眩丸等中成药。

全部796例脑梗死住院期患者的结局指标显示,治愈230例,占28.89%;显效364例,占45.73%;有效137例,占17.21%;无效56例,占7.04%;恶化9例,占1.13%。以上数据说明脑梗死住院期治疗疗效较为确切。本研究结果显示,真实世界中脑梗死住院期患者常合并有高血压病、贫血、冠心病征等。

中国传统医学并无脑梗死的说法,中国传统医学临床上通常将其归于"中风""卒中"范畴,以突然昏仆、不省人事、半身不遂、肢体麻木,伴口眼歪斜、舌謇不语为主要症状[6]。前述统计数据显示,脑梗死住院期活血化瘀类中成药的使用频数最高,说明脑梗死治疗使用的中成药以活血化瘀为主,这正符合了传统医学对于中风病脑脉痹阻或血溢脉外,引起昏仆、不遂的病机的认识。中国传统医学理论中中风病位在脑,病机无外乎风、火、痰、气、虚、瘀六种,属本虚标实、上实下虚之证,急性期虽然有本虚,而标实较为突出,故基本治疗原则是急则治其标[7]。《灵枢·邪客》有言:"补其不足,泻其有余,调其虚实,以通其道而去其邪。"所以临证中主要应用活血化瘀法以祛邪[8]。活血化瘀类药物可以促进血液循环、抑制血小板、抗血栓等,所以能够改善微循环障碍,并改善高血压患者头晕、头痛等症状,长期使用还能够预防缺血性脑卒中、冠心病等并发症[9-10]。可以有效改善缺血部位血液供应,进而减少梗死区域、清除自由基、改善细胞损伤、减少细胞凋亡等,治疗缺血性脑卒中疗效可观[11-12]。基于前述文献,脑梗死住院期患者应用最多的活血化瘀类、益气活血类和理气活血类中成药遵循了中国传统医学理论的指导,符合脑梗死住院期患者常见合并疾病。前述真实世界联合用药规律,遵循了中国传统医学辨证论治的原则及文献中药理作用的描述。为了提高临床治疗效果,本研究整理了大量资料,得到了较为可靠的数据,科学地发掘脑梗死住院期的中成药应用规律,彰显了脑梗死住院期中成药联合应用的合理性与多样性,为脑梗死住院期的中成药应用提供了科学可靠的证据,为后续深入研究奠定了基础。

本研究选择自2014年1月至2015年12月期间在各研究中心住院的脑梗死患者病例数据,通过频数分布与关联规则分析揭示了真实世界中脑梗死住院期患者的中成药联合应用特征,种类上临床主要与活血化瘀类、益气活血类和理气活血类中成药联合应用,为后期相关研究者提供了参考,也给临床药物合理使用提供了科学证据。本研究尚有以下不足：一是本研究未完成中医证候分布特征的研究，中医证候数据缺失，整个研究体系的严谨性受到了影响；二是关联规则数据挖掘结果只是提示潜在相关关系，并不能作为因果关系判定依据，还需要深入研究验证。

参考文献

［1］ 王维治.神经病学［M］.第3版.北京：人民卫生出版社，2021.
［2］ 国家中医药管理局脑病急症协作组.中风病辨证诊断标准（试行）［J］.北京中医药大学学报，1994，17（3）：64-66.
［3］ MAHMOOD S, SHAHBAZ M, GUERGACHI A. Negative and positive association rules mining from text using frequent and infrequent item sets［J］. Sci World J, 2014：1.
［4］ 崔妍，包志强.关联规则挖掘综述［J］.计算机应用研究，2016，33（2）：330.
［5］ 谷建光.关联规则算法研究综述［J］.电子测试，2016（14）：41.
［6］ 涂婷.中医药治疗脑梗死541例数据挖掘研究［D］.成都：成都中医药大学，2017：8-9.
［7］ 韩泰哲.中医药治疗急性脑梗塞研究进展［J］.中医药信息，2010，27（2）：109-111.
［8］ 李硕杰，费智敏，张珏，等.活血化瘀法治疗高血压病研究进展［J］.亚太传统医药，2018，14（4）：89.
［9］ 罗文娥.活血化瘀法在冠心病治疗中的运用［J］.中外医疗，2013，32（36）：196-198.
［10］ 姚水年.活血化瘀法治疗冠心病80例疗效观察［J］.上海中医药杂志，1993（10）：16.
［11］ 郭春宏，任耘.活血化瘀中药注射剂在缺血性脑卒中治疗中的联合应用［J］.天津药学，2014，26（6）：61.
［12］ 张志新，运苟政.辨证使用中成药注射液治疗缺血性脑卒中140例疗效评价［J］.中医临床研究，2014，6（10）：65.

点评

论文对脑梗死住院期患者中成药应用特征的现实情况进行了较为深入的研究，选题具有重要的应用价值。整个研究过程设计严谨，结构完整，方法科学，且所得结论客观。论文对研究的不足之处予以说明，体现了诚实的学术精神。如果能补充相关研究的文献综述，则有助于证明此项研究的创新及价值所在。

多模态隐转喻视角下的图文语篇分析
——以《经济学人》封面为例

麻小晶[*]

摘要：交际媒介的多模态化使得人们在交际活动中拥有了除语言以外的其他非语言符号资源，为语篇意义构建提供了更为丰富的路径。以《经济学人》封面图文语篇为语料，通过定性和定量相结合的方法，从隐转喻理论视角对图文语篇进行解读，旨在分析其意义建构的基本路径以及隐转喻对图文语篇衔接的作用。研究发现，多模态转喻的指称功能是图文语篇构建意义的基础，跨模态隐转喻互动是图文语篇衔接的主要方式，多模态隐喻为语篇构建意义提供丰富资源。

关键词：多模态隐转喻；图文语篇；意义构建

引言

20世纪80年代开始，认知语言学家反对传统修辞学所认为的隐喻和转喻是语言修辞格的观点，认为隐喻和转喻都是人类的认知方式，即通过对一个事物的经验来理解另一个事物的经验，将隐喻和转喻的本质从语言层面提升到了思维层面，二者作为人类基本的认知方式有许多共同之处。在Goossens[1]提出隐转喻（metaphtonymy）的概念之后，越来越多研究开始关注隐喻、转喻之间的联系，有学者提出隐喻和转喻是一个连续体，转喻是隐喻的基础，两者之间存在着复杂的交互作用。然而以往关于隐转喻的研究主要在语言层面，由早期主要关注词汇和句法扩展到语篇层面，隐喻和转喻都发挥着重要的语篇衔接和连贯作用[2]。新媒体的发展带来了新的交际方式和信息传播渠道，人类在交际中拥有越来越多除语言之外的

---

[*] 麻小晶：上海大学外国语学院2019级硕士研究生。

其他符号资源,关于隐转喻的研究对象也应从原来的语言层面拓展到非语言层面。

近年来,多模态隐转喻逐渐应用到新闻话语分析当中,探讨隐喻对话语构建路径的作用以及在多模态语篇中的互动模型。赵秀凤和冯德正[3]批评分析了多模态隐转喻在《经济学人》中对形象的构建,研究指出转喻和隐喻在多模态语篇中的融合与互动更为普遍,提出应该加强对多模态隐转喻的社会维度研究;刘涛[4]从视觉修辞角度证明了隐喻和转喻之间存在普遍的嵌套结构并提出视觉转喻与视觉隐喻的作用模型;杨翕然[5]在视觉隐转喻的视角下系统分析以中美贸易关系为主题的新闻图片,提出了视觉隐转喻的多层选择性意义构建模型。现有关于隐转喻在多模态语篇中的作用模型均是建立在个案分析的基础上提出的,互动模型各具特色,缺乏系统性,但都肯定了多模态语篇中存在复杂隐喻、转喻之间的互动,是多模态语篇意义构建的主要方式。因此本文试图在现有研究的基础上,通过各个理论模型,探索多模态语篇通过隐转喻构建语篇的基本路径。

图文语篇是多模态语篇中最常见的双模态语篇,即图文共现,是目前新闻语篇最普遍的呈现模式。《经济学人》是典型的集文字和图像为一体的双模态图文语篇,常以充满创意、意蕴丰富的封面呈现,封面主要由文字标题和漫画构成,大胆巧妙地传达对国际政治、经济等新闻热点事件的态度和观点,是目前大多数学者进行多模态语篇分析的首选语料。因此,本文以《经济学人》刊物封面为例,在多模态隐转喻的理论指导下对10个封面图文语篇解读,旨在探讨图文语篇意义构建的路径和隐转喻对图文语篇衔接的作用。

1. 理论框架

1.1 多模态隐喻

隐喻和转喻都是人类认知的基本方式,两者都是通过源域和目标域之间的概念映射以达成对事物的理解。隐喻产生的基础是事物之间的相似性,语义冲突是隐喻产生的基本条件,常用表达式 A IS B 来描述概念隐喻的映射过程。隐喻的源域和目的域属于两个不同的认知域,属于跨域映射,一般由源域向靶域映射,具有单向性的特点。

随着认知语言学的隐喻性思维和多模态研究的发展,多模态隐喻研究逐渐兴起。Charles Forceville 是多模态隐喻研究的倡导者,他在1996出版的《广告中的图像隐喻》中,将隐喻分为四类并强调了图像语境对隐喻识别和解读的重要性[6]。冯德正[7]在 Forceville 的隐喻分类基础上对文字和图像隐喻做了进一步的分类,分为跨模态映射(cross-modal mapping)、单模态映射(mono-modal mapping)和多模态映射(multimodal mapping)。前两种都属于单向映射:跨模态映射指源域与目标域分属不同的模态,单模态映射指源域和目标域都属于同一模态。而多模态映射则指同时存在文字映射和图像映射。因此本文将以多模态隐喻分析框架对《经济学人》图文语篇进行隐喻分析,解读语篇中文字和图像复杂多重的隐喻互动,以探求其意义构建路径。

1.2 多模态转喻

与隐喻的跨域映射不同,转喻是在同一理想认知模型(ICM)的映射,构成转喻的基础是事物之间的邻近性,如空间邻近性、时间邻近性和因果邻近性等。通过目标域和源域之间的双向映射,一个概念实体(喻体)可以为另一概念实体(本体)提供心理通道。概念转喻在人类语言交际过程中起到"桥梁"作用,是连接语言信息和各种非语言信息的一种重要手段。转喻思维提高了语言使用和交际的经济性,使人类在运用语言时常常把感知、行为和认知紧密联系起来[2]。基于不同的分类标准,国内外学术界对转喻有多种分类。例如,Panther 和 Thornburg 从语用功能视角将转喻分为三类:指称转喻、谓词转喻和言外转喻。其中指称转喻最为常见,指用一种实体代替另一种实体的指称转换行为,如用 piano 指代弹钢琴的人。Radden 和 Kovecses[8]基于概念的邻近性从原型范畴结构角度将转喻分为整体与部分间和部分与部分间的转喻,两大类转喻下包括更为细致的分类标准,具有广泛的实用分析意义,因此本文将以此转喻类型为框架进行图文语篇的转喻分析。

整体喻部分间的转喻类别可以细分为:事物与部分转喻(America for "United America")、构成转喻(a "glass")、事件转喻(Mary speaks Spanish)、范畴与范畴成员之间的转喻(aspirin for "any pain-relieving tablet")、范畴与特征之间的转喻(white for "white people")、压缩转喻(crude for "crude oil")。

部分与部分间的转喻类别可以细分为:行为转喻(to butcher the cow)、知觉转喻(sight for "thing seen")、因果转喻(slow road for "slow traffic resulting the poor state of the road")、生产转喻(a Ford)、控制转喻(Nixon bombed Hanoi)、领属转喻(He married money)、容器转喻(The bottle is sour)、地点转喻(The whole town shown up)、符号和指代转喻(a self-contradictory utterance)、修饰转喻(Do you love me? — Yes, I do)。

1.3 多模态隐转喻

隐喻和转喻的相互作用已逐渐得到众多学者的重视,国内外关于隐转喻的研究主要有以下5种：Goossens 的隐转喻、Barcelona 和 Radden 提出的隐喻的转喻理据、Riemer 的后转喻和后隐喻、Ruiz de Mendoza 的概念相互作用模式、Geraerts 的隐喻和转喻相互作用棱柱形模式。在多模态语篇分析中,不同学者虽然采取不同的分析框架,但都肯定了在多模态话语意义构建中隐转喻的互动作用,并指出了转喻是隐喻的基础。因此,隐转喻在多模态语篇中意义构建结构的层级是不同的。刘涛也指出图像符号的修辞结构包含三层叙述层：一是源域和目标域,二是转喻层,三是隐喻层。杨翕然提出的视觉隐转喻的多层选择性意义构建模型也将视觉转喻视为底层结构,其次是本体隐转喻、结构隐转喻、空间隐转喻和体态隐转喻。由此,本文将从多模态转喻层级出发,首先识解出图像的源域和目标域,分析图像的指称意义;继而从隐喻层解析图像和文字意义,最后分析图像意义与文字意义之间通过隐转喻达成的衔接互动。

2. 语料收集和分析

2.1 语料来源与分析方法

以英国著名杂志《经济学人》为语料来源,选取了 2020 年 3~4 月间刊物的 10 幅封面(见文末附表)。这一时期全球政治、经济、商业等各领域都受到了新冠肺炎疫情的严重影响。《经济学人》报刊也密切关注此次全球疫情动态,表达对热点话题的态度和观点,封面图文蕴意丰富。

首先分析图文语篇的转喻映射,即识别图像中的源域和目标域。由于目前关于隐喻和转喻的识别尚无科学系统的方法,为尽量避免个人主观性,本研究的隐转喻识别工作由两人合作完成,两人各自识别后讨论决定最后的识别结果,识别过程中通过阅读文本语篇的标题及全文内容加以验证。第二步根据转喻识别结果和 A IS B 的隐喻表达式进行多模态隐喻分析,并根据冯德正的隐喻分类标准进行分类。最后,将识解出的隐转喻置于语篇语境中解读,分析其封面图文语篇意义构建的过程。

2.2 转喻表征结果

通过对图像要素的识解并根据相同的目标域进行分类,10 篇图文语篇中共识解出 8 类(见表1)。结果显示,识别出的源域总频次大于语篇总数,说明一幅图像中涉及多处转喻。其中病毒和地球是出现频率最高的图像元素,通过转喻映射共同指称新冠肺炎疫情在全球蔓延的时事背景。研究发现,转喻在图文语篇中的主要功能是指称,主要表征关系有邻近关系和因果关系,为图文语篇意义构建语义背景。例如,图3(见附录)的"口罩"由因果关系指称"新冠肺炎疫情",简洁明了地构建了图文语篇的背景。在多模态语篇中,转喻的指称功能尤为突出,通过具体的图像表征指称复杂或抽象的概念,从而构建语篇意义。刘涛在《转喻论:图像指代与视觉修辞分析》一文中也指出视觉转喻的本质是图像指代,其功能是"看到原本难以呈现的事物"和"理解原本难以表达的意义"。

表1 《经济学人》中图文语篇的转喻映射

序号	源域	映射	目标域	转喻类型	频次
1	virus	→	Coronavirus	范畴与范畴成员之间的转喻	6
2	mask	→	COVID-19	因果转喻	2
3	pill	→	medicine/treatment	事件转喻	1
4	earth	→	global/globalization	容器转喻/范畴与特征之间的转喻	4
5	leaders	→	government/politics	控制转喻	2
6	arrow diagram	→	economy	符号和指代转喻	1
7	closed noticeboard	→	shut down	行为转喻	1
8	Wall street	→	U.S stock market/financial market	地点转喻	1

2.3 隐喻表征结果

根据概念隐喻的表达式 A IS B,分别解读文字、图像以及经转喻后的文字和图像,共识别出以下9组隐喻(见表2)。其中转喻使用频率最高的源域"地球"也是隐喻中最常用的源域,但是所映射的目标域不同。根据冯德正的隐喻分类标准进行分类,结果发现三大隐喻类型出现频次不一,分别表现为跨模态隐喻5次、单模态隐喻2次和多模态隐喻2次。其中跨模态隐喻使用频率最高,即文字模态和图像模态经常分别作为隐喻的源域和目标域。由此可以认为,图文语篇中通常以跨模态隐喻的方式以实现不同模态的互动,跨模态隐喻是语篇衔接和语义构建的主要手段。其次还发现隐喻总频次小于语篇总数,即说明部分图文语篇并没有构成隐喻,图文语篇表现为图像通过转喻呈现不含隐喻的文字内容,所以可以认为隐喻不是图文语篇构建意义的必需手段。与一图文语篇中包含多处转喻表征结果相比,确定了转喻在图文语篇构建意义上的基础性地位。

表 2 《经济学人》中图文语篇的隐喻映射

序号	源域	映射	目标域	类型
1	earth	→	virus	单模态隐喻
2	economy	→	disease	单模态隐喻
3	earth	→	store	跨模态隐喻
4	fist	→	power	跨模态隐喻
5	leopard	→	survivor	多模态隐喻
6	burden	→	debt	跨模态隐喻
7	crack	→	gap	跨模态隐喻
8	strip	→	goodbye	多模态隐喻
9	road	→	way	跨模态隐喻

3. 图文语篇的意义构建

3.1 单模态隐转喻

单模态映射指源域和目标域属于同一模态,在图文语篇中存在文字隐喻和图像隐喻两种。据表 2,单模态隐喻共出现 2 次(见附表图 2),分别是 earth is virus 和 economy is disease。前者是图像隐喻,后者是文字隐喻。

Earth is virus 这一隐喻中首先进行了范畴和范畴成员转喻,"virus"指称"coronavirus",再基于"virus"和"earth"外形同是圆形的相似性特征构成隐喻,图像将地球和细菌重合,保留了地球表面各大洲、海洋和细菌上的触角。图像的源域和目标域分别与文字的"world""pandemic"呼应衔接,并通过隐转喻互动共同表达了Covid-19成为全球大流行传染病的时事背景。Economy is disease 这一文字隐喻是基于"economic crisis"和"pandemic"都给人类带来危机、急需解决措施的相似性构成隐喻,将世界经济喻指"Covid-19",两者都需要正确的治疗方法解决问题,此处的治疗手段通过图像药丸的视觉要素,完成事件转喻。附图2的语篇意义通过了2次转喻和两次隐喻,转喻的指称功能和语篇衔接功能使得文字和图像之间得以互动,共同表达语篇中心主题,而2次单模态隐喻使得作者用较少的符号资源就能传达出丰富的信息,使图文生动简洁、充满创意。

3.2 跨模态隐转喻

跨模态映射指源域与目标域分属不同的模态,有文字-图像和图像-文字两种情况。经量化统计,跨模态隐喻出现频次最高,且均为图像-文字的跨模态隐喻,包括 earth is store(附表图4)、burden is debt(附表图7)、crack is gap(附表图9)等。

附表图4的隐喻由"歇业告示牌(Closed)"激活,将"地球"喻指"全球的经济实体",表达世界各地人们受新冠疫情影响的现状。附表图7首先进行了转喻映射,即"箭头曲线"指称"经济增长指数",再通过"细菌"与"铅球等圆形重物"的相似性构成隐喻,表达压力的内涵意义。这一图像通过隐转喻映射表达出"债务的压力感",生动形象地对文字部分作了视觉再现。附表图9中"Wall Street"是地点转喻,指称"美国股票金融市场","地表裂缝"通过隐喻引申为"gap",通过副标题得知是指"金融市场和实体经济的差距",构建出"美国金融市场遭遇重创,经济面临危机"的语篇意义。

以上的跨模态隐喻均是由图像作为源域向文字目标域映射,这种跨模态映射使图文语篇意义表达资源更为丰富,在隐转喻机制的互动下图文之间的衔接更加密切,使语篇的主题思想表达更加集中有效。

3.3 多模态隐转喻

多模态映射指文字模态和图像模态同时存在映射,包括 leopard is survivor(附表图6)和 strip is separation(附表图10)。附表图6中文字隐喻映射为 business is creature,即将"企业"喻指"有生命力的物体",或者通过生产转喻将"产品"指代"生产者",表达"企业生存危机"的主题。图像的隐喻映射为 leopard is survivor,"leopard"喻指"生存者",因为"leopard"是一种坚毅、刚强的动物,是丛林中寿命长久的生存者之一。图像隐喻的目标喻与文字隐喻的目标域一致,再结合"豹身上的细菌"转喻指称"新冠疫情",构建出全球"新冠疫情影响下企业面临生存危机"的信息。

附表图10首先通过"地球"转喻指称"全球化"的信息主题,然后"螺旋状上升地球带子(strip)的形状"隐喻了"分离(separation)"的意义。文字模态"Goodbye globalization"中蕴含了 globalization is person 的隐喻映射。通过两种模态的隐转喻互动,"分离"和"Goodbye"在意义上达成衔接。

4. 结论

在多模态隐转喻理论指导下,论文对《经济学人》的10幅封面图文语篇进行解读。研究发现:① 转喻的指称功能在多模态语篇中尤为显著,使多模态转喻成为图文语篇构建意义的基础,是形成图文互动和衔接的必不可少的手段,即文字的意义通过视觉图像和转喻机制而呈现,为语篇意义创建语义背景。② 多模态隐喻虽不是图文语篇的必需手段,但多模态隐喻调动了图文符号资源,可以构建更加丰富的引申意义。③ 图文语篇的意义构建路径分为三步:语言符号和非语言符号构建隐转喻的源域和目标域、多模态转喻促进图文双模态语义互动衔接、多模态隐喻(尤其是跨模态隐喻)构建引申意义,传递比喻的修辞效果。

在隐转喻表征的识解的过程中,论文发现隐、转喻源域和目的域的识别是多模态语篇分析的核心环节,对多模态隐转喻的识解和鉴别存在主观性问题。但目前尚无成熟系统的多模态隐、转喻的识别、解读和分析框架,未来多模态语篇研究应重视多模态隐转喻解读的系统性理论分析框架研究,以提高多模态隐转喻分析的科学性。

附　　表

序号	图 文 语 篇	文章标题和副标题
1		**It's going global** The virus is coming Governments have an enormous amount of work to do

续表

序号	图文语篇	文章标题和副标题
2		The right medicine for the world economy The pandemic threatens an economic crisis Both need fixing
3		The politics of pandemics All governments will struggle Some will struggle more than others
4		Closed The struggle to save lives and the economy is likely to present agonising choices
5		A grim calculus Covid-19 presents stark choices between life, death and the economy They will probably get harder

续表

序号	图文语篇	文章标题和副标题
6		**The business of survival** Some companies won't make it through the crisis Those that do will face a new business climate
7		**After the disease, the debt** Governments will owe vast amounts after the crisis Here's how to deal with it
8		**The 90% economy** Life after lockdowns will be hard in ways that are difficult to imagine today
9		**A dangerous gap** Financial markets have got out of whack with the economy Something has to give

续表

序号	图 文 语 篇	文章标题和副标题
10		**Goodbye globalisation** A more nationalistic and self-sufficient era beckons It won't be richer—or safer

参考文献

[1] GOOSSENS L. Metaphtonymy：the interaction of metaphor and metonymy in expressions for linguistic action[M]//DIRVEN R & PORINGS R(eds.), Metaphor and Metonymy in Comparison and Contrast. Berlin/New York：Mouton de Gruyter, 1990.

[2] 张辉,卢卫中.认知转喻[M].上海：上海外语教育出版社,2010.

[3] 冯德正,赵秀凤.多模态转喻与图像语篇意义建构[J].外语学刊,2017(6)：8-13.

[4] 刘涛.转喻论：图像指代与视觉修辞分析[J].南京社会科学,2018(10)：112-120+128.

[5] 杨翕然.视觉隐转喻视角下的话语构建[J].当代修辞学,2019(5)：80-93.

[6] 赵秀凤.概念隐喻研究的新发展——多模态隐喻研究：兼评 Forceville & Urios-Aparisi《多模态隐喻》[J].外语研究,2011(1)：1-10+112.

[7] 冯德正.多模态隐喻的构建与分类——系统功能视角[J].外语研究,2011(1)：24-29.

[8] RADDEN G, KOVECSES Z. Towards a theory of metonymy [M]//PANTHER K U, RADDEN G. Metonymy in Language and Thought. Amsterdam：John Benjamins, 1999.

点评

论文以《经济学人》10幅封面图文语篇为语料,定性和定量相结合解读隐转喻的意义建构路径及其在图文语篇衔接中的作用。论文观点鲜明,思路清晰,论证充分,叙述清楚,层次分明,结论可信。建议参考文献略有补充。

覆盆子总黄酮降尿酸及抗痛风性关节炎作用研究

史悦悦　郭璐　张晓熙　夏道宗*

摘要： **目的**　对覆盆子总黄酮的最优提取工艺及其降尿酸、抗痛风性关节炎的作用及机制进行研究。**方法**　通过单因素实验和响应面实验得出最优提取工艺,采用腹腔注射氧嗪酸钾足踝关节注射尿酸钠建立小鼠模型,对小鼠踝关节肿胀度,血清TNF-α、IL-1β、尿酸、肌酐、尿素氮含量以及小鼠肾脏尿酸转运蛋白URAT1和ABCG2的表达进行测定,探究覆盆子的抗痛风作用及机制。**结果**　超声提取覆盆子总黄酮的最佳工艺条件为乙醇浓度57%,料液比(g∶mL)1∶24,提取时间34 min,提取功率350 W,提取率为8.08%。覆盆子总黄酮组能够显著降低小鼠踝关节肿胀度、肌酐、尿素氮、尿酸、TNF-α、IL-1β水平,且可显著的降低URAT1表达,提高ABCG2的表达。**结论**　覆盆子总黄酮具有一定的抗痛风作用,其作用机制可能与降低炎性因子及影响尿酸转运蛋白表达水平有关。

关键词： 覆盆子总黄酮;提取工艺;痛风性关节炎

痛风属于代谢性风湿病范畴,与嘌呤代谢紊乱及（或）尿酸排泄减少所致的高尿酸血症直接相关,发病为尿酸钠晶体沉积的关节性疾病[1]。近年来研究表明,痛风的发病率呈逐年上升趋势,这与如今高嘌呤的饮食结构相关[2]。因此在预防和治疗的同时,合理调整饮食习惯与生活方式可有效减少痛风的发作机率。

覆盆子为蔷薇科植物华东覆盆子 *Rubus chingii* Hu 的干燥果实。夏初果实由绿变绿黄时采收,具有益肾、固精、缩尿、养肝名目之功效,收载于2020版《中

---

* 史悦悦,郭璐：浙江中医药大学药学院2018级硕士研究生。
张晓熙：浙江中医药大学药学院2017级硕士研究生。
夏道宗：博士,浙江中医药大学药学院教授、博士研究生导师。

国药典》[3]。近年来有大量研究表明覆盆子中含有黄酮、萜类、挥发油等多种化合物,具有抗氧化、抗肿瘤、降血糖等生物活性。黄酮类化合物作为覆盆子中的主要活性成分,尚不具有成熟且便捷的提取方法,因此致力于覆盆子总黄酮的提取工艺优化研究具有较大应用价值[4]。

覆盆子作为新"浙八味"之一,同时也是国家卫计委公布的药食同源药材,已有大量研究证实了覆盆子具有保护肾脏,抗炎的作用,提示我们覆盆子可能具有抗痛风性关节炎的作用。但相关研究鲜见报道,因此本研究拟采用响应面法优化覆盆子总黄酮的提取工艺,构建急性痛风性关节炎小鼠模型,探究覆盆子提取物对痛风的改善作用。

1. 材料

1.1 药材及试剂

覆盆子总黄酮(覆盆子购自本实验室自制浙江中医药大学中药饮片有限公司,批号20200529,经检测符合质量标准);Mouse IL-1β,Mouse TNF-α, ELISA 试剂盒(美国 Thermo Fisher 公司,批号:MM-0040M1,161044013);肌酐试剂盒(南京建成,批号:20200916);尿素氮试剂盒(南京建成,批号:20200916);Xanthine(Sigma,批号:1002555235);Potassium Oxonate(梯希爱,批号:T6GKM-TA);β-actin、URAT1、ABCG2 抗体购于美国 CST 公司。

1.2 动物

SPF 级雄性 C57BL/6 小鼠,4 周龄,体重(16±2)g 共70只,购自上海 BK 公司饲养于,生产合格证号 SCXK(沪)2017-0005。饲养于浙江中医药大学动物实验研究中心,动物使用许可证号 SYXK(浙)2018-0012。

1.3 仪器

足趾容积测量仪(实验室自制,专利号:ZL201720573173.1);Synergy H1 型多功能微孔板检测仪(美国 Bio-Tek 公司);蛋白电泳系统(Bio-Rad,美国)。

2. 实验方法

2.1 覆盆子单因素和响应面提取工艺优化

2.1.1 样品的制备

覆盆子果实烘干至恒重,粉碎,过40目筛。精密称取一定量的覆盆子粉末,加入乙醇,进行超声提取,减压抽滤后备用[5,6]。

2.1.2 标准曲线制定与含量测定

参考夏道宗等[7]的方法测定总黄酮,以芦丁为对照,于 507 nm 处测定吸光值,取 1 mL 提取液,按照标准曲线的回归方程计算总黄酮含量。

2.1.3 响应面实验

在单因素实验的基础上筛选出提取功率、提取时间、料液比、乙醇浓度作为探索响应面的实验因素,运用 Design－Expert 8.0.5 软件对提取功率(A)、提取时间(B)、料液比(C)、乙醇浓度(D)四个影响因素进行三水平响应面设计[8],见表 1。

表 1 响应面试验因素水平表

水平	因素			
	提取功率 A(w)	提取时间 B(min)	料液比 C(g/mL)	乙醇浓度 D(%)
1	300	30	1∶20	40
2	350	40	1∶25	50
3	400	50	1∶30	60

2.2 动物实验给药及分组

分别准确称取过筛的氧嗪酸钾和黄嘌呤粉末 10 g,用 0.5% 羧甲基纤维素钠溶解,配置成浓度为 28 mg/mL 的氧嗪酸钾和黄嘌呤混悬液。准确称取过筛的尿酸钠粉末 1 g,用生理盐水溶解,配置成浓度为 100 g/mL 的尿酸钠溶液,现配现用。70 只雄性 C57BL/6 小鼠适应环境一周后,随机分为正常组、模型组、秋水仙碱组,别嘌呤组,覆盆子总黄酮低、中、高剂量组,每组 10 只[9]。正常组和模型组灌胃蒸馏水,秋水仙碱组灌胃秋水仙碱(0.65 mg/kg),别嘌呤醇组给予别嘌呤醇(10 mg/kg),覆盆子总黄酮低、中、高剂量组分别给予覆盆子总黄酮为 160 mg/kg、320 mg/kg、640 mg/kg,连续灌胃 7 天。除正常组外,其余各组第 1 天至第 7 天每天腹腔注射氧嗪酸钾(280 mg/kg)和黄嘌呤混悬液(280 mg/kg),正常组注射等体积的 0.5% 羧甲基纤维素钠。在第 6 天灌胃 1 h 后,用灭菌注射器吸取上述配制的尿酸钠溶液 0.025 mL,除正常组外其余小鼠注入踝关节,以对侧鼓起为注入标准,诱导小鼠急性痛风性关节炎模型,正常组注射等体积的生理盐水[10]。

2.3 肾功能相关指标测定

2.3.1 小鼠血清中各物质含量测定

第 7 天通过摘眼球取血法收集小鼠新鲜血液,37℃孵育 1 h,3 500 rpm 离心 15 min 分离血清。肌酐、尿素氮、TNF－α、IL－1β 均用试剂盒,测定其指标[11]。尿酸采用磷钨酸法测定。

2.3.2 肾组织 URAT1、ABCG2 的蛋白表达量测定

将解剖后取得的肾组织裂解后,离心 10 分钟后提取上清液,一部分用 BCA 试剂盒测定蛋白浓度,另一部分用 Loading Buffer 变性后分装,低温－80℃保存[12]。用 SDS－聚丙烯酰胺凝胶电泳将所提蛋白电泳分离后,转膜至 PVPF 膜上,用双色红外激光成像系统显影[13]。

2.4 小鼠踝关节肿胀度与相关炎症因子的测定

2.4.1 小鼠关节肿胀度测定

在第 6 天,用不褪色记号笔在小鼠踝关节上方 0.8 cm 左右处画一道横线,以备测量足趾容积时所需。用足趾容积测量仪测定造模前和造模后的小鼠足趾容积[14]。造模后,观察小鼠右后足肿胀情况,并于注射后 2 h、4 h、6 h、10 h、24 h 测定足趾容积,按下列公式计算:

$$肿胀度(\%) = \frac{致炎后足趾容积 - 致炎前足趾容积}{致炎前足趾容积} \times 100$$

2.4.2 关节腔炎症因子测定

ELISA 检测小鼠踝关节组织中炎症因子含量:取小鼠踝关节,称重,按 1∶10(g/mL)的比例加入生理盐水,在冰上用匀浆器研碎,以 4℃、3 000 rpm 离心条件离心 10 min,收集上清,IL－1β、TNF－α 的含量按对应的 ELISA 试剂盒说明书进行测定。

3. 统计学分析

所有数据均使用 SPSS17.0 统计软件进行处理,数据以 $\bar{x} \pm SEM$ 表示,组间的差异按照方差分析方法进行检验分析,并且用最小显著法检验进行两两比较,$P<0.05$ 时有统计学意义。

4. 实验结果

4.1 响应面方差分析

应用 Design – Expert 8.05 软件设计进行实验,分析得 OD 总值与提取功率(A)、提取时间(B)、液料比(C)、乙醇浓度(D)的二次回归方程为:$Y = 7.83 - 0.14B - 0.44C + 0.23D + 0.51AC + 0.40BC + 0.23CD - 0.41A^2 - 0.25B^2 - 1.23C^2 - 0.19D^2$。根据表 2 的分析结果可得此模型($P<0.001$)具有显著性差异,并且失拟项($P = 0.5565>0.05$)差异不显著,相关 $R^2 = 0.9631$,说明此模型选择合适,可以用此回归方程确定最优提取工艺。同时从表 2 中可以看出 B、C、D、AC、BD、CD、A^2、B^2、C^2、D^2 都具有显著性差异,且各因素的影响顺序为:液料比(C)>乙醇浓度(D)>提取温度(B)>提取时间(A)。且由图 1 可以看出液料比和提取功率对结果的影响较大,液料比和提取温度次之,这与方差分析的结果相一致。根据软件分析得到预测的最优条件结合实际微调为乙醇浓度 57%、液料比(g∶mL)1∶24、提取时间 34 min、提取功率 350 W。按照以上实验条件对覆盆子进行三次平行试验通过显色换算所得黄酮提取率为 8.08%[15-17]。

表 2 响应面二次模型的方差分析

来 源	平方和	自由度	均方	F 值	P 值(Prob > F)
模型	15.44	14	1.1	26.96	<0.0001**
A-提取功率	0.049	1	0.049	1.21	0.2903
B-提取时间	0.24	1	0.24	5.75	0.031*
	2.29	1	2.29	55.93	<0.0001**
C-液料比	0.64	1	0.64	15.63	0.0014*
D-乙醇浓度	0.055	1	0.055	1.35	0.2647
AB	1.05	1	1.05	25.68	0.0002**
AC	0.14	1	0.14	3.44	0.0849

续表

来源	平方和	自由度	均方	F值	P值(Prob > F)
AD	0.66	1	0.66	16.04	0.001 3**
BC	0.042	1	0.042	1.03	0.328
BD	22.0	1	22.0	5.29	0.037 4*
CD	1.1	1	1.1	26.83	0.000 1**
A^2	0.41	1	0.41	9.92	0.007 1**
B^2	9.81	1	9.81	239.92	<0.000 1**
C^2	0.23	1	0.23	5.51	0.034 2*
D^2	0.57	14	0.041		
残差	0.41	10	0.041	0.98	0.556 5
失拟项净误差	0.17	4	0.041		
总离差	16.01	28			

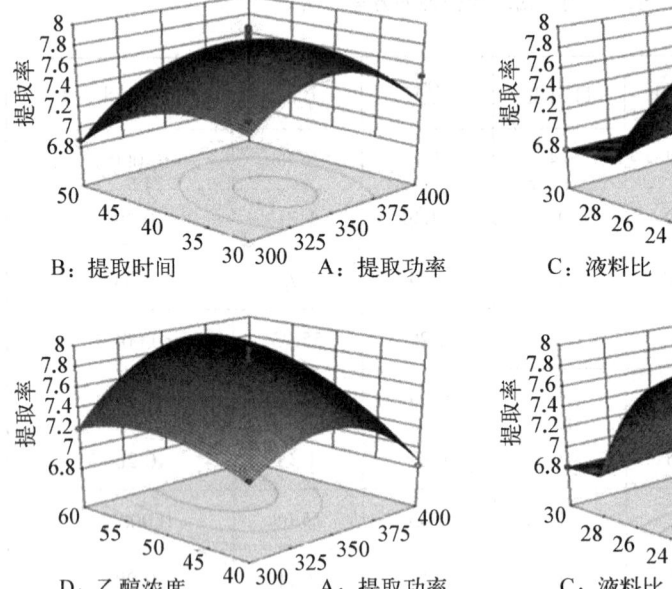

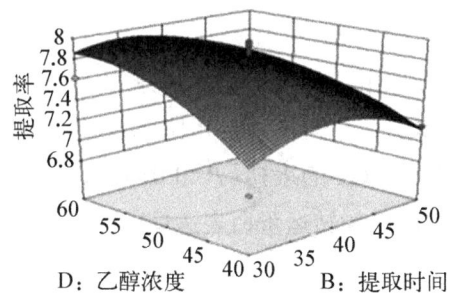
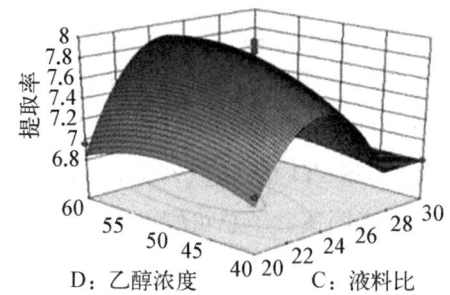

图1 提取功率(A)、提取时间(B)、料液比(C)、乙醇浓度(D)之间的交互作用

4.2 覆盆子总黄酮对小鼠中血清肌酐、尿素氮和尿酸的影响

血清肌酐、尿素氮为肾功能指标,其变化指示肾功能的改变。由图2可得模型组尿酸水平与正常组相比具有显著性差异($P<0.01$),模型组的尿酸水平比正常组高接近4倍,表示此模型造模成功。从图2中可以看出覆盆子总黄酮中、高剂量组与模型组相比具有显著性差异($P<0.01$),且覆盆子总黄酮对小鼠降尿酸作用具有剂量依赖性,剂量越高其降尿酸作用越明显。如图2所示,与正常组相比,模型组小鼠血清肌酐、尿素氮水平明显升高,具有显著差异($P<0.01$)。与模型组相比,给药组中高剂量小鼠血清肌酐显著降低($P<0.05$)。覆盆子总黄酮低中高组能降低小鼠血清中尿素氮水平,但小鼠尿素氮只有高剂量组的显著降低($P<0.05$)。

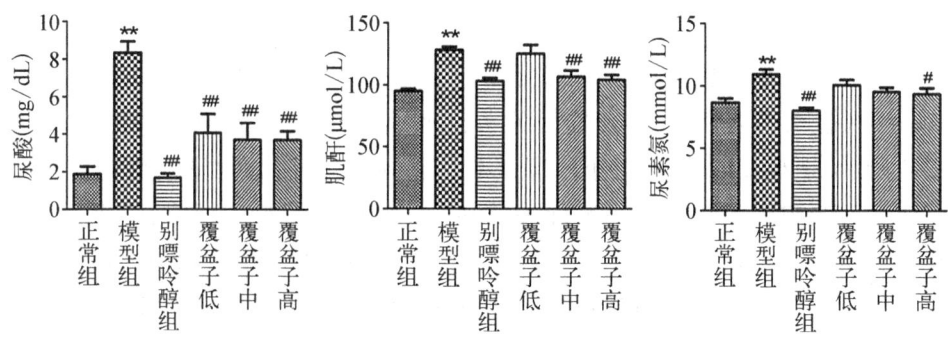

图2 覆盆子总黄酮对尿酸、肌酐、尿素氮水平的影响

注:** 与正常组相比,差异显著($P<0.01$);## 与模型组相比,差异显著($P<0.01$);# 与模型组相比,差异显著($P<0.05$)。

4.3 覆盆子总黄酮对高尿酸血症小鼠尿酸转运蛋白 URAT1 和 ABCG2 的蛋白表达水平的影响实验结果

如图 3 所示,与正常组相比,模型组的肾组织 URAT1 表达水平显著升高($P<0.01$),ABCG2 表达水平显著降低($P<0.01$)。与模型组相比,给药组能显著降低 URAT1 的表达($P<0.01$),显著升高 ABCG2 的表达($P<0.01$)。以上实验结果表明覆盆子总黄酮可通过影响肾组织中尿酸转运蛋白表达量来起到保护肾脏及促进尿酸的排泄。

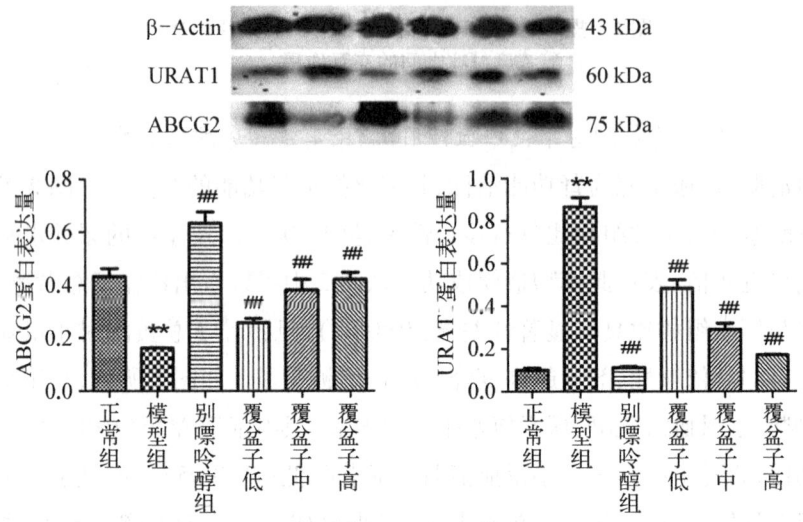

图 3　覆盆子总黄酮对尿酸转运蛋白 URAT1 和 ABCG2 的蛋白表达水平的影响

注:** 与正常组相比,差异显著($P<0.01$);## 与模型组相比,差异显著($P<0.01$);# 与模型组相比,差异显著($P<0.05$)。

4.4 覆盆子总黄酮对小鼠足趾容积和炎症因子的相关指标

痛风性关节炎的病理表象为关节红肿、疼痛,炎症因子水平上升。如图 4 所示,造模 2 h 后,各组小鼠踝关节均有肿胀,说明急性痛风性关节炎模型建立较为成功。正常组小鼠踝关节在 2 h 时肿胀度最大,随后逐渐减小,其余各组小鼠在造模后直至 4 h,肿胀度不断增加,在 4 h 达到最大值,之后的时间点测定时肿胀度有所降低。与正常组比较,在造模 2 h—24 h 之间,模型组小鼠踝关节肿胀度增加;与模型组比较,覆盆子各剂量组在造模后其小鼠踝肿胀度有所下降。且相较于模型组,覆盆子各剂量组的炎性因子 TNF‑α 含量显著降低($P<0.01$),覆盆子中高剂量组的 IL‑1β 含量显著降

低($P<0.01$)。以上实验结果表明覆盆子总黄酮可通过调节炎性因子来达到抗关节炎的作用。

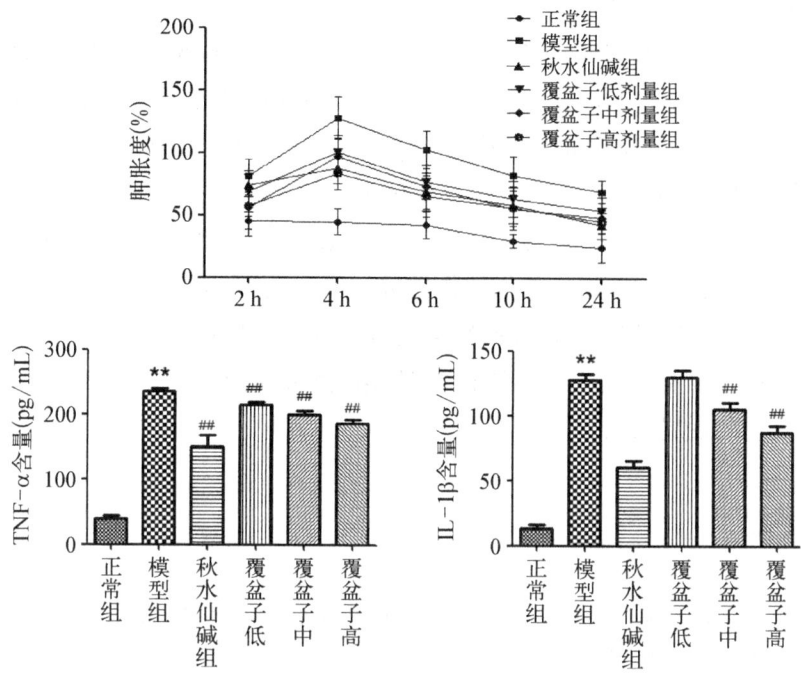

图4 覆盆子总黄酮对小鼠踝关节肿胀度的影响

注：** 与正常组相比,差异显著($P<0.01$);## 与模型组相比,差异显著($P<0.01$);# 与模型组相比,差异显著($P<0.05$)。

5. 讨论

现代生活方式,高压力、快节奏,加上高蛋白高嘌呤饮食的习惯,高尿酸血症引起的痛风发病率不断增高,其严重影响患者的生活质量及工作效率[18-19]。在过去的50年里,治疗都采用传统的非甾体类药物,此类传统用药,易出现肾毒性、胃肠道出血及反复性[20-22]。覆盆子作为药食同源重要药品,其优势在于低毒性高疗效,在高尿酸血症和痛风的研究中有良好的研究前景。

覆盆子黄酮类化合物现阶段自然提取率低,前期研究多以正交为方法,论文运用响应面法优化工艺准确可靠,考察所建立模型的可信度参数较多,显示出较其他方法更多的优势。以中药覆盆子的基础研究为切入点,优化所得覆盆子黄酮提取物的提取工艺为乙醇浓度57%、液料比(g/mL)1∶24、提取时间34 min、提取功率350 W,提取率为8.08%。

痛风性关节炎的病理表象为关节红肿、疼痛。实验模型较少将高尿酸症与痛风性关节炎相结合共同探究。论文将高尿酸血症模型与痛风性关节炎模型相结合,更大程度上的模拟痛风所致的病理特征,而造模小鼠的踝关节肿胀度、肌酐、尿素氮、尿酸、IL-1β、TNF-α等指标也相较于正常小鼠显著升高,可在一定程度表明本实验方法设计合理有效。研究通过对炎症各指标及氧嗪酸钾所致高尿酸血症所引起的肾损伤的保护作用进行考察,表明覆盆子能有效地减少炎症,并可通过调节肾组织中的尿酸转运蛋白表达来促进尿酸的排泄,从而起到抗痛风的作用。说明覆盆子总黄酮在肾脏代谢类疾病及痛风性关节炎中有较好的效果及良好的发展前景。

参考文献

[1] 中华医学会风湿病学分会.原发性痛风诊断和治疗指南[J].中华风湿病学杂志,2011,15(6):410-413.

[2] 邓雪玉.痛风和高尿酸血症药物治疗研究现状[J].中国处方药,2020,18(1):24-26.

[3] 国家药典委员会.中华人民共和国药典[S].北京:中国医药科技出版社,2020:399.

[4] 张亨.覆盆子酮的化学合成研究进展[J].乙醛醋酸化工,2014,5(9):12-19.

[5] 马智超,翟春梅,怀雪,等.响应面法优化山荆子果实总黄酮的提取工艺[J].中医药学报,2018,46(5):45-49.

[6] 吕丹,唐克慧,王宇弛,等.同步提取山楂皮中总多酚、总黄酮和三萜类物质的工艺优化[J].河南工业大学学报(自然科学版),2018,39(5):69-75.

[7] 夏道宗,于新芬,王慧铭,等.麦冬总黄酮提取的响应面法优化及抗氧化性研究[J].中华中医药杂志,2009,24(12):1629-1632.

[8] 高雪梅,祁岳,张志,等.响应面法优化酸藤子叶总黄酮的超声提取工艺[J].黑龙江畜牧兽医,2018,45(17):167-170.

[9] 孙海滨,于梅.高尿酸血症动物模型研究进展[J].黑龙江中医药,2018,47(4):130-131.

[10] 裘忆雪,刘永杰,张笛,等.建立高尿酸血症性肾损害小鼠模型的实验研究[J].中国比较医学杂志,2018,28(9):46-54.

[11] 陈锡铖.金丝草水提物降低慢性肾衰小鼠血肌酐、尿素氮活性及成分研究[D].福建农林

大学,2013.

[12] 刘淼.荔枝核总黄酮对高糖联合TNF-α诱导大鼠肾小球系膜细胞的增殖作用及机制研究[D].长春中医药大学,2016.

[13] 夏燕,陆光辉,黄琼,等.ABCG2基因rs3114018单核苷酸多态性与武陵山地区痛风及高尿酸血症的相关性研究[J].中国免疫学杂志,2018,34(7):1054-1058.

[14] 陈莹,杨路,冼培凤,等.不同蜂针剂量对佐剂性类风湿性关节炎大鼠血清TNF-α、IL-1β、IL-6的影响[J].中华中医药学刊,2017,35(5):1151-1154.

[15] 夏道宗,于新芬,王慧铭,等.麦冬总黄酮提取的响应面法优化及抗氧化性研究[J].中华中医药杂志,2009,24(12):1629-1632.

[16] 马趣环,石晓峰,沈薇,等.响应面分析法优化雪松松针多糖提取工艺研究[J].中华中医药杂志,2018,33(3):1106-1110.

[17] 李武超,吕惠卿,陈学智,等.响应面优化山竹果皮总黄酮的超声提取工艺及抗菌作用研究[J].中华中医药杂志,2017,32(8):3699-3702.

[18] 陈玲.中医治疗急性痛风性关节炎的研究进展[J].大众科技,2019,21(10):77-79.

[19] 南亚婷,照日格图,陈慕芝,等.痛风的中医治疗研究进展[J].风湿病与关节炎,2019,8(12):72-75.

[20] CHEN X, GAO Q, ZHOU L, et al. MiR-146a alleviates inflammation of acute gouty arthritis rats through TLR4/MyD88 signal transduction pathway[J]. Eur Rev Med Pharmacol Sci, 2019, 23(21):9230-9237.

[21] DOSS H M, DEY C, SUDANDIRADOSS C, et al. Targeting inflammatory mediators with ferulic acid, a dietary polyphenol, for the suppression of monosodium urate crystal-induced inflammation in rats[J]. Life Sci, 2016, 148(1):201-210.

[22] KIÇIK A, TÜZÜN E, ERDOĞDU E, et al. Neuroinflammation Mediators are Reduced in Sera of Parkinson's Disease Patients with Mild Cognitive Impairment[J]. Noro Psikiyatr Ars, 2020, 57(1):15-17.

点评

论文对覆盆子总黄酮降尿酸及抗痛风性关节炎作用进行了较为深入的研究,选题具有很强的应用价值。研究的目的明确、方法科学、所得结论较为客观。文献参考丰富,且在文中有对应。但缺乏国内外相关研究综述,难以定位其创新性。另外使用的SPSS版本较低。

社交媒体报道对女性医护人员印象的固化
——以《人民日报》与"央视新闻"微博为例

田蕾馨[*]

摘要：选取热门社交媒体"微博"作为研究对象，以《人民日报》与"央视新闻"两大官方媒体的微博为语料，从表征视角出发，结合话语分析理论与传播学理论，研究对女性医护人员印象的固化。在标题语气方面，媒体多用感叹语气与祈使语气，表达出"心疼"与"感动"的情感态度；在标题指称方面，报道者多用家庭角色来表征女性医护人员，没有将她们的职业放在突出位置；而在正文内容方面，"牵挂"和"思念"的主题占比最高。由此可见，社交媒体在报道中未能合理地建构女性医护人员的形象，反而向受众传达了"女子本弱"这一错误观念。论文从媒体和受众两个角度着手，试提供相应的解决对策。

关键词：女性；媒体话语；医护人员；表征

引言

随着社会的发展和思想的解放，女性形象已经取得了极大的改观，女性走出家庭，步入各行各业，成为社会运转的中坚力量。然而，"女子本弱"这种观念依然根深蒂固，难以消除，即使在女性占比较高的医护人员中，相关报道也透露出了这种看法。论文即针对这个话题，从热门社交媒体"微博"中获取语料，从表征视角出发，结合话语分析理论和传播学理论，来阐明媒体报道中对女性医护人员倾向性的刻画，并给出供参考的女性形象建构路径，为认知性别平等提供借鉴。

---

[*] 田蕾馨：上海大学外国语学院 2019 级硕士研究生。

1. 文献综述及分析框架

在以往的研究中,研究者多从收入、教育、法律、语言、广告等角度出发,来揭露性别差异这一问题。收入方面,王美艳通过计量方法分析了中国城镇存在的工资性别差异,表明女性职工处于相对不利的劳动力市场地位[1]。喻术红从法律的角度定义了就业性别歧视这一概念,通过阐述其产生根源及危害性来呼吁对劳动法的完善[2]。刘伯红、卜卫以一千余广告样本为对象进行研究,发现三分之一的广告中有性别差异的倾向[3]。刘泽云从教育收益率着手,利用中国城镇居民住户调查数据,得出了"低教育水平职工中的工资性别歧视程度更高,导致不同教育水平的女性之间的工资差异比男性更大"这一结论[4]。潘建从造字、词汇结构、谚语俗语等方面研究了汉语中的性别差异,同时与英语中的性别差异进行了比较[5]。目前,国内鲜有研究者以社交媒体报道为对象进行相关的研究。于惠淑、解娜曾以网络娱乐新闻为例,探析了媒体对女性片面性报道的原因[6],却也未涉及更加严肃、官方的新闻报道。

综上所述,目前国内关于社交媒体新闻报道中性别差异的研究比较少见。而社交媒体作为基于用户关系的内容生产与交换平台,在如今这个互联网时代蓬勃发展,具有举足轻重的作用。人们不仅通过社交媒体分享意见、经验或观点,而且还以此作为获取新闻信息的主要渠道。这就意味着社交媒体承担了更多的社会责任,反映并影响着某个群体的意识形态。

论文的分析框架参考了唐青叶、吴草于 2016 年发表的《中国主流媒体对明星吸毒报道的研究》[7],从表征视角出发,结合话语分析理论和传播学理论,来探究社交媒体对女性医护人员形象的表征,并提供较为合理的女性形象建构路径。Halliday 和 Matthiessen(1999)认为,语言具有表征经验的功能,但经验中的各种范畴和关系并不是自然"赋予"的结果,我们的语言并不是被动地反映经验,而是以词汇语法为动力主动地建构各种范畴和关系[8]。也就是说,话语既能表征社会现实,也影响着社会现实的构建[9]。这体现了话语分析中的意识形态观,意识形态被认为是建立和维持权利关系、支配和剥削的手段,常借助语言手段隐含在语篇中,成为自然化的常识。而新闻话语一定程度上代表着社会群体的意识形态,形成的是高于个人表征的社会表征,因而受到极大的关注。此处的"社会表征",是由法国社会心理学家莫斯科维奇(S. Moscovici)首先提出的一个概念。他把"社会表征"定义为"拥有自身的文化含义并且独立于个体经验之外而持续存在的各种预想（preconceptions）、形象（images）和价值（values）所组成的知识体系"[10]；而 Martin 和 George 将社会表征理解为是表征的主体或载体以及表征的客体和社会群体的实际场景三者相互支持的系统[11]。目前,社会表征理论得到了以 Van Dijk 为代表的认知话语分析学派的高度重视并被应用到实际的新闻话语研究之中。

2. 微博媒体对女性医护人员形象的表征

微博是目前国内最为流行的社交媒体之一,具有强大的便捷性、传播性和原创性,用户可以在任何时间、任何地点即时发布信息,其传播速度远远超过传统纸媒及其他网络媒体。随着微博的影响力与日俱增,从而渗透到政治、经济、文化各个领域,典型的事件有"微博反腐""微博打拐""微博扶贫"等,可见其在人们生活中的影响力。

论文选取的语料来自"微博"上最为权威、受众面最广的两大官方媒体,分别是"央视新闻"微博与《人民日报》微博。"央视新闻"的粉丝量达 1.08 亿人,《人民日报》的粉丝量更是高达 1.15 亿人（统计时间为 2020 年 3 月 30 日）,二者是人们从网络获取官方新闻消息的最主要来源。这两大媒体在新冠疫情防控期间有关女性医护人员的报道内容具有相当高的代表性,代表着整个社交媒体的宣传风向。具体而言,论文统计了 2020 年 1 月 1 日至 2020 年 3 月 30 日间"央视新闻"与《人民日报》发表的有关女性医护人员的报道,共计 124 条微博,其中"央视新闻"67 条,《人民日报》57 条。

2.1 微博标题的语气分析

标题永远是一则新闻最为吸引眼球的部分,Van Dijk 曾在对新闻语篇的分析框架进行阐述时指出:"'标题+副题'总括新闻语篇并阐明其语义宏观结构。"[12]因此,标题是整个新闻语篇的概括,体现了其核心内容。微博标题相当于传统的新闻标题,但有所区别的是,微博标题中还包含"话题",是微博的一大特色功能。用户以"#话题词#"的形式发布信息,即可生成包含该话题词的超链接,而阅读量和讨论量足够大的话题将登上微博的热搜榜单,获得平台上的最高关注度。

在汉语中有四种语气：陈述语气、疑问语气、祈使语气和感叹语气。陈述语气用来陈述一件事实,疑问语气用来发出疑问或者询问情况,祈使语气是直接表达命令、请求等,感叹语气则用来表示惊讶和赞叹等。通过分析微博标题的语气,来获知整个新闻的情感态度及隐藏的意识形态。在搜集到的语料中,运用最多的是陈述语气与感叹语气相结合,其中也不乏祈使语气。如:

例1:【#护士长面部浮肿勒出压痕#你的样子让人心疼!】(2020年1月29日)

例2:【#抗疫一线的面孔#心疼!】(2020年2月5日)

例3:【#6岁哥哥霸气开导想护士妈妈的弟弟#看哭!妈妈坚守一线】(2020年2月23日)

例4:【#武汉医院隔离区真实记录#慢慢看完!】(2020年2月27日)

例5:【#新冠肺炎老小孩患者#这些护士照顾着。转起!说声辛苦了!】(2020年3月5日)

例6:【#最美的她#转!致敬】(2020年3月8日)

标题中频繁出现的感叹语气和祈使语气能够迅速抓住阅读者的注意力,奠定整个语境的情感基调,并引发群众的认同和共鸣。从以上例子可以看出,大部分的标题都以"心疼""感动"为主要的情感态度,表达对女性医护人员的怜惜和感激之情。这就反映出,媒体报道者传达出的潜在意识形态是:女性是柔弱的,奋战在一线的女性医护人员也不例外,但是她们的付出令人十分敬佩,她们的专业水平和敬业精神值得赞叹。这样的宣传话语标题本质上是夸赞女性医护人员出色的抗疫表现,只是通过煽情来实现媒体想要的宣传效果。

2.2 微博标题的指称分析

话语分析汲取了语言社会符号观的思想,认为语言本质上是一种意义资源,或称意义潜势,语篇是人们根据语境从意义潜势中选择的结果,是意义潜势的实例化[13]。语言使用者用什么样的语言符号来表征其言说对象具有理据性,对于同一个客观事物,不同的语言符号表达会产生不同的效果,并演绎出不同的组合规则和行事逻辑[14]。因此,从媒体用何种语言符号来指称女性医护人员可以了解到其报道的宣传重点。

在搜集的语料中,大量的微博语篇都采用"女儿""妻子"和"母亲"这三个社会符号来表征女性医护人员,相比较她们的"医生""护士"的身份,后者采用较少。例如,"央视新闻"于2020年2月8日发布的【#2岁宝宝翻柜子找妈妈#护士14天未回家】这条微博,叙述了四川一名女护士的2岁儿子因太过想念自己的妈妈而在家里到处翻找的故事,侧重了"妈妈"的身份。类似的还有,【#一线护士与女儿隔离带相见#】(2020年2月4日);【#8岁男孩和妈妈说的话让记者哽咽#】(2020年3月7日);【#赴汉抗疫护士与儿子隔空对话#泪目!】(2020年2月13日);【#不让播名字怕妈妈担心的护士#】(2020年3月23日);【#承诺包一年家务的丈夫怎么样了#】(2020年3月10日);【#丈夫陪出征武汉的妻子剃光头#】(2020年2月10日)……如此多的报道都将侧重点放在了"女儿""妻子"和"母亲"这三种身份上,看似温馨感人的故事背后,反映的是媒体对女性医护人员家庭角色的强调。因此,虽然报道在赞扬其辛苦与无私,宣传女性医护人员的勇气、敬业与贡献,实则加深了人们对女性传统定位的印象。

2.3 微博正文的内容分析

在"央视新闻"与《人民日报》124条微博语料中,正文的主题大致可以分为以下四类:(1)与家人有关;(2)与外貌有关;(3)与工作有关;(4)其他(主要包括日常的分享以及护士的流泪场景)。具体统计结果如表1所示:

表1 "央视新闻"与《人民日报》124条微博的内容分类

	家 人	外 貌	工 作	其 他
央视新闻	28	4	10	25
《人民日报》	21	7	10	19
总 计	49	11	20	44

从表1可以看到,"央视新闻"与《人民日报》官方媒体微博报道最多的是女性医护人员与她们的家人,分别发表了28条和21条与之相关的微博;其次是其他类,包括展示护士生活状态或者在镜头中流泪的场景等等,共计44条;接着是对女性医护人员工作时的真实记录,共计20条;最后是有关她们外貌受损的报道,共计11条。从这一结果可以得知,两大官方媒体微博将女性医护人员与家人之间的互动作为最主要的报道内容,有关她们战疫现场的报道数量较少,突出了女性医护人员的家庭角色。再以2020年3月8日"央视新闻"发布的关于妇女节的微博为例,其文案如下:

【#最美的她#转!致敬】她们是医生、是护士,也是女儿、妻子和妈妈。她们是战疫一线最坚强的战士,也有最柔软的爱意、最深沉的思念。#2020妇女节#,

感受这份温暖而坚韧的巾帼力量,向每一位平凡岗位上不平凡的她致敬!(9张配图上的艺术字分别为"背影""不舍""思念""隔空拥抱""许愿""惦念""比心""传承"及"临时妈妈")

妇女节的设立初衷是为了庆祝女性在经济、政治和社会等领域作出的重要贡献和取得的巨大成就,以2020年湖北抗疫一线为例,医护人员中有50%以上的女性,一线女护士更是超过了90%。9张配图中仅有最后一张"临时妈妈"是关于她们在抗疫时的工作场景,其余均是关于她们的孩子、丈夫与母亲的图片。因此,这条微博在彰显女性医护人员在疫情抗击中的卓越贡献的同时,文案中的"柔软""思念""不舍"等字眼,表征了"女子本弱"的观念,并不符合妇女节的精神内涵。这一点在"央视新闻"于同一天发布的另一条微博中体现得尤为明显,其标题是【其实#脱下防护服我也是个女孩#】,该话题的阅读量达1 645.8万次,影响力之广可见一斑,但由于其"赞颂女性医护人员"的主题与温暖煽情的表述,赋予了"女孩其实不勇敢"很强的隐蔽性,难以被人察觉。

另外值得注意的一点是,在124条微博中有11条是关于"外貌"方面的报道,达到了有关女性抗疫工作纪实微博的半数之多。如【#武汉90后光头护士#:用我的及腰长发,换你的健康平安】(2020年1月28日)、【西安#医疗队女队员集体理平头和光头#】(2020年2月9日)、【支援武汉女护士的#除夕与初六对比图#,令人泪目!】(2020年1月30日)、【心疼! #医护人员脸上的勒痕#】(2020年2月3日)等,都是将宣传点放在她们身为女性的"牺牲"上,也从侧面反映出社会对女性外貌的审视,带有性别差异的视角。

3. 讨论:问题与对策

从以上的分析中可以看出,社交媒体对女性医护人员的报道,即使是微博上的官方媒体,拥有众多的粉丝量和极高的关注度,也在报道她们在抗疫中的光辉形象时,笔墨较多地用在了强调女性家庭角色和温柔弱小的形象上,这无形之中强化了人们对女性"主内""柔弱""胆小"的印象,不利于构建正确的性别差异视角。

郭淑娟认为,新闻话语在新闻文本的基础上既呈现了新闻从业人员对事件本身的表达与构建,又反映出受众透过文本对真实事件的理解与认知[15]。因此,通过媒体来建构一个全新的当代女性形象,须得从媒体及受众两方面着手。

首先是媒体方面，根据 Van Dijk 的新闻结构理论，一则新闻话语可以用以下这张格局图来展示：

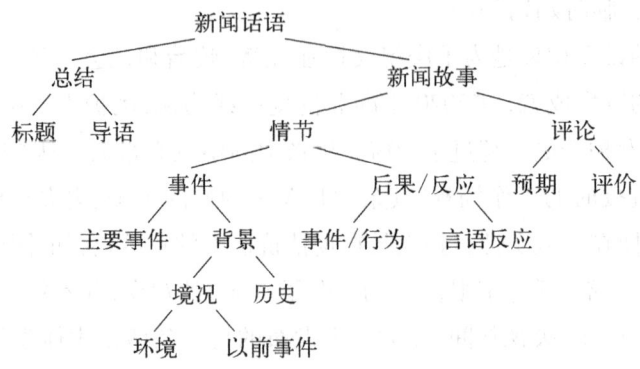

图 1　梵·迪克新闻话语格局

注：图片截取自丁和根的《梵·迪克新闻话语结构理论述评》。

图 1 的读法是自上而下、从左向右。从图 1 可以看出，标题是阅读者最先关注到的部分，所以在建构女性形象时，须在标题的撰写上十分谨慎，要用合适的社会符号来指称女性，并且注意信息的选择和语气的使用。比如在宣传女性医护人员时，重点就应放在其专业水平和敬业精神上，不应过多地对其家庭角色进行强调，而弱化她们对社会的实际贡献。紧随标题之后的是新闻故事本身，在其若干次范畴之中，"背景"具有认知功能，能够激发阅读者记忆中关于类似事件的情景再现，也就是 Van Dijk 所说的"情景模型"，而新闻理解的目标就是更新这些模型，将其与其他新闻情景模型联系起来[16]。因此，从"背景"这个范畴入手，将女性如今的成就与以往的事件串联到一起，能够有效地更新人们对女性形象的传统认知，意识到女性群体发生的巨大变化。此外，"后果"范畴也能起到非常关键的作用，比如在报道中，媒体若能够更多地从康复患者的角度进行叙述，来展现女性医护人员的努力成果，就能更好地向阅读者证明她们的专业素质，从而产生对她们的尊重与敬佩之情。报道者应充分利用媒体话语公信力强、影响力大的特点，展现当代女性果敢、自信、独立的魅力。

受众方面，在这样一个信息爆炸的时代，阅读者应注重培养自身的批判性思维，提高对性别差异问题的敏感度，在阅读涉及女性形象的新闻报道时，要意识到新闻本身承载着报道者的情感态度，能够用清醒的头脑去判断媒体话语是否全面地提供了信息。同时，由于当今网络的便捷性与开放性，在社交媒体平台上常出现"百家之语",阅读者应理性地思考,不能盲目跟风。

4. 结语

论文从新闻标题的语气、指称和正文内容三个方面入手,探讨了《人民日报》与"央视新闻"两大微博官方媒体报道中对女性医护人员形象的表征。在标题语气方面,媒体主要的情感态度为"心疼"与"感动",通过大量的感叹语气与祈使语气来引发公众的共鸣;在标题指称方面,报道者多用"女儿"、"妻子"和"母亲"这三个社会符号来表征女性医护人员,体现了对女性家庭角色的突出刻画;在正文内容方面,占比最大的主题为"牵挂"与"思念",强调的是女性的"柔弱"与"牺牲"。由此可见,社交媒体在报道女性医护人员相关新闻时,潜在的意识形态固化了人们对女性的印象。真正地赞美女性医护人员在例如抗击疫情工作中的巨大贡献,赞美女性医护人员的专业水平、同理心和无私奉献,而不是通过"心疼"与"感动"的文字来引发公众对女性奉献的认同。希望在今后的媒体报道中,报道者应合理地选择信息,平衡其宣传内容,充分展现当代女性的自信与独立、智慧与担当。

参考文献

[1] 王美艳.中国城市劳动力市场上的性别工资差异[J].经济研究,2005(12):35-44.

[2] 喻术红.反就业歧视法律问题之比较研究[J].中国法学,2005(1):129-136.

[3] 刘伯红,卜卫.我国电视广告中女性形象的研究报告[J].新闻与传播研究,1997(1):45-58+96.

[4] 刘泽云.女性教育收益率为何高于男性?——基于工资性别歧视的分析[J].经济科学,2008(2):119-128.

[5] 潘建.英汉语言性别歧视的比较研究[J].外语与外语教学,2001(3):14-16.

[6] 于惠淑,解娜.网络娱乐新闻对女性的性别歧视——以娱乐新闻为例[J].青年记者,2010(35):14-15.

[7] 唐青叶,吴草.中国主流媒体对明星吸毒报道的研究[J].中国药物滥用防治杂志,2016,22(3):153-157.

[8] HALLIDAY M A K, MATTHIESSEN C M I M. Construing Experience through Meaning: A Language-Based Approach to Cognition[M]. London: Cassell, 1999.

[9] 单胜江.新闻语篇的批评性话语分析[J].外语学刊,2011(6):78-81.
[10] 管健,乐国安.社会表征理论及其发展[J].南京师大学报(社会科学版),2007(1):92-98.
[11] MARTIN W, BAUER G. Towards a paradigm for research on social representations[J]. Journal for The Theory of Social Behavior,1999,29(2).
[12] 楚军,周军.报纸新闻标题的功能研究[J].四川外语学院学报,2006(4):89-93.
[13] 张德禄,郭恩华.多模态话语分析的双重视角——社会符号观与概念隐喻观的连接与互补[J].外国语(上海外国语大学学报),2013,36(3):20-28.
[14] 唐青叶.叙利亚危机的媒体话语与话语政治分析[J].阿拉伯世界研究,2014(5):64-80.
[15] 郭淑娟.新闻话语中的意识形态建构[J].当代传播,2011(1):37-39.
[16] 丁和根.梵·迪克新闻话语结构理论述评[J].江苏社会科学,2003(6):199-203.

点评

论文以《人民日报》与"央视新闻"微博为例,结合话语分析理论与传播学理论,对社交媒体报道女性医护工作者刻板印象进行了探讨,并提出了相应的解决对策,具有一定的现实意义。论文视角新颖,观点鲜明,思路清晰,结构合理,写作比较符合论文规范。

汉语道歉话语策略性别差异实证研究

——以工龄10年内的当代青年为例

王婧文[*]

摘要：研究以道歉话语为例，采用定性和定量相结合的研究方法，考察了当代男性和女性青年（工龄10年内）在不同权势关系、社会距离、冒犯严重程度的交际语境中的礼貌观。统计了频数、百分比并进行了显著性差异运算。分析表明，当代青年呈现出积极的礼貌观，其中，男性青年倾向于简单直接的道歉，更关注自己的面子，注重言语传递信息的功能；女性青年情感细腻丰富，倾向于选择以他人为中心的复杂道歉话语，关心被冒犯者的感情，维护他人的面子，注重言语维系情感的功能。研究还发现一种有趣的"机智型"道歉策略，即冒犯者以幽默巧妙化解尴尬，降低矛盾等级。

关键词：道歉话语策略；性别差异；礼貌观

引言

道歉是人们日常生活中常见的言语行为。人在社会中，不断地与他人进行接触和交流，都有一种渴望与他人建立良好社会关系的需求，当互动关系处于非平衡状态时，一方的言行给另一方造成一定的威胁甚至伤害，进一步的交流合作有可能终止，此时，发出冒犯行为的一方如果意识到自己的过失，且有意修复对听话人造成的损失，即出现道歉行为。Holmes[1]（1990）说，道歉是当说话人冒犯了听话人，用来维护听话人的面子，并且弥补冒犯的后果，进而恢复和谐的一种言语行为。人际互动过程中的性别差异也是诸多语言学家、社会学家、心理学

---

[*] 王婧文：上海大学外国语学院2019级硕士研究生。

家等普遍关注的课题。很多学者都认为女性言语与男性言语存在差别（Baron, 1986; Ariliss, 1991）。Lakoff[2]（1973）从词汇和句法的角度对"女性语言"给予关注和思考。近二十年来，关于"女性是否比男性更礼貌"这一问题引起了国内外学者的广泛热议（如 Coates, 1998、2004; Holmes, 1995、1998、2003; Pan & Zheng, 2017）。其中，Holems[3]（1995）提出女性比男性更礼貌，因为女性比男性更关注互动的情感功能。Mills[4]（2003）反对"女性比男性"更礼貌的观点，指出，"礼貌"不是话段的属性，它更像是行为社区发展、确认和竞争的"行为和策略体系"[4]（Mills, 2003）。研究以道歉为例，通过问卷调查，从权势关系、社会距离和冒犯严重程度三个维度对不同性别当代青年的道歉观念进行考察，结合前人的研究，以期呈现当代青年在礼貌方面的性别差异并探讨主要成因，揭示男女之间的认知差异，为减少人际冲突，实现更高效与成功交际提供有益参考。

1. 文献综述

"男女在语言使用上的差异很早就为人类学家、历史学家和语言学家所注目（祝畹瑾,1992）。"[5]20 世纪 70 年代以来，诸多语言学家如 Lakoff, Holmes, Coates 等对男女性别语言差异的问题作了深入的探讨。研究表明，男女在言语方面确实存在差异，不仅在语音、词汇、语法、话题、话轮转接等存在差异，女性语言倾向于较为间接、委婉、含蓄，而男性语言更为直接、明确。目前，国内外学者对请求（Houck, 1992; Macaulay, 2001; 段成钢, 2008）、称赞（Herbert, 1990; 权立宏, 2004; 冯江鸿, 2003; 魏耀章, 2001）、拒绝（Beebe, et al., 1990）、邀请（Homels, 1995）、致谢（Eisenstein & Bodman, 1986）和道歉（Chamani, 2014; Holmes, 1989、1995）等言语行为的性别差异进行了广泛研究。Holmes（1990）运用民族志的研究方法，收集了 183 个新西兰以英语为母语的人的自然对话并建立语料库，应用定性和定量相结合的方式，发现性别差异对道歉策略的选择有显著影响，总体上来说，女性比男性更多的使用道歉话语。Tata[6]（2000）的研究结果显示女性更关心他人的面子，易使用缓和性道歉语（mitigating apology）。

近 20 年来，国内关于道歉话语的研究也呈雨后春笋之势。学者们对道歉话语进行了多维度的性别差异分析，研究方法也不断更新，如定性与定量研究，语料收集有田野调查、民族志调查、问卷调查，语篇补全测试、访谈、角色扮演等。潘小燕[7]（2004）采取实录法，记录了受观察者在三种不同的语境下的道歉话语行为,共收集语料 53 条,受观察者中男性 25 人,女性 28 人,并对实验数据进行了显著性差异测量,得出结论,女性比男性更容易道歉,更爱使用程度副词,如"真""十分"等。郭敏[8](2005)采用语篇补全测试的问卷调查方法,调查对象是某大学大二学生,回收有效问卷 130 份,结合三个社会语用因素(社会距离,冒犯程度和受话人性别),利用方差分析方法,得出结论:男性侧重将道歉视为面子威胁的行为,而女性侧重将道歉作为维护人际关系策略。李洋[9](2009)也使用语篇补全测试和单项选择评估测试,受试者由 30 名大学生组成,研究结果表明男女受试者在道歉策略的选择上有较大的差异。侯香勤[10](2012)采用问卷调查与访谈的形式,对汉语语境中男女致歉言语策略进行定量、定性分析后,发现女性比男性使用较多的致歉。张晓洁[11](2012)以反映当代大学生校园生活的电视剧和小说为语料来源,探索中国大学生汉语道歉话语行为的性别差异,研究表明,男女大学生总体上具有相似的道歉策略使用频率,且男大学生较女大学生更多地使用承担责任策略、提出补偿策略和正式直接道歉策略,而女大学生更频繁地使用解释说明策略。李梦欣[12](2019)采用问卷调查法,考察了当代男女大学生在道歉必要性和道歉郑重程度方面的性别差异,研究表明,女性展现出比男性对道歉必要性的重视,而男生和女生在道歉郑重程度上不存在显著性差异。

由上所知,一些学者在数据分析时使用了简单的百分比或频数比较(李洋,2009;张晓洁,2012),且受试者大多以当代大学生为主,忽略了已经进入社会工作的当代青年,而参与到社会工作的成年期是一个人社会化的重要阶段。故本研究对象以大学毕业已工作(10 年内)的当代青年为主,以期完善此领域的研究。

2. 理论框架

根据 Brown 和 Levinson[13](1987)所说,礼貌就是"典型人"(model person)为满足面子需求所采取的各种理性行为。而"面子"即是一个社会成员意欲为自己挣得的在公众中的"个人形象"(the public self-image),它分为消极面子(negative face)和积极面子(positive face)两类。消极面子是指不希望别人强加于自己,自己的行为不受别人的干涉、阻碍。积极面子是指希望得到别人的赞同、喜爱。在社会交际中,既要尊重对方的积极面子,又要照顾对方的消极面子,才能使社会交往能得以顺利进行。同时,Brown 和 Levinson 指出,有些言语行为具有固有的威胁面子的性质,也就是说,有些言语行为本质上与说话人或听话人的面子需求背道而驰。道歉即是一种威胁说话人积极面子的言语行为。当说话人意识到自己的所作所为有意或者无意冒犯了听话人时,说话人就需要采取言语或者非言语的方式去维护对方的面子,通过道歉这一言语行为修复两人之间的关系。Brown 和 Levinson 认为威胁面子行为的因素主要有以下三个因素:① 说话人和听话人之间的"社会距离"(social distance);② 说话人和听话人之间的"相对权势"(relative power);③ 特定的文化中,言语行为本身所固有的强加的绝对级别(absolute ranking of imposition)。

M. Owen[14](1983)与 A. Trosborg[15](1987)等学者对道歉语都进行过研究。他们根据自己的观察与实验对道歉策略进行了详尽的总结与归纳。本研究将使用 A. Trosborg(1987)归纳的七种道歉策略(见表1)。策略的选择就是说话者对所估算的威胁面子行为的冒犯程度的"编码"[16](何兆熊,1999),故说话者对道歉策略的选择,一定程度上反映出说话者的礼貌观。研究从 Brown 和 Levinson 提出的威胁面子行为的三个因素出发,对当代青年所使用的道歉策略进行考察。

表1 道歉话语的使用策略分类

序号	策略	解释	举例
策略1	0策略(拒绝道歉)	冒犯者否认自己有任何责任	"我对此事一无所知。"
策略2	减轻责任策略	冒犯者承认自己有责任,但通过多种手段辨明自己只应负部分责任	"这并不都是我的错,小王也有责任。"
策略3	认可应负责任策略	冒犯者认可自己的责任	"我承认是我忘了,你责怪我是应该的。"
策略4	解释说明策略	冒犯者对冒犯行为进行解释说明	"对不起,我来晚了,因为路上塞车。"
策略5	直接道歉策略	冒犯者明确地表示自己的歉意	"真的很对不起,请你原谅。"
策略6	采用补偿手段策略	冒犯者采用补偿措施来弥补冒犯的不良后果	"我的上衣不能借给你。不过,这条裙子可以借给你。"
策略7	保证将克制自己策略	冒犯者承诺将来的表现	"我保证以后再也不迟到了。"

续表

序号	策略	解释	举例
策略 8	表达对听话者关心策略	为了安慰被冒犯者,冒犯者表现出对对方处境的关心来缓和自己的冒犯程度	"你等了很久了吧?累了吧?"

其中,策略 5 属于直接道歉策略(direct apology strategies),策略 2、策略 3、策略 4、策略 6、策略 7 和策略 8 属于间接道歉策略(indirect apology strategies),间接道歉策略又可以分为自我中心道歉策略(self-oriented apology strategies)和他人中心道歉策略(other-oriented apology strategies),前者包括策略 2、策略 3、策略 4 和策略 7,后者包括策略 6 和策略 8[17](王海萍,2003)。

3. 实验设计

研究采取定性和定量研究相结合的方法,考察不同性别的当代青年的礼貌观,旨在回答以下两个问题:

(1)在汉语文化背景下,男性和女性在道歉话语的策略使用上是否存在显著差异?如果存在这些差异,为什么?

(2)在汉语文化背景下,在"道歉"这一言语行为的实施上,女性是否比男性更礼貌,为什么?

围绕着这两个主要的研究问题,笔者采用问卷调查法,使用"问卷星"平台在线收集语料。问卷设计最初采用"语篇补全测试"(Discource-completion Test)的形式,结合贾玉新(1997)设计的道歉话语行为 DCT 问卷并进行了修改。问卷由两部分组成,第一部分是受试者基本信息,第二部分由 15 个情景组成,且与受试者日常生活密切相关,要求受试者结合自己的经历和感受做出相应的道歉话语行为。在此问卷设计中,15 个情景围绕着不同权势关系及不同社会距离下,人们在不同冒犯程度的情景下所做的道歉展开。为了测试问卷设计的合理性与合适度,问卷先在小范围内预测。根据受试者反馈,开放式的语篇补全形式,需要受试者以"填空题"的形式自主作答,而不是"选择题",由于受试答题过程中付出的心力提高,导致问卷回收率不高,且问卷的有效性和真实性大大降低。故,初步试验后,笔者根据 A. Trosborg(1987)总结归纳的八种道歉话语策略,结合初步实验中被试者的回答,给出相对应的八种道歉话语,并在每个情景中给出一个可选的填空题选项,如果被试发现以上选项里没有合适的道歉话语,即可填写自己有可能发出的道歉话语。

问卷调查的对象为当代大学本科毕业工作 1~5 年内的青年共 266 人(排除在校学生),回收问卷 266 份,排除工龄大于 10 年的工作人员以及作答时间小于 1 分钟的问卷,共回收有效问卷 150 份,其中男性 63 人,女性 81 人。工作地区大多集中在中国南部、中部和西部地区的大中小城市。

4. 数据分析

在统计运算中,为了测量当代青年在社会权势、社会距离和冒犯程度三个变量对受试者道歉观念的影响,笔者将 15 个情境分成 8 组,其中按照冒犯者之于被冒犯者的社会权势分为 3 组,分别为,社会权势为上对下:Q1,Q10,Q14;社会权势平等:Q5,Q6,Q8;社会权势为下对上:Q2,Q3,Q4;按照冒犯者和被冒犯者的社会距离分为 2 组:社会距离较远:Q7,Q11,Q12;社会距离较近:Q9,Q13,Q15,运用单因素方差分析(One-Way ANOVA)和双因素方差分析法(Two-Way ANOVA)来计算社会权势、社会距离以及冒犯程度是否对不同性别的当代青年在道歉策略选择上有显著影响。

在数据整理过程中,笔者发现,有部分受试者选择了"填空"选项,并给出了自己认为合适的道歉话语。笔者根据 A. Trosborg(1987)总结归纳的八种道歉话语策略对其进行归类整理,且发现受试者填写的道歉话语中出现了一种新的道歉策略,即,"机智型"道歉策略(详见后文分析),笔者将此道歉策略列为策略 9,并进行了相关计算。

4.1 当代青年道歉话语策略总体特征

表 2 和图 1 分别汇报了当代男性和女性青年在以上 15 种情境下道歉话语策略的整体统计结果。通过表 2 和图 1 可知,整体上来说,当代青年在道歉话语中,较多的选择策略 6(27.7%)和策略 8(24.1%),即"采取补偿手段策略"和"表达对听话者关心策略",且女性使用策略 6(29.9%)和策略 8(25.4%)的频数皆大于男性使用策略 6(24.9%)和策略 8(22.4%)的频数,通过表 3 可知,当代男性青年和女性青年在道歉话语策略 6 的使用呈现显著性差异(Sig. = 0.039<0.05)。通过图 1 可知,男性在策略 1、策略 2、策略 3、策略 5、策略 9 的使用频数上均高于女性(2.1%>1.3%,2.7%>1.0%,10.2%>5.9%,14.7%>11.6%,0.9%>0.2%),且

在策略 2 和策略 3 的使用上呈现显著性差异(表 4:Sig. = 0.020<0.05,Sig. = 0.019<0.05),即"减轻责任策略"和"认可应负责任策略"。

表 2　十五种情境下男性青年和女性青年所使用的道歉话语策略频数

策略	男性		女性		总计	
	No.	%	No.	%	No.	%
策略 1	21	2.1%	16	1.3%	37	1.6%
策略 2	27	2.7%	13	1.0%	40	1.8%
策略 3	101	10.2%	74	5.9%	175	7.8%
策略 4	110	11.1%	146	11.6%	256	11.4%
策略 5	146	14.7%	146	11.6%	292	13.0%
策略 6	247	24.9%	377	29.9%	624	27.7%
策略 7	107	10.8%	165	13.1%	272	12.1%
策略 8	222	22.4%	320	25.4%	542	24.1%
策略 9	9	0.9%	3	0.2%	12	0.5%
总计	990	100%	1 260	100%	2250	100%

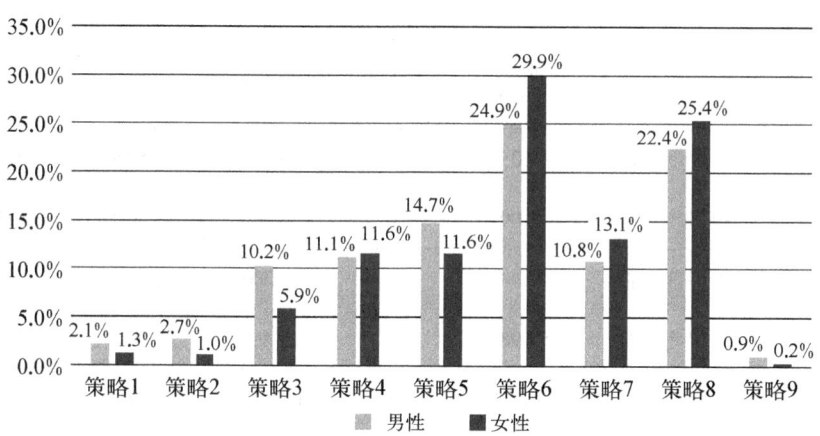

图 1　各种情境中,男性青年和女性青年所使用的道歉话语策略选择百分比

表3 单因素方差分析(One-Way ANOVA)结果(各个策略)

策略	平方和	自由度	均方	F	显著性
策略1	.374	1	.374	.633	.427
策略2	2.452	1	2.452	5.516	.020
策略3	10.823	1	10.823	5.640	.019
策略4	.146	1	.146	.060	.807
策略5	7.242	1	7.242	2.636	.107
策略6	26.270	1	26.270	4.347	.039
策略7	.080	1	.080	.046	.831
策略8	6.088	1	6.088	.997	.320
策略9	.023	1	.023	.204	.653

4.2 不同语境中当代青年道歉话语策略性别差异分析

4.2.1 权势关系与道歉话语策略的应用

为了检验社会权势、性别及其交互作用对当代青年道歉话语策略的影响,笔者使用双因素方差分析(Two-Way ANOVA),分析结果见表4:

表4 主体间效应检验(性别 * 社会权势)

源	因变量	Ⅲ类平方和	自由度	均方	F	显著性
性别	冒犯程度较高	14.057	1	14.057	4.526	.034
	冒犯程度中等	23.091	1	23.091	11.135	.001
	冒犯程度较低	3.080	1	3.080	1.083	.299
社会权势	冒犯程度较高	55.983	2	27.992	9.012	.000
	冒犯程度中等	286.447	2	143.224	69.066	.000
	冒犯程度较低	70.158	2	35.079	12.338	.000

续表

源	因变量	Ⅲ 类平方和	自由度	均方	F	显著性
性别*社会权势	冒犯程度较高	2.952	2	1.476	.475	.622
	冒犯程度中等	2.234	2	1.117	.539	.584
	冒犯程度较低	.274	2	.137	.048	.953

如表 4 所示,当冒犯程度较高(Sig. = 0.034<0.05)和冒犯程度中等(Sig. = 0.001<0.05)时,性别对男性和女性青年在道歉话语策略选择上影响显著。由(Sig. = 0.000<0.05)可知,社会权势对男性和女性青年在道歉话语策略的选择上影响高度显著。而性别*社会权势的交互作用效应对男性和女性青年在道歉话语策略的选择上没有显著影响(Sig. = 0.622>0.05,Sig. = 0.584>0.05,Sig. = 0.953>0.05)。

A. 权势关系为上对下,且冒犯程度不同

表 5　单因素方差分析(One-Way ANOVA)结果(社会权势关系为上对下)

冒犯程度	平方和	自由度	均方	F	显著性
冒犯程度较高	12.577	1	12.577	2.568	.111
冒犯程度中等	12.114	1	12.114	4.330	.039
冒犯程度较低	.514	1	.514	.155	.694

由表 5 可见,当冒犯程度中等时,不同性别的当代青年在社会权势关系为上对下的交际语境中,在道歉话语策略的选择上存在显著差异(Sig. = 0.039<0.05),在冒犯程度较高和较低的交际语境中,不存在显著性差异(Sig. = 0.111>0.05,Sig. = 0.694>0.05)。

在上对下的权势关系中,选择策略 6("采取补偿手段策略"),策略 7("保证将克制自己策略"),策略 8("表达对听话者关心策略")的青年的比例较高,即不管是男性还是女性,都认为应该道歉,意识到自己冒犯了对方,威胁到对方的

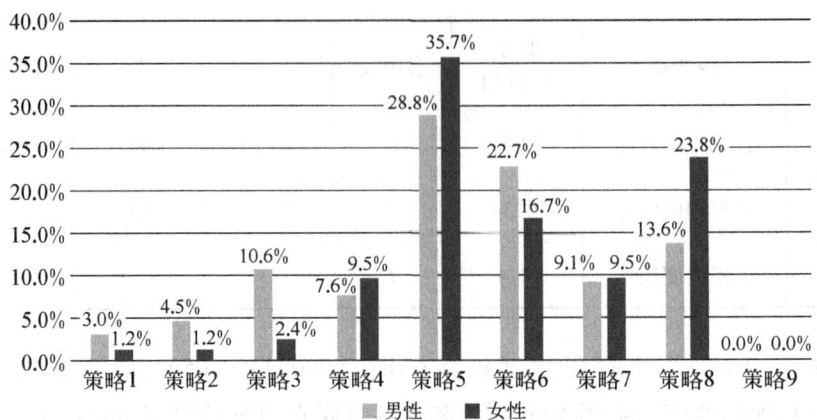

图 2　社会权势关系为上对下、冒犯程度中等时,男女青年道歉话语策略选择百分比

面子,欲采取补偿措施,并表达对听话者的关心。且当冒犯程度中等时,女性青年在策略 5("直接道歉策略")和策略 8("表达对听话者关心策略")的选择上比例显著高于男性,即女性青年认为在冒犯程度中等,作为高权势的冒犯者应该郑重并且有诚意的向被冒犯者表达歉意,挽回对方的面子。值得注意的是,此种交际环境中,男性青年在策略 1("0 策略"),策略 2("减轻责任策略"),策略 3("认可应负责任策略"),策略 6("采取补偿手段策略")的选择上显著高于女性青年。

B. 权势关系平等,且冒犯程度不同

表 6　单因素方差分析(One-Way ANOVA)结果(社会权势关系平等)

冒犯程度	平方和	自由度	均方	F	显著性
冒犯程度较高	2.837	1	2.837	1.376	.243
冒犯程度中等	10.779	1	10.779	5.188	.024
冒犯程度较低	.801	1	.801	.341	.560

由表 6 可见,当冒犯程度中等时,不同性别的当代青年在社会权势关系平等的交际语境中,在道歉话语策略的选择上存在显著差异(Sig. = 0.024<0.05),在

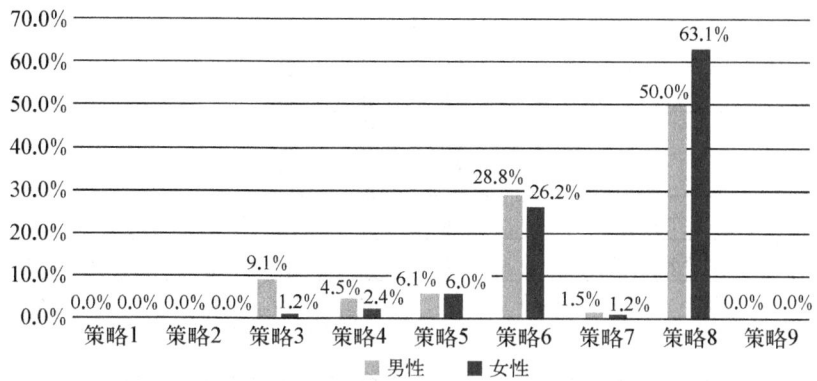

图3　社会权势关系平等、冒犯程度中等时,男女青年道歉话语策略选择百分比

冒犯程度较高和较低的交际语境中,不存在显著性差异(Sig. = 0.243>0.05, Sig. =0.560>0.05)。

当冒犯者与被冒犯者权势关系平等时,如同事或者同学,整体上,策略6("采取补偿手段策略")的选择比例较高,即不管是男性还是女性,都认为应该道歉,且应采取补偿措施。当冒犯程度中等时,女性青年在策略8("表达对听话者关心策略")的选择上显著高于男性青年,且男性青年在策略3("认可应负责任策略")的选择比例上显著高于女性青年。

C. 权势关系为下对上,且冒犯程度不同

表7　单因素方差分析(One-Way ANOVA)结果(社会权势关系为下对上)

冒犯程度	平方和	自由度	均　方	F	显著性
冒犯程度较高	1.596	1	1.596	.676	.412
冒犯程度中等	2.432	1	2.432	1.807	.181
冒犯程度较低	2.038	1	2.038	.710	.401

由表7可见,当冒犯者之于被冒犯者的社会权势为下对上时,如普通职员之于公司领导,晚辈之于长辈,学生之于教师,无论冒犯程度如何,不同性别的当代青年在道歉话语策略的选择上不存在显著差异(Sig. = 0.412>0.05,Sig. =

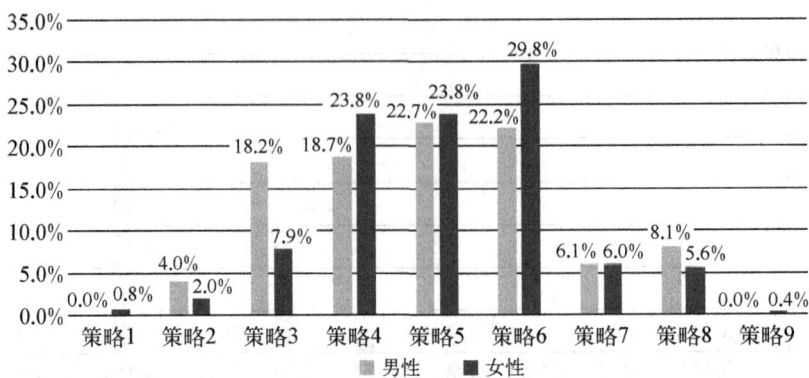

图 4　社会权势关系为下对上、冒犯程度不同时,男女青年道歉话语策略选择百分比

0.181>0.05,Sig.=0.401>0.05),策略 4("解释说明策略"),策略 5("直接道歉策略"),策略 6("采取补偿手段策略")的选择比例较高,在此种交际语境中,选择"拒绝道歉"、"减轻责任策略"的比例较低,且较少的表达对被冒犯者关心。同样的,男性青年在策略 3("认可应负责任策略")的选择上显著高于女性青年,女性青年在策略 6("采取补偿手段策略")的选择上显著高于男性青年。

4.2.2　社会距离与道歉话语策略的应用

为了检验社会距离、性别及其交互作用对当代青年道歉话语策略的影响,笔者使用双因素方差分析(Two-Way ANOVA),分析结果见表 8:

表 8　主体间效应检验(性别 * 社会距离)

源	因变量	Ⅲ 类平方和	自由度	均方	F	显著性
性别	冒犯程度较高	7.714	1	7.714	3.768	.053
	冒犯程度中等	19.330	1	19.330	6.350	.012
	冒犯程度较低	2.272	1	2.272	.799	.372
社会距离	冒犯程度较高	50.603	1	50.603	24.716	.000
	冒犯程度中等	5.741	1	5.741	1.886	.171
	冒犯程度较低	48.312	1	48.312	16.984	.000

续表

源	因变量	Ⅲ类平方和	自由度	均方	F	显著性
性别*社会距离	冒犯程度较高	7.923	1	7.923	3.870	.050
	冒犯程度中等	.327	1	.327	.108	.743
	冒犯程度较低	13.646	1	13.646	4.797	.029

如表8所示,当冒犯程度中等(Sig.=0.012<0.05)时,性别对男性和女性青年在道歉话语策略的选择上影响显著。当冒犯程度较高(Sig.=0.000<0.05)和较低(Sig.=0.000<0.05)时,社会距离对男性和女性青年在道歉话语策略的选择上的影响高度显著。当冒犯程度较低时,虽然性别与社会距离的交互作用Sig.=0.029<0.05,但在此条件下,性别对于男性和女性青年在道歉话语策略的选择上没有显著影响(Sig.=0.372>0.05),故性别与社会距离的交互作用影响不显著。

A. 社会距离较远,且冒犯程度不同

表9 单因素方差分析(One-Way ANOVA)结果(社会距离较远)

冒犯程度	平方和	自由度	均方	F	显著性
冒犯程度较高	15.636	1	15.636	8.226	.005
冒犯程度中等	7.313	1	7.313	2.137	.146
冒犯程度较低	2.391	1	2.391	.556	.457

由表9可知,当冒犯者与被冒犯者社会距离较远时,如各种情境下的陌生人,当冒犯程度较高时,男性青年和女性青年在道歉话语策略选择上呈现显著性差异(Sig.=0.005<0.05),且在此种交际语境中,女性青年在策略6("采取补偿手段策略"),策略8("表达对听话者关心策略")的选择上显著高于男性青年;男性青年在策略4("解释说明策略")和策略5("直接道歉策略")的选择频率上显著高于女性青年。

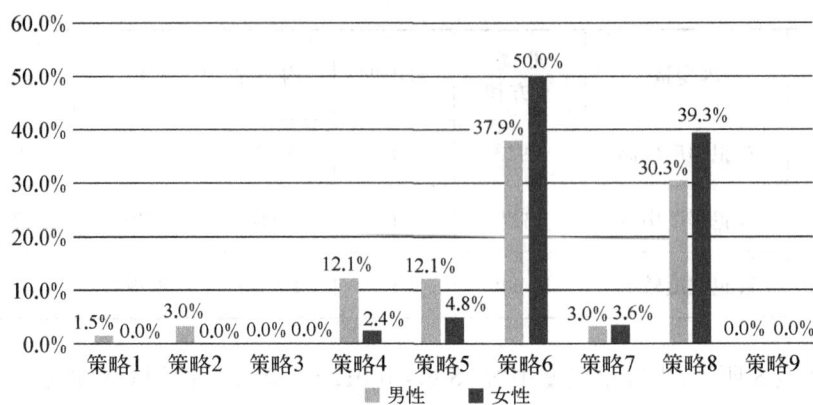

图5 社会距离较远、冒犯程度较高时,男女青年道歉话语策略选择百分比

B. 社会距离较近,且冒犯程度不同

表10 单因素方差分析(One-Way ANOVA)结果(社会距离较近)

冒犯程度	平方和	自由度	均方	F	显著性
冒犯程度较高	.001	1	.001	.000	.986
冒犯程度中等	12.344	1	12.344	4.628	.033
冒犯程度较低	13.527	1	13.527	9.763	.002

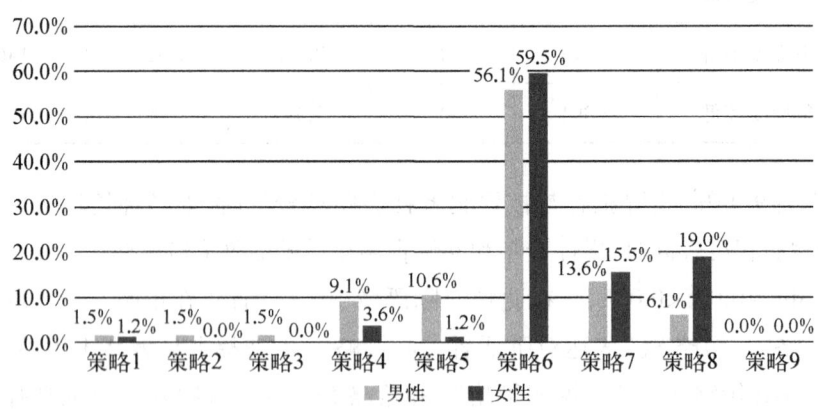

图6 社会距离较近、冒犯程度较低时,男女青年道歉话语策略选择百分比

由表10可知,当冒犯者与被冒犯者社会距离较近时,如好朋友,当冒犯程度较低时,男性青年和女性青年在道歉话语策略选择上呈现显著性差异($Sig.=0.002<0.05$),且在此种交际环境中,策略6("采取补偿手段策略")的选择比例最高,男性青年在策略4("解释说明策略")和策略5("直接道歉策略")的选择上显著高于女性青年,女性青年在策略8("表达对听话者关心策略")的选择中显著高于男性青年。

5. 讨论

根据上文数据分析结果可知,在各个策略水平上,女性青年在策略6("采用补偿手段策略")的选择频率上高于男性青年,且差异显著;而男性青年在策略2("减轻责任策略")和策略3("认可应负责任策略")的选择上高于女性青年,且差异显著。且在多种不同的交际语境中,女性青年在策略8("表达对听话者关心策略")的选择频率上都高于男性青年。权势关系对男女青年在道歉话语策略的选择上影响显著,且当权势关系为上对下时,如公司领导之于公司职员,长辈之于晚辈,男性青年在策略1("0策略"),策略2("减轻责任策略")和策略3("认可应负责任策略")选择上显著高于女性青年,而女性青年认为此时仍然应该郑重、真诚的道歉。社会距离对男女青年在道歉话语策略的选择上影响显著,且当社会距离较远,冒犯程度较高和较低时,男性青年更多选择策略4("解释说明策略")和策略5("直接道歉策略"),差异显著,女性青年更多选择策略6("采用补偿手段策略")和策略8("表达对听话者关心策略"),差异显著。此结果与郭敏(2005)、张晓洁(2012)、李梦欣(2019)的研究结果基本一致。

综上所述,结合不同权势关系以及不同社会距离下各个冒犯水平的不同交际语境中,男性青年和女性青年对道歉话语策略选择的统计结果,研究主要有以下发现:

第一,在相同的交际语境中,男性青年更倾向于使用以自我为中心的道歉话语策略,话语形式简单直接,注重言语传递信息的功能;女性青年更倾向于使用以他人为中心的道歉话语策略,且使用复杂形式的道歉话语,注重言语维系情感的功能。道歉是一种"负礼貌"行为,威胁说话人的面子,维护听话人的面子。一个人越顾及和维护他人的面子,越表现的有礼貌,对自己的面子威胁越大。在道歉话语中,男性倾向于以自我为中心,简单直接的道歉,承担应负责任,而女性倾向于采取较复杂的道歉策略,选择礼貌程度较高的表达方式(Holmes,1995)。传统观念对男女性别行为的期待有所不同,社会更期望女性的行为举止更礼貌。如以下情境:

[1] 朋友有事不能去上课,请你帮忙向老师请假,但你忘记了,你会如何跟朋友说?

大多数男性和女性青年选择策略6,即提出补偿策略,如"对不起啊,忘记帮你请假了,我现在去跟老师说一声",而女性青年在策略8的选择上显著高于男性,如"对不起啊,忘记帮你请假了,你别担心,应该没事的",面对关系亲近的朋友,一旦失信更应该真心诚意地表达歉意维系感情;而男性青年倾向于简单直接的道歉,表示不必如此拘谨和正式,且两性对冒犯程度的认知不一样,男性青年认为如此小事不必介怀,而女性青年情感丰富,审美能力强,自我表达的自由度较大,倾向于以他人为中心,尽管是很小的冒犯,也会郑重、认真的道歉,关心是否伤及对方的感情。同时,女性倾向于使用复合式道歉策略,通常是直接道歉策略在前,间接道歉策略在后。

第二,男性青年和女性青年对社会权势和社会距离都很敏感,男性青年在道歉话语中注重维护自己面子,承担社会责任,保持个人社会形象和声誉;女性青年在道歉话语中以同理心出发,情感丰富细腻,注重维护对方的面子,倾向于郑重道歉。根据 Van Dusen & Spies[18](2003)的观点,职位更高的人比较不情愿道歉,因为道歉本身就是威胁说话人积极面子的行为,道歉即承认个人弱点,是一种妥协行为,不利于领导形象的树立。而本研究数据分析结果显示,当道歉者之于被道歉者的社会权势为上对下时,大多数当代青年仍然认为要真诚的道歉。这说明,随着时代的发展,中国青年越来越注重独立、平等、自由等价值观,作为领导、长辈更应该树立榜样,为集体利益以身作则。值得注意的是,此种交际语境中,男性青年对策略1、策略2、策略3和策略6的选择显著高于女性青年,作为权势较高的一方,男性青年选择间接地提供经济或者其他方面的补偿,但郑重的道歉有损作为领导者的威严,如以下情境:

[2] 假设你是某大型活动的负责人,以为志愿者(学生)带领外籍嘉宾进错了会议室,因而十分严厉的责怪了该志愿者。事后发现是自己的日程表未更新,错怪了该志愿者,你会如何处理这件事?如何跟该志愿者说?

在此情境中,80.66%的男性和女性青年认为应该诚恳道歉,而7.5%的男性青年(女性青年:2.2%)选择不再提及此事,或者通过辩解提出对方也负有责任,进而减轻自己的责任,如"日程表有变,你应该跟我及时沟通的";而女性青年倾向于使用"非常"、"很"等强势词加深自己的歉意,如"非常诚恳地向你道歉,由于我没有发现日程表更新错怪了你",以此表达自己的真诚,补救自己的过失,照顾对方的面子,进而得到对方的谅解,以恢复和谐的人际关系。

第三,研究发现受试者还倾向于采取"机智型道歉策略",以出其不意、幽默的方式巧妙化解尴尬,降低矛盾等级,在挽回对方面子的同时,又维护了自己的面子。如以下情境:

[3] 采访现场,假设你是某记者,你不小心将咖啡洒到了受访人的衣服上,你会如何跟他说?

在此情境中,有受试者给出"天啊天啊天啊,第一次看到您太激动了!实在不好意思!"这种敏捷、跳跃式的道歉话语,冒犯者从一个意想不到的视角出发,制造惊奇感,巧妙化解人际冲突,这正是人对于事物的洞察力、机智敏感以及把握智慧和才能的一种表现。

6. 结语

研究以道歉话语为例,考察了当代青年在涉及不同权势关系、社会距离和冒犯严重程度的交际语境中的礼貌观,分析冒犯者道歉话语策略的选择,并探讨了造成差异的原因。由以上文可知,当代男性和女性青年均呈现出积极的礼貌观,继承了中华民族的传统美德,道歉不是出于被动地展现被社会所赋予的角色和地位,而是出于和谐人际关系或个人形象的维系,是一种主动承担责任、积极构建社会身份的选择[19-20](陈新仁,2013、2014)。同时,研究也揭示了具体语境中男性青年和女性青年礼貌观念的差异,语言是社会文化的一面镜子,可以反映语言使用者的认知状态、文化心理、价值取向以及社会规范等等。可以看到,当代青年继承了中华民族谦和好礼、修己慎独的传统美德,同时,人们也应理解和尊重不同性别之间的认知差异、表达方式,以促进跨性别交际的和谐沟通。

参考文献

[1] HOLMES J. Apologies in New Zealand English [J]. Language in Society, 1990,

19(2):155-199.

[2] LAKOFF R. Language and woman's place [J]. Language in Society, 1973, 2(1): 45-80.

[3] HOLMES J. Women, Men and Politeness [M]. London and New York: Longman Group Limited, 1995.

[4] MILLS S. Gender and Politeness [M]. Cambridge: Cambridge University Press, 2003.

[5] 祝畹瑾.社会语言学概论[M].长沙:湖南教育出版社,1992.

[6] TATA J. Implicit Theories of Account-Giving: Influence of Culture and Gender [J]. International Journal of Intercultural Relations, 2000, 24(4): 437-454.

[7] 潘小燕.汉语道歉言语行为的性别差异研究[J].西南交通大学学报(社会科学版),2004(1):89-92.

[8] 郭敏.汉语道歉策略的性别差异研究[D].成都:西南交通大学,2005.

[9] 李洋.中国大学生道歉策略的性别差异研究[D].青岛:中国海洋大学,2009.

[10] 侯香勤.汉语致歉策略性别差异研究[J].华文教学与研究,2012(3):89-95.

[11] 张晓洁.中国大学生汉语道歉言语行为的性别差异研究[D].杭州:浙江大学,2012.

[12] 李梦欣.当代中国大学生礼貌观性别差异调查与分析[J].外语研究,2019(1):37-43.

[13] BROWN P, LEVINSON S C. Politeness: Some Universals in Language Usage [M]. Cambridge: Cambridge University Press, 1987.

[14] OWEN M. Apologies and Rememdial Interchanges [M]. The Haugue: De Gruyter Mouton, 1983.

[15] TROSBORG A. Apology strategies in natives / non-natives [J]. Journal of Pragmatics, 1987, 11(2): 147-167.

[16] 何兆熊.新编语用学概要[M].上海:上海外语教育出版社,1999.

[17] 王海萍.汉语道歉言语行为之研究[D].上海:上海外国语大学,2003.

[18] VAN DUSEN V, SPIES A. Professional apology: dilemma or opportunity [J]. American Journal of Pharmaceutical Education, 2003, 67(4): 114.

[19] 陈新仁.语用身份:动态选择与话语构建[J].外语研究,2013(4):27-32.

[20] 陈新仁.基于社会建构论的语用能力观[J].外语研究,2014(6):1-7.

[21] 段成钢.汉语礼貌语言使用的性别与年龄差异研究[J].语言教学与研究,2008(3):57-63.

[22] 冯江鸿.英汉赞扬及其应答的相别语用比较[J].外语研究,2003(2):18-24.

[23] 贾玉新.跨文化交际学[M].上海:上海外语教育出版社,1997.

[24] 权立宏.汉语中男女在称赞语和称赞语回应使用上的差异分析[J].现代汉语,2004

(1): 62-69.

[25] 魏耀章.恭维语的性别差异研究[J].西安外国语学院学报,2001(1):1-5.

[26] 张亭亭.汉语言语交际中称赞语的性别差异研究[D].北京:北京语言大学,2007.

[27] ARLISS L P. Gender Communication [M]. Englewood Cliffs, NJ: Prentice Hall, 1991.

[28] BARON D. Grammar and Gender [M]. New Haven: Yale University Press, 1986.

[29] BEEBE L M, TAKAHASHI T, ULISS-WELTZ R. Pragmatic transfer in ESL refusal. On the Development of Communicative Competence in a Second Language [M]. New York: Newbury House, 1990.

[30] COATES J. Language and Gender: A Reader [M]. Oxford: Blackwell, 1998.

[31] COATES J. Women, Men and Language: A Sociolinguistic Account of Sex Differences in Language [M]. Harlow: Pearson Educational Limited, 2004.

[32] CHAMANI F. Gender differences in the use of apology speech act in Persian [J]. International Journal of Linguistics, 2014(6): 46-63.

[33] EISENSTEIN M, BODMAN J W. "I very appreciate": expressions of gratitude by native and non-native speakers of American English [J]. Applied Linguistics, 1986, 7(2): 167-185.

[34] HOUCK N. Cross-cultural Pragmatics: Requests and Apologies [C] // BLUM-KULKA S, HOUSE J & KASPER G. Studies in Second Language Acquisition. Norwood, NJ: Ablex, 1992: 217-218.

[35] HERBERT J. Sex-based differences in compliment behavior [J]. Language in Society, 1990, 19 (2): 201-224.

[36] HOLMES J. Sex differences and apologies: one aspect of communicative competence [J]. Applied Linguistics, 1989, 10(2): 194-213.

[37] HOLMES J. An Introduction to Sociolinguistics [M]. Cambridge: Cambridge University Press, 1991.

[38] MACAULAY M. Tough talk: indirectness and gender in requests for information [J]. Journal of Pragmatics, 2001, 33(2): 293-316.

[39] PAN F, ZHENG B. Gender difference of hedging in interpreting for Chinese government press conferences: a corpus-based study [J]. Across Language & Cultures, 2017, 18 (2): 171-193.

点评

论文以道歉为切入点,结合定性和定量方法,从权势关系、社会距离、冒犯程

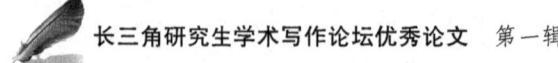

度等方面分析道歉话语策略的选择,考察当代青年的交际语礼貌观。作者对相关领域的研究前沿有较好了解,掌握并能熟练运用量化研究工具,数据挖掘细致,结论分析得当。如能在理论层面进一步深化,可进一步提升本文的理论和实践价值。

长三角一体化发展背景下基于长三角中心区的城市规模结构和经济地理格局分析

王星皓[*]

摘要：长三角中心区是包括上海、江苏、浙江、安徽在内的27个城市组成的城市地域，是推动长三角一体化发展的驱动地和基本盘。基于城市流强度，采用城市首位律、位序-规模法则、莫兰指数分析和空间插值法等研究方法，对长三角中心区城市规模结构和经济地理格局进行分析。研究发现总体上长三角中心区城市中心区中等城市进一步发育，空间集聚程度略有上升，但内部差距进一步拉大；区域中心度高值地区转移，形成"江苏高、浙江中、安徽低"的格局；上海作为长三角的绝对中心城市，对长三角中心区发展的带动作用明显；经济沿长江发展轴往上游发展趋势明显。最后基于以上结论，在空间层面对促进长三角一体化发展提出一些建议。

关键词：长三角一体化发展；城市规模结构；经济地理格局

引言

长江三角洲地区位于中国长江的下游地区，是长江入海之前形成的冲积平原，是中国经济发展最活跃、开放程度最高、创新能力最强的区域之一。长三角区域是"一带一路"与长江经济带的重要交汇地带，在中国国家现代化建设大局和开放格局中具有举足轻重的战略地位，是中国参与国际竞争的重要平台、经济社会发展的重要引擎、长江经济带的引领者，是中国城镇化基础最好的地区之一。长三角区域总体发展状况良好，但内部发展水平差异较大，2018年11月，

---

[*] 王星皓：西安外国语大学人文地理研究所2018级硕士研究生。

党中央决定将支持长江三角洲区域一体化发展并上升为国家战略,长三角区域发展迎来重大发展机遇。

根据中共中央、国务院发布的《长江三角洲区域一体化发展规划纲要》,长三角城市群包括上海市、江苏省、浙江省、安徽省全域(面积35.8万平方公里)。以上海市,江苏省南京、无锡、常州、苏州、南通、扬州、镇江、盐城、泰州,浙江省杭州、宁波、温州、湖州、嘉兴、绍兴、金华、舟山、台州,安徽省合肥、芜湖、马鞍山、铜陵、安庆、滁州、池州、宣城27个城市为中心区(面积22.5万平方公里),辐射带动长三角地区高质量发展。

根据弗里德曼的核心-边缘理论,在区域经济增长的过程中,核心区域和边缘区域存在不平等的发展关系,核心区域居于统治地位,边缘区域在发展中依赖于核心区域。当工业产值在经济中的比重达到25%至50%时,经济发展进入工业化成熟阶段,核心区域对边缘区域起着支配和控制作用;创新都几乎由核心区域流向边缘区域,而劳动力则由边缘区域流向核心区域[1]。2018年,长三角地区总体上第二产业占GDP的比重达到42.65%,此时核心区域和边缘区域的相互联系达到最强,而且核心地区部分中心城市如上海、南京、杭州的第三产业占比更是达到60%以上,资金、技术、信息从中心城市向外的流动进一步加强。因此,在长三角城市群发展过程中,中心区的带动作用至关重要,研究中心区的城市和经济地理格局对于推动长三角地区一体化发展具有重要意义。

1. 研究创新点

以城市流强度作为研究长三角中心区城市规模结构和经济地理格局的基点,因此首先介绍城市流的基本概念。城市流是指城市间人流、物流、信息流、资金流和技术流等空间流在城市群区域内所发生的频繁的、双向的和多向的流动现象,反映了城市集聚与辐射的状态以及城市规模结构不断变化完善的过程。城市流强度(F)是城市外向功能量(E)与其所产生的实际影响力(N)之积,表示城市对外联系与辐射的能力。某个城市是否具有外向功能量,取决于该城市中某一部门从业人员的区位熵(LQ),有:

$$LQ_{ij} = \frac{Q_{ij}/Q_i}{Q_j/Q}$$

式中 LQ_{ij} 为 i 城市 j 部门的从业人员区位熵；Q_i、Q_{ij} 分别为 i 城市总从业人员、i 城市 j 部门从业人员数量；Q、Q_j 分别为全国总从业人员、全国 j 部门从业人员数量。当 $LQ_{ij}<1$ 时，i 城市 j 部门无外向功能量，即 $LQ_{ij}=0$；当 $LQ_{ij}>1$ 时，i 城市 j 部门有外向功能量。

此时 i 城市中分配于 j 部门的从业人员比例高于全国平均水平，即 i 城市 j 部门是具有专业化程度的部门，可以为自身以外的其他区域提供服务。i 城市 n 个部门的总外向功能量（E_i）为：

$$E_i = \sum_{i=0}^{n} E_{ij}$$

i 城市的影响力即功能效率（N_i）以从业人员的人均 GDP 表示：

$$N_i = GDP_i / Q_i$$

式中：GDP_i 为 i 城市 GDP 总量。城市流倾向度（K_i）是反映 i 城市总功能外向程度的物理量：

$$K_i = E_i / Q_i$$

由上得到 i 城市的城市流强度[2]：

$$F_i = GDP_i * K_i$$

关于城市流的研究成果丰富，研究范围包括中国各大城市群。其中包括从整体层面着眼的城市流研究，卢万合、刘继生（2010）对中国十大城市群 99 座城市的外向型功能量、城市流强度和城市流倾向度进行计算[3]；叶磊、欧向军（2012）通过对中国 15 个主要城市群城市流强度与结构的分析，从城市流视角探讨中国城市群对外服务功能空间分布特征及其增长情况[4]。也有具体分析中国主要城市群的城市流强度情况，如张虹鸥等（2004）研究珠江三角洲城市群城市流的强度大小[5]，李光勤等（2006）基于城市流的研究方法分析成渝城市群空间联系现状[6]；刘建朝、高素英（2013）采用经济联系强度模型与城市流模型对京津冀城市群进行了实证研究[7]。还有学者基于城市流强度方法对两个不同城市群的空间联系进行比较分析，如王彬燕等（2015）以城市流强度理论为基础论证哈长、辽中南城市群的发展进程、特征、问题和发展方向[8]；李慧玲（2016）基于城市流强度的分析方法，对京津冀城市群和长三角城市群 2004—2013 年经济联系进行动态变化对比分析[9]。

从以上分析可以看出,国内对城市流的研究分析主要用于分析城市群内部空间联系分布特征,较少用于城市规模体系的分析。雷菁(2006)利用计算城市流强度的方法来划分江西省中心城市规模等级体系[10],但也仅限于城市流强度上的横向比较,而没有应用城市首位度、城市金字塔、位序-规模法则等划分城市规模体系的科学方法。实际上城市流表示了城市对外联系和辐射的能力,反映了城市外向强度的大小,也是城市区域经济影响力大小的体现。区域等级越高的城市,其城市流强度相应越大。因此,用城市流来划分区域城市规模等级、分析城市群经济地理格局具有一定的科学性。

本研究抛弃原有单一的人口指标划分城市规模等级的做法,创新性地采用了城市流强度这一科学指标作为衡量城市中心度的指标,基于 2004—2018 年共 18 年的面板数据,使用城市首位度和位序-规模法则分析长三角城市群城市规模等级的演进,并据此分析该地区的经济地理格局,以便对推动长三角地区一体化发展提出切实合理的建议。

2. 城市体系规模结构分析相关理论及文献综述

2.1 城市首位律理论

城市首位律是马克·杰斐逊(M. Jefferson)在 1939 年对国家城市规模分布规律的一种概括,利用非农业人口规模对一个国家或区域的城镇体系进行分析研究,主要通过 2 城市指数、4 城市指数和 11 城市指数表征研究区域中城市发展要素在最大城市的集中程度。通过以下公式计算:

$$S_2 = P_1/P_2$$

$$S_4 = P_1/(P_2 + P_3 + P_4)$$

$$S_{11} = 2P_1/(P_2 + P_3 + \cdots + P_{11})$$

其中 S_2,S_4,S_{11} 为 2 城市指数、4 城市指数和 11 城市指数;P_1、P_2、P_3、P_4、…、P_{11} 分别为位序在第 1、2、3、4、…、11 位的城市非农人口规模;一般认为,$S_2>2$,$S_4>1$,$S_{11}>1$ 时,属于首位分布;$2<S_2<4$ 时,属于中度首位分布;$S_2>4$ 时,属于高度首位分布[11]。

20 世纪 80 年代,严重敏、宁越敏(1981)将城市首位度的概念引入中国以后,城市首位度的研究进展不断取得突破。20 世纪八九十年代,我国学者对城市首位度的研究主要集中于研究我国城市化的省际差异(许学强、叶嘉安 1986)、城镇体系的划分(顾朝林 1992)等方面,进入 21 世纪以后,学界对城市首位度的研究取得了新的进展并赋予了新的内涵,如卢学法、申绘芳(2007)首次提出了经济首位度、产业首位度、科技首位度、人才首位度和文化首位度的概念[12],张璇(2012)在此基础上引入了城市功能首位度和生态首位度的概念[13],朱军、刘艳(2015)构建了城市首位度的评价指标[14],等等。

2.2 位序-规模法则

位序-规模法则由德国经济学家奥尔巴赫于 1913 年提出,齐普夫于 1949 年对此进行了修正,认为城市规模结构分布可以用公式 $P_r = P_1/r^q$ 表示,其中 P_r 表征了一定区域内城市人口规模排在第 r 位的人口数,P_1 是排在第一位的城市人口规模,r 表示人口规模为 P_r 的城市位序。他认为一个区域内城市规模分布近似服从指数为 1 的帕累托分布,也就是说 q 值近似等于 1。为了方便计算,对上述模型进行变形可以得到公式 $\ln R_1 = \ln P_1 - a\ln P_r$,其中 a 被称为 Zipf 指数。当 $a=1$ 时,表示城市体系内部人口分布较为合理;当 $a<1$ 时,表示人口分布集中,中小城市发育不足;当 $a>1$ 时,表示人口分布平均,大城市分布不足[15]。

我国基于位序-规模法则的城市规模结构的研究成果十分丰富,其中长三角城市群是研究热点之一。程开明(2007)使用长三角城市群 2004 年的人口数据,运用城市首位度、位序-规模法则和二倍数规律等方法,对长三角地区城市体系进行了研究[16]。蒲英霞(2009)基于 1984—2002 年人口面板数据对长三角 16 座地级市的城市规模分布的演变进行了较为系统的研究[17]。孙贵艳(2011)基于长江三角洲城市群 1989—2007 年各市县(区)非农业人口资料,运用位序-规模法则等方法对长三角城镇体系发展中的规模结构及空间结构特征分析研究[18]。韩欢(2013)基于 2011—2010 年面板数据研究分析了长三角整体城市人口和经济规模分布演变规律[19]。晁静(2020)基于多源夜间灯光数据,运用标准差、位序-规模法则、等级钟、马尔科夫转移矩阵等方法对 1995—2015 年长江经济带三大城市群规模差异及规模结构演变特征进行比较分析[20]。

3. 城市规模结构分析

3.1 基于城市首位度的分析

经过计算,基于城市流强度计算的城市首位度如表 1 所示。2004—2018

年长三角城市群中心区城市的城市首位度、4 城市指数和 11 城市指数均略有上升。只有在 2017 年长三角中心区城市满足真正的中度首位分布（$S_2>2$，$S_4>1$，$S_{11}>1$），其余年份均不满足首位分布的情况。值得指出的是，大部分年份首位城市为上海，第二位城市为苏州，而 2011 年和 2012 年正好相反。可以看出，2001—2010 年上海在长三角区域影响力逐渐增大，在经历 2011、2012 年的短暂失落期后，2013 年开始上海重新发挥了自身的影响力，发挥了越来越强的示范引领作用，并且保持对其他城市合理的优势，避免过度集聚发展，一家独大。

表 1　2004—2018 年长三角城市群中心区城市首位度变化表

年 份	城市首位度	4 城市指数	11 城市指数
2004	1.11	0.66	0.60
2005	1.56	0.93	0.88
2006	1.27	0.80	0.77
2007	1.18	0.75	0.75
2008	1.28	0.80	0.78
2009	1.29	0.56	0.66
2010	1.23	0.73	0.77
2011	1.06	0.59	0.60
2012	1.16	0.62	0.60
2013	1.16	0.63	0.67
2014	1.24	0.68	0.74
2015	1.25	0.69	0.74
2016	1.32	0.74	0.77
2017	2.85	1.41	1.33
2018	1.42	0.74	0.78

3.2 基于位序-规模法则的分析

从表2中可以看出，2004—2018年长三角城市群中心区城市城市体系的结构容量 lnA 总体来说呈现上升趋势，从 7.435 4 上升到 9.598 7，表明长三角中心区城市城市对外联系度总体上升的趋势明显，城市间影响和联系越来越明显。图1显示长三角中心区城市流强度的位序-规模曲线随着时间呈现平行向前推进的趋势，但曲线随着 x 轴（城市位序）的变化，位序规模曲线向前推进的间距有所差异，表明不同位次的城市用地规模增长速度有所差别[21]。

表2展示2004—2018年长三角中心区城市 Zipf 指数总体呈现出波动上升的趋势，从 1.088 9 上升到 1.129 8。2004—2012年 Zipf 指数总体下降，在此期间长三角中心区城市群城市规模分布集中度上升，高位次城市作用突出，中间位序的城市发育不够成熟，各城市间存在一定的差距[22]；2013—2018年 Zipf 指数触底反弹并不断上升，在此期间长三角中心区城市体系分布趋向分散，中等城市进一步发育，大城市垄断地位下降，城镇体系整体发育进一步成熟。从图1中可以看出，2004—2018年第二梯队城市（第3—16位城市）之间差距及其与头部城市（头2位城市）差距进一步缩小，但与位居其后的第三梯队城市差距进一步拉大，且内部整体的标准差也进一步增加，说明长三角中心区城市群的影响力在发展中逐渐出现分层级的现象，且内部差异进一步扩大。

表2 2004—2018年长三角中心区城市位序-规模分析表

年　份	Zipf 指数	ln A	R^2
2004	1.088 9	7.435 4	0.862 5
2005	1.067 6	7.673	0.867 9
2006	1.080 6	7.781 9	0.876
2007	1.045 4	7.866 3	0.878 9
2008	0.994 8	7.953 7	0.866 4
2009	1.089 2	8.377 7	0.899 1

续表

年 份	Zipf 指数	ln A	R^2
2010	0.999 5	8.317 9	0.896 5
2011	0.954 9	8.405 3	0.918 1
2012	0.928 8	8.506 9	0.888 1
2013	1.034 1	8.899 6	0.877 8
2014	1.070 3	9.089 3	0.882
2015	1.054 6	9.142 4	0.886 9
2016	1.061 9	9.250 9	0.892 7
2017	1.292 1	9.213 1	0.938 8
2018	1.129 8	9.598 7	0.864 5

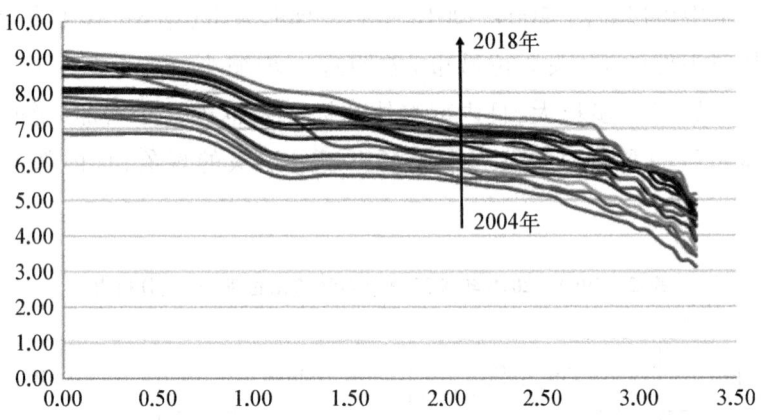

图1　2004—2018年长三角中心区城市城市流强度位序-规模对数曲线

4. 经济地理格局分析

　　区域经济地理分析主要分析方法包括区域差异可视化分析、空间自相关分析方法、空间插值分析。分析长三角中心区城市的经济地理格局，可以更好地揭示长三角区域一体化进程中的区域内部差异，为政策和规划的制定提供依据。

4.1 区域差异可视化分析

用 arcgis 软件将长三角中心区城市城市流强度进行可视化分析,使用自然断点法对其进行分级,可以得出长三角中心区城市中心度从 2004—2018 年出现了热度区域北移趋势。城市流强度共分为 12 个小的等级,按照"高-中-低"的分类方式分为 3 个等级,可以得出 2004 年长三角中心区高热度区域除了苏州、上海、无锡以外,主要分布在其南部地区,包括杭州、绍兴、台州、宁波、金华、温州等浙江城市,北部和西部地区大部分城市中心度属于中低中心度等级。2008、2013 年的中心度情况显示,北部江苏地区城市中心度普遍上升,包括南通、泰州、扬州、镇江、常州、南京,西部的安徽城市合肥也出现中心度等级上升,而南部的浙江城市中心度普遍下降,苏州、上海、无锡继续保持较高的中心度。2018 年长三角中心区中心度等级体系彻底形成"江苏高、浙江中、安徽低"的结构,高中心度区域彻底从南部转移到北部,江苏省城市的中心度普遍属于中高等级;南部浙江城市的中心度虽有所下降,但大多数仍保持在中等级别;西部安徽城市除了合肥以外,普遍属于低中心度等级。

4.2 空间自相关分析

空间自相关分析是在考虑区域内各空间单元空间属性关联的基础上,对区域内空间单元的某一属性与相邻空间单元同一属性的相关程度进行考量的分析方法,可以很好地揭示区域内相邻空间单元的相互作用,从而发现空间集聚或异化现象[23]。

空间自相关分析包括全局自相关分析和局部自相关分析,全局相关性分析是对区域内所有空间单元的整体相互联系程度进行分析,用于判断区域的某一属性在空间上的相关程度,但无法回答区域属性的空间聚集格局。局部相关性分析是针对区域内的单个空间单元,计算其某一属性与相邻空间单元同一属性的相关程度,进而计算出具有某种特征的集聚区,从而揭示出经济地理空间格局的基本特征[26]。

从表 3 可以看出,从 2004—2018 年长三角中心区城市流强度的全局莫兰指数经过下降又重新回升的过程,从 2004 年的 0.326 80 到 2018 年的 0.357 88,略有回升。而 z 得分也从 3.353 55 上升到 3.828 22。这一结果表明长三角中心区内部各地级市区域影响力的空间相关程度增强,区域联动发展程度有所上升,各地级市经济发展的相关程度有所提升。

表 3　2004—2018 年长三角中心区城市城市流强度全局莫兰指数分析

	2004 年	2008 年	2013 年	2018 年
全局莫兰指数	0.326 80	0.278 99	0.354 87	0.357 88
预期指数	-0.038 46	-0.038 46	-0.038 46	-0.038 46
方差	0.011 86	0.010 45	0.011 50	0.010 72
z 得分	3.353 55	3.105 05	3.668 11	3.828 22
p 值	0.000 80	0.001 90	0.000 24	0.000 13

在对长三角中心区城市城市流强度进行局部莫兰分析以后，可以得出，2004年城市中心度"高-高"集聚区包括上海和嘉兴两座城市，表示在高城市中心度城市集聚的片区中表现突出的城市；"低-高"集聚区包括南通市范围，表示在高城市中心度城市集聚的片区中表现较差的城市；"低-低"集聚区包括南京市和安徽的合肥、马鞍山、芜湖、铜陵、池州、安庆等城市，表示在低城市中心度城市集聚的片区中表现较差的城市，其余城市均属于"不显著"地区。到了 2008 年，"高-高"集聚区新增了苏州市，原有"低-低"集聚区中马鞍山和南京脱离队伍，马鞍山成为"不显著"地区的一分子，南京变为唯一一个"高-低"集聚区的城市（表示在低城市中心度城市集聚的片区中表现突出的城市）。2013—2018 年长三角中心区城市中心度整体格局最终确定下来，南通和上海、苏州一起组成长三角中心区的"高-高"集聚区，嘉兴市成为"高-低"集聚区的城市，安徽省合肥、芜湖、铜陵、安庆、池州等城市组成"低-低"集聚区，其余城市均属于"不显著"地区。

纵观长三角中心区城市中心度局部莫兰格局的演进，可以发现，在高中心度城市集聚地区中，上海一直独领风骚，苏州和南通先后崛起，共同推动长江入海口附近地区成为长三角地区城市中心度最高的区域；上海和嘉兴在高中心度地区的相对地位下降明显，成为该地区"灯下黑"的"洼地"；位于长三角中心区偏上游的南京发展加快，相对周边地区地位上升，逐渐摆脱"低-低"集聚区的泥潭，并带动马鞍山市的发展，逐渐融入长三角中心区整体发展格局的大流；长三角中心区西部的合肥、铜陵、芜湖、安庆、池州等安徽城市则一直是该地区整体中心度发展的"低洼地区"，较低中心度的城市集中连片分布。

4.3 空间插值分析

空间插值常用于将离散点的测量数据转换为连续的数据曲面,它包括内插和外推两种方法。前者是通过已知点的数据计算同一区域其他已知点的数据,后者则是通过已知区域的数据,求未知区域的数据。常用的内插方法包括反距离加权、全局多项式、径向基函数、克里格内插法等等。

用空间插值法计算出 2004—2018 年长三角中心区城市城市流强度年均增长水平的地区分布,可以看出,城市中心度年均增长较快的城市主要分布在江苏的长江一带和长江以北地区,包括扬州、泰州、南通、镇江、常州等城市,另外安徽的合肥、芜湖和浙江的舟山中心度年均增长也较快。年均增长率低值地区主要分布在南部和西部地区,比较显著的包括浙江省杭州、金华、台州、温州、湖州和安徽省宣城、安庆、滁州、马鞍山等。

2004—2018 年长三角中心区城市城市流强度相对增长水平,可以得出相对增长幅度比较大的地区集中在长江入海口地区,其中的上海、苏州、南通分成明显的三个等级,这三个城市的增长幅度占总体的 44.79%。其余地区与长江入海口地区相比有明显差距,包括江苏的其他城市地区、浙江地区和安徽地区。其中安徽(除合肥外)地区是低值的集中连片地区,包括滁州、马鞍山、芜湖、铜陵、池州、安庆等城市,这些城市的增长幅度仅占总体的 4.36%。合肥、南京市是低值连片地区中表现相对突出的城市,有希望成为引领相对落后地区发展的增长极。

5. 总结和建议

5.1 研究成果总结

根据上述分析结果,可以总结出 2004—2018 年长三角中心区城市中心度发展的几个显著特点:

第一,总体情况分析。总体上长三角中心区城市中心区中等城市进一步发育,空间集聚程度略有上升,但内部差距进一步拉大。

2004—2018 年长三角中心区所有城市城市流强度均有所提升,2004—2012 年区域内大城市作用较为突出,区域中小城市发育不足;2013—2018 年区域内第二梯队城市进一步发育,进一步缩小与头部城市的差距,但是与身后第三梯队城市的差距拉大,形成明显的等级分层,区域内整体城市中心度差距进一步拉大。空间聚集度方面经历了先下降上升的过程,总体空间集聚程度略有上升,区域联动发展程度有所上升。

第二，分区情况分析。区域中心度高值地区转移，城市中心度形成"江苏高、浙江中、安徽低"的格局。

2004—2018年区域中心度方面，浙江城市相对地位下滑明显，中心度高值地区从南部浙江地区逐渐转移到北部的江苏地区。安徽城市则一直处于区域中心度的低值地区，低中心度城市集中连片，因此相对于安徽而言，浙江城市在中心度方面还是具备一定优势，城市中心度形成"江苏高、浙江中、安徽低"的格局。

第三，中心城市分析。上海作为长三角的绝对中心城市，对长三角中心区发展的带动作用明显。

作为带动长三角地区发展的龙头，上海的优势地位明显，2004—2018年城市中心度大部分年份都位居区域第一，且期间中心度增长幅度占总体的21.77%。但并未由此在区域中形成一家独大的格局，在城市首位度方面一直保持与其他城市较为合理的优势，而且通过自身的发展带动长江入海口苏州、南通等城市甚至整个苏南地区城市区域影响力的提升，为区域发展起到很好的示范和引领作用。

第四，经济沿长江发展轴往上游发展趋势明显。

上海作为发展的龙头带动了周边城市中心度的提升，同时长江沿线的镇江、常州、泰州城市中心度也有较高的提升。位于较上游的南京和合肥中心度也进一步提高，特别是南京的发展逐渐融入区域发展的主流并进一步带动马鞍山的发展。但是位于区域最上游的安徽部分城市中心度仍然较低，中心度低值城市集中，在区域中的影响力较低，所占分量较轻。

5.2 推进长三角区域一体化发展的建议

长三角中心区是长三角地区区位和经济发展条件最佳的区域，是推动长三角一体化发展的驱动地和基本盘，肩负着辐射带动非中心地带融入长三角一体化发展潮流的使命。根据以上分析发现的长三角中心区发展过程中存在的问题和趋势，从空间发展层面提出推进长三角区域一体化发展的建议，并参考《长江三角洲区域一体化发展规划纲要》提出的主要发展轴线和都市圈，提出以下三点建议：

第一，重点强化沿江发展带的带动作用，打造合肥、安庆两大增长极，推动上游安徽地区融入长三角整体发展格局

安徽一直是长三角中心区发展相对薄弱的环节，近年来城市中心度值、年均和相对增长率都较低，对于安徽非长三角中心区的城市吸引带动力不足。近年

长三角地区发展中,长江发展轴的发展带动作用明显,是长三角一体化发展最重要的依靠轴线。未来推动长三角西部城市的发展,除了进一步强化南京的影响力、中心地位和辐射能力以外,更重要的是将合肥和安庆两个门户城市打造成为安徽本土的两个重要增长极,加快构建现代化产业体系,打造长三角地区高质量发展的中心区和辐射带动皖西北、皖西南地区的区域重点城市,推动安徽城市融入长三角一体化发展的总体格局。

第二,加快建设沪舟甬沿海大通道,增强上海南向辐射力

近年来浙江城市在长三角中心区的相对地位下降,中心度高值地区转向江苏地区。沪舟甬沿海大通道作为跨杭州湾的重要交通要道,有助于重构长三角区域一体化联动发展新格局,形成上海-舟山-宁波世界级组合港群和国际航运中心一体化支撑性重大引擎,并推动上海、杭州、宁波三大都市圈一体化发展,形成上海南向都市连绵区,此举有助于加强上海向南的辐射能力,沿着沿海发展带和沪杭金发展带,将发展红利遍及浙江省全域。

第三,进一步加强沿海发展带向北辐射作用,打造盐城成为苏北发展桥头堡

苏北地区近年经济社会发展较快,但与苏南地区仍有较大差距。苏北地区唯一纳入长三角中心区的盐城市的城市中心度在中心区城市当中不算出众,年均和相对增长率也较低。近年上海的发展有力带动了北边的南通市中心度的提高,未来需要进一步发挥沿海发展带向北功能强度的发挥,将盐城作为上海产业服务对外辐射的重要接受地和沿海发展带的关键节点城市,把盐城打造成为苏北发展桥头堡,加强盐城的区域影响力和功能地位,引领苏北经济进一步发展,融入江苏省乃至长三角发展的主流。

参考文献

[1] 王宝强,陈腾,尹海伟,张博.基于"核心-边缘"理论的海峡西岸经济区空间结构解析[J].城市发展研究,2010,17(1):60-65.

[2] 王彬燕,王士君,田俊峰.基于城市流强度的哈长与辽中南城市群比较研究[J].经济地理,2015,35(11):94-100+116.

[3] 卢万合,刘继生.中国十大城市群城市流强度的比较分析[J].统计与信息论坛,2010,25(2):60-64.

[4] 叶磊,欧向军.我国主要城市群的城市流动态比较[J].城市发展研究,2012,19(6):

6-11.

[5] 张虹鸥,叶玉瑶,罗晓云,叶树宁.珠江三角洲城市群城市流强度研究[J].地域研究与开发,2004(6):53-56.

[6] 李光勤,张明举,刘衍桥.基于城市流视角的成渝经济区城市群空间联系[J].重庆工商大学学报.西部论坛,2006(4):29-33.

[7] 刘建朝,高素英.基于城市联系强度与城市流的京津冀城市群空间联系研究[J].地域研究与开发,2013,32(2):57-61.

[8] 李慧玲,戴宏伟.京津冀与长三角城市群经济联系动态变化对比——基于城市流强度的视角[J].经济与管理,2016,30(2):9-16.

[9] 雷菁,郑林,陈晨.利用城市流强度划分中心城市规模等级体系——以江西省为例[J].城市问题,2006(1):11-15.

[10] 温小军,刘祖文,康俊锋,易秀娟,王星皓,叶小军.江西赣南地区城镇体系规模分布和结构研究[J].江西理工大学学报,2017,38(5):1-6.

[11] 雷仲敏,康俊杰.城市首位度评价:理论框架与实证分析[J].城市发展研究,2010,17(4)·33-38.

[12] 张璇.城市首位度的理论内涵与体系构建研究[J].企业导报,2012(16):11-13.

[13] 朱军,刘艳.城市首位度的内涵和研究状况概述及评价体系构建[J].大众科技,2015,17(3):181-183.

[14] 李小鹤,郭正光.财政独立性视角下中国各省城市人口齐普夫(Zipf)指数分布检验[J].科技促进发展,2019,15(2):176-182.

[15] 程开明.长三角城市体系分布结构及演化机制探析[J].商业经济与管理,2007(8):56-61.

[16] 蒲英霞,马荣华,马晓冬,顾朝林.长江三角洲地区城市规模分布的时空演变特征[J].地理研究,2009,28(1):161-172.

[17] 孙贵艳,王传胜,肖磊,金凤君.长江三角洲城市群城镇体系演化时空特征[J].长江流域资源与环境,2011,20(6):641-649.

[18] 韩欢.长三角城市群规模分布及其演变研究[D].宁波大学,2013.

[19] 晁静,赵新正,李同昇,青雨馨.基于多源夜间灯光数据的长江经济带三大城市群规模结构动态比较[J].地理与地理信息科学,2020,36(1):44-51.

[20] 周晓艳,韩丽媛,叶信岳,姚丽,王柏源.基于位序规模法则的我国城市用地规模分布变化研究(2000年~2012年)[J].华中师范大学学报(自然科学版),2015,49(1):132-138.

[21] 丁长发,谢晓琼.福建省城市规模结构之研究——基于首位度和位序-规模法则的视角

[J].发展研究,2017(3):35-43.
[22] 尹海伟,孔繁花.城市与区域规划空间分析实验教程(第三版)[M].东南大学出版社:南京,2018:326.

 点评

  论文对长三角一体化发展背景下基于长三角中心区的城市规模结构和经济地理格局进行了分析,提出了重点强化沿江发展带的带动作用、增强上海南向辐射力、打造盐城成为苏北发展桥头堡等建议。选题及结论具有一定新意,论文研究视角新颖,论证科学,论据充分,写作质量较高。

下 编

中国服饰企业的供应链柔性研究
——以森马电商为例

白冰峰　高峻峻　董北松[*]

摘要：选取连续多年入围中国时尚零售企业百强榜单、美国波士顿咨询(BCG)"转型群英录"中唯一入选的服饰企业森马作为研究案例，研究森马服饰过去十年面对市场环境的快速变化，在电子商务拓展、全渠道零售、时尚内容整合以及供应链数字化的管理流程中，做出的关键决策、核心变革。森马在中国服饰品牌面向电商与新零售转型发展中具有很强的典型性和代表性，本案例的研究能对其他服饰企业起到一定借鉴作用。

关键词：电子商务；新零售；供应链管理；数字化；森马服饰

引言

2000年至2010年被誉为中国服饰零售行业的"黄金十年"，2010年以后，行业进入到品牌零售商格局转型的竞赛时代，至2020年，对于前后十年的变化，服装行业一度被看作"芳华已逝，面目全非"，利润率的持续降低与越来越高的消费者要求让不少传统劳动密集型的服饰企业陷入迷途和危局。就在这样的大环境下，浙江森马服饰的表现依然强劲：

2013年，森马服饰净利润超过10亿元；

2016年，森马年度营业额突破100亿元；

2017年，WPP集团公布了BrandZ"最具价值中国品牌100强"入围名单，森

---

[*] 白冰峰、董北松：上海大学管理学院2019级硕士研究生。高峻峻：上海大学悉尼工商学院教授、博士生导师。

马以 2.43 亿美元的品牌价值在列;

2018 年,森马线下门店数量接近 10 000 家;

2019 年,天猫"双 11"当天,森马电商销售额突破 13.8 亿元,实现 20.3% 的增长率。

面对近十年来复杂多变的市场环境,森马发展依然势如破竹,业绩规模和品牌声誉迅速增长,令人惊喜。服饰行业的产业链冗长、复杂,创业和守业都是一个艰难的赛道,而森马却在国际品牌环伺、线上平台争抢份额的局势下逆势稳健增长,成为难得的可以与国际品牌过招的企业。

企业高速发展的背后是一系列审时度势的坚定决策,时间回溯到 2010 年,外界看来已是一家成功服饰企业的森马,决定重新上路,回到渠道、营销、运营本身,围绕零售的本质,为整个行业上演一个风险与机遇并存的转型故事。

然而,专注、高效、生动的商业实践并不意味着森马服饰发展的平坦无阻,在电子商务和新零售的大背景下,作为由线下转型的传统服饰品牌,森马如何有效地利用线下资源和渠道,处理好线上的冲突,改善品牌、渠道和营销能力,又如何以数字驱动决策,实现匹配新零售的柔性供应链管理,将直接影响到其行业竞争力。

总而言之,森马在较短的时间内取得如此大的转型发展成绩,是一个了不起的成功。森马在电子商务拓展、品类品牌的全渠道零售、时尚内容整合以及供应链数字化方面的创新能力,被认为是森马持续成功的根本要素,也是服饰行业基于消费者需求做数字化转型的重点所在,得到业内广泛认可。那么,森马是如何做到这一切的呢?

1. 发力电商:从迎难而上到后来居上

1.1 临危受命

2011 年,以优衣库、Zara、H&M 为代表的外资服饰企业开始在国内零售市场大放异彩,攻城略地,迅速抢占市场份额,国内服饰企业情势危急。对比这些强势登陆的外资品牌,除了产品设计、品牌文化等软实力,国内服饰企业在运营与供应链系统的硬实力上也远远落后。举例而言,当时即便森马和美特斯·邦威这两个国内服饰品牌的佼佼者,从产品设计到面向市场销售的时间跨度大概也在 2 至 3 个月,而 Zara 和 H&M 的供应链导入周期却只要 2 周,差距不可谓不大。

对于时尚行业而言,速度就是时尚品牌的生命线。伴随森马在外资企业速度冲击下的节节败退,国内服饰行业长期以来挤压的问题例如款式老旧、品牌定位模糊、供应链效率低下等问题也在 2012 年集中爆发。刚刚上市的森马遇到前所未有的行业危机,"去库存"成为公司救急的当务之需。传统清理库存只有两种方式,门店大甩卖和外贸,前者损害品牌形象,后者难以收回成本。在这样的背景下,森马电商应运而生,承担的使命就是拯救公司业务危机,清理库存。

1.2 线上专供

基于森马深耕中国本土市场多年的品牌效应,加上三四折的价格优势,电商的好处很快彰显,线上零售势如破竹。电商发展速度惊人,森马的运营危机也悄然袭来。由于是传统线下门店起家,发起线上渠道以后,门店和电商供应共享同一盘货的行为不断触犯线下加盟商的利益,导致矛盾加剧。2014 年上半年,森马线上与线下冲突已经到了不可调和的地步。

面对这样的状况,森马电商管理团队闭门会议,经过集体决策,诞生了线上专供款,电商主打两倍左右加价倍率,讲究性价比的爆款,借此实现森马线上线下差异化产品管理,这是森马电商成立以来第一个具有象征意义的发展拐点。线上专供策略启动以后,森马电商迎来飞奔式发展,当年营收接近 10 个亿,2015 天猫"双 11"购物节中,森马电商以近 4 个亿的当日销售额,在服饰品牌商的线上销售中名列前茅。

1.3 大森马战略

随着电商业务的一路高歌猛进,森马高层认为清理库存绝非长期生存之道,电商已经不再只是有关滞销库存与卖货渠道的问题,而应该成为未来十年森马品牌的新零售资源平台,打通线上线下,实现真正意义上的供应链协同。由于线下门店的空间限制,有限的陈列品类无法形成丰富的产品线,而这方面"虚拟无形"的线上拥有天然的优势,电商顺势成为这场森马服饰转型升级的发动机。

2016 年,森马迎来第二个具有重要意义的战略拐点,正式启动"大森马战略",扩充品类,反哺线下。在此基础上,森马零售不再局限于主营的服饰品类,进一步丰富了箱包、鞋帽、内衣等品类名目,满足用户的需求广度。此后五年,森马电商的业绩持续稳步提升(见图 1)。

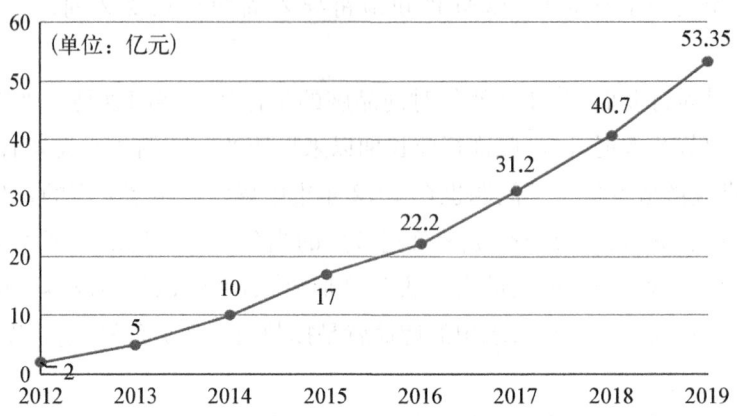

图1 森马电商年度业绩增长曲线

资料来源:森马集团财务年报。

2019年,森马电商业务继续保持快速发展的态势,全年实现营业收入突破50亿元,占据森马集团总销售收入的三成,电子商务已经成为森马举足轻重的业务渠道,即使横向对比国内时尚零售百强[1]、服饰品类排名第一的安踏,其线上销售收入占比不到两成[2]。无疑,在中国传统服饰品牌领域,森马已经成为转型互联网零售的一道亮丽风景线(见图2)。

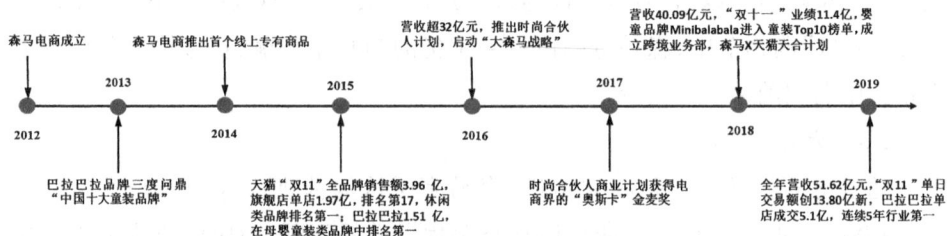

图2 森马电商发展历程关键事件及阶段划分

资料来源:森马官方微信公众平台。

从为解决过季库存的森马电商正式成立、到线上专供款的打造,再到品类扩充、反哺线下这三大战略,森马借助互联网迭代思维的电商打法,从最初"去库存"的临时救场销售渠道临危受命、小步快跑,到运营战略的不断创新,森马电商过去八年的品牌互联网之路,是中国传统服饰品牌拥抱变化、面对互联网时代、拥抱需求经济最具代表性的缩影。

森马发力电商,从迎难而上到后来居上,是明智之举,也是成功之路。随着大数据与人工智能等信息技术的推进,服饰电商与新技术融合应用必将深入发展,未来,电子商务对服饰企业的驱动将由渠道驱动向数字驱动转变,不断引领数字时尚产业的创新发展[3]。

2. 单聚焦、多品牌与全渠道:打造"护城河"优势

美国著名投资人沃伦·巴菲特最早提出了"企业护城河"概念,他洞悉到每一家企业,想要经营得久一点,最终都需要去构建自己的"护城河"。所谓护城河,就是说企业要有持续的竞争优势,它们就像城堡外宽阔的护城河,里面还有游弋的鳄鱼,保护企业不受竞争的侵蚀。同时,《巴菲特的护城河》一书提出,护城河是企业能够长期保持竞争优势的结构性特征,是竞争对手难以复制的品质。

对于森马而言,如何构建自己的护城河优势?总的来说,森马更加关注的是企业无形资产与网络效应,将核心优势扎根于企业战略之中。2016年以后,森马进一步明晰了自己的企业愿景:成为全球领先的时尚服务提供商。为了实现这一目标和愿景,森马提出"单聚焦+多品牌+全渠道"的企业运营战略,打造护城河优势。

2.1 单聚焦

过去、现在、未来,森马将儿童服饰业务板块确定为公司长期的核心战略方向,构建儿童服饰多品牌集群,围绕儿童生活方式,进行产品创新及品类扩张,从时尚度、功能性、科技感等维度升级产品穿着体验,打造产业护城河。过去三年以来,童装收入在森马服饰整体营收的绝对值和增长率都同比新高(见图3),童装收入由2017年的63.22亿元,占比总营收的一半到2019年的126.63亿元,占比超过65%,护城河优势日益凸显。

2.2 多品牌

基于自持、收购、授权等方式,森马通过多品牌矩阵的产品组合覆盖从高端到大众、成人到儿童、休闲到时尚的各类服饰用品细分市场。森马集团旗下目前拥有森马、Balabala、JUICY COUTURE、Catimini、Absorba、Mini Balabala、Jason Wu、MARC O'POLO等众多服饰品牌,基本形成了多元化、梯度化的品牌矩阵,能够满足各类消费者的服饰需求。

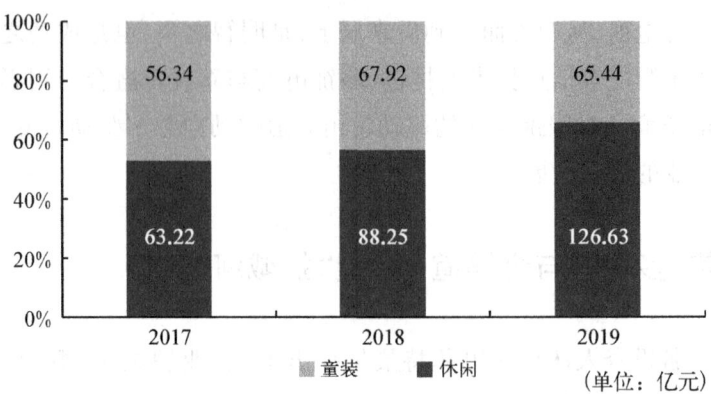

图3 近三年森马产品分类的营收状况

资料来源：笔者依据相关信息整理[4]。

鉴于中国新中产阶级不断壮大,森马近年来一直在加速布局中高端市场[5],通过收购建造多品牌"护城河"。以 Marc O'Polo 为例,在森马集团的支持下,2014 年正式进军中国市场开设首家门店,每年的销售增幅保持在 90% 以上,并入驻天猫、京东两大电商平台开设线上旗舰店。

品牌管理于森马的竞争优势有着非同一般的意义,服饰作为典型的 2C 消费品,"品牌"是建立产品与消费者连接的重要媒介,因此我们认为服饰企业的护城河最终还是抽象于"品牌"[3]。

2.3 全渠道

森马早期的销售网点以街面店铺为主,但随着销售渠道网络的不断扩展,目前已经涵盖了百货商场、主流购物中心、直营门店、加盟门店、电子商务、移动电子商务等各种形态。线下,截至 2019 年末森马已经在海内外拥有超过一万家门店。线上,森马电商与淘宝、天猫、唯品会等电商平台积极开展深度合作。在服饰这个竞争白热化、快速变化、不确定性强的赛道,森马已经构建出全渠道的零售体系[6]。

3. 内容运营：从电商渠道到资源整合平台

移动互联网时代,服饰销售渠道的多样化、碎片化是全行业的普遍痛点,渠道渗透力的挖掘深度对企业运营尤为关键。如果说发力电商,聚焦品类、品牌的全渠道零售是在森马营销管理上做出的战略决策，那么，依靠营销渠道精进的森马是否全然解决了不确定性日增时代下的消费者痛点？基于对销售渠道的深刻理解，森马从时尚内容平台资源整合的运营方面给出了自己的方案。

森马早期对电商渠道的理解与国内其他服饰企业存在明显差异，认为电商本身也要形成资源整合的平台。2016年，森马启动时尚合伙人计划，邀请当红明星、设计师，以及时尚领域内有影响力的达人成为品牌"股东"，进行内容平台的合作打造。例如邀请某明星作为签约的第一位时尚合伙人，其全程参与同款服装的产品企划工作，并在天猫森马旗舰店首发。活动四天，日均进店人数超过百万，带动全店销售额超过两千四百万元。

这是一项大胆又极具创意的营销变革，合伙人会实际参与到产品开发、企划推广与联合营销这一完整的产品链条中，让自身气质与品牌深度融合。通过合伙人亲自参与服装设计、品牌策划以及粉丝互动，拉近了品牌与消费者的距离。这种"品牌+合伙人"的商业模式，开启了森马电商内容营销的新模式。随后，时尚合伙人计划也收获了"电商界奥斯卡"之称的金麦奖的荣誉认可。

2017年预热"双11"，森马基于时尚内容资源、电商营销流量以及供应链能力，童装品牌巴拉巴拉联合 The Emoji Movie 推出联名款产品，将 Emoji 表情虚拟现实（AR）技术同服饰有机结合，促使时尚内容运营平台的运营有了更多的新鲜玩法。对这场创新表现，供应链总监刘长伴描述为，服饰电商的发酵可以强化森马在时尚行业的优势特征，而供应链管理是森马创业以来的传统优势，当时尚内容结合优质供应链，时尚内容运营平台的打造便水到渠成。

2019年以来，随着直播、网红达人等新营销模式的风潮乍起，森马表现冷静，并不盲目的大规模切入风口，而是将电商直播的效应服务于自身时尚内容运营平台的资源打造中来，推出"森马 Live"内容导购频道，发挥品牌协同效应。

对于森马的运营而言，电商是带货渠道也是自身品牌理念的时尚内容平台，是品牌与消费者情感内容传播与交融的载体，同时也是营销资源聚合的创新商业实践。时尚合作人服务粉丝并最终转化为销售的过程之中，其与森马也实现了深度的价值共创。

4. 推动数字化建设，深化新零售供应链改革

不管如何转型升级，零售的生存本质终究根基于流通，而实现流通的唯一归

属在于企业的供应链系统。至于新零售的降本增效种种,供应链的生态化一体化改革必须贯穿始终。若想成为中国规模最大的服饰企业,"底盘"必须扎实,所谓底盘是服饰企业的内功心法,即商品的研发和运营体系,而运营体系的核心就是供应链。

供应链管理对于当下中国服饰零售企业的重要性,不言而喻,传统零售和虚拟电商都在强化供应链数字化的转型与升级,而森马却又是这两者综合的集成体,这注定了供应链建设在森马体系中的战略定位与意义。

2019年"双11"购物节的大促过后,阿里巴巴供应链研究中心的负责人希疆感慨,森马的惊艳表现,赢在了高效的运营管理,更准确地说,是赢在了基于供应链管理为核心的数据运营。背后,浸润了森马推动数字化建设,深化新零售供应链改革的决心、力量与变革。

4.1 供应链变革

森马分别于2014、2016、2017年不遗余力地对其供应链管理体系进行了三次重大调整(见图4)。

图4 森马供应链发展的三次战略变革

4.1.1 集中式供应链变革

2014年,森马对供应链进行第一次的梳理整合,将原有松散型供应链转向集中式供应链,精简供应商数量,实施"供应商减半策略",由四百家降至两百家。一方面是考虑到供应商的综合质量,森马早期不同供应商提供的品类丰富度、产品质量等参差不齐,尤其线上渠道开辟并且业务蒸蒸日上的时候,一些上游供应商的订单响应、信息同步等问题凸显,已经影响到了供应链上下游的整体绩效,森马迫切需要优胜劣汰,整合性价比高的供应商。另一方面是需求固定的前提下,同少量的供应商合作意味着单个合作规模的扩大,有利于森马提升价格、货款周转等方面的话语权。

从某种意义上来说,少即是多,精简即是改善。在森马启动电商业务两年以来,清理库存虽已不再是业绩目标导向,但早期库存沉积遗留下来的杂乱SKU(Stock Keeping Unit,标准产品单位)数量已经超过八千。对此,时任森马集团副总经理的郑洪伟曾在一次内部会议中强调,库存转型路上森马需要警惕美特斯·邦威式烦恼,只转型而无改革,转型也需大刀阔斧,雷厉风行。

此时,2011年步入营收巅峰,此后开始业绩衰退的知名服饰品牌美特斯·邦威,连续三年饱受过量库存类目的弊端。"不走寻常路"的美邦追求 ZARA 式的快时尚,但是快时尚的重心不是"如何多",而是"怎样快",与国外顶级品牌在营销、渠道、运营以及供应链能力仍不对等的状况下,一味追求结果的快时尚,终将是失衡的狂奔。

2014年底,森马正式完成产品单元精简的革新,缩减近四成的产品数量,完成集中式供应链的战略大调整。

4.1.2　快反式供应链变革

2015年"双11"后,森马电商总经理邵飞春向内部全体员工发出名为"向优衣库学习致敬"的总结信:在优衣库面前,我们还是小学生。号召全员向国际品牌优衣库学习供应链管理,对标先进,而非盲目排外。

坚定地向优衣库学习的号召并非口号空喊,而是中国服装市场的流行趋势仍在不确定性中波动,这波动的源头是消费者个性化需求的提升。2015年首先受到冲击的森马赖以起家的传统休闲服装,关店数量超过三百家,营业收入比重下滑明显。

2015年冬天刚过,森马再次对供应链体系进行第二次调整,核心议题是加快供应链体系的反应速度。2016年开始,森马逐步将原先每个季度一次的订货会改为一季两次,同时将三成产品进行现货发货,这正是为了进一步降低订货占比,加快货品周转,进而更好地满足消费者的即时需求。

4.1.3　柔性化供应链变革

2017年,森马在供应链方面又有新的大调整,向供应链全链条发动变革。具体来讲,森马供应链网络进行了长单转短单的改革,缩短产品周期,产品设计周期从原来的8到10个月转变为2个月,同时提升现货比率,逐渐向"一半现货、一半期货"的柔性模式转换,其中,基础款主要面向期货,时尚款主要面向现货。

森马供应链通过与核心供应商在产品制造周期上的调整(淡季生产基本

款,将产能预留给需要翻单的产品)、对数据管理能力的提升、选择性开拓拥有供应链调整能力、具备快反翻单生产经验的优秀供应商加入等方式,全面提升公司的快反翻单能力,打造匹配森马新零售的供应链柔性能力(见图5)。

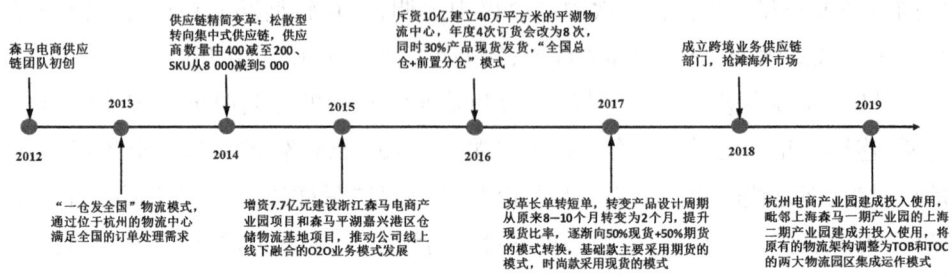

图5　森马电商供应链发展历程关键事件及阶段划分

4.2　供应链数字化

4.2.1　供应链的大数据应用

大数据应用,并非仅为国内互联网电商公司的专属,森马拥有自己的稳健节奏。供应链前端的销量预测和补货层面,森马大幅提升收集分用户数据、定制促销与销售计划的效率,利用大数据分析持续改善线上线下的消费者体验。库存管理阶段,森马物流接入大数据运用,基于数据分析进行商品组合存储和仓间货品调拨,来减少拆单比率和提高发货速度。基于大数据的应用,森马电商订单的平均出库时长缩短了3至5小时,这在分秒必争的服饰电商中是难能可贵的表现。

4.2.2　数据驱动供应链决策,让听得见炮声的人来指挥战斗

数据驱动的运营方面,森马积极尝试借助外力,合作共赢,打造天猫-巴拉巴拉爆款的机动供应链是一个鲜活的决策案例。借助与天猫的合作,2019年森马成功打造出童装的一款轻薄羽绒服爆品,单款销量15万件。设计方案的实现并非易事,背后是生产供应链的改变,营销端借力天猫电商平台的海量需求预测数据做出智能选品,运营端森马团队积极与上游工厂打通库存层面的ERP(企业资源计划)系统对接,进而实现全流程的深度供应链协同,以此满足个性化的商品的供货需求。

数据驱动的组织层面,森马构建自下而上的灵活决策和反馈机制,让听得见炮声的人参与决策。森马让基层员工反馈供应链数据系统中采购、库存、物流、配送等信息和建议,此时,系统不再只是执行工具,也是基础单元的决策工具,为基层员

工提供拍板的机会。在森马电商总经理邵飞春眼中,每个森马仓库打包员的工作都是有温度的,这种温度会通过产品形象传递给森马的每一个消费者。一线员工是与消费者接触距离最近,也是接触最多的,让基层员工拍板的决策更能贴合消费者的需求,更能接近消费者,这样的决策不仅准确,决策过程也会很敏捷。

4.3 供应链精益化

供应链总监刘长伴在内部运营分析会上多次强调,建立在商品单元供应链上的运作效率是服饰零售最核心的能力需求。供应链计划对于服饰企业尤为关键,俗话说,兵马未动,粮草先行。森马内部有一套完整的供应链商品计划系统,可以快速捕捉到线下线上用户的消费偏好,借助数据分析深度了解市场动态,分析市场容量与竞争格局,最终对商品进行精益计划。

针对供应链生产管理,森马采用日本精益管理中经典的准时制生产方式(JIT),大大减少了上游工厂原材料的准备储量,减少储存费用,也有利于及时暴露生产线上的弊端,促进生产水平、作业效率和货品周转的流程改善,进而提高从生产、运输、销售到消费者这一过程的运转效率。

森马在供应链变革中不断重新塑造供应网络,力争从设计、生产到物流、仓储、门店、消费者的全流程的供应链精益化,打造商品供应链全流程覆盖的"圆形自我中心模式",通过数字化创新挖掘消费者需求的广度与深度,推动同供应商协同的嵌入式产品创新,实现大数据驱动的概率优化。把供应、需求、生产打造成为以消费者为中心的"圆形闭环",从战略、战术到执行层面协同供应链计划系统。

5. 结论

回顾森马服饰过去十年之路,从森马电商的建立和发展,打造"护城河"优势、多品牌矩阵以及全渠道的布局,到时尚内容平台的资源整合,再到围绕全渠道构建匹配电商节奏的柔性供应链,森马经历了从迎难而上到后来居上的攀登历程。总经理邱坚强将其总结为"森马做成中国的ZARA、H&M的升级之战[7]",艰苦而光荣。但不管如何"升级",森马始终紧紧围绕零售业的本质发力电商、内容平台、全渠道零售,数字化建设以及供应链改革,这些都是在运营效率和消费者体验方面的持续精进,依靠数据驱动,摒弃传统服饰企业陈旧、同质化严重的老路,提高新零售背景下服饰企业的数字化创新能力[8]。

当然,森马也面临重重挑战。深耕三四线城市多年并且在未来继续下沉渠道的森马,面对电商企业、其他服饰品牌纷纷加大渠道下沉力度的环境下,如何保证快时尚节奏,又不失品牌黏性,是亟待解决的问题。归根结底,未来智慧零售时代,持续蓬勃发展的零售企业必须既有线下门店的运营管理能力、供应链管理能力,还要有互联网科技的应用能力[9-10]。前两项森马通过内部运营与管理创新在服饰行业具备较强的竞争优势,最后一项能力也是森马在新零售时代正在强化的,也是森马继续高歌猛进的关键所在。

关于未来,森马会继续推进移动互联网时代的支撑、强化、拓展业务及场景与规模的大数据建设,构建集团级的信息共享平台。围绕新零售和数字化,扩大时尚合伙人的范围与合作形式,积累市场营销的各类 IP 资源,建立童装品牌专属的电商团队,统一线上线下的会员制度架构,实现更为优质的全渠道服务。

参考文献

[1] 邱琼.2019—2020 年中国服装电子商务发展报告[R].北京:中国国际电子商务中心研究院,2020.
[2] 周惠宁.这个北欧服饰品牌收入增幅逾 90%,背后推手森马集团做对了什么?[EB/OL].时尚商业快讯,2018-08-29.
[3] 护城河研究系列之纺服篇:服装公司如何实现长青[EB/OL].东方财富网,2019-06-12.
[4] 钱瑜.森马构建全渠道零售体系,启动种子店铺计划[J].北京商报,2019(7).
[5] 覃金妹.森马电商引领时尚与生活方式升级[R].中国上海:中国服装网,2018.
[6] 赵正.美特斯·邦威走失"风格跑道"[J].商学院,2018(9):45-48.
[7] 中欧商业评论.从迎难而上到后来居上,森马的供应链进化之路[EB/OL].2020-08-18.
[8] 李梦军,荆兵.永辉超市:从"生鲜超市"向科技转型[J].清华管理评论,2018(9):94-104.
[9] 中国连锁经营协会.中国时尚零售百强企业榜单[R].中国:北京,2020.
[10] 波士顿咨询.转型群英录.森马:依托核心优势,应对市场变化[EB/OL].2020-05-11.

点评

论文以服饰企业森马为研究案例,描述森马服饰过去十年面对市场环境的快速变化,叙述森马发力电子商务的迭代过程,森马的全渠道、多品牌布局以及电商渠道到资源整合平台的内容创业。森马推动数字化建设、深化新零售供应链改革的经验值得研究。论文选题新颖,主旨明确,结构清晰,论述较合理,结论有一定的实践意义。

浅析系统性红斑狼疮与巨噬细胞的联系

陈可玥　范雪敏　李荣群*

摘要：系统性红斑狼疮（systemic lupus erythematosus，SLE）作为一种累及多器官、多系统损伤的自身免疫性疾病，发病机制尚不明确，针对SLE发病机制和治疗方法的研究一直是受各界关注的前沿课题，目前越来越多的研究聚焦于巨噬细胞与SLE之间的相关性。就SLE与巨噬细胞的关系、巨噬细胞表型和功能分析、巨噬细胞移动抑制因子及巨噬细胞衍生趋化因子等方面予以论证，为SLE病因学研究提供理论思路，为促进巨噬细胞成为SLE的治疗靶点提供更有力的证据。

关键词：系统性红斑狼疮；巨噬细胞；移动抑制因子；衍生趋化因子

SLE是一种常见的自身免疫性疾病，可以累积全身各系统和器官，造成多系统器官损害，以T、B淋巴细胞活化，生成大量自身抗体，激活补体，免疫复合物清除障碍为特征[1]。SLE的发病机制目前尚不明确，但有大量的研究可以显示，遗传、内分泌、感染免疫异常等因素与SLE的发病关系密切[2]。已有对SLE的研究更多关注于特异性免疫方向，目前随着人们更多地深入了解非特异性免疫，发现其与特异性免疫共同参与自身免疫性疾病的发病机制，非特异性免疫在SLE中的作用越来越被人重视。单核-巨噬细胞特别是巨噬细胞（Mφ），是参与非特异性免疫的重要细胞。巨噬细胞能够吞噬、杀灭病原微生物和处理、清除损伤及衰老的细胞，在多种疾病的免疫应答中发挥重要作用，但其发生异常也可能破坏机体组织，参与自身免疫性疾病如SLE的发生发展[3]。针对SLE发病机制和治疗方法的研究一直是受各界关注的前沿课题，目前越来越多的讨论侧重于

---

* 陈可玥,范雪敏：浙江中医药大学基础医学院2018级硕士研究生。李荣群：医学博士,浙江中医药大学副教授,硕士生导师。

Mφ 与 SLE 之间的相关性,并且有研究显示 SLE 患者相较于健康人群,体内巨噬细胞相关表面分子、免疫调节和吞噬功能显示异常,巨噬细胞有望成为改善治疗 SLE 的靶点[4]。

1. 系统性红斑狼疮介绍

系统性红斑狼疮是一种以免疫系统异常活化和自身抗体的异常增多为特征的一类炎症性自身免疫疾病。SLE 多发病于育龄期女性,目前全世界的发病率约为 40~70/10 万,在中国的发病率约为 30~70/10 万,SLE 在女性人群为 113/10 万,男女之比约 1:9[6]。随着现代治疗水平的提高,SLE 病人 5 年生存率从 20 世纪 50 年代的 44%提高到现在的 82%,但患者的平均寿命仍只有 44 岁[7]。SLE 临床表现复杂,常可致皮肤、血液、关节、肾脏等多器官、多系统受累。前期研究表明,SLE 患者自身免疫异常导致组织及血管壁损伤加上抗磷脂抗体的作用使其处于血栓前状态,产生多种症状及并发症[8],如面部蝶形红斑、紫癜、甲周皮肤红斑、脾肿大、贫血、赘生性心内膜炎、心肌炎、心包炎、狼疮性肾炎、肾硬化、肺出血梗塞等一系列表现[9],该病病程长,绵延反复,甚至可造成致死性损害,严重损害患者健康和生活质量[10]。SLE 病因复杂,发病机制还未明确,目前临床对于这一类疾病仍以糖皮质激素、抗疟药、免疫抑制剂、非甾体类抗炎药等治疗为主,但临床作用有限,治愈效果不佳,而且毒副作用较大[11]。目前对 SLE 的病因研究普遍认为其与遗传、感染、药物、环境、激素水平等多方面因素有关。SLE 几乎累及免疫系统的各个部分,免疫学机制十分复杂,特异性免疫及固有免疫均参加其发病发展过程。过去的研究以特异性免疫在 SLE 的发病机制中的作用较多,包括自身耐受缺陷,大量激活自身反应性 T、B 淋巴细胞,T、B 细胞凋亡障碍,生成大量自身抗体,免疫复合物清除障碍[8]。不过随着对非特异性免疫的认识逐步深入,其在 SLE 发病机制中的作用受到广泛关注。

2. 系统性红斑狼疮与巨噬细胞的关系

非特异性免疫又称为固有免疫或先天免疫,是人类在漫长进化过程中形成的一系列防御机制,其中执行非特异性免疫作用的细胞主要包括:单核-巨噬细胞、树突状细胞、中性粒细胞、嗜酸性粒细胞、嗜碱性粒细胞、自然杀伤细胞、自然杀伤T细胞、γδT细胞、B1细胞和肥大细胞等[3]。单核-巨噬细胞是非特异性免疫系统中的重要组成细胞,包括骨髓中的前单核细胞、外周血中的单核细胞、以及组织中固定或游走的巨噬细胞。Mφ来源于血液中的单核细胞,是一种异源吞噬细胞,能发挥抗原、提呈作用,并且在炎症和感染的免疫反应过程中发挥关键作用,是机体非特异性免疫的重要因素,对于维持免疫稳态至关重要。研究表明巨噬细胞功能的异常,导致免疫稳态破坏,诱发自身免疫病[12-14]。巨噬细胞在机体自身免疫的启动和SLE的发展中发挥广泛的作用,有研究表明SLE患者体内巨噬细胞表型、免疫调节能力和吞噬功能相较于健康人均明显异常,可见巨噬细胞异常影响SLE的发病[15,16]。SLE发展往往受累肾脏,研究表面Ⅳ型狼疮肾炎患者的肾脏组织中巨噬细胞表达高水平提示患者预后不良,并且将狼疮模型鼠体内巨噬细胞清除可明显减缓其疾病活动度[17,18],以上结果可见巨噬细胞在SLE发病进程中意义重大,并且在狼疮性肾炎的发病机制中有十分关键的作用。

2.1 巨噬细胞表型和功能分析

SLE是一种经典的自身免疫病,免疫细胞过度活化为其显著特点,巨噬细胞不仅在固有免疫中发挥抗感染作用,它在免疫调节方面也发挥了一定的作用。由于巨噬细胞分化程度、外界激活因子以及解剖学定位的多样性,是一种具有可塑性和多能性的细胞群体,因此巨噬细胞表现出复杂的异质性,其在不同组织甚至相同组织,表型和功能方面也存在很大的差异[19,20]。

目前根据活化状态和发挥功能的不同,巨噬细胞主要可分为M1型即经典活化的巨噬细胞(classically activated macrophage),和M2型即替代性活化的巨噬细胞(alternatively activated macrophage)[21,22]。M1型巨噬细胞主要分泌促炎因子,功能以发挥促炎为主,常见M1型巨噬细胞的表面标志有:HLA-DR、CD197等[23]。巨噬细胞在γ干扰素(interferon-γ,IFN-γ)、肿瘤坏死因子-α(tumor necrosis factor-α,TNF-α)和脂多糖(LPS)等因子作用下,发挥宿主防御的功能,分泌白细胞介素(interlukin,IL)-1、IL-12、IL-23、TNF-α、活性氧(ROS)、活性氮(RNS)等趋化因子,主要针对微生物的炎症反应,发挥宿主免疫的功能,也会对机体正常组织造成炎症损伤[24]。

M2型巨噬细胞的作用以降低炎症反应,发挥机体组织的修复功能为主,常见M2型巨噬细胞表面标志有:CD206、CD209和CD301等[24]。巨噬细胞可在IL-4、IL-10、IL-13和转化生长因子-β(transforming growth factor-β,TGF-β)等作用下,发生向 M2 型极化,可分泌 TGF－β、表皮细胞生长因子(Epidermal Growth Factor,EGF)、血管内皮生长因子(vascular endothelial growth factor, VEGF)及其他因子,主要在炎症反应后期发挥抗炎的作用,促进纤维变性和创伤的修复[25]。

在机体不同生理状态或者疾病发生时,巨噬细胞会表现出不同的类型。经研究证实,SLE 患者体内与 M1 相关的一些炎性介质在机体中表达显著上调[26]。另一方面,M2 为一类具有免疫抑制功能的巨噬细胞。CD163 是一种 M2 重要的表面标记,它可以通过释放如 IL－10 等抗炎细胞因子发挥抗炎作用[27],而在 SLE 中的巨噬细胞 CD163 表达量显著下降;表明了在 SLE 患者中巨噬细胞中存在 M2 的极化缺陷[15]。提示 SLE 患者存在巨噬细胞免疫调节障碍。

2.2 巨噬细胞移动抑制因子

巨噬细胞移动抑制因子(macrophagemigration inhibitory factor,MIF)也称为糖基化抑制因子,是一种前炎症因子,由 114 个氨基酸组成,在迟发型超敏反应过程中可抑制巨噬细胞迁移,在各物种间持高度保守[28]。MIF 大多由单核巨噬细胞及 T 细胞产生,在免疫、炎症反应及抗感染等过程中有十分重要的作用。目前有研究表明,MIF 能够通过对巨噬细胞功能的激活、调节淋巴细胞的活化、促进多种细胞因子的分泌与表达等其他途径参与 SLE 的发病过程[29]。

随着对 MIF 的研究逐渐深入,目前普遍认为 MIF 是非特异性免疫的重要参与者,MIF 以免疫调节为主要功能,能活化淋巴细胞,促进某些细胞因子分泌和表达,如 IL－1、IL－6、IL－8、TNF－α、IFN－γ 等[30-33],这些细胞因子在 SLE 中均有重要作用。固有免疫应答中,通过自分泌和旁分泌的形式,来源于巨噬细胞的 MIF 能刺激其自身的合成,同时也刺激其他促炎症介质合成;MIF 还以提高巨噬细胞内杀伤活性的方式,促进产生过氧化氢,增强一氧化氮释放和磷脂酶 A2 的表达,进而起到促炎作用[33]。MIF 缺失的巨噬细胞减少促炎症细胞因子的生成,大多可能是因为降低 Toll 样受体(Toll-like receptor,TLR)－4 的表达和核因子κB 的活性[34]。目前国内外的研究均证实,MIF 水平在 SLE 患者血清中明显升高,并且 MIF 水平与疾病严重程度呈正相关[29]。狼疮肾炎(LN)主要由免疫复合物介导的慢性炎症所导致,巨噬细胞及单核细胞浸润的多少可评价炎症程度,反映肾小球的损害程度。而 MIF 可刺激巨噬细胞的活化,高水平的 MIF 导致肾巨噬细胞的聚集,促进肾小球的增殖,加重了蛋白尿程度[36],可见 MIF 介导了 SLE 的器官受损。

大量研究证实,MIF 作用广泛,特别在维持免疫调节、细胞凋亡及与糖皮质激素和性激素的相互作用中,均表明其与 SLE 有着明显的相关性[35],而且 MIF 能以表达细胞因子、激活巨噬细胞和活化 T 细胞以及阻碍糖皮质激素效应等各种途径导致 SLE 的发生发展,提示拮抗 MIF 可能会为治疗 SLE 提供新策略。

2.3 巨噬细胞衍生趋化因子

趋化因子又称趋化性细胞因子,是分子质量大部分介于 7~15 kD、可诱导的一类细胞因子,主要由单核巨噬细胞、B 细胞、T 细胞、内皮细胞、成纤维细胞等分泌,根据趋化因子分子氨基端保守的半胱氨酸(C)的数量及序列位置,可其分为 4 个亚类:CXC 类、CC 类、CX3C 类和 C 类(C 代表半胱氨酸,X 代表任意氨基酸),其中 CC 类趋化因子和 CXC 类趋化因子家族的成员数量最多[37]。巨噬细胞衍生趋化因子(macrophage derived chemokine,MDC)是由巨噬细胞、树突状细胞以及活化的 B 细胞所产生的 CC 亚类趋化因子之一,其与受体 CCR4 结合进而发挥生物活性。近年来的研究表明,MDC 在 Th2 相关疾病损害中呈现高表达,MDC 可引起树突状细胞和 Th2 细胞的趋化移动,在 Th2 细胞向炎症部位补充和 Th2 相关的免疫反应调节中有至关重要的作用[38]。而自身免疫性疾病如 SLE 的发病于 Th1 细胞和 Th2 细胞的相对比例有密切的联系,MDC 直接参与调控 Th 细胞分化,进而影响 SLE 的发病[39]。

有相关研究证实,MRL/lpr 狼疮小鼠肾组织中的巨噬细胞、活化的 B 细胞以及树突状细胞,可分泌大量 MDC,主要引起单核细胞和 Th2 细胞向肾脏组织趋化迁移,造成肾小球系膜细胞增殖和肾小管间质持续性的自身免疫损伤[42]。由此可见,狼疮小鼠肾组织中 MDC 的高水平表达,导致肾脏中包括 T 细胞在内的单个核细胞大量浸润,可能是在 LN 发生和进展的过程中作为关键因素之一。

CC 类趋化因子作为主要的趋化因子家族之一,在趋化迁移免疫细胞中发挥重要作用。CCL2 又称为单核细胞趋化蛋白 1(MCP-1),作用于受体 CCR2,主要趋化未成熟的树突状细胞、T 淋巴细胞、单核细胞和 NK 细胞。有研究证实,CCL2/CCR2 信号轴介导单核细胞向炎症部位浸润,与胰岛素抵抗、动脉粥样硬化以及类风湿性关节炎等炎症疾病联系密切[40],提示 CCL2 的过量表达增加巨噬细胞的浸润,进而增进 SLE 发病。因此 CC 类趋化因子家族中的成员 CCL2 介导炎症免疫细胞的趋化迁移,参与 SLE 的发生发展。趋化因子及其受体与 SLE 的发病有紧密的联系,它们能够精准调控白细胞向炎症组织的趋化迁移,因此它们对免疫细胞所产生的影响及对疾病的病理生理学作用是未来研究关注的方向[41]。

3. 总结与展望

SLE 作为一种累及多器官、多系统损伤的自身免疫性疾病,具有潜在的致死性,但发病机制尚不明确,其病因和治疗方法是各界关注的热点。大量研究表明,巨噬细胞参与组织稳态和炎症反应,能够帮助组织炎症修复或引起组织炎性损伤,而其功能的异常会诱发自身免疫系统疾病,如参与 SLE 的发病和进展过程。表现在 SLE 患者体内与 M1 相关的一些炎性介质在机体中表达显著上调以及在 SLE 患者中巨噬细胞中存在 M2 的极化缺陷;MIF 能够通过表达细胞因子、活化 T 细胞、激活巨噬细胞以及阻碍糖皮质激素的效应等各种途径导致 SLE 的发生发展;趋化因子及其受体能够精准调控白细胞向炎症组织的趋化迁移从而导致 SLE 的发病。了解巨噬细胞在调节炎症作用中涉及信号级联反应的确切机制,可能为利用巨噬细胞调节和控制自身免疫性疾病提供新的思路,而未来进一步深入的研究将为巨噬细胞成为 SLE 的治疗靶点提供更有力的证据。

参考文献

[1] 于成成.NLRP3、NLRP1 炎性体信号通路在系统性红斑狼疮、类风湿关节炎免疫机制中的作用[D].山东大学,2013.

[2] 董玉梅.系统性红斑狼疮的诊断标准及治疗研究进展[J].临床医药文献电子杂志,2017,4(44):8711-8712.

[3] 黄湛.CD226~+NK 细胞参与系统性红斑狼疮疾病进程[D].中国科学技术大学,2011.

[4] JIA ZHILIN, HE JIAO. Paeoniflorin ameliorates rheumatoid arthritis in rat models through oxidative stress, inflammation and cyclooxygenase 2[J]. Experimental and therapeutic medicine, 2016, 11(2).

[5] BUKHARI M, HARRISON B, LUNT M, et al. Time to first occurrence of erosions in inflammatory polyarthritis: results from a prospective community-based study[J]. Arthritis and rheumatism, 2001, 44(6): 1248-1253.

[6] ZHENG Z H, GAO C C, WU Z Z, LIU S Y, LI T F, GAO G M, LIU Z S. High prevalence of hypovitaminosis D of patients with autoimmune rheumatic diseases in China [J]. Am J Clin Exp Immunol, 2016 Jun 1, 5(3): 48-54.

[7] 张伟娟.ALD-DNA 诱导 SLE 的新机制：巨噬细胞极化及其作用[D].复旦大学,2010.

[8] 常晓萍.系统性红斑狼疮患者 ER、IL-10、Blys 的表达与临床相关性研究[D].天津医科大学,2009.

[9] 陈宏.T 细胞相关细胞因子对自身免疫性疾病的致病机制研究[D].天津大学,2012.

[10] ZHAO MING, ZHOU YIN, ZHU BOCHEN, et al. IFI44L promoter methylation as a blood biomarker for systemic lupus erythematosus[J]. Annals of the Rheumatic Diseases, 2016, 75(11): 1998-2006.

[11] 吴海竞,陆前进.系统性红斑狼疮发病机制的研究进展[J].皮肤科学通报,2018,35(3): 249-257+235.

[12] 董妍君,李卫东,屠呦呦,等.双氢青蒿素对 BXSB 狼疮小鼠自身抗体产生、TNF-α 分泌及狼疮性肾炎病理改变的影响[J].中国中西医结合杂志,2003,(9): 676-679.

[13] MU X, WANG C. Artemisinins-a promising new treatment for systemic lupus erythematosus: A descriptive review[J]. Curr Rheumatol Rep, 2018, 20(9): 55.

[14] 陈红波,项晓骏,范军芬,等.双氢青蒿素对 MRL/lpr SLE 小鼠 CD4~+T 细胞基因组 DNA 甲基化水平的影响研究[J].浙江医学,2018,40(9): 899-901+928.

[15] 陈纬纬,邓伟,张卓亚,等.系统性红斑狼疮患者巨噬细胞表型和功能初步研究[J].现代免疫学,2018,38(2): 100-103+119.

[16] MA C, XIA Y, YANG Q, et al. The contribution of macrophages to systemic lupus erythematosus[J]. Clin Immunol, 2019, 207: 1-9.

[17] CHEUNSUCHON BOONYARIT, INCHAROEN PIMPIN, CHAWANASUNTORAPOJ RATANA, et al. Glomerular macrophage is an indicator of early treatment response in diffuse proliferative lupus nephritis[J]. J Med Assoc Thai, 2013, 96 Suppl 2: S246-51.

[18] CHALMERS S A, CHITU V, HERLITZ L C, et al. Macrophage depletion ameliorates nephritis induced by pathogenic antibodies[J]. J Autoimmun, 2015(57): 42-52.

[19] GORDON S, TAYLOR P R. Monocyte and macrophage heterogeneity[J]. Nat Rev Immunol, 2005, 5(12): 953-964.

[20] GORDON S. Macrophage heterogeneity and tissue lipids[J]. The Journal of Clinical Investigation, 2007, 117(1): 89-93.

[21] GORDON S. Alternative activation of macrophages[J]. NatRev Immunol, 2003, 3: 23-35.

[22] MANTOVANI A, SICA A, LOCATI M. Macrophage polarization comes of age[J]. Immunity, 2005, 23(4): 344-346.

[23] MUELLER C K, SCHULTZE-MOSGAU S. Histomorphometric analysis of the

phenotypical differentiation of recruited macrophages following subcutaneous implantation of an allogenous acellular dermal matrix[J]. International Journal of Oral and Maxillofacial Surgery, 2010, 40(4): 401-407.

[24] 周宪宾,姚成芳.巨噬细胞 M1/M2 极化分型的研究进展[J].中国免疫学杂志, 2012,28(10): 957-960.

[25] WYNN THOMAS A, BARRON LUKE, THOMPSON ROBERT W, et al. Quantitative assessment of macrophage functions in repair and fibrosis[J]. Current Protocols in Immunology, 2011, Vol. Chapter 14: Unit14.22.

[26] LEE E Y, LEE Z H, SONG Y W. CXCtO and autcimmune diseases[J]. Autoimmun Rev, 2009, 8(5): 379-383.

[27] MANTOVANI A, BISWAS S K, GALDIERO M R, et al. Macrophageplasticity and polarization in tissue repair and remodelling[J]. J Pathol, 2013, 229(2): 176-185.

[28] MERK M, MITCHELL R A, ENDRES S, et al. D-dopachrome tautomerase (D-DT or MIF-2): Doubling the MIF cytokine family[J]. Cytokine,2012,59(1): 10-17.

[29] 黄宇,曲航,黄琴.巨噬细胞移动抑制因子在系统性红斑狼疮中的研究进展[J].医学综述,2020,26(3): 433-437+442.

[30] CALANDRA T, BERNHAGEN J, MITCHELL R A, et al. The macrophage is an important and previously unrecognized source of macrophage migration inhibitory factor[J]. J Exp Med, 1994, 179(6): 1895-1902.

[31] CALANDRA T, BERNHAGEN J, METZ C N, et al. MIF as a glucocorticoid-induced modulator of cytokine production[J]. Nature, 1995, 377(6544): 68-71.

[32] BACHER M, METZ C N, CALANDRA T, et al. An essential regulatory role for macrophage migration inhibitory factor in T-cell activation[J]. Proc Natl Acad Sci U S A. 1996, 93(15): 7849-7854.

[33] LUE H, KLEEMANN R, CALANDRA T, et al. Macrophage migration inhibitory factor(MIF): Mechanisms of action and role in disease[J]. Microbes Infect, 2002, 4(4): 449-460.

[34] ROGER T, DAVID J, GLAUSER M P, et al. MIF regulates innate immune responses through modulation of Toll-like receptor 4[J]. Nature, 2001, 414(6866): 920-924.

[35] 郭学华,吴华香.巨噬细胞移动抑制因子和系统性红斑狼疮[J].浙江医学,2006(4): 307-309.

[36] IKEZUMI Y, HURST L A, MASAKI T, et al. Adoptive transfer studies demonstrate that macrophage can induce pmteinuria and mesangial cell proliferation[J] Kidney

Int, 2003, 63(1): 83-95.

[37] 朱娜.二甲双胍对 LPS 诱导的巨噬细胞趋化因子表达的调节及其机制的探讨[D].南昌大学,2016.

[38] 刘海娜,吴春玲,蒋莉,张晓莉,李舒帆,王晓非.系统性红斑狼疮患者血浆巨噬细胞衍生趋化因子水平及临床意义[J].中华风湿病学杂志,2005(3):142-144.

[39] SOLTÉSZ P, ALEKSZA M, ANTAL-SZALMÁS P, et al. Plasmapheresis modu-lates Th1/Th2imbalance inin patients with systemic lupus erythematosus according to measurement of intracytoplasmic cytokines[J]. Autoimmunity, 2002, 35 (1): 51-56.

[40] FIDAN E, ONDER ERSOZ H, YILMAZ M, et al. The effects of rosiglitazone and metformin on inflammation and endothelial dysfunction in patients with type 2 diabetes mellitus. Acta Diabetol, 2011, 48(4): 297-302.

[41] 刘海娜.巨噬细胞衍生趋化因子在系统性红斑狼疮发病中的作用[D].中国医科大学,2008.

点评

此文论述 SLE 与巨噬细胞的关系、巨噬细胞表型和功能分析、巨噬细胞移动抑制因子及巨噬细胞衍生趋化因子等,分析如何利用巨噬细胞调节和控制自身免疫性疾病,旨在为 SLE 病因学研究提供理论思路,有利于促进巨噬细胞成为 SLE 的治疗靶点。论文选题新颖,论证层次清晰,叙述条理流畅。作者进行了大量的文献考证,能在已有基础上作出推进创新,研究具有一定的应用价值。

学术创新三部曲：研典、追踪、交汇
——袁影教授访谈录

郭蒸颖　王新月[*]

摘要：袁影教授提出了理论创新的三部曲：深研本领域的经典，追踪核心概念的演变，交汇界内、跨界或中西相关范畴；并论及了团队集思对完善学术创新的功效与路径。这些独到的创新之法都是在她自身科研经历与多年研究生创新培养的基础上逐一总结而来，富有切实性与推广性。

关键词：学术创新；研典；追踪；交汇

近年来学术创新备受关注，南京大学叶继元教授指出："不论是高层次的原始创新，还是集合创新、应用创新，抑或是低层次的移植创新，总是要有新意。没有新意，便无所谓'学术'。"[1]可是，对于初涉研究的学习者而言，如何进行有价值的创新是学术探索中的最大难关。因此，2020年10月1日，笔者有幸邀请到苏州大学外国语学院袁影教授对如何有效开展学术创新给予建议和指导。兹据访谈整理成文，以飨读者。

郭：袁老师，您好！非常感谢您今天拨冗接受采访。作为您的学生，本人一直关注着您在西方修辞学领域的各种创新性成果，所以今天想向您请教有关学术创新的问题。您认为创新有哪些切实可行的途径吗？

袁：谢谢你提出的这一重要问题！创新是一个十分广泛的话题，它包含了理论创新、方法创新、应用创新等等。这些创新都很有价值，但比较而言理论创新尤其重要，因为这"是解决'论点'问题的"，而论点"一定要有新意，具有前沿性"。①聚焦理论创新，我认为（西方修辞学的研究）可以从以下三个方面进行突

---

[*] 郭蒸颖，王新月：苏州大学外国语学院2019级硕士研究生。
① 出自《学术创新能力培养的几点思考——王寅教授访谈录》（详见参考文献）此篇访谈录中，王寅教授反复强调理论创新的核心地位，视其为所有创新中的首要。

破:第一个方面是对本领域源头经典的细研,我们称之为"研典",这是创新必不可少的勘探工作;第二个方面是"追踪",就是考察领域核心概念在整个研究史中的演变轨迹,以提炼出普遍性的关键元素;第三个方面为"交汇",这里主要是指相关范畴间的界内交汇、跨界交汇以及中西交汇。

1. 研典:创新之根基

郭:袁老师,如您上述所言,理论创新可以从三方面切入。那么接下来想请教您是怎样看待"研典"的?从这一方法出发又该如何进行创新呢?

袁:"研典",刚才提到是指对本领域(如西方修辞学)经典要著的精细研读,这是我们深入这一学科极其重要的基础。通过本领域典籍的反复研读,才能把握核心范畴的基本特征,并有可能察觉这些范畴所存在的问题或其研究的空间所在。比如说亚里士多德的《修辞学》、西塞罗的《论雄辩家》、昆体良的《论雄辩家的教育》、伯克的《动机修辞学》、佩雷尔曼等的《新修辞学:论论辩》,这些重要作品(这里仅举古典和当代两个时期的)都是我们这一学科不能不读的经典之作。现在,许多人为了省事、求快,往往跳过这些经典转而依靠二手资料、甚至是三四手,泛泛了解其中的理论就开始做相关研究了。但是,如果不研典而仅关注间接资料中涉及的一星半点,就不能明白这些理论的来龙去脉,更不可能发现其问题所在,也就无法做出具有突破性的理论研究。我自己在读博期间,通过对亚里士多德的《修辞学》(*Rhetoric*)进行反复研读,发现里面的"修辞推论"/"修辞三段论"(Enthymeme/Rhetorical Syllogism)是西方修辞学中极为复杂的一个概念,已有的相关论述出入较大。要掌握此概念就需要从源头上仔细地推敲亚氏本人在书中是如何阐释其定义及特征的。如果只是依靠二、三手文献,就难以确切地、整体性地把握这个概念。因此,我不仅反复通读亚氏《修辞学》(甚至将全书手录了一遍)①,还对相关"修辞推论"的章节(如第一卷第二章)进行了难

---

① 经典著作是值得手录的,因为在这个过程中你会比阅读时更加全神贯注,容易注意到更多的细节、触发更多的联想。明代文学家张溥每读好书都要进行七录,并将他家乡太仓的书屋起名为"七录斋"。致力演绎巴赫的大提琴家、华东师范大学音乐学院吴和坤院长,曾花费大量时间几乎手录了他演奏的每一首巴赫作品的曲谱,并认为这是十分值得的付出。我对亚氏《修辞学》的手录始自2017年2月7日,终于2018年7月29日,中间因伦敦访学,停了数月;全书绝大部分章节我都恭敬地加以摘录并作了细心核对,过程中还记下了各种发现和心得。此外,我对经典还下过些翻译的功夫,如与团队成员合作了《西方修辞学经典选译——核心概念地图集》。

计其数的精细研读,直到透彻地弄清"修辞三段论"的两大特征——省略性与或然性。通过细研本领域经典,一方面,较易发现其他学者相关研究中的失误或漏洞所在;另一方面,我也能察觉亚里士多德在讲这个概念时,什么地方是比较模糊的,或什么地方他并没有细化下去,这就是我们可以继续深入研究的所在。比如说,亚氏在书中并没有清晰说明修辞推论有哪些形式,而只是简要概述为"修辞三段论的命题数常常少于常规三段论",那到底是少一个还是两个命题呢? 由于他的含糊其词,很多人认为修辞三段论比常规三段论只少了一个命题。而通过仔细考察亚氏前后(不同的章节中)所给出的例子,我发现修辞三段论可以省略一个命题,也可以省略两个,而且所省的可以是前提也可以是结论,并且还可以不省略,因为亚氏在描述时说的是"常常",并且书中出现了(或然性而)完整的修辞三段论。因此,基于对亚氏相关表述及示例的精细辨析,我在 2006 年(读博期间)于本领域权威的学术期刊《修辞学习》(现更名为《当代修辞学》)发表了《解析"修辞推论"——亚里斯多德〈修辞学〉核心概念》,首次提出了从完整到各种省略的七种修辞三段论形式。而之后的深化研究和系列发表,都是建立在这一研典根基上的[①]。

郭:我们发现老师对西方修辞学的另一个核心概念,"争议点"(Stasis),所作的系列创新性研究,也是建立在研典基础上的。您主要通过精研西塞罗的《论雄辩家》(*De Oratore*)、《论题》(*Topica*)等著作中的相关阐述,发现了他分类中有失清晰性与可操作性的地方,因此,您对"争议点"的划分进行了适当调整和补充,建立了一个更方便当代应用的争议点体系。原来研读经典对于理论创新是如此关键! 研究者要对西方修辞学或自身领域的核心理论进行富有新意的探索,就必须首先从源头上加以辨析。

2. 追踪:创新之稳途

王:老师,您刚刚谈论了精研典籍是理论创新的重要基础,那么"追踪"又有着怎样的具体内涵,在学术创新过程中发挥着怎样的作用呢?

袁:"追踪"可以分为两个方面——追踪核心概念意涵的流变和追踪当代相关前沿研究。追踪义涵流变要求对所研概念在每一历史时期主要代表作中的含

[①] 袁影,蒋严.论"修辞情境"的基本要素及核心成分[J].修辞学习,2009 (4):1-8.
朱琳,袁影.修辞"在场":佩雷尔曼的辞格论辩观[J].福建师范大学学报,2016 (4):41-47.

义进行考辨,而后对各时期的含义加以汇总比较,这样不仅能集合此概念的各种意涵,还可以发现其中的核心语义维度或勾勒出其义涵的总体演化趋势。这是一种集已有研究之大成的创新,可能就是前面叶继元教授所提到的"集合创新"(他在文中未加展开)。我和你师姐余思思合作的《"情感诉求"方法体系探微》[2]采用的就是这一追踪法:通过系统梳理西方古今修辞学各时期代表作中的"情感诉求"(Pathos)理论,将诉诸情感的主要途径和方式加以汇总,再进一步提炼整合出了较为全面的"情感诉求"方法体系。而追踪当代前沿,从逻辑上讲,应该属于追踪流变,但由于西方修辞学的历史跨越了两千五百多年,对这么长的学术史整个地加以追踪有时会力不从心或效果不尽人意,那么可以考虑选取某一历史时期进行考察,一般来说,当代的前沿性研究尤其需要追踪(在了知概念源头的情况下)。我与你的另一位师姐王妞合作的《亚里士多德"人品诉诸"的当代阐释》[3],所用的就是这种追踪方法。我们在研典后,发现亚氏在《修辞学》中关于"人品诉诸"(Ethos)虽然论及"明智""美德""善意"三个要素,但每个要素的具体所指不清,给理解和应用造成了困难;而当代对这一概念却有着不少丰富的阐发,于是我们就聚焦当代前沿性研究中对这三个要素的理解,为各要素抉择出了较具共识的代表性子要素,这样不仅明确了人品诉诸/人格诉求的具体所指,而且确保了这样的阐释在当代的适用性与可操作性。总体来看,"追踪"是一条较为稳当而相对易行的创新之路,如果有足量的一手资料和时间投入,这样的理论创新,即便是初入门者也是完全可期的。

王:以前听您提到过这两位师姐在读研之前并没有修辞学的基础,但在导师指引下,通过"追踪"之法就做出了具有创新性的理论研究,这很值得我们起步阶段的研究生学习。其实,我与蒸颖目前正按您所提倡的这个方法,分别对西方修辞学中的"谋篇"(Arrangement)与"论题"(Topos)两大概念进行追踪;从希罗时期、中世纪、文艺复兴、启蒙时期直到现当代的演变脉络现已基本厘清,希望在此基础上,我们对这两个核心范畴的丰富内涵也能有一个把握,探索当代的语篇分析具有新意的经典修辞范畴。

3. 交汇:创新之源泉

王:关于前两种创新方式,我们已经基本了解。但有关"交汇"相关范畴的具体方法还不太清楚,请问您是如何运用"交汇"法进行理论创新的?

袁："交汇"所产生的新意往往最为显著。"交汇"形式是多层面的,包括界内交汇、跨界交汇、中西交汇等。界内交汇是指本领域(如修辞学)界内范畴之间的结合性研究;跨界交汇是指修辞学与语言学、社会学、心理学等学科之间在相关概念上的融合;中西交汇是指对中西方相近修辞概念的会通。我的一些发表文章就分属于这三种交汇性创新。界内范畴交汇的典型文章有《"西塞罗'争议点'系统与博克'戏剧五元"》[4],这是借用美国修辞学家伯克(Burke, K.)影响广泛的"戏剧五元"(Dramatic Pentad)对西塞罗"争议点"体系中宽泛的行动争议点下属加以改造,使整个系统趋于完备并具有更强的可操作性。又如,在 *Stasis Salience and the Enthymemic Thesis*[5](《争议点的凸显与主旨修辞推论》)一文中,我将"修辞推论"和"争议点"两个界内核心范畴进行结合,阐述了作为中心论点的主旨修辞推论是如何限制(作为论据的)争议点的选择和主次安排;以及如何从受到凸显的争议点推导出全文的主旨论点等不乏新意的发现。此外,"逻辑诉求""人格诉求""情感诉求""谋篇布局""凯洛斯""在场""认同"等范畴间的各种交汇也都是可以产生新意的潜在论题。

郭：袁老师,您这种对学术创新的敏锐度让我们从中受益匪浅。在"双一流"建设中也越来越强调跨学科的重要性,您以上所述均为西方修辞学界内交汇的相关例子,那您能再详细介绍一下修辞学可以如何进行跨界交汇创新吗?

袁：好的,跨界研究的创新空间极其宽广,因为存在许许多多的学科或领域。我认为,寻找交汇点可以首先关注我们较有基础的相邻学科,如语言学、文学、社会学、心理学等。修辞学与语言学中的语用学尤为接近,易于找准跨界的交汇点。我与蒋严老师(现任教于伦敦大学亚非学院)在《外语教学与研究》上发表的《修辞三段论与寓义的语用推导》就是将修辞学与语用学中的重要对象创新性地联系在一起加以研究[6]。通过修辞三段论,我们将语用界原来步骤繁多的寓义推导进行了高效简明的推理刻画;而通过语用推导中的表面无关联话语,我们发现修辞三段论还存在一种新形式,即将之前提出的七种修辞推论形式拓展为了八种。可见,这种学科间的创新交汇是互益的关系,可以对各自的理论范畴加以丰富和发展。再如,那篇《论"用典"的权威授加功能》[7]则是将修辞学与相邻的社会学进行了结合。我在考察"用典"的人格功能时,借助了德国社会学家韦伯(Weber, M.)的权威结构理论,对修辞人格中"明智"(Good Sense)下的"权威"要素进行了丰富。韦伯在代表作《社会和经济组织理论》中阐述了三类权威:依合法规则施令的法理权威(Legal Authority)、依神圣传统行使的传统权威(Traditional Authority)、因超凡品质而具有的魅力权威(Charismatic Authority);借助这一分类,就可以有力地得出引经据典对于确立言者的权威、实现其人格诉求所起的关键作用。我们不难看出,在与相邻学科的交汇中修辞学的理论得到了丰富或细化。这也符合"新文科建设需要各个学科交流、交叉、交融,文科不仅要与理、工、农、医等学科交叉,更需要打破其内部的学科壁垒。"①

郭:您举的例子正好体现了国家对新文科的期待。我还注意到您在《修辞学"争议点"理论的认知解析与应用》[8]中借助认知语言学大家 Langacker 在《认知语法基础》[9]一书中提出的两层突显观:侧面与基体(Profile-Base)、射体与界标(Trajector-Landmark),相应地提出了争议点在语篇中的取舍与主次安排两大运用策略。这样看来,跨界交汇可以源源不断地进行理论创新啊!我通过研读您的一些论文,发现您也创新性地将西方修辞学的理论与我国相关修辞概念进行了联系,请问这是不是一种中西交汇呢?

袁:是的,中西交汇是我这几年来特别关注的。中西修辞学里有些范畴较为相近,两种传统对它们各有理解和论述,那么这些论述就值得比较。如,汉语修辞学中的"错综"辞格与文艺复兴时期伊拉斯谟(Erasmus, D.)所论的言辞"丰裕"(Copia)较为相似,我在《"错综"与"丰裕"的中西交汇》[10]研究中发现,这两个范畴具有较强的兼容性,源于《易经》、代表局部与整体两大变化的"错"和"综"是对言辞丰富法更为简准的命名,而伊氏的"丰裕"分类有助于挖掘和整理汉语"错综"手法,并且"错综"格的定义也需要结合"丰裕"理论予以增补。这种融合中西相关术语进行的考察,对于拓展人文社会科学中的概念研究不失为一条富有成效的探索路径,有助于甄别命名、完善界定并构建既具普遍性又含本土性的要素语义网络。再如,《中西"时机"观考辨》[11]一文中,我通过比较《论语》与《伊索克拉底文集》中的修辞"时机"与"凯洛斯"(Kairos,后者所用术语),发现:无处不在的时机之用是两者的共识;但《论语》更重失时的性质、误机的原因、契机与否的结果,而伊氏《文集》则尤为关注应机之策。可见,中西时机观的融合有助于全面把握这一通用范畴的内涵。基于这一交汇思路,我与你们的另两位师姐继续深入中西"时机"观的比较,发表了《从先秦典籍探析古希腊"凯洛斯"范畴中"适时"与"适度"修辞准则》[12],通过《周易》《孟子》《鬼谷子》中的相关要语,对"凯洛斯"范畴中的两大基本要素进行了丰富和细化。这一中西交汇

---

① 刘曙光.新文科与思维方式、学术创新[J].上海交通大学学报,2020(2):18-34.

的过程,其实也是将西方理论本土化的过程。

郭:袁老师,我们发现您近年指导的研究生论文也主要是中西交汇式的,如《修辞问句的逻辑诉求功能研究——〈文心雕龙〉中反问句的修辞推论解析》[13]和《提喻的人格诉求功能研究——以〈孟子〉中的"君子"为例》[14],可见,中西交汇也有着广阔的创新前景。

袁:是的,但挑战性也很强,需要我们长期深入中西相关典籍的考察。

郭:刚才您总共从三方面向我们具体介绍了如何对西方修辞学进行理论创新。那么我想请问一下,您提到的"研典"、"追踪"以及"交汇"这三部曲之间是否存在着一定的联系呢?这三者联系起来又是如何进行理论创新的呢?

袁:你问得非常关键。这三方面是存在着必然联系的。首先,"研典"贯穿理论创新的始终。对于初入门的研究生来说,细读领域中的经典是打好创新基础的关键。即便是资深研究者,读典仍然是很重要的。因为当你反复研读时,你就会觉察之前未注意到的要义或产生新的联想或发现需深入研究的模糊之处。这就像欣赏苏州园林一样,我特别喜欢的沧浪亭,在不同的年份、不同的季节、不同的时辰、不同的天气、不同的心境下,游了可能有百次之多,从不厌倦,可以说每次的体会都有所不同,经常会有新的发现或感悟。"追踪"与"研典"是密切相连的,往往在我们研读经典对某一概念产生兴趣而要深入探究时就需要进行追踪,厘清它的来龙去脉,一般通过考察各个时期的代表作来揭示其演化过程。比较而言,"交汇"的理论创新难度是最大的,因为要做出真正有价值的界内交汇,需要对领域内的诸多核心范畴及其研究史有相当深入的认识,这就有赖于长年的研典或追踪功夫。跨界交汇不仅需有本领域的根基还应对所跨领域有相当认识,至少是读过些该领域的相关经典,才能免于牵强或空泛,最好是两个领域的研究者进行合作探索(《修辞三段论与寓义的语用推导》就是这样的合作)。而中西交汇,就需要具备两种修辞学传统的根基或素养才可能找准恰当的交汇点;但如果是将西方的某一修辞理论用于分析中国的语料(最好是典籍中的),以所得发现来补充或修正该理论,则相对易行些,上面你提到的两篇硕士论文就属于这一类中西交汇。

4. 集思:创新之完善

王:老师,您刚才在跨界交汇中提到合作对学术创新的重要性。那您可以进一步谈谈团队合作的具体模式以及它是如何在创新过程中发挥作用的吗?

袁: 我确实非常注重团队合作。"合作"有广、狭两义,狭义上主要指合作撰写论文,而广义上可包括提供资料、建议、甚至质疑等各种相关帮助,我认为团队合作中这两种方式都是需要的。所谓"团队"也有大、小之分。小团队主要由导师及其指导的研究生组成,这是较为稳定的;而大团队,是指因某项研究所需,邀请国内外的相关专家学者来集思广益,这是临时性的,一般与小团队结合在一起发挥作用。这种多层面的团队合作我在加拿大滑铁卢大学访学期间感受颇深。曾获《自然》《科学》刊发书评的《语言学战争》(*The Linguistics Wars*)的作者、Randy Allen Harris 教授,每周都有几小时与团队成员一起讨论学生与他及其同事合作的论文。成员中除了较为固定的数人小团队外,他还通过 Skype 现场反复咨询其他国家的相关学者,针对这一篇 3 人合作文章(学生是第一作者,他是第二作者)的修改讨论竟持续了数月之久。而在他的那些新意迭出的独著中均列有一长串的致谢名单,这些专家我相信是他实实在在咨询过的。可见创新是需要团队的集思和验证的①。现在我也努力效仿他的做法,至少要在小团队内对大家的新研究进行反复讨论、推敲,直到能为所有成员基本接受。与大团队成员的交流,如果有条件也要尽力争取,如那倩与我合作发表的《〈文心雕龙〉中反问句的修辞推论解析》就曾咨询过美国加州大学的赵和平教授,他是运用西方修辞理论研究《文心雕龙》的国际知名学者,赵教授仔细通读了这篇文章,不仅充分肯定了我们的研究,还提供了诸多宝贵的修改意见。此外,大团队成员还有期刊审稿人,我们投的是国外学术期刊(往往反馈信息丰富),获得了两位匿名评审的不少具体修改建议,我们十分重视,对论文又作了相应的调整和完善。那倩以此为基础的硕士论文在盲审时,三位双盲专家均给出了难得的优秀等级,这在很大程度上也是得益于多层面的团队合作②。

王: 原来团队合作对于学术创新也是这么关键,难怪您经常线上线下召集大家研讨交流呢,假期里也没有中断;而且还十分注重研讨的环境,线下或是在

---

① 苏格兰启蒙运动领袖坎贝尔(Campbell, G.)的传世名作《修辞哲学》(*The Philosophy of Rhetoric*)即得益于他所创立的阿伯丁哲学社团(Philosophical Society of Aberdeen)。该社团由约 10 人组成,每月聚会两次,交流所撰新稿;这部被誉为 18 世纪最重要的修辞学著作,其章节几乎都为团里的成员们反复讨论过,整个过程持续了 10 多年之久。

② 除了集思以外,盲审前,我不仅逐句审阅过她的学位论文,还将其章节分给团队成员,请他们逐字仔细核读各个部分以排除各种可能存在的漏失;其他研究生的论文也都是这样及时得益于团队的合力相助。

我们老东吴大学古色古香的办公楼里,或是在苏城有名的书屋、图书馆那些优美温馨的咖啡吧中,在这样的氛围里,大家思维敏捷、特别容易受到激发。

郭:袁老师,衷心感谢您能抽出时间来接受采访并详细回答了我们的各种问题。您围绕研典、追踪以及交汇三大方面对修辞学这一学科的理论创新阐发了自己的诸多见解。您提出的这"三部曲"不仅给我们学习修辞学的研究生许多启发,也会给其他领域的莘莘学子很大的启迪。我们坚信您给出的这些宝贵建议将对如何进行学术创新以及培养创新性思维具有重要意义。再次感谢您接受本次访谈!

总结

彭影教授提出了学术创新的三部曲:研典、追踪、交汇。研典是创新的根基;追踪是创新的稳途;交汇是创新的源泉。三者存在着必然的联系,研典贯穿始终,追踪深入探索,交汇跨界考察,而团队合作、集思完善也是学术研究创新的关键所在。

(衷心感谢华东师范大学音乐学院院长吴和坤教授为文章标题抉择了"三部曲"的比喻,以及罗明安先生对英文部分所提供的宝贵建议。)

参考文献

[1] 叶继元.以学术规范促进学术创新[J].图书馆论坛,2019(3):1.

[2] 余思思,袁影."情感诉求"方法体系探微[J].外国语言文学,2017(3):187-196.

[3] 王妞,袁影.亚里士多德"人品诉诸"的当代阐释[J].外国语言文学,2014(4):217-223.

[4] 袁影.西塞罗"争议点"系统与博克"戏剧五元"[J].当代修辞学,2012(2):75-81.

[5] YUAN, YING, RANDY ALLEN HARRIS, YAN JIANG. "Stasis Salience and the Enthymemic Thesis"[J]. Language and Semiotic Studies, 2017(3):103-124.

[6] 袁影,蒋严.修辞三段论与寓义的语用推导[J].外语教学与研究,2010(2):97-103.

[7] 袁影.论"用典"的权威授加功能[J].苏州大学学报,2017(2):153-159.

[8] 袁影,崔淑珍.修辞学"争议点"理论的认知解析与应用[J].外国语言文学,2009(2):87-94.

[9] LANGACKER, RONALD W. Foundations of Cognitive Grammar vol. I: Theoretical

Prerequisites[M].Stanford:Stanford University Press,1987.

[10] 袁影."错综"与"丰裕"的中西交汇——《文心雕龙》语言艺术研究[J].社会科学战线,2019(7):156-163.

[11] 袁影.中西"时机"观考辨——《论语》与《伊索克拉底文集》比较[J].中国比较文学,2016(3):183-193.

[12] 马银欢,那倩,袁影.从先秦典籍探析古希腊"凯洛斯"范畴中"适时"与"适度"修辞准则[J].外国语言文学,2019(6):564-577.

[13] NA,QIAN,YING YUAN.Logical Function of Rhetorical Questions:An Enthymematic Analysis of RQs in The Literary Mind and the Carving of Dragons[J].Linguistics and Literature Studies,2019(7):156-163.

[14] 袁影,马银欢.《孟子》中"君子"提喻的人格诉求功能[J].国文天地,2019(10):45-50.

[15] 刘曙光.新文科与思维方式、学术创新[J].上海交通大学学报,2020(2):18-34.

[16] 刘玉梅等.学术创新能力培养的几点思考——王寅教授访谈录[J].山东外语教学,2015(6):3-10.

[17] R.马丁.论权威——兼论M.韦伯的"权威三类型说"[J].罗述勇,译.国外社会科学,1987(2):30-32,13.

[18] 吴朝晖."双一流"建设的三重协奏曲[J].中国高等教育,2019(Z1):37-39.

[19] 袁影.解析"修辞推论"——亚里斯多德《修辞学》核心概念[J].修辞学习,2006(5):23-30.

[20] 袁影.修辞批评新模式构建研究[M].上海:上海外语教育出版社,2012.

点评

论文以苏州大学外国语学院袁影教授长期耕耘的修辞学领域为出发点,围绕理论的创新问题对袁教授展开访谈,提炼出理论创新的三部曲,即深研本领域的经典,追踪核心概念的演变,交汇界内、跨界或中西相关范畴,并论及团队集思对完善学术创新的功效与路径。论文主题明确,格式规范,内容清楚,所提炼的创新之法眼光独到,富有切实性与推广性。

品牌道歉声明中的权势与亲密关系构建
——基于级差系统视角的分析

华逸聪*

摘要：研究国际品牌的道歉声明，以系统功能语言学评价理论中的级差系统为理论基础，分析语势、聚焦情况及其对建构权势与亲密关系的影响。有利于将公众对道歉声明的感性认识上升到理性认识。研究发现：品牌道歉声明多运用增强语势和锐化来建构权势，但对亲密关系构建较少。有时由于语境和搭配的影响，还会产生反效果。

关键词：级差系统；道歉声明；权势；亲密关系

引言

《牛津高阶英汉双解词典》用了"apologia"的词义，把道歉定义为"辩解中的言语"。声明则是机构或个人就有关自身权益的事件信息公开表明立场与主张的文书。从功能来看，官方道歉声明一方面需要建构权势，将自身意识形态施加给读者，从而获得谅解维护自身权益，另一方面需要与读者建构亲密关系，让读者更加信服，能更加隐蔽地逃避责任，达到维护形象的目的。

"权势因素"和"亲密关系"是由社会心理学家 Brown 和 Gilman(1960)最先提出并引进了社会语言学中。权势是指由于地位、财富等差异，一方在话语中占据强势位置。直白地说，拥有了话语权势就意味着掌控话语权，控制话语进程，在话语中影响弱势一方。而亲密关系则指在话语中双方处于联系紧密、互为伙伴。官方道歉声明中离不开这二者的平衡。

评价系统是"目前描写语篇中价值评判的最完善模型"（Thompson &

---

* 华逸聪：上海大学外国语学院 2019 级硕士研究生。

Hunston,2006:308)。评价系统分为介入(engagement)、态度(attitude)和级差(graduation)三个子系统。其中,级差系统在整个评价系统中占有重要地位,级差性是态度、介入及其各子系统的典型属性。

级差反映态度的加强与衰弱,是对态度的分级(王振华、马玉蕾,2007:19-23)。级差系统分为语势(force)和聚焦(focus)。语势上,作者可通过量化(quantification)和程度化(intensification)实现语势的增强或减弱。量化是对数量、形态、跨度方面的操作,程度化是对质量、过程的操作。聚焦上,作者可通过锐化(sharpen)或钝化(soften)来适应自身目的(如图1)。

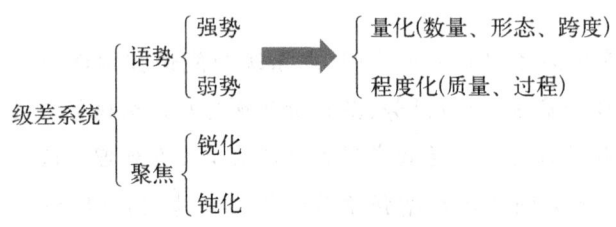

图1 级差系统理论框架图

1. 文献综述

1.1 对官方声明的研究现状

国外学者 Catenaccio、Cotter、Smedt、et al.(2011)、Choi(2012)、Brennan(2013)、Wickman(2014)等分别从语用学、新闻学、公共关系学、修辞学等角度对声明的语言特点与语篇结构等进行过研究。其中,Catenaccio 等学者还特别提出对声明语篇的研究不仅要关注它作为新闻产品的属性,还要关注它作为话语过程的属性(discursive processes)。

国内学者多对官方声明进行批评话语分析(杨丽婷,2012;张雪英,2016),还有从公共关系(高鹏,2007)、有效性(丁齐英、王飞、汪峰,2017)、对话性(孟超,2018)等角度对声明作用进行探讨。值得注意的是从道歉角度进行分析的仅有一篇(祁、肖、Dániel,2019)。

1.2 对级差系统的研究现状

国外学者多集中于评价理论的整体研究。理论研究中,马丁(Martin)、怀特(White)创立的评价理论是较有影响力的评价研究(刘婷婷、徐加新,2018)。

实践运用上,西方学者研究评价理论在各类语篇上的运用(Korner, 2000; Susan, 2006)。

国内学者也多集中于评价理论的整体研究(刘世铸、韩金龙,2004;张先刚,2007;司显柱、庞玉厚,2018)。级差系统主要运用于分析级差系统在不同文本体裁上的体现,如文学文本(付晓丽,付天军 2009)、社论(王燕,柳福玲,张文静 2014)、工作报告(司炳月,高松 2019)等。还有探究级差系统在不同交际场景下的运用的,如辩论(董敏 2012)、网络点评(吕文萍 2015)、演讲(刘盛华,李霞 2017)等。

1.3 总结

由上述所得,声明作为话语过程,拥有权势的主体,势必将自己意识形态影响另一话语主体。话语分析能更好地探索一方选择如此措辞的原因及话语的影响。现有对声明的语言学研究集中在语用学话语分析上,且聚焦于其他语体,对道歉声明这一语体的研究较少。运用评价理论研究不同文本体裁较为普遍,但以单个级差系统来进行研究的较少。据所查找到的文献,对级差系统在构建权势与亲密关系是如何平衡的,偏离这一平衡所产生的效果关注也不多。因此,本研究旨在用评价理论下的级差系统来对道歉声明进行研究,分析道歉声明中级差资源的分布及其在构建权势与亲密关系上的作用,尤其是二者平衡失当带来的反效果。为读者提供解读声明新视角,为企业提供官方声明写作借鉴。

2. 品牌道歉声明中的级差资源、权势与亲密关系

2.1 级差资源的总体分布

本研究所选语料为 7 个品牌的道歉声明 8 份,其中 CK 占据两份。由于汉语特性及发布渠道限制,所有语料均有简短,多小句的特点。狭义的小句指一种句子以下的语法单位(Otto, 1924),广义的小句既可以代表一个句子,也可以发挥分句的功能(邢福义,1995)。本研究以广义的小句为分类单位,它在语义上建构一个情形,在认知层面表达事件概念(何伟、王敏辰,2019)。

据统计,该 8 份官方声明共计 68 个小句(35 个句子)。其中,涉及语势子系统下强化弱化的共 28 个小句,涉及聚焦子系统下锐化钝化的共 17 个小句,二者都不涉及的共 28 个小句,两者都涉及的共 5 个小句。

从上图2可以得出：第一，存在级差资源的小句占官方声明的大部分；第二，在极差的两个子系统中，语势系统的使用频率较高，且数值与聚焦系统相差较大。第三，综合运用两个子系统的数量较少。

由数据可知，品牌方广泛运用了级差系统。一方面用增强立场阐述来树立权势，提高道歉声明的权威性；一方面运用降低姿态表达友好，取悦读者，减少读者对权势的抵触与反抗。同时在传达态度的过程中，语势资源运用更多，说明道歉声明的主要目的是凸显语篇立场，向读者表明决心，达到权势的构建，最大限度地影响读者，达到辩解的目的，而不是聚焦或弱化事件本身。

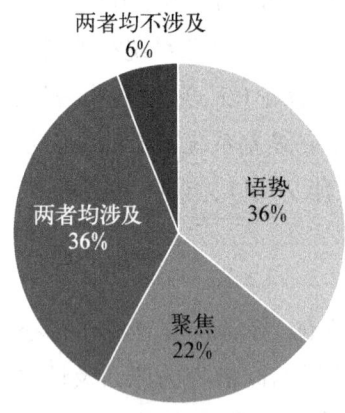

图 2　级差资源总体分布

2.2　语势资源

宏观来看，涉及语势的 28 个小句均为语势的强化，没有涉及语势的弱化。这 28 个小句中共有 30 处（量化 21 处，程度化 9 处）语势的增强。微观上来看，这 8 份品牌声明涉及量化中的数量（number）和跨度（extent），程度化中的质量（quality）和过程（process）。具体分布如下：

量化	数量	百分比	跨度	百分比
21处（70%）	13	61.9%	8	38.1%

程度化	质量	百分比	过程	百分比
9处（30%）	1	11.1%	8	88.9%

图 3　语势资源分布

2.2.1　量化分析

（1）数量

品牌道歉声明通过数量的语势强化影响读者的情感判断，维护自身的权威。

例 1：并<u>再次</u>检查<u>所有</u>与中国领土描述相关的信息准确性。（CK 声明）

例 2：并<u>再次</u>确认<u>所有</u>与中国领土描述相关的信息的准确性。（CK 声明）

例 3：主动在全球范围的<u>所有</u>渠道将所涉商品下架。（Coach 声明）

例4：该T恤已于7月24日在Versace范思哲官方所有销售渠道下架并销毁。（Versace声明）

"再次"指再一次或第二次，表示动作的反复性，"所有"表示全部，一点都不剩下。这两个词语显示出品牌方弥补措施涉及范围之广，力度之彻底，态度之仔细。首先维护自身品牌权威，塑造自己专业的形象，给读者以强烈的说服力。同时，暗含品牌之前也有仔细检查信息的含义，使得权势进一步加强，影响读者对品牌的情感。

例5：我们也重申Calvin Klein完全尊重和支持中国主权和领土的完整。（CK声明）

例6：Versace范思哲重申，我们热爱中国。（Versace声明）

例7：我们也重申Calvin Klein完全尊重和支持中国主权和领土完整。（CK声明）

3份声明均运用了"重申"一词来加强申辩。"重申"一词非常正式，同时也体现了反复性，预设了曾经品牌的立场也是维护中国主权和领土完整的。使得立场的阐述更加强烈，更加深刻地影响读者的态度，达到权势建构。并且由于这种热爱中国的情感与读者的情感高度契合，呼唤读者共鸣，达到了亲密关系的建构。更容易获得读者的谅解，减少对声明施加的品牌意识形态的反抗。

例8：我们由此对广大消费者的感情造成的伤害表示万分歉意。（Coach声明）

例9：我们感到万分抱歉。（施华洛世奇声明）

例10：万分感谢各界人士监督。（施华洛世奇声明）

以上三个例子均借用"万分"来表达情感，但在情感种类上有所差异。例8和例9以这一副词表达与道歉这一消极感情相连，达到权势建构的目的。品牌方掌握着话语权，是拥有权势的一方。因此他们的道歉能减轻对读者面子的威胁程度，以退为进，传达了更加鲜明的态度立场。而例10与感谢这一积极情感相联系，比抱歉更加技高一筹。"感谢"隐含着认可、赞许，给读者以"以德报德"的印象。拥有权势的一方的道谢更容易提升读者对自身地位的认知。但实际上这种以退为进的手法本质上还是品牌方构建权势的一种手段，通过放低姿态，恭维读者，使得读者更容易接受其思想，既维护了自身形象又达到了获得体谅的目的。

（2）跨度

通过时间跨度上的语势强化，品牌声明通过强调立场、决心、情感的惯常性来建构权势和亲密关系。

例11：COACH <u>一贯</u>尊重并维护中国主权及领土完整。（Coach 声明）

例12：纪梵希品牌<u>一贯</u>尊重中国主权。（纪梵希声明）

例13：Fresh 馥蕾诗<u>始终</u>坚持一个中国的原则。（Fresh 声明）

例14：施华洛世奇<u>从来</u>坚决维护中国的主权和领土完整。（施华洛世奇声明）

"一贯""始终""从来"表示一定时间空间范围内，某种状态行为保持不变。在上述例子中，各品牌意在说明品牌对中国的尊重一直没有发生改变，直接说明了品牌从前对中国主权的态度是认可尊重的，突出比较此次风波的可信度不大，逃避责任。这是一种隐藏的权势，就像一个信誉好的人往往更容易获得信任，品牌塑造以前的信誉，目的是让读者接受现在的过失是无心的，甚至是无中生有的。

例15：我们将<u>一如既往</u>地为中国顾客提供优质的产品与服务。（Coach 声明）

"一如既往"是品牌建构权势与亲密关系相协调的佐证。Coach 声明中否认了对中国主权问题的模糊，强势表达了此次风波自身没有实际责任，是权势的体现。然而风波不会影响品牌初心，愿意与读者一直保持良好关系。品牌意在做出友好亲近姿态，更容易获得读者原谅。

2.2.2 程度化分析

（1）质量

质量强化是对性质或是品质的程度强弱进行描述（刘立华，2010）。其强化方式主要是采用语法强化词对形容词和副词质量进行分级。

例16：我们<u>非常</u>遗憾林允与她的团队单方面停止与 Calvin Klein 的合作。（CK 声明）

在30处语势增强描述中，仅有1处涉及质量。CK 因发布"中国特供"声明遭代言人解约后再发声明，不但模糊了事件焦点：道歉声明仅仅发布在中国社交媒体上，还推卸责任。级差系统能使阅读者理解并相信这种价值立场，并将它纳入自己的评判标准中（吕文萍 2015），这是 CK 品牌建构权势的核心目的。然而由于自身傲慢，建构权势过程中太过强硬，忽视读者的情感诉求，完全打破了与读者间的亲密关系，因此这份道歉声明一经发出，读者的愤怒之情愈演愈烈，微博回复中言辞更加激烈。

（2）过程

强化动作过程能对话语的语势资源进行分级,达到渲染话语意图的目的(刘盛华,李霞 2017)。

例 17：对此我们<u>深</u>表歉意。（纪梵希声明）

例 18：我们为此次争议事件<u>深</u>表歉意。（Versace 声明）

例 19：我们<u>深刻</u>认识到这次问题的严重性。（Coach 声明）

例 20：我们<u>一定</u>立即纠正并引以为戒。（纪梵希声明）

例 17 至例 20 通过"深刻""一定"等词的情感诉诸,强化了品牌方认错态度的真诚和表达决心的坚定这一过程,达到了建构权势的目的。

2.2.3 总结

品牌道歉声明运用了丰富的语势资源,且全部都采用了加强语势策略,具体通过量化与程度化来控制话语,维护自己的权势。其中量化所占比例较高,而程度化所占比例较低,这是由于量化作用面较广,能在阐述立场、致歉、展示决心及体现这三者的惯常性上发挥巨大的作用。程度化作用面较窄,因为声明鲜少涉及品质与动作。

通过态度的分级,大大提高了道歉声明的情感感染力和可信度,能更大程度地影响读者的情感判断,体现控制话语的权势关系。但在建构亲密关系上的努力较少,道歉态度中隐含着强硬,甚至在有些语境中完全割裂了亲密关系,因而道歉声明的可接受度大打折扣。因此,道歉声明在建构权势,表达立场的同时要关注与读者的心理距离,适当建构亲密关系来获得读者的谅解。

2.3 聚焦资源

在 17 处聚焦资源中,有 8 处锐化,9 处钝化。品牌方均衡使用两种策略调节权势与亲密关系。

2.3.1 锐化分析

聚焦系统中的级差词用于调节范围量值,锐化类似舞台上的聚光灯,其目的在于强调和限定(何伟 2016)。通过将读者注意力聚焦某处,达到提高自身形象但又维护与读者亲密关系的目的。

例 21：<u>对于</u> Calvin Klein 美国网站内语言/国家分类选项造成误解。（CK 声明）

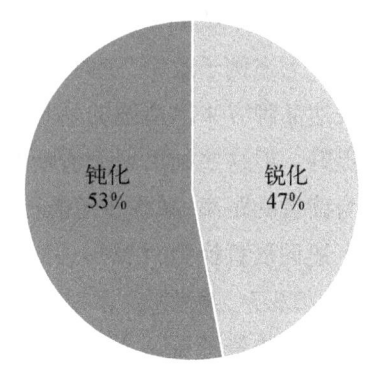

图 4 聚焦资源分布

例22：关于今日引起部分网友讨论的海外市场纪梵希印花T恤中的错误而引发大家的关注。（纪梵希声明）

例23：就Fresh 馥蕾诗英文官方网站上国家（地区）分类选项造成的误解。（Fresh 声明）

例24：并再次检查所有与中国领土描述相关的信息准确性。（CK 声明）

例25：并再次确认所有与中国领土描述相关的信息的准确性。（CK 声明）

例21、22、23通过添加范围限定词，且放在声明开篇，将读者注意力聚焦在造成风波的原因上，营造坦诚相待的感觉，通过表示自己的真诚、直面争议，能够破除读者对品牌"心虚"的负面印象，从而拉近与读者距离。例24、25出现在句子中间，将读者注意力聚焦于矛盾主体，表达后续整改承诺，既显示自身拥有商品信息控制权，达到传播自身意识形态、构建权势的目的，又安抚读者情绪，表现出积极合作的意愿。

例26：我们对于由此造成的影响深表歉意。（Versace 声明）

例26将聚光灯投射在"由此造成的影响上"，体现了品牌方的共情能力，显示出理解公众愤怒的姿态，将自己置身于读者一方，尝试与读者结盟。

2.3.2 钝化分析

级差系统中的聚焦源自Lakoff（1972）对模糊语概念的探讨。在8份语料中，钝化主要用于模糊时间。

例27：我们将会即时修正。（CK 声明）

例28：立刻采取紧急措施。（Coach 声明）

例29：我们已第一时间全力与亚瑟士总部积极沟通。（亚瑟士声明）

例30：尽快更正相关问题。（亚瑟士声明）

例31：我们一定立即纠正并引以为戒。（纪梵希声明）

上述例子运用"及时改正"的策略，采用不同的词汇来表达"马上"的意思，表达品牌方采取措施的及时性，给读者痛改前非的正面印象，使得品牌形象得到提升。但这些词语缺乏清晰的检验时间节点，容易被理解为外交辞令，从而拉大与读者的距离，减少了道歉声明的可信度。若在发布声明前做好了补救措施，将上述词语替换为"已经"，品牌方的权势将得到进一步巩固。

2.3.3 总结

聚焦资源在这8份品牌道歉声明中的数量与语势资源相比较低，说明道歉声明的主要目的是表达立场，而非聚焦矛盾。聚焦资源中锐化和钝化的数量则相差不大,品牌方能综合运用两种手段构建权势,并与读者保持恰当的心理距离。

道歉声明运用锐化手段将读者注意力聚焦于矛盾中心点,使得情感表达、立场表明更为直接,通过构建权势更加能影响读者的思想观念。同时显示出积极友好的态度,理解读者感情,建立与读者的亲密关系。但是一些汉语词语的模糊性与钝化相结合,容易模糊态度,使得构建的权势遭到抵消,与读者的亲密关系也遭到冲击。比如"尽快"一类词的不确定性让读者难以信服,联系到品牌本身还没有实质性举动的社会语境,声明的可信度进一步下降,不能成功构建权势。因此要达到维护自身利益,提高品牌形象的目的,道歉声明应尽量使用确切化表述来构建权势,通过权威性的表达传达意识形态,影响读者判断。综合情感体恤、主动回应等策略来缩短与读者的距离,营造亲密氛围。

3. 结论

论文研究选取 8 份品牌道歉声明,通过总结评价理论中级差资源的分布情况,分析了级差资源在道歉声明中构建权势和亲密关系的作用。研究发现:第一,语料的语势资源占比大且均为语势加强,聚焦资源较少,其主要目的是增强情感,坚定立场,构建权势。第二,语势资源中的量化与程度化对阐述立场、表示歉意、表达决心起到了强化作用。由于量化在这三者上可操作层面更广,因此量化的频率更高。道歉声明在构建权势的努力上较大,在拉近亲密关系上有所欠缺。甚至因为转移焦点,割裂与读者的亲密关系,影响权势建构。第三,聚焦资源下的锐化与钝化对点明矛盾,起到了积极作用。但其模糊性容易使得权威性受到影响,传递意识形态的效果将会削弱。因此道歉声明不但要主动表明态度立场,维护品牌形象,通过构建权势影响读者的态度思想,还要注意与读者保持亲密但适当的距离,减小读者对权势的抵触。在这个中和的过程中尤其要注意语境和词语搭配,以免起到反效果。由于此样本容量小,且汉语级差判定与英语存在很大不同,本研究还有待进一步的完善与改进。

参考文献

[1] BRENNAN N, MERKL-DAVIES D, BEELITZ A. Dialogism in corporate social

responsibility communications: Conceptualizing verbal Interaction between organizations and their audiences[J]. Journal of Business Ethics, 2013(4): 665 – 679.

[2] BROWN R, GILMAN A. The Pronouns of Power and Solidarity [G]//GIGLIOLI P P (ed.). Language and Social Context. New York: Penguin Books,1960. 252 – 282.

[3] CATENACCIO P, COTTER C, SMEDT M, GARZONE G, et al. Towards a linguistics of news production[J]. Journal of Pragmatics, 2011(43): 1843 – 1852.

[4] CHOI J. A content analysis of BP's press releases dealing with crisis[J]. Public Relations Review, 2012(3): 422 – 429.

[5] KORNER K. Negotiating Authority: The Logogenesis of Dialogue in Common Law Judgments [D]. University of Sydney. 2000.

[6] LAKOFF G. Hedges: A Study in Meaning Criteria and the Logic of Fuzzy Concepts[J]. Proceedings of the Chicago Linguistics Society, 1972(8): 183 – 228.

[7] OTTO JESPERSEN. The Philosophy of Grammar[M]. London: George Allen and Unwin LTD, 1924.

[8] SUSAN H. The persuasive power of prosodies: Radiating values in academic writing[J]. Journal of English for Academic Purposes.2006(5): 37 – 49.

[9] THOMPSON G, HUNSTON S. Evaluation in text [M]. BROWN K (ed.). Encyclopedia of Language & Linguistics (2nd edn.). Oxford: Elsevier, 2006: 305-312.

[10] WICKMAN C. Rhetorical framing in corporate press releases: The case of British Petroleum and the Gulf Oil Spill[J]. Environmental Communication, 2014(1): 3 – 20.

[11] 丁齐英,王飞,汪峰.中国产品伤害事件的危机声明发布有效性分析(英文)[J].中国科学技术大学学报,2017(3): 221 – 230.

[12] 董敏.从级差系统分析辩论话语的人际意义[J].外语研究,2012(3): 14 – 20.

[13] 付晓丽,付天军.英语文学语篇的级差系统分析——以《呼啸山庄》为例[J].河北师范大学学报(哲学社会科学版),2009(3): 115 – 119.

[14] 高鹏.成也声明,败也声明[J].国际公关,2007(2): 52.

[15] 何伟.基于评价系统理论的汉语评价词典构建[J].江汉学术,2016(6): 118 – 122.

[16] 何伟,王敏辰.英汉语小句结构对比研究[J].上海交通大学学报(哲学社会科学版),2019(3): 116 – 137.

[17] 刘立华.评价理论研究[M].北京:外语教学与研究出版社,2010: 238.

[18] 刘盛华,李霞.级差视角下反恐演讲话语的人际意义——以 The Way Forward in Afghanistan and Pakistan 为例[J].牡丹江大学学报,2017(1): 6 – 8+12.

[19] 刘世铸,韩金龙.新闻话语的评价系统[J].外语电化教学,2004(4): 17 – 21.

[20] 刘婷婷,徐加新.评价理论研究综述[J].英语教师,2018(24):9-13.
[21] 吕文萍.网络酒店点评的级差资源分析[J].内蒙古师范大学学报(哲学社会科学版),2015(5):133-135.
[22] 孟超.突发事件中官方声明的立场与对话解读:介入视角[J].外语教学,2018(2):42-48.
[23] 祁福鼎,肖婷婷,Dániel Kádár.到底是声明还是道歉——日语公开道歉的研究[J].外语与外语教学,2019(3):56-66+145.
[24] 司炳月,高松.外宣文本中英级差资源分布与翻译——以2019年政府工作报告双语文本为例[J].上海翻译,2019(5):14-20.
[25] 司显柱,庞玉厚.评价理论、态度系统与语篇翻译[J].中国外语,2018(1):96-102.
[26] 张先刚.评价理论对语篇翻译的启示[J].外语教学,2007(6):33-36.
[27] 王燕,柳福玲,张文静.中英社论语篇级差资源比较研究——以《人民日报》和《纽约时报》为例[J].新闻传播,2014(17):52-54.
[28] 王振华,马玉蕾.评价理论:魅力与困惑[J].外语教学,2007(6):19-23.
[29] 邢福义.小句中枢说[J].中国语文,1995(6):420-428.
[30] 杨丽婷.从CDA角度分析菲律宾总统关于香港人质事件的官方声明[J].牡丹江大学学报,2012(1):183-187.
[31] 张雪英.福喜食品安全事件官方声明的批评话语分析[J].景德镇学院学报,2016(1):66-70.

 点评

论文运用评价理论分析了国际知名品牌的8份道歉声明,总结评价理论中级差资源的分布情况,分析级差资源在道歉声明中构建权势和亲密关系的作用。研究发现,品牌道歉声明多运用增强语势和锐化来建构权势,但对亲密关系构建较少,甚至有时受到语境和搭配的影响产生反效果。论文选题新颖,语料分析详细,结论具有一定应用价值。

俄罗斯电影《八次初遇》局部会话结构分析

金 玄[*]

摘要：电影中的语料真实，语言环境具体，贴近日常交际生活。具体从语用学的角度来看，电影会话语料具有较强的语用教学意义，即对于外语学习者来说，具有重要参考价值。会话是人类最原始的语言使用形式，是话语的最基本、最重要的形式。语言结构的各个方面都是以运用中的会话为中心组织的。分析会话结构，可以揭示会话构成的规律，揭示自然会话的连贯性，并且有益于话语意义的准确理解。由于涉及研究的电影会话语料有限，本文不做关于整体结构的研究，研究重点主要在于局部会话结构上面。本文将俄罗斯电影《八次初遇》的会话语料为研究对象，参照萨克斯（H. Sacks）、谢格罗夫（E. A. Schegloff）等学者的会话分析框架，试考察电影中对话轮的构成与转换、相邻对、话语重叠以及插入序列等局部会话结构。

关键词：《八次初遇》；会话分析；话论；局部会话结构

引言

关于会话分析，最早是由萨克斯（H. Sacks）、谢格罗夫（E. A. Schegloff）、杰弗逊（G. Jefferson）等学者开展。20世纪60年代到70年代，学者们以会话和谈话为研究对象，从大量的真实语言资料中寻找反复出现的模型，从中探索自然语言的构成规律，目的是揭示话语的语用规律以及会话的组织结构，并探讨会话参与者是如何使用语言和非语言要素进行言语交际、理解会话生成的[1]。会话分

---

[*] 金玄：哈尔滨理工大学外国语学院2019级硕士研究生。

析是围绕生成言语行为语列及语列顺序问题进行的。会话结构研究分为两方面：一是对会话整体结构的研究，即把会话过程看作是一个整体，怎样开始、结束，过程如何；二是对会话局部结构的研究，即一次会话活动是由参加者接连交替的局部发言所构成的，不同发言者之间的联系，如何构成连贯的话语，它们如何进行更迭[2]。以下则主要是关于后者的研究。

1. 话轮的构成

会话的基本单位是话轮。说话人从发话到结束被看作是一个话轮，如果会话不断进行，一个话轮终止之后，另一个话轮又可以开始，直到整个会话结束。在 AB 双方参加的会话中，话轮交替呈"A – B – A – B – A – B"的形式。通过对电影《八次初遇》中出现的所有会话语料进行分析，会话参与者的话论大多是由简短句子构成。构成话轮的话语单位形式，大体上分为单句和复句两种，以下为关于该电影话轮构成与转换的典型实例分析，话轮由 T 代表。

    1.1   由词语、短语、句子构成的单句话轮

    例 1. **T1**：Режисёр：Казанцева, ты что, в этом году "Тэффи" получила?

          T2：Вера：Простите…

          T3：Режисёр：Тогда с какого постоянно опаздываешь…значит так ещё одно опоздание, и будешь в Челябе, на региональном новости в 4 утра читать!

          T4：Вера：Хорошо.

    例 2. **T1**：Подруга：Вера ты чего дома не ночевала?

          T2：Вера：Ночевала.

          T3：Подруга：Ты меня чего лечишь?

          T4：Вера：Не ночевала.

会话例 1 和会话例 2 分别是女主人公维拉与导演、与朋友的简短对话。两段对话中可以看出，会话例 1 的 T2、T4，会话例 2 的 T2 均为由词语构成的单句话轮。会话例 1 的 T1、T3，会话例 2 的 T1、T3 话轮是由一个句子构成的单句话轮，会话例 2 中的 T4 则是由短语构成的话轮。

    1.2   由复句构成的话轮

    例 3. **T1**：Никита：Не пешком же мы сюда пришли. Кто-то же нас привёз.

T2：Вера：Слушайте, я стараюсь забыть это и вас как страшный сон. Почему вы мне все время напоминаете.

例 4. **T1**：Никита：Вы точно рылись в моих штанах. Откуда вы знаете, что у меня ровно 1200?

　　　　T2：Вера：Да ни где я не рылись. По вашим физическим данным понято, что вы больше не унесёте.

从以上这两组女主人公维拉和男主人公尼基塔之间的对话中可以看出，例 3 和例 4 的所有话轮都是由一个复句构成的单句话轮。

2. 话轮转换

　　会话的一个特点是说话人的轮换(turning-taking)，即参与会话的人在整个会话过程中轮流说话。根据 Sacks 等学者在 1974 年对大量日常对话的研究中得出结论，认为话轮转换系统主要涵盖了以下几种交接规则：（1）在一个话轮中，说话人明确指定下一个，并且放弃话轮，那么被指定说话者说话时，就是话轮转换的位置。（2）在一个话轮中，说话人没有指定下一个说话者，在话轮结束时，可以是会话参与者自主选择说话，也可以是说话人继续说话。（3）在一个话轮中，说话人没有选定下一个说话者同时也没有结束话轮的情况下，另一个会话参与者争取话轮，则话轮转换[3]。

例 5. **T1**：Никита：Не ужели так сложно прийти вовремя?

　　　　T2：Вера：Может, для вас это просто, а деловому человеку приходится крутиться как белке в колесе.

　　　　T3：Никита：Значит я все правильно сделал.

　　　　T4：Вера：Что именно?

　　　　T5：Никита：Орешки заказал. Вы сейчас их погрызете, силы восстановите, и вперед, в колесо.

　　从上述对话中可看出，T1 是男主尼基塔对女主维拉的提问话轮，属于说话者自主选择下一位说话者，并且放弃了话轮，话轮转到女主维拉。T2 话轮作为女主维拉的陈述句话轮，在 T2 话轮结束时没有指定下一个说话者，视为自主放弃话轮。男主尼基塔的 T3 话轮为 T2 话轮的言语反馈，属于是在上一说话者没有指定下一说话者的情况下，会话参与者自主争取话轮，从而话轮位置发生转变。T3 话轮尾部,尼基塔没有明确指定下一个说话人并且停止说话,下一个说话者维拉以 T4 话轮接着完成会话。T4 话轮符合转换情况中的说话者明确选定下一个说话者,下一个说话者接着说话,维拉在 T4 话轮中明确选定尼基塔为下一个说话者,话轮转到 T5。在 T4 中维拉选完说话者后,话轮位置发生转变。

例 6. **T1**：Вера：До центра.

  T2：Таксист：800 рублей.

  T3：Вера：Мы чего, на самолёте, что ли полетим.

  T4：Никита：Шеф, я согласен.

  T5：Вера：Могли бы женщине и уступить.

以上为女主维拉、出租车司机、男主尼基塔三个会话参与者之间的一组对话。T1 话轮是女主维拉向出租车司机询问乘车费用时说出的。句式层面上,T1 是由短语构成陈述句,但是在语用意义上,T1 可被理解为"维拉向司机询问价钱"的一种问句。因此,T1 符合话轮转换的第一条规则,即说话者明确指定下一个说话者,司机作为下一个说话者接话。司机在 T2 话轮进行 T1 话轮的言语反馈后自主放弃话轮,T3 自主选择接话并且没有选择下一个说话者,T4、T5 均选择自主参与会话,并且都没有指定下一个说话者。

3. 相邻对及其他会话结构

相邻对(adjacency pair)是会话结构的一种基本组成单位,是指两个说话者各说一次话所构成的对子,萨克斯(H. Sacks)和谢格罗夫(E. A. Schegloff)提出相邻对应具有以下特征:相邻对是一前一后两个话轮,这两个话轮是相邻的由不同的说话者分别说出的,顺序分别是第一部分(始发语)和第二部分(应答语),特定的第一部分(始发语)要有特定的第二部分(应答语)相匹配[2]。

3.1 相邻对

相邻对包括"问候—问候""提问—回答""陈述—反应""邀请—接受/谢绝""抱怨—否认/道歉""道歉—否认/抚慰""请求—答应/拒绝""提议—接受/拒绝"等,其中"提问—回答"是最典型的语列。相邻对中第一配对部(提问、邀请、请求、提议等)规定了第二配对部的产生,具有刺激功能,而第二配对部(回答、接受/谢绝、答应/拒绝等)具有反应功能[4]。

① "问候—问候"相邻对

例 7. Доктор: Никита Андреевич, здравствуйте!

　　Никита: Здравствуйте!

例 8. Никита: Привет! солнышко.

　　Илона: Привет.

② "问—答"相邻对

例 9. Никита: Извините, не подскажете, где уход?

　　Охрана: Там, где и вход.

例 10. Никита: Сколько здесь сахар?

　　Вера: 5, как вы просили.

③ "陈述—反应"相邻对

例 11. Доктор: Ой смотрю, вечеринка удалось.

　　Никита: Удалось.

例 12. Олёша: Никитос, я с такой бомбой познакомился.

　　Никита: Очень интересно…

④ "抱怨—道歉"相邻对

例 13. Пациент: Доктор, мы уже час вас ждём!

　　Никита: Простите, сейчас секунду.

⑤ "请求—答应"相邻对

例 14. Пациент: Мы опять тортиков объелись, помогите нам пожалуйста.

　　Никита: Сейчас я пройду, секундочку.

⑥ "道歉—抚慰"相邻对

例 15. Никита: Извините, перепутал.

　　Пешеход: Ничего, бывает.

3.2 相邻对的繁化结构

相邻对作为会话的基本组成单位,具有其繁化结构。通过对俄罗斯电影《八次初遇》的会话语料进行分析,发现该会话语料中,大致包含话语重叠、插入语列、修正机制、后续话步等 4 种相邻对的繁化结构。以下内容是关于上述 4 类相邻对繁化形式的典型实例分析。

3.2.1 话语重叠

Шведова 曾对话语重叠做过深入的研究,并列出了多种重叠类型。这里分析的是作为相邻对繁化形式的话语重叠,专指该会话语料相邻对中重复第一配对部,并构成第二配对部的词语[4]。

例 16. Никита：Илоночка, честное слово, поверь, правда, заболтались с лёшей.

Илона：Заболтались… заболтались… врун! в глаза!

例 17. Илона：Смотри, какие красные!

Никита：Красные!

会话相邻对例 16 和例 17 是尼基塔和他的女友伊洛娜之间产生的,从两个例子中可以看出,两个接话者即相邻对的第二配对部均重复了第一配对部的词语:"Заболтались"和"Красные"。相邻对例 16 和例 17 均体现了增强话语表现力的话语重叠功能。例 16 的重叠表示对提问人的不悦和气愤情绪;例 17 中的重叠则包含"赞同上一说话者说话内容"的主观情态意义。两者都通过话语重叠增添了话语的表情色彩。

3.2.2 插入序列

在实际会话中,人们有时并不会直接回答提问,而是在"提问(Q)—回答(A)"会话格式中添加另一组问答话轮,即插入语列(insertion sequences),插入语列可以表现各种语用功能,可以充当应答语的条件或前提,可以是一个缓答/认证或证实的过程,也可以是一个疑惑/解惑的过程。

例 18. Никита：То есть вечер у тебя свободен？（Q^1）

Вера：А что тебя так интересуют мои планы на вечер？（Q^2）

Никита：Ничего, просто я тебя вечером никогда не видел.（A^2）

Вера：Ну к Терехову в бутик за платьем собиралась.（A^1）

会话中的问话人是尼基塔,听话人则是女主维拉。维拉在做出第一话轮的回答之前,为了进一步明确对方即尼基塔的问题,向他提了一个问题 Q^2,待尼基塔回答自己问题之后,维拉才应尼基塔的要求作出回答,既在第一话轮和第四话轮的始发语和应答语之间插入了缓答语列（Q^2、A^2）。

例 19. Никита：А где дом？（Q^1）

Милиционер：Чей？（Q^2）

Никита：Наш дом. Ну здесь дом стоял, куда он делся？（A^2）

Милиционер：А вот этот! Ну ещё утром тю-тю, Выставка закончилась, все разобрали и увезли.（A^1）

警官对于尼基塔提出的问题 Q^1 没有立即回答,而是向对方提出问题 Q^2,目的是为了进一步了解对方提问的内容。在尼基塔做出对 Q^2 的说明 A^2 之后,警官才对始发语 Q^1 作出回答。

3.2.3 修正机制

话语分析中的会话修正是言语交际过程中会话者意识到话语存在问题而不能有效实现交际意图后,会话双方经过互动协商而最终解决会话问题的过程[5]。修正可分为自我修正和对方修正,且具有以下特征(T1,T2,T3 分别表示第一、第二、第三话轮):

T1(包含可修正的话)= 第一次机会:主动自我修正

T1 和 T2 的过渡间隔= 第二次机会:主动自我修正

T2= 第三次机会:对方修正或促使对方在 T3 作自我修正

T3= 第四次机会:在 T2 对方的促使下作自我修正

需要指出,一些修正现象可以形成插入序列或嵌入序列,Jefferson(1972)把它称为旁侧序列。旁侧序列是在会话过程中听话人的一方认为说话人的话中有需要澄清或需要修正的地方,从而打断说话人正在说的话向他提出疑问而产生的,它是在说话人说完一句话后提出的[2]。如下例中的听话人是男主尼基塔,他发现伊洛娜的话 T1 中存在需要明确的地方,从而向伊洛娜提出疑问 T2 以促使对方做出修正,得出 T3,属于第四次机会的自我修正:

例 20. **T1**:Илона:Слушай, Соколов, скажи мне, только честно, я что на девочку похожа?

T2:Никита:В смысле?

T3:Илона:А ты почему не позвонил? Я между прочим, в олновалась всю ночь не спала.

3.2.4 后续话步

在"提问—回答""请求—拒绝/接受"等对话结构中常常出现后续话步(follow-up move)。后续话步的语用功能包括对对方提供的信息进行评述,或对对方提供信息的行为表示感谢,表明获知了所期待的信息,是一个信息反馈标志[6]。

例 21. **T1**:Доктор:Что-то передам?

T2:Вера:А можно, я ему записку оставлю? У вас нет бумажка?

T3:Доктор:Хорошо. Есть.

T4：Вера：Спасибо！

T5：Доктор：Я передам.

上述会话是值班医生和女主维拉之间产生的。T2 话轮中维拉问值班医生自己是否可以留言,并且要求了一张留言用的纸。医生在 T3 话轮中做出了肯定的回答。在这一相邻对中可以看出,T2 话轮的前一句可看作是请求话轮,后一句是提问话轮,T3 话轮的前一句是接受话轮,后一句则是回答话轮。随后出现后续话步 T4,既是维拉获知所期待的信息后对信息提供者表示感谢的话轮,发挥了交际的积极语用作用。

4. 结语

会话分析充分重视日常交际,试图在真实语言资料中寻找反复出现的特有交际模型,体现出其中蕴含的每一个细节,既解释会话参与者是如何使用语言和非语言要素进行言语交际、理解会话生成的问题[4]。此外,会话分析强调交际是具有其特定规律和组织性的。因此,它的研究一向是围绕生成言语序列结构以及话轮设计来进行的。本研究则是通过萨克斯(H.Sacks)和谢格罗夫(E.A.Schegloff)等学者提出的会话分析模式,对电影《八次初遇》中出现的局部会话结构进行考察,探讨了话轮发生转变以及扩展言语序列产生的原因。通过分析发现,电影《八次初遇》中会话参与者的话轮大多是由简短句子构成;构成话轮的话语单位形式,大体上是单句和复句两种;会话参与者的话轮是由大量的相邻对构成,其中包括"问候—问候""问—答""陈述—反应""抱怨—道歉""请求—答应""道歉—抚慰"六种基本形式的相邻对,也包括话语重叠、插入序列、修正机制、后续话步等相邻对的繁化形式。总而言之,本研究试图通过考察该影片中的话轮设计和序列结构来展现言语交际的组织性和连贯性。而揭示隐藏于自然会话中的组织性和连贯性指引人们准确理解话语含义。

参考文献

[1] 索振羽.语用学教程[M].北京:北京大学出版社,2000:184.

[2] 王宏军.会话结构的语用研究方法述评[J].天津外国语学院学报,2006(5):67-69.

[3] 卜凡凡.访谈节目《可凡倾听》局部会话结构分析[J].视听,2019(9):62.

[4] 徐翁宇.俄语会话分析[J].中国俄语教学,1997(2):21、22-23.
[5] 罗忠.网络会话修正机制探析[J].北京城市学院学报,2018(4):51.
[6] 王艺霏.听力语篇中会话结构的语用分析及其对英语教学的启示[J].文教资料,2018(30):228.

点评

论文以俄罗斯电影《八次初遇》的会话语料为研究对象,参照萨克斯(H. Sacks)、谢格罗夫(E. A. Schegloff)等学者的会话分析框架,从局部会话结构角度分析了该电影中话轮构成与转换,相邻对及其他会话结构等。文章语料真实,角度较新,结构基本完整,语言较为流畅。建议增加对文献研究的回顾和归纳,增强研究的理论深度,优化论证思路,并提供外国语料的汉语译文。

"战争与儿童"主题小说中"孩子"形象对比分析

——以《团的儿子》和《小兵张嘎》为例

孟立伟[*]

摘要：苏联作家卡塔耶夫的《团的儿子》与中国的《小兵张嘎》，两部作品作为中苏在20世纪战争文学中的代表作品，都选取了"孩子"形象作为主人公，通过叙事情节展现了孩子的革命成长，其对"孩子"形象的塑造既有共同点，又有差异性。论文借助对比分析法，将两部作品中的"孩子"形象的特点进行对比分析，挖掘作品背后的文化内涵。

关键词：战争；"孩子"形象；《团的儿子》；《小兵张嘎》

20世纪上半叶，"孤儿"和"浪浪儿"的形象大量出现在文学作品中，并与战争主题紧密相连，"战争与儿童"题材，有苏联作家卡塔耶夫的《团的儿子》、帕乌斯托夫斯基的《草原雷雨》、班台莱耶夫的《在小渡船上》、伏隆科娃的《从城里来的小姑娘》等等；在中国有徐光耀的《小兵张嘎》、管桦的《小英雄雨来》（原名《雨来没有死》）、吕庆庚的成名作《小砍刀的故事》（《小砍刀传奇》），延安时期陈模创作的革命传统纪实小说《少年英雄王二小》、李心田的《两个小八路》，著名儿童文学作家邱勋的少年英雄故事长篇小说《烽火三少年》、华山的中篇小说《鸡毛信》等等。这一主题创作的影响力可见一斑[1]。

在这一系列描写"战争与儿童"主题的小说中，《团的儿子》（«Сын полка»）和《小兵张嘎》可谓是最具代表性的作品。《团的儿子》是苏联作家卡塔耶夫的作品，讲述了苏联红军某炮兵连在一个深夜邂逅四处流浪的孤儿瓦尼亚的故事。瓦尼亚聪明倔强，深受骑兵战士们的喜爱。当时战争非常激烈，红军准备将瓦尼

---

[*] 孟立伟：哈尔滨理工大学外国语学院2019级硕士研究生。

亚送往后方,但瓦尼亚几次想方设法逃回,几经曲折加入了红军,并乔装打扮协助侦察兵深入敌军后方勘察地形,又带领红军找到敌军的司令部避弹所歼灭德兵,立下了赫赫战功,被战士们亲切地称为"团的儿子"。该作品深受人们喜爱,于1945年获得斯大林奖金,并入选"全球儿童文学典藏书系"。《小兵张嘎》由中国电影编剧、著名小说家徐光耀创作编写,出色地塑造了一个在战火中成长起来的爱国少年张嘎子的人物形象。小说曾被译成英、印、俄等多种文字,深受国内外的好评,荣获第二次全国少年儿童文艺创作一等奖,并入编《百年经典》系列丛书。

这两部小说虽诞生于不同国家作者的笔下,但无论是在主题选取或是形象塑造上都具有极大的相似点,本研究选取了"全球儿童文学典藏书系"发行的《团的儿子》以及国内《百年经典》系列作品《小兵张嘎》作为研究文本,从对比研究的角度入手,首先对"孩子"一词在俄、汉语中的词源及释义进行分析,在此基础上探寻两部作品中的"孩子"形象特点的异同,并尝试剖析其代表的深层文化内涵[2]。

1. 俄汉语中"дети/孩子"的词源及释义

词语的词源,即词语的内部形式保留着事物最原始的概念,指示了词汇语义进一步的发展方向,是词语产生各种可能的联想意义的基础,正是这些联想意义形成了不同的语义[3]。借助于词源及词典释义的分析可以更加全面准确地阐释"孩子"一词分别在俄罗斯和中国的民族文化中的反映。

1.1 俄语 дети 的词源及释义

《Этимологический словарь русского языка 俄语词源词典》(1986)指出,дети 一词最早可溯源至古斯拉夫词根 dětь,意为"动物的幼崽"。根据词源学家的观点,该词根带有"性别义素"(сема пола),词语"дева/少女"、"девочка/女孩"、"дочь/女儿"皆由此衍生而来。但词源学研究者也指出,这些词语在诞生初期,并不具备"年龄义素"(сема возраста)[4]。古斯拉夫语中的"дети"的含义只强调亲缘关系中哺育与被哺育的生理特征,对于年龄则没有明确的界定。

《Большая Советская энциклопедия 苏联大百科词典》(1957)中"дети"一词的定义被划分为两部分:第一部分指未成年人,这一阶段被认为是孩子的童年时期,且有明确的阶段特征:1岁以下为婴儿期,1至3岁为学龄前阶段,3至7岁为入托阶段,7至12岁为小学阶段,12至14岁为初中阶段,14至17岁为高中阶段；而 дети 的第二部分含义为"已满法定成年年龄的人",这一阶段的孩子被视为父母的法定继承人。可见在该词典中,其释义模糊了"性别义素",而在此基础上增加了"年龄义素",并具备划分明确的"阶段特征"。

在什维多娃和奥日科夫主编的《Толковый словарь Ожегова/奥日科夫俄语词典》(1990)中对 дети 的词典释义如下:1)单词"ребёнок"、"дитя"的复数形式,指少年时期之前处于幼年阶段的小男孩、小女孩们,例:Театр для детей/儿童剧院;Дети дошкольного возраста/学龄前儿童;2)指儿子、女儿,例:Мои д/我的孩子们;У него двое детей/他有两个孩子。此处的 дети 在具备表征主体年龄的功能同时,还突出了其承担的社会角色,义项2则可归入亲属词的范畴。可见 дети 一词的含义愈来愈宽泛。

而《Большой современный толковый словарь русского языка/现代俄语详解大辞典》(2012)中的 дети 释义则更加宽泛,共有4个义项:1)处于少年时期前的男孩或女孩。<口>动物幼崽;2)与父母相对而言的儿子或女儿,不受年龄限制;3)后代;年轻一辈;4)<转>涉世未深或行为举止天真的成年人。

通过对以上4部权威俄语词典中的 дети 释义进行分析,我们可以发现其释义主要包含以下几个核心语义特征:1)具有年龄表征含义,指未成年时期的小男孩、小女孩,或成年后的青年等。2)具有家庭属性,可指父母的儿子和(或)女儿及其他后代。3)具备社会属性,可以用来指称某一类特定的社会阶级,如年轻的一辈人。4)具备转义,如指涉世未深或举止天真的成年人。此外,通过按照词典编撰的时间顺序列举其词典释义,不仅揭示了 дети 的核心语义特征,还能体现出其释义随着时代变化而动态发展的过程。可以看出随着社会和语言文化的发展,俄语中 дети 一词的表意功能经历了由较为单一到日趋完善的发展过程。дети 不断被赋予了新的含义,并逐渐演变成了一类与人类社会生活紧密相关的名词。

1.2 汉语中"孩子"的词源及释义

在汉语中,词语"孩子"在战国初期首次出现,其记录在典籍《墨子·明鬼下》中:"播弃黎老,贼诛孩子",译为"抛弃老人,屠杀孩童",此时的"孩子"可以用来表征人的年龄,且与"老人"相对。

汉语中的"孩子"由两个汉字组成,即"孩"与"子"。汉字"孩"与"子"在古汉语和现代汉语的释义发生了一定的改变。在古字典《说文解字》中相应的解释为:汉字"孩"指婴儿或婴儿笑,释义略少;汉字"子"为象形文字,其词源释义为"婴儿、儿童、幼仔"。二字释义的共同点为都可表示人的幼年阶段,但年龄范围的界定尚不明晰。在《现代汉语词典(第7版)》中,汉字"孩"意为"孩童、儿童",可引申为"子女,男孩儿,孩提(指幼儿时期)"。汉字"子"的释义则要丰富得多,其详细注解如下:1)子为地支的第一位;2)古代兼指儿女;3)专指儿子;4)指女婿;5)子孙后代;6)谓国君的继承人,嗣君;7)泛指继承人,后继人;8)尽到做子女的义务和责任;9)卵;10)幼小的。可见在现代汉语中,"孩"的词典释义仍较为单一,而"子"的释义则丰富得多。二者均可用来表示"子女、人的幼小时期、后代",但"子"具有了表征年龄以外的功能,如古代用来记录时间的符号"地支子",说明其语义功能得到了补充和完善。

随着社会和语言文化的发展,二者各自具备的某些古时旧有的义项已失去了实用性,在现代汉语中,"孩子"一词逐渐演变成了固定表达的词语,意为"儿童、子女",即较幼小的未成年人(年龄比"幼年"小,通常为0—14岁之间)以及亲属关系词"儿子"和"女儿",通常与弱小无助的特征紧密相连,表义更加具体明晰。

1.3 俄语汉词源及释义对比

通过分别对俄语和汉语中"дети/孩子"的词源及词典释义进行分析,发现其核心概念基本相同,具有2个共有的语义特征:1)释义越来越具体且细化,指称范围明晰;2)在家庭层面和社会层面的语义被凸显出来,按照年龄范围加以界定,表示人的幼年时期。不同点为在俄语中,除基本义外,дети还具备丰富的象征含义,应视具体情况加以区分地理解,且俄语语义多于汉语语义,表意范围更加宽泛。

总之,无论是在俄罗斯还是在中国,"孩子"一词始终是社会关系中十分重要词汇,与社会的发展紧密相连。因此对"孩子"形象的异同点进行对比分析,有助于剖析其背后代表的丰富的深层文化内涵。

2. "孩子"形象的对比分析

《团的儿子》被誉为苏联版的《小兵张嘎》,可见两部作品在主题选取、人物塑造、情节展开等多方面具有相似之处,但因两国具体国情不同,所以细微之处也存在差别。下文将着重对两部作品中的"孩子"形象进行对比,试析其异同点。

2.1 相同点

2.1.1 身世悲惨——"孤儿"

战争使得无数无辜的孩子失去亲人,致使孤儿的数量的急剧增加,这是战争的不良后果之一。大部分旨在反映残酷战争的文学作品都关注到了这一现象,选取"孤儿"形象作为作品主人公,通过展现孩子在战争中的悲惨命运来反映现实的残酷,《团的儿子》和《小兵张嘎》就是这样两部作品。

在《团的儿子》中,作者主人公瓦尼亚(Ваня)第一次被部队发现时衣不蔽体、浑身是伤地睡在堑壕里,作者将当时的情景描述为"Картина, которую они увидели, была проста и вместе с тем ужасна/他们看到了一派简单却可怕的景象",可知瓦尼亚的处境多么糟糕,然而令人心痛的还有瓦尼亚的家境:Отец погиб на фронте в первые дни войны. Деревню заняли немцы. Мать не хотела отдавать корову. Мать убили. Бабка и маленькая сестрёнка померли с голоду. Остался один. Потом деревню спалили. Пошёл с сумкой собирать куски…/小男孩的父亲在战争初期死在前线上,村子被德国人占领了,母亲由于不想上交母牛而被打死,奶奶和妹妹饿死了,只剩他自己一个人。随后村子被烧毁了,他就开始带着袋子乞讨……至此,作者完全交代了瓦尼亚的孤儿身份,不仅令读者万分同情小主人公的遭遇,还直面战争的残酷无情,同时也为下文瓦尼亚参军的情节做了铺垫。

在作品《小兵张嘎》中,主人公张嘎的幸福家庭也因战争支离破碎,"老奶奶没有儿,儿子在事变那年给鬼子打死了;张嘎子没有妈,妈在他5岁那年病死了。老奶奶只有这个孙子,孙子也只有这个老奶奶"。嘎子只与奶奶相依为命,然而好景不长,在一次敌人的大扫荡中,奶奶为了掩护在家养伤的八路军战士,不幸牺牲,年仅13岁的张嘎也成了孤儿。至此小主人公张嘎也成了战火年代中万千悲苦儿童命运的缩影。

因此,两部作品在"孩子"形象塑造方面的共同点之一是主人公同为"孤儿"。两个小主人公出身相同、年纪相仿(瓦尼亚12岁,张嘎13岁)、家庭背景相似,且同因战争成为"孤儿",都是代表千万不幸儿童的典型人物。战争改变了他们的生活,敌人的铁蹄践踏了他们年幼的幸福时光,张嘎失去了相依为命的奶奶,瓦尼亚也失去了父母和妹妹,独自流浪。这种身份设定既反映了当时的社会现实,也可引起读者的强烈悲愤共鸣。

2.1.2 优秀的个人品质

两部作品对"孩子"形象刻画的相同之处还在于瓦尼亚和张嘎身上具备一

系列相同的优秀个人品质,诸如聪明、勇敢、极强的荣誉感等。在战火纷飞的年代,虽没有家人的呵护和引导,但两位小主人公仍然向着正义和善良努力地成长。瓦尼亚和张嘎所具有的这些金子般的品质与无情的战争形成了鲜明的对比,使得"孩子"形象更加丰满,更具吸引力。

首先,瓦尼亚和张嘎在后期都成长为优秀的侦察员,这得益于他们都具有聪明灵活的头脑以及敏锐的洞察力。在《团的儿子》中,司令起初并不同意将瓦尼亚留在部队,而是决定将其送到后方,而瓦尼亚凭借着聪明的头脑以及出色的侦查天赋两次成功逃过了老侦察员比杰卡的看守,逃回了部队。老侦察员比杰卡作战经验丰富,从未有俘房从他手下脱逃,而小小的瓦尼亚成功避开了他的看守,这不禁令比杰卡赞叹不已:"Ах, *хитрый*! Ну же, я вам скажу, и лисица! Ничего не скажешь — силён! / 啊,真狡猾呀! 我告诉你,真是个小狐狸! 毫无疑问——真厉害!"而后当瓦尼亚第一次正式加入作战时,也正是发挥了自己的聪明才智才能成功从敌人手中逃脱。此外,文中还多次出现夸赞瓦尼亚机智聪明的词句,如"какой *шустрый*! / 多么聪明伶俐""*бойко* / 机智的""Уж больно *смышлёный* паренёк, Прирождённый разведчик / 那个令人心痛的机灵的小伙子是个天生的侦察兵"等,都从侧面表现了瓦尼亚的聪明机智。

而在作品《小兵张嘎》中,作者在开篇第一句便交代了张嘎聪明伶俐的性格特点:"白洋淀边一个小水庄子里,有个聪明伶俐的孩子,叫张嘎。"而随着下文故事情节的发展,同样展现了张嘎的侦查天赋。年纪虽小,但从未误过一次正事,"有时蹲在直通据点的路口,有时爬上叶茂枝稠的大树,有时隐在雾罩露垂的青稞中,有时掩在鸦寞雀静的房角下,那一对小眼睛,总是瞪得圆圆的,滴溜溜一直转到天黑。每次发现敌情,都有他个清清楚楚的报告儿,没有一回误过事情"。可见张嘎年纪轻轻,但洞察力极强,难怪队长夸赞他:"这聪明的小脑袋瓜,是个天生的侦察员胚子。"

其次,瓦尼亚和张嘎都具备勇敢无畏的精神。在战争年代,最令人钦佩的当属勇敢无畏、无惧危险的牺牲精神。而在两部作品中,这种宝贵精神也得到了充分彰显,主人公瓦尼亚和张嘎虽年纪尚轻,但却从未表现出半点贪生怕死、懦弱无能。在作品《团的儿子》中,叶戈罗夫中士考虑到瓦尼亚的安全,反对他留在部队,坚持派人将他送到后方,在半路上瓦尼亚跳车逃回了部队,坚持要参军打仗,这时负责护送瓦尼亚的上等兵比杰卡不禁感叹道:"*Смелый*, чертёнок! *Ничего не боится*. Настоящий солдат! / 小鬼头,真是勇敢! 无所畏惧,是个真正的战士!"而当部队需要侦查前方敌人的情况时,瓦尼亚又主动要求为侦察兵带路,即使战士们如何强调这是一件十分危险的事,瓦尼亚也不惧怕,"Ваня очень просился. Он так жалобно повторял: Дяденька, возьмите меня с собой! Ну что вам стоит? …/这是瓦尼亚自己要求的。他苦苦哀求:"叔叔,带上我吧!你们犹豫什么呢?"最后瓦尼亚终于如愿加入了侦查队伍,并出色完成了任务。

在作品《小兵张嘎》中,张嘎也是一个勇敢坚决的孩子。当奶奶不幸牺牲后,在张嘎家养伤的八路军战士钟叔叮嘱张嘎要成为一个勇敢的人,张嘎十分坚决地回应了钟叔。"你要当得起勇敢、坚决的小英雄啊!""那是当然!""小嘎子也听见了自己的回答,一股热血,陡地从心里涌腾起来。"而当张嘎见到疑似特务出现时,即使手里只有一把假手枪也毫不犹豫地冲了出去,"说时迟,那时快,他把草筐一甩,蹿过去大吼一声道:'不许动!举起手来!打死你狗汉奸!……'吼着,伸手就去那小子腰里拔枪。"可见当时小张嘎完全将个人安危置身事外,令读者在感叹其勇敢的同时不禁捏了一把冷汗。而当组织需要时,张嘎则表现出了同瓦尼亚一样的坚决和勇敢,面对其他同志的担心,"小嘎子又开口了:'流血就流血呗!老钟叔给鬼子抓了去,还喊共产党万岁呢!'"可见在两位作者笔下,张嘎与瓦尼亚两位小主人公同为不惧牺牲、勇敢无畏的小英雄。

再次,两位小英雄都具有极强的荣誉感。他们对待上级下达的任务总是格外认真,渴望得到肯定,并不断向着成为一名合格的战士的目标努力。在《团的儿子》中,当瓦尼亚第一次射出一枚炮弹时,他深深地为自己感到骄傲,"И Ваня стал *гордиться* первым орудием так же сильно, как он раньше *гордился* командой разведчиков. И это яснее всего показывало, что у него душа настоящего солдата. Ибо какой же хороший солдат не *гордится* своим подразделением! /瓦尼亚开始深深地感到自己以第一炮为荣,就像他之前以侦察兵首长为傲一样。这一切都清楚地表明了瓦尼亚已经拥有了颗真正的战士的心。要知道,哪名好战士不是以自己所在部队为骄傲的呢?"这种荣誉感始终激励着瓦尼亚,帮他一次又一次获得成长。

而在《小兵张嘎》中,张嘎同样以加入部队为荣,"特别使小嘎子称心满意的,是他真的当了小侦察员!每到一个宿营地,部队刚一隐蔽好,他就先去村边上放哨巡风了。小小一个新战士,居然成了保障部队安全的眼睛。这使他在同志们面前,够多么显赫呀!这可实在是一件了不起的光荣!"而当后来张嘎蜕变成了一名优秀战士并获得荣誉时,张嘎却显得格外害羞,"他忸怩地回过头去,却见区队长和石政委都站在台上,也朝他微笑着,他猛然心中一动,忙舒开两臂,朝着他们热烈地鼓起掌来,于是台上台下更加暴风雨似地鼓成了一片"。这种质朴羞涩的"忸怩"更加衬托出了张嘎内心的紧张和激动,于是他"猛然"心中一动,享受着这当之无愧的荣耀。正是这种极强的荣誉感,时时鞭策着两位小主人公不断向前。

2.1.3 收获成长

虽然瓦尼亚和张嘎都具有悲惨的身世,但他们正式加入革命组织开始,两个小主人公的命运就发生了转折。瓦尼亚先是充当侦察兵,带着同志们成功潜入敌人阵地,虽不幸落入敌手,但誓死没有透露半份情报,被救出后调到了炮兵连正式加入战斗,赢得了战争的最终胜利。当战争结束后,瓦尼亚被送往苏沃洛夫军事学校接受教育。在这一系列过程中,瓦尼亚从一个流浪的"孤儿"成为一名坚强勇敢的革命小英雄。而张嘎则同样在八路军队伍中收获了成长。他怀着为奶奶报仇的心愿加入队伍,但却在与同志的相处中一次次感受到了革命党人的铁骨真情,他们一起开会、宣传、打游击、做侦查……张嘎从一个生性顽劣的孩子成长为遵守铁纪的军人,从对党不了解、不熟悉到正式成为一名共产党员,张嘎从一个莽撞少年成长为一名革命后备军战士,彻底完成了军事觉悟的质变。

2.2 不同点

2.2.1 "孩子"形象所反映的国情不同

优秀的文学作品多是成功地塑造了典型人物形象,反映了一定历史时期社会生活的本质或某些方面的本质[5]。在《团的儿子》中,瓦尼亚作为流浪儿,是部队在清理战场时的意外发现。而通过进一步了解可知,"Три года жил Ваня, как бродячая собака, без дома, без семьи/瓦尼亚像流浪狗一样过了三年,没有住处,没有亲人"。他始终在独自流浪,没有家人,也碰不到"自己人"。

而在《小兵张嘎》中,"当时正是抗日战争最残酷的 1943 年,日本鬼子对冀中人民发动的'五一'大扫荡,过去也就是一年光景,人们已从'无村不戴孝,户户闻哭声'的年月,转入'出门必过路,夜观岗楼灯'的阶段了。各村庄已大体编就保甲,向据点一天一度地派着'联络员'……"张嘎家正是共产党联络员交换情报的地点之一,张嘎的奶奶正是为了掩护联络员"钟叔"不幸牺牲,张嘎也从未中断同游击队的联系。这充分体现了中国抗战时期共产党人与万千群众的密切联系,正是共产党人始终团结人民群众、依靠人民群众、发展人民群众,才为战争的最终胜利创造了有利条件。

因此瓦尼亚加入作战队伍具有很强的随机性和偶然性,而张嘎进入游击队则是一种必然。这种偶然和必然的差别也正是不同国情的具体体现。

2.2.2 "少年英雄"形象具有差异

瓦尼亚和张嘎后期虽都成长为令人敬佩的"少年英雄",但其形象塑造仍有不同之处。瓦尼亚是沉稳的"小大人",有着本不该属于这个年纪的老成和压抑。瓦尼亚深知,"А первое правило настоящего разведчика — лучше знать да молчать, чем знать да болтать/作为一个真正的侦察兵,第一条规则就是——知道什么时候沉默,什么时候闲谈"。所以纵使他心中有无数疑问,沉甸甸的规矩依旧压抑着孩子的天性,"Ване хотелось расспросить Ковалёва о многом … Но воинская дисциплина не позволяла ему первому начинать разговор со старшим/瓦尼亚有很多问题想仔细询问科瓦列夫……但是军纪不允许他首先就开始同老兵这样交谈"。可见风餐露宿、四处漂泊的生活使得瓦尼亚看惯了世间冷暖,属于孩童的天真顽皮的天性早已消失不见,这种趋向完美的"少年英雄"形象的塑造使得读者在感叹其听话乖巧的同时,还能强烈感受到残酷的生存环境对于孩子身心的莫大伤害,从而更多的是心疼和怜惜。

而相比之下,嘎子则是不完美的"少年英雄",他天性顽皮,当他好奇开会内容时,则会忍不住偷听,情急之下还破门而入,"他静悄悄来到那个窗根,把窗纸舔了个窟窿,瞄着眼一瞧,喝,有六七个人哩:老罗叔、大个李、通讯员杨小根,以及几个平常顶受人敬重的人。就听大个李隆隆地响着膛音儿说:'……这一次战斗必然打得大,鬼子也一定多。我保证带领我的副射手,把两挺机关枪使用好,掩护同志们顺利地冲上去,好好收拾一下他狗日的!'"'噢,'小嘎子明白了,'他们在这儿也讨论打仗呢!'心里不由得有些上火,便闯闯几步,一边往里闯,一边喊叫道:'好哇!你们在这儿商量打仗,也不叫我一声儿!'"偷听开会和硬闯会议室的行为显然违反了军中纪律,但正是一份莽撞和冲动却将张嘎对革命事业的认真展现得淋漓尽致。同时,对于张嘎缺点的描写将孩童的天真可爱展现得淋漓尽致,使得张嘎这一人物形象更加丰满,令"孩子"形象更加贴近生活,深入人心。

3. 结语

《团的儿子》和《小兵张嘎》两部作品作为战争主题文学的代表作,都通过刻画"孩子"形象、讲述孩子的革命成长故事,塑造了永不磨灭的抗战小英雄形象。两部作品在"孩子"形象的塑造方面既存在相似之处,也具备差异。

相同之处具体表现在以下三点:

1)瓦尼亚和张嘎同为年纪相仿、命运相似的"孤儿";

2)虽经历了悲惨的童年,但在瓦尼亚和张嘎身上仍可以发现一系列相似的金子般的品质,如聪明机智、勇敢无畏、极具荣誉感等,这些品质在战争年代显得尤为可贵;

3)二人都因某种巧合进入部队,并实现了命运的转折。部队生活无异于赋予了二人"重生",他们在部队中完成了各自的转变,收获了成长,蜕变成了合格的栋梁之才。

但其形象塑造也存在差异。《团的儿子》更侧重于塑造完美的少年英雄形象,以此来反映战争带给孩子们心理上的迫害与压抑;而《小兵张嘎》则更倾向于塑造不完美的英雄形象,通过在前期展现张嘎所具有的孩子顽皮淘气的天性,与后期更加成熟稳重的张嘎形成对比,来展现张嘎在部队中的成长蜕变。同时,两个"孩子"形象又代表了两个国家的特定时期的社会背景。

《团的儿子》和《小兵张嘎》作为中苏反映20世纪上半叶战争主题儿童文学的代表作,其塑造的"孩子"形象均为时代的产物,是万千遭受战争迫害但仍努力成长的孩子们的缩影。通过对比两部作品中"孩子"形象的异同,更加亲近地感知两个国家的不同历史现实,加深文化的理解。

参考文献

[1] 牟桑进.浅谈文学语言的艺术特征及其社会属性[J].安徽文学(下半月),2010(11):74-75.

[2] 韦苇.俄罗斯儿童文学论谭[M].长沙:湖南少年儿童出版社,2015:117.

[3] 李卓君.语言文化学视角下的俄语观念词"труд"研究[D].上海外国语大学,2017.

[4] Калюжкая И.А, Концепт «Детство» в немецкой и русской лингвокультурах: дис, канд, филол, наук[D]. Волгоград, 2007.

[5] 黄加强.浅谈文学作品中人物形象的分析[J].新教育时代电子杂志(教师版),2015(19):351.

 **点评**

论文以"战争与儿童"为主题,着眼特定历史背景下的儿童文学作品,选取《团的儿子》和《小兵张嘎》这两部中苏在20世纪战争文学中的代表作品,借助对比分析法探讨两部作品中的"孩子"形象的特点,以挖掘作品背后的文化内涵,从而加深对两国历史文化的理解。论文主题明确,思路清晰,结构合理。建议补充文献综述,增强案例分析的相关度和学术性,形成有较高价值的研究结论。

The Effects of Word Exposure Frequency and Second Language Proficiency on Second Language Incidental Vocabulary Learning in the High Constraint Context

Qu Huiyu[*]

Abstract: Two research questions were posed as follows: in the high constraint context, 1) does different word exposure frequency affect the effects of IVL? 2) do different levels of learners' second language proficiency influence the effects of IVL? To address these two questions, this study designed a mixed experiment using E-prime 2.0. The participants of the current study were 103 students of a university in Shanghai. In the experiment, participants were instructed to first read some high constraint sentences presented on the screen and then complete the semantic relatedness judgment task. Their accuracy and response time of the judgment task were recorded, collected and analyzed to probe into the effectiveness and efficiency of IVL. A few important findings were generated. Firstly, it was uncovered that both word exposure frequency and second language proficiency had significant influence on the effects of IVL in the high constraint sentence context. Secondly, it was found that three encounters with new words was ideal and sufficient for the achievement of IVL in the high constraint context. To be more specific, three times of word exposure were both conducive for low proficiency learners to enhance the effectiveness of IVL and favorable for high

---

[*] Qu Huiyu: School of Foreign Languages, Tongji University, master's degree cadidate of the class of 2019.

proficiency learners to improve IVL efficiency.

Keywords: Second language incidental vocabulary learning; word exposure frequency; second language proficiency; the high constraint sentence context

1. Introduction

Vocabulary acquisition research has traditionally focused entirely on the learning process of vocabulary itself (Sang, 2015). It was not until the 1980s that some researchers began to realize that most vocabulary is learned incidentally except for the first few thousand common words which are intentionally acquired (Nagy, Herman & Anderson, 1985). This way of vocabulary acquisition is conceptualized as incidental vocabulary learning (IVL) or incidental vocabulary acquisition (IVA). In the past few years, the significance of IVL has been largely confirmed by numerous scholars in the field of SLA (Elley, 1989; Newton, 1995; Paribakht & Wesche, 1999; Laufer & Hulstijn, 2001; Pulido, 2003). Since numerous scholars agree that great amounts of reading can effectively enlarge the vocabulary (Hulstijn, 2001), the research of IVL in reading accounts for a large proportion in the IVL research field, according to one survey done by Gai (2003). IVL in reading refers to the process that learners inadvertently acquire new words while performing some reading tasks. In this process, reading comprehension is the main activity while vocabulary acquisition is not the object of intentional learning but only a "by-product" (Laufer & Hulstijn, 2001). To explore the effective and efficient way of IVL, researches have collectively probed into various factors affecting IVL in reading (Mason & Krashen, 2004), including the learner's second language (L2) proficiency levels, the annotation types, the reading purposes, etc.

However, a number of factors remain unresolved in the field of IVL (Deng, 2017). One of the key unsettled issues is the number of word exposures for successful vocabulary acquisition (Huckin & Coady, 1999). Many researchers have evidenced that only sufficient exposures to the word can foster IVL (Saragi,

Nation, Meister, 1978; Herman, Anderson, Pearson, Nagy, 1987; Rott, 1999; Waring & Takaki, 2003; Webb, 2007), but an empirical solution to the specific number of word exposures has yet to be provided. The current study acknowledges the absent consideration of contexts as the main hindrance to the discussion about word exposure frequency. Previous studies which researched on the word exposure frequency took the initiative applying different types of reading materials, including stories, novels and sentences; nonetheless these attempts failed to evaluate the degree of contextual constraints, which may be the cause of the unresolved issue. It has been found from both first language (L1) and L2 research that the degree of sentence contextual constraints can influence the effects of IVL (Borovsky, Kutas & Elman, 2010). However, few studies have captured a glimpse of the word exposure frequency in the context. Previous research also paid attention to the influence of learners' L2 proficiency on the effects of IVL (Pulido, 2003; Shao, 2006; Wang, 2016), but little research has explained how word exposure frequency and learners' L2 levels interact in shaping IVL in a high or low constraint context.

In the light of the above-mentioned problems, it is necessary to take the factor of contextual constraints into account when talking about the effective or sufficient word exposure frequency. Therefore, the current study aimed to explore the effects of word exposure frequency on IVL in the high constraint sentence context. Additionally, the learner's L2 proficiency was covariated in the study to test the interaction and individual effect exerting upon IVL.

2. Research Methodology

2.1 Participants

One hundred and three participants took part in this experiment voluntarily. All of them were Chinese college students who learn English as a foreign language. The participants were divided into two groups according to their English proficiency which was evaluated by their College English Test (CET) levels. According to Syllabus for College English Test (2016), the CET is used to make a scientific measurement of Chinese undergraduate students' comprehensive English ability. Fifty-one participants who passed CET Band 6 were grouped into the high proficiency English learners and the other fifty-two participants who passed CET Band 4 but failed CET Band 6 were sorted into the low proficiency group.

2.2 Experiment Design

This study adopted a mixed experimental design, with English proficiency (high, low) as a between-subject factor and the number of sentences containing pseudo-words (one, two, three, or four) as a within-subject factor. The dependent variables were participants' response time and accuracy of the semantic relatedness judgment task after sentence reading. Operationally, the effects of IVL were examined by participants' performance on the designed semantic relatedness judgment task. To be more specific, participants' accuracy and response time of the semantic relatedness judgment task were recorded and analyzed to evaluate the effects of IVL.

2.3 Materials

2.3.1 Pseudo-words and semantically related/unrelated words

The discussion of pseudo-words and semantically related/unrelated words applied in this study is inseparable from the depiction of the corresponding real words. The current study randomly selected 30 real words from the word list provided by the research of Ma et al. (2019) which discussed the effects of proficiency levels and sentence constraints on L2 IVL. Ma et al. chose 120 high-frequency concrete nouns whose word frequency, concreteness and familiarity had all been rated by scientific databases or volunteers with the same background as the participants. After the selection of 30 real words, the corresponding pseudo-words and semantically related/unrelated words, which were also adopted from Ma et al.'s study, were matched with the selected real words. After carefully matching, each real word owned one pseudo-word and one semantically related/unrelated word. For instance, for the real word "movie", its corresponding pseudo-word was "speath" and its semantically related word was "film".

2.3.2 Sentences

Four high constraint sentences were made up for each real word which always appeared at the end of the sentence. When a sentence is highly constrained, it is effortless to deduce the meaning of the vocabulary at the end of the sentence in the light of the sentence meaning. For instance, for the word "movie", one of the high constraint sentences can be "What about going to the cinema to see a movie?". In order to rate the constraint of the 120 constructed sentences, 10 college students with the same background as the participants were invited to have a cloze test. In this cloze test, they were asked to complete the 120 sentences with the last words removed. The result signified that for each sentence, the percentage of times that participants could fill in the right word was over 86.67%, which convincingly verified the high constraints of the 120 designed sentences. The above 10 participants were also invited to rate the difficulty degree of these sentences using a 5 - point scale (1 = very easy, 5 = very difficult) after they completed the cloze test. The score was 1.47, which ensured that the participants of this study can readily understand all these sentences. Finally, the real words in these sentences were all replaced by their corresponding pseudo-words to form a new 120 - sentence group called experimental sentences.

Then, the 120 experimental sentences were split into four sentence lists, each of which contained one of four conditions (30, 60, 90, or 120 sentences, representing the pseudo-words would repeat 1, 2, 3, or 4 times). Each participant would be required to read only one of the four sentence lists.

2.4 Procedure

The experimental procedure was encoded by using E-prime software 2.0. The whole experiment was conducted in a quiet environment and participants were provided with timely instructions. This study applied a whole sentence presentation paradigm and participants were asked to read the sentence present on the screen carefully and to understand the meaning of the sentence. Experimental sentences were presented to participants in a random order. Participants could move on to the next sentence at any moment by pressing the space bar, which enabled participants themselves to control their reading speed. Sentences ending with the same pseudo-word were regarded as one group, which may contain 1, 2, 3, or 4 sentences. After each group of sentences came a semantic relatedness judgment task. With reference to previous studies (Chen, Zhang & Ma, 2019), a question mark prompt ("?") would appear on the screen for 2000 ms before the semantic relatedness judgment task. According to the instructions, participants were asked to judge whether the pair of words presented on the screen was semantically related or not. If participants agreed that the two words were semantically related, they would be instructed to press "F" for "Yes", otherwise they would press "J" for "No". Both the accuracy and the response time of the semantic relatedness judgment task were recorded.

To confirm that all participants had understood the experimental requirements correctly, participants were asked about their understanding of the term "semantic relatedness" after the whole procedure finishes.

3. Results and Discussion

3.1 Multivariate Analysis of Variance

Multivariate analysis of variance (MANOVA) was conducted through Statistic Package for Social Science (SPSS) 23.0. The results of multivariate tests were shown in Table 1. In this study, the outliers shown in the Box-plots were all removed and not included in the results of this study.

Table 1 Multivariate Tests

Effect		Value	F	Sig.
Proficiency	Wilks' Lamba	.91	4.38	.016
Frequency	Wilks' Lamba	.78	3.62	.002
Proficiency * Frequency	Wilks' Lamba	.89	2.06	.060

As Table 1 shows, the significance value of L2 proficiency was 0.016 and that of word exposure frequency was 0.002, both of which were lower than 0.05. The significance value of the interaction of L2 proficiency and word exposure frequency was 0.060 ($p>0.05$). The results indicated that both L2 proficiency and word exposure frequency significantly affected the outcome of the semantic relatedness judgment task, and their interaction appeared to be marginally significant. In other words, there seemed to be weak interactive effects between learners' L2 proficiency and word exposure frequency, but each of them had a crucial influence on the effects of IVL independently. Therefore, the main effects of both two variables should be inspected.

Table 2 Tests of Between-Subjects Effects

Source	Dependent Variable	Type III Sum of Squares	Mean Square	F	Sig.
Proficiency	Accuracy	481.64	481.64	7.42	.008
	Response time	8 510 492.08	8 510 492.08	3.52	.064
Frequency	Accuracy	893.69	297.90	4.59	.005
	Response time	21 781 346.13	7 260 448.71	3.01	.035

Table 2 above illustrates the results of tests of between-subjects effects. As Table 2 displays, for the variable learners' L2 proficiency, the significance value of accuracy was 0.008 ($p<0.05$) and that of response time was 0.064 ($p>0.05$). The results indicated that different levels of learners' proficiency led to significantly different results of accuracy and caused marginally significant difference in response time. For the variable word exposure frequency, the significance value of accuracy was 0.005 and that of response time was 0.035, both lower than 0.05, indicating that different frequency of word exposure had a considerable impact on both accuracy and response time. Since the pseudo-word exposure frequency varied from one time to four times, post hoc multiple comparisons were employed to locate the difference. Table 3 shows the results of post hoc multiple comparisons using Tukey HSD post-hoc procedure.

Table 3 Post Hoc Multiple Comparisons

Tukey HSD

Dependent Variable	(I) Frequency	(J) Frequency	Mean Difference (I−J)	Sig.
Accuracy	One time	Two times	−6.25	.059
		Three times	−7.73*	.006
		Four times	−8.97*	.001
	Two times	One time	6.25	.059
		Three times	−1.48	.931
		Four times	−2.71	.698
	Three times	One time	7.73*	.006
		Two times	1.48	.931
		Four times	−1.23	.951
	Four times	One time	8.97*	.001
		Two times	2.72	.698
		Three times	1.23	.951
Response time	One time	Two times	1 574.18*	.007
		Three times	886.91	.190
		Four times	433.93	.769
	Two times	One time	−1 574.18*	.007
		Three times	−687.27	.470
		Four times	−1 140.25	.092
	Three times	One time	−886.91	.190
		Two times	687.27	.470
		Four times	−452.98	.745

续表

Dependent Variable	(I) Frequency	(J) Frequency	Mean Difference (I−J)	Sig.
Response time	Four times	One time	−433.93	.769
		Two times	1 140.25	.092
		Three times	452.98	.745

The results of post hoc multiple comparisons (Table 3) indicated that for accuracy, the significant difference among word exposure frequency existed between "One time" and "Three times" as well as between "One time" and "Four times". The significance value of "One time" with "Three times" was 0.006, and 0.001 with "Four times", both lower than 0.05, which showed that the difference between "One time" and other two exposure frequency were statistically significant. The significance values of other groups of comparison were all higher than 0.05, indicating no significant difference existed under these conditions. Similarly, for response time, the difference between "One time" and "Two times" was significant ($p=0.007$, <0.05) and there were no other significant differences.

In conclusion, MANOVA displayed that both learners' L2 proficiency and the frequency of pseudo-word exposure had significant effects on the participants' performance on the semantic relatedness judgment task, i.e. the effects of IVL, although the degree of significant effects varied among accuracy and response time.

3.2 One-way Analysis of Variance

The one-way analysis of variance (ANOVA) was employed to provide further details about the influence of different L2 proficiency and of different word exposure frequency.

Table 4　ANOVA of Different L2 Proficiency

			F	Sig.
L1 vs H1	Between Groups	Accuracy	6.58	.017
		Response time	2.73	.112

续表

			F	Sig.
L2 vs H2	Between Groups	Accuracy	1.86	.189
		Response time	.01	.913
L3 vs H3	Between Groups	Accuracy	.38	.545
		Response time	5.81	.024
L4 vs H4	Between Groups	Accuracy	3.20	.088
		Response time	.59	.450

Notes: L/H represents the low or high proficiency level of participants; the numbers 1 to 4 refer to the different word exposure frequency.

Table 4 illustrates the influence of different levels of L2 proficiency on participants' performance. For accuracy, the significance value of "L1 vs H1" was 0.017, lower than 0.05, while the significance values of other three conditions were all higher than 0.05. The results indicated that in terms of accuracy, different levels of L2 proficiency had significantly different effects only when participants were exposed to the pseudo words once. For response time, the significance value of "L3 vs H3" was 0.024 ($p<0.05$) and those of other three conditions were higher than 0.05, indicating that there existed significant difference between low and high proficiency when participants were exposed to the pseudo-words three times.

Table 5 ANOVA of Different Word Exposure Frequency

			F	Sig.
Low Proficiency	Between Groups	Accuracy	4.47	.008
		Response time	1.54	.219
High Proficiency	Between Groups	Accuracy	1.23	.309
		Response time	5.13	.004

Table 5 displays the influence of word exposure frequency on the performance of participants of the same L2 level. For the group of low proficiency, the significance value of accuracy was 0.008 ($p<0.05$) and of response time was 0.219 ($p>0.05$). For the group of high proficiency, the significance value of accuracy was 0.309 ($p>0.05$) and of response time was 0.004 ($p<0.05$). Therefore, there was significant difference among different word exposure frequency for the low proficiency group from the perspective of accuracy. Similarly, for the high proficiency group, significant difference also existed among different frequency of word exposure from the response time perspective. A Bonferroni post-hoc procedure was employed to locate the difference among different groups. Table 6 and Table 7 are the results of multiple comparisons of low and high proficiency group respectively.

Table 6 Multiple Comparisons of Low Proficiency Group

	(I) Frequency	(J) Frequency	Mean Difference (I−J)	Sig.
Accuracy	One time	Two times	−5.11	1.000
		Three times	−10.50*	.021
		Four times	−10.50*	.021
	Two times	One time	5.11	1.000
		Three times	−5.39	1.000
		Four times	−5.39	1.000
	Three times	One time	10.50*	.021
		Two times	5.39	1.000
		Four times	.00	1.000
	Four times	One time	10.50*	.021
		Two times	5.39	1.000
		Three times	.00	1.000

As Table 6 shows, for the accuracy of the low proficiency group, the significance values of "One time" with "Three times" and with "Four times" were both 0.021, lower than 0.05. The significance values of other groups of comparison were all higher than 0.05. The above results indicated that from the accuracy perspective, the significant difference among word exposure frequency for the low proficiency group came from the differences between "One time" and "Three times" as well as between "One time" and "Four times".

Table 7 Multiple Comparisons of High Proficiency Group

	(I) Frequency	(J) Frequency	Mean Difference (I − J)	Sig.
Response Time	One time	Two times	938.70	.357
		Three times	1 186.95	.122
		Four times	−443.31	1.000
	Two times	One time	−938.70	.357
		Three times	248.25	1.000
		Four times	−1 382.02*	.032
	Three times	One time	−1 186.95	.122
		Two times	−248.25	1.000
		Four times	−1 630.27*	.009
	Four times	One time	443.31	1.000
		Two times	1 382.02*	.032
		Three times	1 630.27*	.009

Similar to Table 6, Table 7 reveals that the significant difference among word exposure frequency for the high proficiency group derived from the differences between "Two times" and "Four times" and between "Three times" and "Four times". The significance values of these two pairs were respectively 0.032

and 0.009, both of which were lower than 0.05. In other words, for the high proficiency group, the response time would be markedly different when participants were exposed to the pseudo-words two times or three times compared with the condition when they were exposed to the words four times.

3.3 Discussion

From the above data analysis, findings need to be further explicated.

First of all, the results of multivariate tests (Table 1) suggest that both two factors involved in the current study, learner's L2 proficiency and word exposure frequency, have significant impacts on the effects of IVL in the high constraint sentence context. Furthermore, little interaction was found between two factors. In other words, there may be no joint and interconnected contributions of word exposure and proficiency to successful IVL. One of the possible reasons for this can be that the high constraint contexts applied in the present study can provide sufficient information for learners, even those with low L2 proficiency, to acquire word meanings. Previous studies also attested to the crucial role of context in inferring word meanings (Mondria & Boer, 1991; Huckin & Coady, 1999). On the other side, Table 1 shows that the significance value of the interaction of L2 proficiency and word exposure frequency was 0.060, which indicated a marginally significant result. This exploratory result was an initial attempt to demystify the interconnectedness of the two variables and to some extent, underscored the interaction between word exposure frequency and learners' L2 proficiency.

In the following parts, the results of accuracy and those of response time were discussed in more detail, since these two indicators reflect different aspects of the results: the indicator of accuracy foreshadows the effectiveness of IVL while the indicator of response time predicates the IVL efficiency.

3.3.1 The Results of Accuracy

The results of ANOVA (Table 4) unveil that when exposed to the words once, participants of different L2 proficiency levels had significantly different performance on the semantic relatedness judgment task. This finding is in line with previous studies (Zahar, et al., 2001; Pulido, 2003; Shao, 2008; Wang, 2016; Chen, et al., 2019) that learners' L2 proficiency can affect the effects of IVL. The significantly different performance may derive from high proficiency learners' making better use of existing knowledge to infer word meanings and to promote vocabulary acquisition. As Knight (1994) claimed, advanced participants demonstrate better word guessing skills and better vocabulary retention in his research.

For low proficiency participants, the results of ANOVA (see Table 5 and Table 6) indicate that different word exposure frequency can lead to different effects of IVL. Due to their weaker L2 knowledge, participants of low proficiency got a relatively low accuracy rate. However, increasing word exposure frequency can provide them with more information to infer the meaning of words and make comparisons, which helped them perform better on the semantic relatedness judgment task with higher accuracy. Judd (1978) justified that the effects of IVL can be enhanced as the word exposure frequency increases. When new words were repeated three times, the accuracy of semantic relatedness judgment task was significantly different with the accuracy when new words appeared once only. However, after three times, more word exposure times did not cause significant difference any more. Just as Horst et al. (1998) claimed, there is an upper limit for the improving effects of IVL brought about by the increasing word exposure frequency. To sum up, IVL can have an important impact on low proficiency learners when they are exposed to new words three times in the high constraint sentence context.

For high proficiency participants, different word exposure frequency led to the same IVL effects, as Table 5 reveals. As mentioned before, high proficiency learners may take advantage of their existing knowledge while learning new words. Due to their great command and understanding of L2 knowledge, participants of high proficiency level could master over 90 percent of the new words when they were exposed to these words only once. When the frequency of word exposure continued to increase, the accuracy of semantic relatedness judgment task still rose, but there was no significant difference among the accuracy rate because of the already high rate of the one-time exposure. Therefore, for high proficiency learners, more word exposure times may simply be icing on the cake for IVL and do not lead to some substantial improvements on the effects of IVL in the high constraint sentence context.

The above discussion also reflects some limitations of the current study. Although the results of ANOVA have indicated that there was no significant difference in the accuracy of high proficiency participants with the word exposure frequency increasing, the descriptive statistics did show that the average accuracy rate went up with the exposure frequency. Due to the limited word exposure frequency in the current study, whether the average accuracy will continue to rise when participants are exposed to new words five or more times remains unclear.

3.3.2 The Results of Response Time

The results of ANOVA (Table 4) show that when exposed to the words three times, participants of different L2 proficiency levels had significantly different performance on the semantic relatedness judgment task. This is probably because that with the word exposure frequency increasing, the gathered information becomes rich, and hence high proficiency learners need less time to infer word meanings whereas low proficiency ones spend a longer time making comparisons among a wealth of information. This assumption is supported by previous electrophysiological studies that learners with different language levels had different ways of information processing. For instance, Elston-Güttler, Paulmann, and Kotz (2005) claimed that the level of language proficiency is an important factor in L2 semantic processing. Additionally, Ferguson and Cane (2015) have found in their study that the high L2 proficiency group elicits more negativity over the posterior hypothalamic area than the low L2 proficiency group in counterfactual conditionals.

For low proficiency participants, there was no significant difference in the response time of different word exposure frequency, as Table 5 shows. Because of their limited existing L2 knowledge, learners of low proficiency tend to spend a large amount of time to infer the meaning of new words when exposed to the words once only. When new words are repeated several times, they still need a long time to make comparisons. Previous studies displayed that the first encounter with a new word may provide learners with a hypothesis or guess, and then the subsequent encounters will offer further confirmation or rejection (Medina, Snedeker, Trueswell

& Gleitman, 2011; Trueswell, Medina, Hafri & Gleitman, 2013). Therefore, no matter how many times they are exposed to pseudo-words, low proficiency participants always need relatively long response time to perform the semantic relatedness judgment task, which explains why no significant difference existed among different word exposure frequency for the low proficiency group.

For high proficiency participants, their abundant L2 knowledge can promote their IVL with a relatively short time even though they are exposed to the words once. When the word exposure frequency increases, high proficiency participants spend less time to finish the semantic relatedness judgment task since they have collected enough information to infer word meanings. As Gollan et al. (2011) indicated, high L2 word frequency can lead to fast vocabulary access. However, when they were exposed to words four times, the response time grew significantly longer, as Table 1 and Table 8 indicate. This is probably because when participants are exposed to words four times, they receive excessive information and the brain has too much to process, which lengthens their response time of the judgment task. Previous studies have evidenced that high working memory load has negative impacts on both working memory span (Zhang, Xu & Bai, 2010) and involuntary attention (Wang, Hu & He, 2012). Therefore, there is reason to believe that for high proficiency learners, excessive word exposure will not enhance the efficiency of IVL but waste learners' energy instead in the high constraint sentence context.

In summary, the current study found that it may not require 8 or even 20 exposures as in previous studies (Saragi, et al., 1978; Herman, et al., 1987; Waring & Takaki, 2003) to achieve IVL and two or three encounters with new words is enough in the high constraint sentence context. There are two other points worth mentioning in the current study. For one thing, the speed-accuracy trade off (SAT) has an inevitable impact on participants' performance on the semantic relatedness judgment task. SAT refers to the interchange relationship between reaction speed and accuracy. That is, the pursuit of speed will reduce accuracy while improving accuracy will sacrifice response speed. Therefore, it is necessary for the current study to evaluate the effects of IVL from the perspectives of both accuracy and response time of the semantic relatedness judgment task. For another, the results of the current study only indicate that in high constraint sentence contexts, a few word exposure times can establish a preliminary form-meaning mapping relationship. However, multiple word exposures and repetition of words are essential for the establishment of a solid relationship between form and meaning.

4. Conclusion

4.1 Major Findings

The current research aimed to explore the influence of word exposure frequency and L2 learners' different proficiency on the effects of IVL in the high constraint sentence context. In addition, the effects of IVL were evaluated by participants' accuracy and response time of the designed semantic relatedness judgment task. Major findings of the present study were summarized as follows.

Previous studies have affirmed the significant roles of word exposure frequency and learners' proficiency levels in the research filed of IVL (Rott, 1999; Pulido, 2003; Shao, 2006; Luo, 2012; Wang, 2016). However, the various types of contexts were hardly considered when discussing the influence of the above two factors. The current study thus focused on the high constraint sentence context and revealed that different word exposure frequency and learners' different L2 proficiency can significantly influence the effects of IVL in the high constraint sentence context.

Moreover, the current study disentangled that in the high constraint sentence context, it may not require 8 or even 20 exposures as in previous studies (Saragi, et al., 1978; Herman, et al., 1987; Waring & Takaki, 2003) to achieve IVL and a few encounters with new words is enough. The present study also indicated that in high constraint sentence contexts, low proficiency learners can achieve the same IVL effects as high proficiency ones as long as the appropriate frequency of word exposure is provided.

Last but not least, the current study has made an initial attempt to explore the specific number of word exposures needed to achieve IVL in the high constraint sentence context. The experiment results indicated that for low proficiency learners, three times of word exposure can improve the accuracy of semantic relatedness judgment task while both two and three times of word exposure can efficiently shorten the task response time of high proficiency group. However, providing the word exposure frequency exceeds three times, the accuracy of low proficiency learners is not increased, nor the response time of high proficiency learners continues to shorten. Therefore, it can be concluded that in the high constraint sentence context, three times of word exposure is conducive for low proficiency learners to enhance the effectiveness of IVL and for high proficiency learners to improve IVL efficiency.

4.2 Limitations and Suggestions

Although detailed analysis and great efforts have been made in the current study, some limitations are still unfolded here. Firstly, the participants in this study are only 103 college students in a university of Shanghai. Considering the limited samples in the current study, the research conclusions may not be directly generalized to situations of all Chinese college students. Therefore, additional participants should be recruited to examine the generalizability of the experimental findings. Future studies can also recruit subjects from vocational universities or other social groups to promote the comprehensive research. Secondly, the limited word exposure frequency and the simple division of learners' L2 proficiency levels in the current study are another concern. Whether more word exposures or multiple proficiency levels will change the findings in this study still needs further verification. Finally, the carry-over effect is noteworthy in the current study. In the experiment, the semantic relatedness judgment task was presented after each sentence group of the same pseudo-word, which may confound the effects of the judgment task. To be more specific, after several semantic relatedness judgment tasks, participants may be able to infer the meaning of pseudo-words more consciously while reading sentences since they might have predicted the subsequent judgment tasks. Thus, in future studies, the semantic related judgment task can be presented after participants read all the designed sentences, which can inspect the more pure influence of word exposure frequency on the effects IVL.

References

[1] BOROVSKY A, KUTAS M, ELMAN J. Learning to use words: event-related potentials index single-shot contextual word learning[J]. Cognition, 2010(2): 289 – 296.

[2] ELLEY W B. Vocabulary acquisition from listening to stories [J]. Reading Research Quarterly, 1989(2): 174 – 187.

[3] FERGUSON H J, CANE J E. Examining the cognitive costs of counterfactual language comprehension: evidence from erps[J]. Brain Research, 2015: 252 – 269.

[4] GOLLAN T H, SLATTERY T J, GOLDENBERG D. Frequency drives lexical access in reading but not in speaking: The frequency-lag hypothesis[J]. Journal of Experimental Psychology: General, 2011(2): 186 – 209.

[5] HERMAN P, ANDERSON R, PEARSON P, NAGY W. Incidental acquisition of word meaning from expositions with varied text features[J]. Reading Research Quarterly, 1987: 263 – 284.

[6] HORST M, COBB T, MEARA P. Beyond a clock orange: Acquiring second language vocabulary through reading[J]. Reading in a Foreign Language, 1998: 207 – 223.

[7] HUCKIN T, COADY J. Incidental vocabulary acquisition in a second language: A review [J]. Second Language Vocabulary Acquisition. 1999(21): 181 – 193.

[8] HULSTIJN J H. Intentional and incidental second language vocabulary learning: A reappraisal of elaboration, rehearsal and automaticity [M]//ROBINSON P (ed.). Cognition and Second Language Instruction. Cambridge: Cambridge University Press. 2001: 258 – 286.

[9] JUDD E I. Vocabulary teaching and TESOL: a need for reevaluation of existing assumption [J]. TESOL Quarterly, 1978: 12 – 76.

[10] KNIGHT S. Dictionary use while reading: The effects on comprehension and vocabulary acquisition for students of different verbal abilities [J]. Modern Language Journal, 1994(3): 285 – 299.

[11] LAUFER B, HULSTIJN J. Incidental vocabulary acquisition in a second language: the construct of task-induced involvement[J]. Applied Linguistics, 2001(1): 1 – 26.

[12] MASON B, KRASHEN S. Is form-focused vocabulary instruction worthwhile? [J]. RELC Journal, 2004(2), 179 – 185.

[13] MEDINA T N, SNEDEKER J, TRUESWELL J C, et al.. How words can and cannot be

learned by observation[J]. Proceedings of the National Academy of Sciences, 2011(22): 9014-9019.

[14] MONDRIA J M, BOER W. The effects of contextual richness on the guessability and the retention of words in a foreign language[J]. Applied Linguistics, 1991: 249-267.

[15] NAGY W E, HERMAN P A, ANDERSON R C. Learning words from context[J]. Reading Research Quarterly, 1985(2): 233-253.

[16] NEWTON J. Task-based interaction and incidental vocabulary learning: a case study[J]. Second Language Research, 1995(2): 159-176.

[17] PARIBAKHT T S, WESCHE M. Reading and "incidental" L2 vocabulary acquisition: an introspective study of lexical inferencing[J]. Studies in Second Language Acquisition, 1999(2): 195-224.

[18] PULIDO D. Modeling the role of second language proficiency and topic familiarity in second language incidental vocabulary acquisition through reading[J]. Language Learning, 2003(2): 233-284.

[19] ROTT S. The effect of exposure frequency on intermediate language learners' incidental vocabulary acquisition and retention through reading[J]. Studies in Second Language Acquisition, 1999: 589-619.

[20] SARAGI T, NATION P, MEISTER G F. Vocabulary Learning and Reading[J]. System, 1978: 72-78.

[21] TRUESWELL J C, MEDINA T N, HAFRI A, et al.. Propose but verify: fast mapping meets cross-situational word learning[J]. Cognitive Psychology, 2013(1): 126-156.

[22] WARING R, TAKAKI M. At what rate do learners learn and retain new vocabulary from reading a graded reader?[J]. Reading in a Foreign Language, 2003: 130-163.

[23] WEBB S. The effects of repetition on vocabulary knowledge[J]. Applied Linguistics, 2007(1): 46-65.

[24] 陈宝国,张媛玥,马腾飞.高限制性句子语境条件下词汇接触次数和二语熟练度对词汇习得的影响[J].心理与行为研究,2019(2):153-159.

[25] 邓阳.二语词汇附带习得研究30年综述[J].教育界,2017(12):66-68.

[26] 盖淑华.英语专业学生词汇附带习得实证研究[J].外语教学与研究,2013(4):43-47.

[27] 罗静.二语词汇附带习得研究综述[J].大江周刊:论坛,2012(1):101-102.

[28] 全国大学英语四、六级考试委员会.大学英语考试大纲[M].上海:上海外语教育出版社,2016.

[29] 桑旭.词汇附带习得研究综述[J].都市家教月刊,2015(4):263.
[30] 邵艳春.不同阅读目的对词汇附带习得的影响———一项基于 SPSS 统计分析的调查研究[J].外语电化教学,2006(3):60-63.
[31] 王婷,胡媛艳,何华敏.工作记忆负荷对无意注意的影响[J].心理科学,2012(5):1060-1064.
[32] 王秀丽.词汇水平对英、汉注释词汇附带习得影响的研究[J].牡丹江大学学报,2016(1):40-43.
[33] 张丽华,徐微,白学军.加工负荷和加工时间对工作记忆广度任务成绩的影响[J].辽宁师范大学学报,2010(3):43-47.

点评

基于用 E-prime 2.0 设计的混合实验,论文研究探讨在高限制性句子语境中不同的词汇接触次数是否影响词汇附带习得的效果,以及不同学习者的二语水平是否影响词汇附带习得的效果,指出在高限制性句子语境中词汇接触次数和学习者的二语水平是影响词汇附带习得的两个重要因素。论文主题明确,语言流畅,结论对于英语学习有一定的启发意义。建议明确界定相关标准,调整文献综述结构,文献搜索紧跟当代研究前沿。

酒店网络关注热度时空特征及影响因素

——以西安市三星级以上酒店为例

孙涵宇　谢珊　张婷伟　段兆雯*

摘要：随着Web2.0的快速发展，旅游网络平台中各酒店的网络关注度已成为旅游者选择入住酒店的重要参考。基于此，论文以西安市371家三星级以上酒店为研究对象，通过从携程旅行网获取酒店网络关注度数据，对酒店网络关注热度时空特征和影响因素展开研究。研究发现：1) 2016—2018年，西安市三星级以上酒店网络关注数量总体上呈现先递增后下降的时间演化趋势；2) 西安市三星级以上酒店网络关注热度空间分布以钟鼓楼商业区为核心，整体呈现"大集聚、小分散"的分布格局；3) 不同级别酒店网络关注热度空间集聚差异性较为明显；4) 大型国际性会展活动的举办、城际交通的进一步完善是影响酒店网络关注热度时间分布的主要因素，而交通便利性、旅游景区(点)邻近性、商业购物场所邻近性是影响酒店网络关注热度空间分布的主要因素。

关键词：网络关注热度；时空分布特征；影响因素；三星级以上酒店；西安市

引言

酒店业作为旅游产业的重要组成部分之一，已成为衡量区域经济发展水平和对外开放程度的重要指标。随着中国城市经济的快速发展和城市化的不断推进，酒店数量逐年呈现增长态势。在互联网大数据时代背景下，中国酒店产业的

---

* 孙涵宇,谢珊,张婷伟：西安外国语大学旅游学院·人文地理研究所2019级硕士研究生。
段兆雯：管理学博士,西安外国语大学旅游学院教授。

发展已逐步向信息化、智能化转变,这导致旅游者在信息收集及购买行为方面发生了改变,网络关注数量和评价内容直接影响到旅游者购买酒店产品的决策,进而成为酒店管理者预测旅游者流量、了解旅游者消费偏好及行为的重要信息数据,也成为酒店产业经济研究和行业实践的热点之一。论文以中国西安市三星级以上酒店为研究对象,探讨酒店网络关注度的时空分布特征及其影响因素,以期把握游客对酒店产品的消费偏好,为酒店管理者店面选址、营销策略的制订以及政府管理部门制订酒店产业规划提供有益的参考与借鉴。

1. 文献综述

1.1 网络关注度研究

目前,Gawlik E 等学者们发现网络关注度对预测消费者流量、影响消费者购买意愿以及提升消费者满意度等方面都有积极的作用。目前中国学者们更注重网络关注度的实证研究,主要利用百度指数数据或网络爬虫数据,对区域旅游网络关注度的时空分布特征、旅游景区网络关注度时空分布特征及影响因素展开研究。

1.2 酒店空间布局研究

酒店空间布局的研究一直是城市地理、经济地理和人文地理学的研究热点。20 世纪 80 年代,Wall 等学者们将商业区位理论、集聚经济理论引入对酒店空间布局研究之中,如商务型、经济型酒店大都分布于城市的边缘城区和外环地带,区位条件优越、生态环境优良的佛罗里达、拉斯维加斯和夏威夷等地区是美国酒店选址的热点区域。Urtasun A 等发现城市中不同级别酒店空间集聚程度具有较明显的差异性,大城市中高星级酒店空间分布集聚特征明显,主要集中在城市 CBD;中低档酒店往往分布在高级别酒店周围、交通枢纽周边;经济型酒店则主要集中在交通线、交通枢纽、高等学校等位置;而城市边缘地带酒店分布几乎为零。Puciato D 等学者们从不同视角研究影响酒店业空间布局因素,现有研究结果表明除了土地价格、顾客需求、酒店企业自身发展目标之外,当地经济、社会、文化发展水平,交通通达度、商业业态的多元化、旅游资源、旅游业的发展程度、法律和监管框架以及当地国际化和城市化水平等都会影响到酒店的布局。

综上所述,学者们运用百度大数据、Google 趋势等网络数据对酒店业时空分布规律的研究成果趋成熟,但这些研究往往忽视了旅游者的需求。论文以旅游者的需求为出发点,利用在旅游专业网站上所收集到的酒店网络关注度数据,对旅游者选择入住酒店的区位偏好及其影响因素进行探讨。

2. 研究设计

2.1 研究区域及研究对象

西安位于中国中部关中平原,北邻渭河,南邻秦岭,是世界举世闻名的四大古都之一。西安其境内拥有秦始皇陵及兵马俑、汉长安城未央宫遗址、唐长安城大明宫遗址、大雁塔、小雁塔、兴教寺塔等世界级人类文化遗产,1981年西安被联合国教科文组织指定为"世界历史名城"。1978年到2018年,西安累计接待海内外游客14.35亿人次,其中,接待海外游客2 474.49万人次,实现旅游总收入11 909.24亿元,西安旅游业逐步壮大并已成为西安五大支柱产业之一。西安市共有新城、碑林、莲湖、雁塔、未央、灞桥、阎良、临潼、长安、高陵、鄠邑等11个区和周至、蓝田2个县(如图1),总面积10 108平方公里。截至2019年12月,西安市共有三星级以上酒店共868家,绝大多数酒店主要集中分布于西安市主城区,所以论文的研究对象最终确定为西安市主城区内莲湖区、碑林区、雁塔区、未央区、新城区、灞桥区以及长安区北部等7个区域共371家酒店,其中三星级酒店数量为199家,四星级酒店数量为127家,五星级酒店数量为45家。

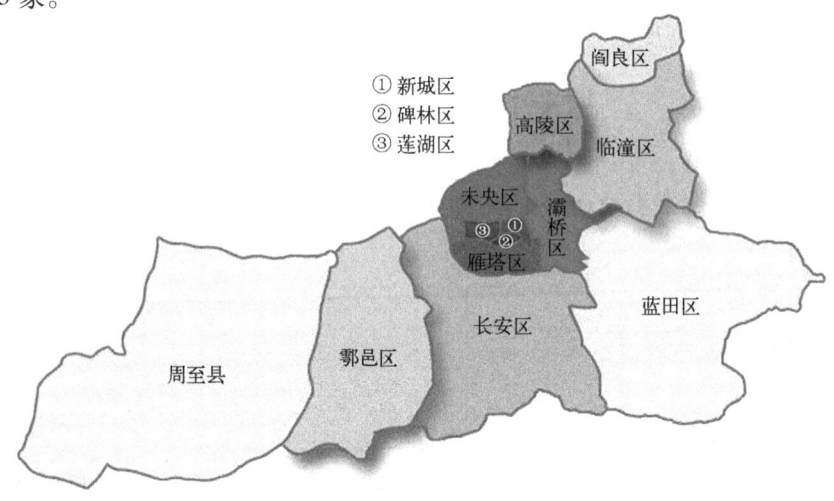

图1 西安市行政区划简图

2.2 数据获取及处理

携程旅行网成立于1999年,它是中国领先的酒店预订服务中心,在国内外有60万家会员酒店可供预订,注册会员可以享受携程旅行提供的各种形式的住宿预订服务。2016年携程旅行网评论功能上线,会员可以通过网站发布个人评论和感受。首先,本研究从携程旅行网收集西安三星级酒店名称、地址、详情页链接等数据信息,整理后发现与研究区域、评论时间(2016—2018)相吻合的三星级以上目标酒店共376家。其次,利用GPSspg xGeocoding工具,批量获取目标酒店的经纬度数据,并经过坐标纠偏后加载进ArcGIS10.1中,与西安市行政区划与道路信息进行叠加,结果显示371家酒店都分布在西安市绕城高速以内及周边,只有5家酒店位于距离西安市主城区较远的长安区西北部,详见图3。为保证分析数据的代表性并结合《西安市土地利用总体规划(2006—2020年)调整完善方案》,最终确定了371家酒店作为本研究的对象。第三,利用网络爬虫技术对所确定的371家酒店的星级、住客点评数量、发表评论时间、住客推荐指数等进行获取。为了保证研究数据的真实性,防止"刷单"现象,本研究剔除重复关注等无效网络数据,最终收集旅游者有效评论条数456 256条,具体详见表1。第四,运用ArcGIS10.1软件Spatial Analyst tools中的"密度分析"功能模块测算西安市三星级以上酒店网络关注热度分布规律。通过已知点分布推测面上分布概率。阴影程度越深,空间分布密度越高。假设酒店项目数据$P_1, P_2, \cdots\cdots, P_n$为连续分布$P(x)$,则任意酒店项目点x处的密度估计为:

$$X_n = \frac{1}{n \cdot h} \sum_{i=1}^{n} wi = \frac{1}{n \cdot h} \sum_{i=1}^{n} k\left(\frac{P-P_1}{h}\right)$$

式中:h为搜索半径;n为酒店的个数;$k(p)$为酒店规模核密度函数;X_n为估计密度。

3. 研究结果

3.1 酒店网络关注热度时空演化特征

从表1可知,2016—2018年西安市三星级以上酒店网络关注数量整体呈上升态势。其中,2016—2017年酒店网络关注数量急速上升,2018年酒店网络关注数量缓慢下降。

表1 西安市三星级以上酒店网络关注数量表

年份 \ 酒店级别	三星	四星	五星
2016	29 251	39 261	22 306
2017	65 497	81 815	45 303
2018	58 246	78 196	36 381
总计	152 994	199 272	103 990

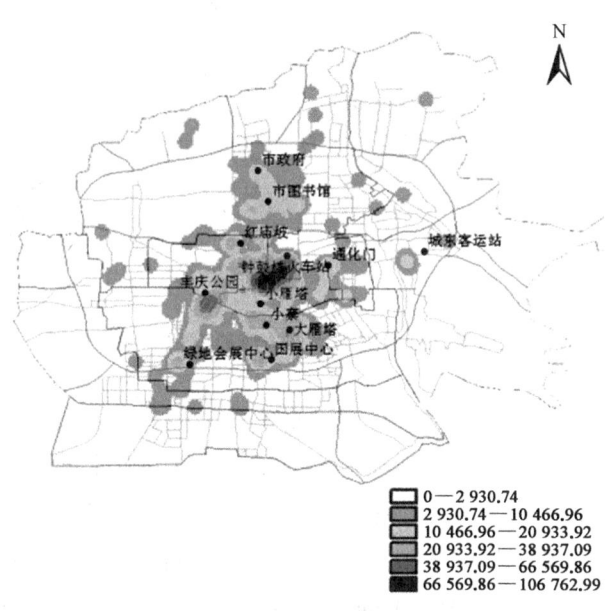

图2 西安市三星级以上酒店网络关注热度和密度简图

由图2可知,西安市三星级以上酒店网络关注热度主要集聚在钟鼓楼商业区,并以圈层形式向外扩展的状态,在丰庆公园、小寨—大雁塔、火车站、红庙坡、绿地会展中心、国展中心等地形成6个次级核心区,总体呈现出"大集聚、小分散"特征,而不同星级酒店的网络关注热度空间集聚差异性较明显。

3.1.1 三星级酒店网络关注热度时空演化特征

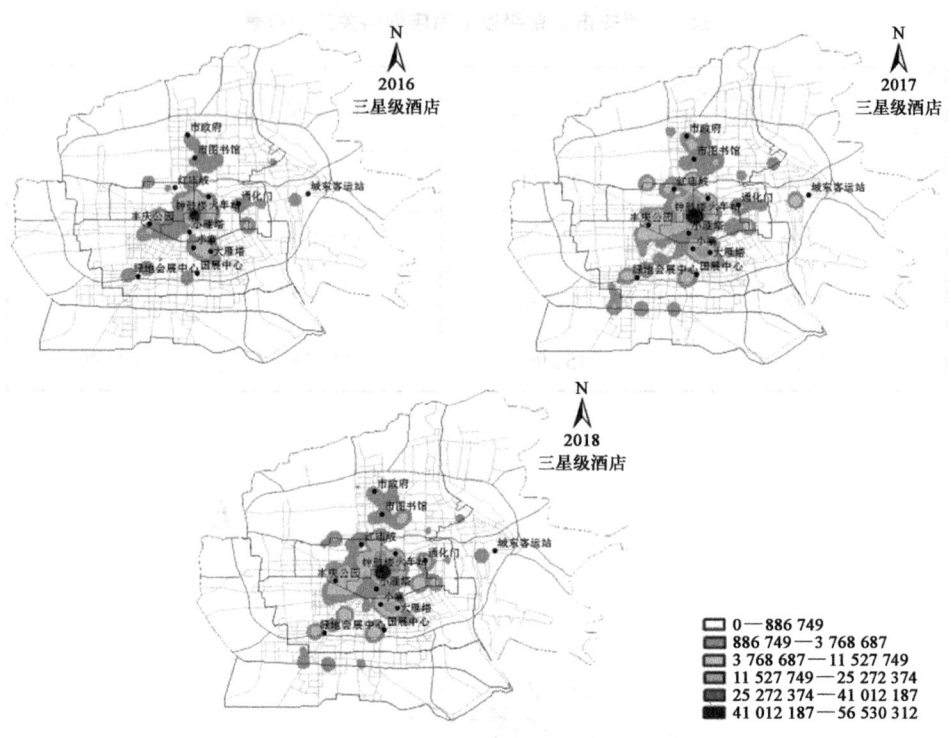

图 3　西安三星级酒店网络关注热度空间集聚特征

从图3可知,2016年三星级酒店网络关注热度核心区域为钟鼓楼商业区,并以钟鼓楼为中心点向四周辐射形成了一个1 000米的左右的圆,无其他核心圈层出现;2017年网络关注热度整体范围扩大,且各商业区之间的联系越来越紧密,网络关注热度范围以钟鼓楼为中心向外扩张2 000米,并形成小寨—大雁塔次级核心区;2018年网络关注热度空间范围呈现出缩小的态势,以钟鼓楼商业区与小寨-大雁塔为核心及次级核心区域,但市政府、市图书馆、城东客运站、红庙坡等区域的网络关注热度明显下降。整体上看,从2016—2018年西安三星级酒店网络关注度空间分布特征呈现"单核心"向"双核心"发展态势。

3.1.2 四星级酒店网络关注热度时空演化特征

从图4可知,2016年西安四星级酒店网络口碑关注热度核心区域为钟鼓楼

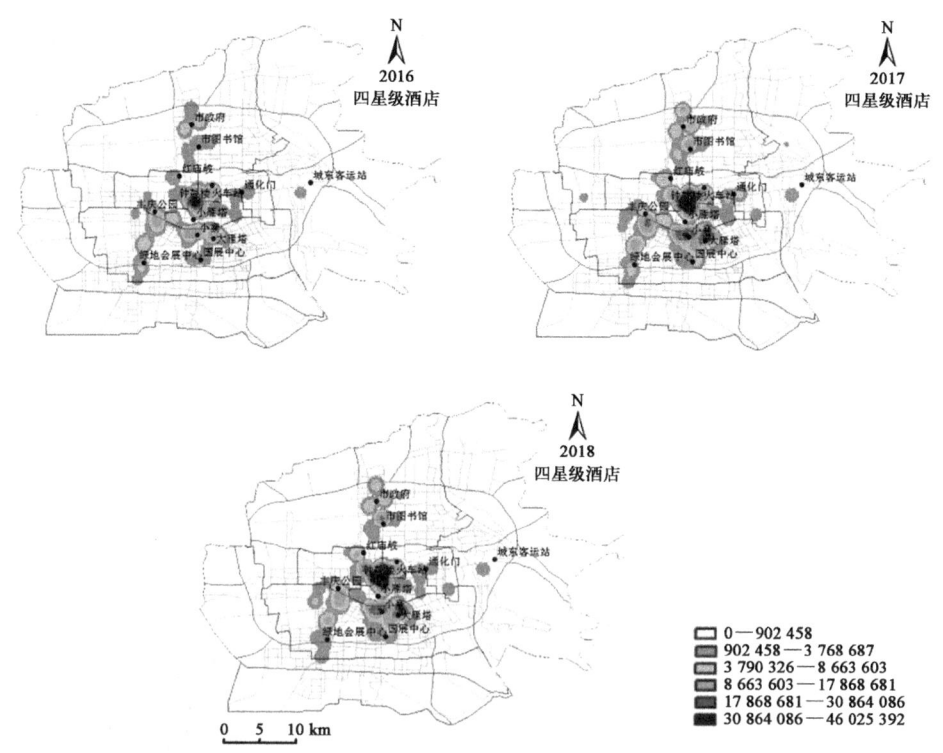

图 4　西安四星级酒店网络关注热度空间集聚特征

商业区,并以钟鼓楼为中心点向四周辐射形成了一个 1 000 米的左右的圆。虽然小寨—大雁塔、丰庆公园等 2 个区域酒店网络关注度数量较多,但空间集聚特征不明显;2017 年四星级酒店的网络关注度数量有所提升,除钟鼓楼商业区外,小寨—大雁塔、丰庆公园等区域酒店网络关注程度加强并逐渐形成次级核心区域。绿地会展中心、市图书馆、市政府、红庙坡等区域也成为消费者网上搜寻酒店的主要区域;2018 年钟鼓楼、大雁塔、市图书馆等区域网络关注数量依然呈现出上升趋势,而小寨、丰庆公园酒店网络关注数量开始出现下滑趋势,绿地会展中心区域和火车站等区域酒店网络关注数量下降明显。整体来看,从 2016—2018 年西安市四星级酒店的网络关注热度空间特征呈现"单核心"向"一心两翼"发展态势。

3.1.3　五星级酒店网络关注热度时空演化特征

从图 5 可知,2016 年西安五星级酒店网络关注热度主要集中在 3 个核心圈层。其中,以钟鼓楼为中心形成 3 个核心圈层:钟鼓楼东北侧直径 1 000 米的核

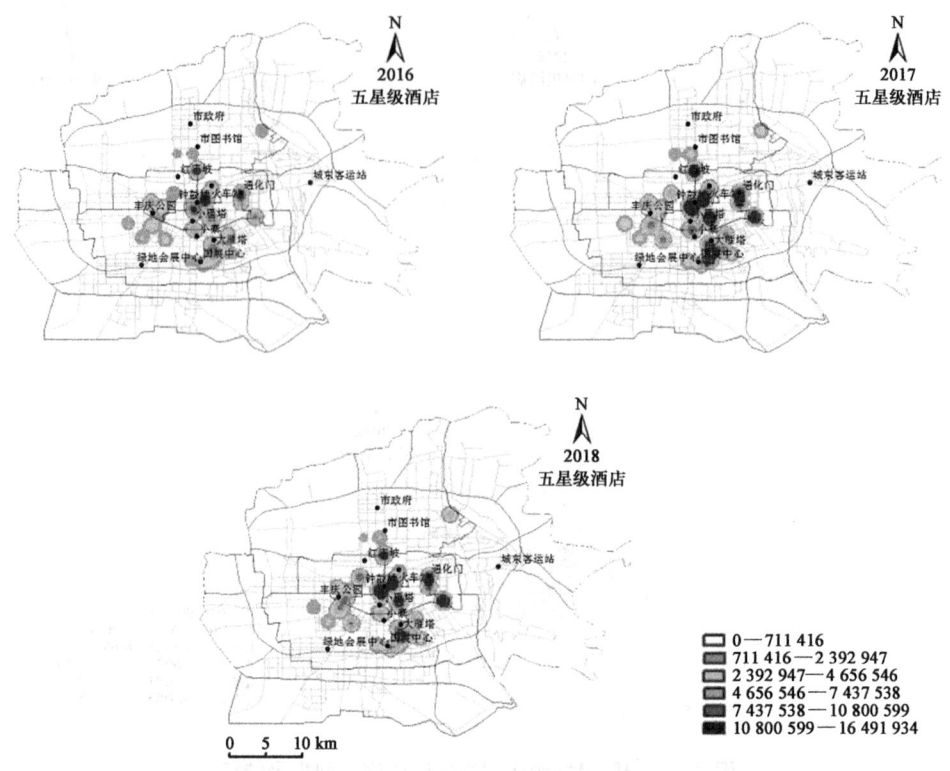

图 5　西安五星级酒店网络关注热度空间集聚特征

心圈层、钟鼓楼西南侧直径 200 米的核心圈层和通化门核心圈层。而红庙坡、丰庆公园、大雁塔、小雁塔、小寨区域则成为酒店网络关注热度的次核心区域。2017 年五星级酒店的网络关注热度空间呈现扩展趋势。其中,钟鼓楼东北侧与西南侧两个核心区域连接为一个整体区域;酒店关注热度逐渐由钟鼓楼向其周边扩展,红庙坡、小雁塔、大雁塔等区域的网络关注热度迅速增强,由次级核心区域转变为核心区域;2018 年五星级酒店网络关注热度与 2017 年相比,核心区域没有发生明显的变化,但是丰庆公园、国展中心区域的网络关注强度有所下降。整体来看,从 2016—2018 年西安五星级酒店网络关注热度空间范围逐渐扩大,呈现出"多核心"特征。

3.2　西安市三星级以上酒店网络关注热度时空影响因素

3.2.1　酒店网络关注热度时间分布影响因素

从表 1 可知,2017 年西安市三星级以上酒店的网络关注数量达到顶点,随后在2018年开始缓慢下降,这主要由于西安大型国际性活动的举办和城际交通的进一步完善,提升了西安市的城市形象,吸引了大量游客前来旅游。

(1)大型国际性会展活动的举办。从表1可知,西安市三星级以上酒店的网络关注热度在2016—2018年呈现先急速递增又缓慢下降的趋势。2017年西安市为了提升城市旅游形象,先后举办多项大型国际性活动,如首届世界西商大会、首届全球硬科技大会、西安国际马拉松等,吸引全球游客前往西安旅游。在这些大型国际活动举办期间,西安酒店需求数量激增,网上预订人数迅速上升。

(2)城际交通进一步完善。2017年,西兰高铁、西成高铁的先后开通,使得兰州、成都到西安的交通旅行时间分别由原来的8个小时、16个小时缩短为3个小时和4个多小时。交通旅行时间的缩短,使得城际的旅游更加快捷,促使成都和兰州的市民到西安旅游人数大幅度增加。

3.2.2 酒店网络关注热度空间分布影响因素

(1)交通便利性。西安市三星级以上酒店网络关注热度主要集中的区域如钟鼓楼、丰庆公园、小寨—大雁塔、市政府、市图书馆、火车站、红庙坡、城东客运站、国展中心等地,公共交通网络发达、通达性好,这不仅能提高酒店的入住便利性,也降低旅游者的交通成本。

(2)旅游景区(点)邻近性。旅游景区(点)作为旅游活动的核心承载物,是吸引旅游者到旅游目的地旅游的直接动力,而酒店与旅游景区(点)之间物理距离,是旅游者选择入住酒店的重要决策因素之一。酒店邻近旅游景区布局,能够节省旅游者往返住宿地和景点之间的交通费用和时间成本。西安三星级以上酒店网络关注热度集中的核心区域钟鼓楼,是回民街、钟楼、鼓楼等西安传统景点的集聚区域;而次级核心区大雁塔-小寨周边有大雁塔北广场、大兴善寺、陕西省历史文化博物馆、慈恩寺、曲江遗址公园、大唐芙蓉园等西安高级别旅游景点。

(3)大型商业购物场所邻近性。"吃""购"和"娱"不仅是旅游者的需求,同时也是旅游者在旅游过程中的重要活动内容。西安市三星级以上酒店网络关注度的核心区域钟鼓楼、小寨-大雁塔等地区除了交通便利、邻近旅游景区之外,同时也是西安市重要的商业中心聚集地,如西安开元商城、西安世纪金花购物中心、民生百货、西安小寨赛格国际购物中心、西安金莎国际购物广场、飞炫广场、百汇市场、新乐汇、大悦城等,都是西安市民及旅游者主要的购物、餐饮和娱乐场所。

4. 结论及讨论

基于网络口碑研究酒店的时空分布特征,对探讨酒店服务业的区位规律和旅游者住宿偏好具有一定的实践和理论意义。研究基于西安市三星级以上酒店的旅游者网络口碑评价数据,对不同级别酒店的网络口碑关注度、网络口碑得分进行了时空角度的探索。研究发现:(1)从网络关注数量分析可知,西安市三星级以上酒店整体受关注数量呈现先急速上升后缓慢降低趋势。(2)西安市三星级以上酒店网络关注热度核心区域均为钟鼓楼地区,关注区域范围与酒店等级成正比。(3)西安不同星级酒店网络关注热度时空特征差异性较明显。(4)大型国际性会展活动的举办、城际交通的进一步完善是影响酒店网络关注热度时间分布的主要因素,而交通便利性、旅游景区(点)邻近性、大型商业购物场所邻近性是影响酒店网络关注热度空间分布的主要因素。

由于携程旅行网的评论功能上线时间为 2016 年,所以本研究仅选取了 2016—2018 年的网络关注度数据进行时空的分析,研究数据较为有限,结论有待进一步深入地探讨。后续研究将采用线上数据收集与线下问卷调查相结合的方式,增加调查样本的数量,使研究结论更加全面和客观。

参考文献

[1] DINIS, GORETE, CARLOS COSTA, OSVALDO PACHECO. The use of Google Trends data as proxy of foreign tourist inflows to Portugal[J]. International Journal of Cultural and Digital Tourism, 2016, 3(1): 66 – 75.

[2] SKADBERG, YONGXIA X, ANDREW N. SKADBERG, JAMES R. KIMMEL. Flow experience and its impact on the effectiveness of a tourism website[J]. Information Technology & Tourism, 2007, 7(3 – 4): 147 – 156.

[3] DAVIDSON, ANDREW P, YINGMIAO YU. The Internet and the occidental tourist: An analysis of Taiwan's tourism websites from the perspective of western tourists[J]. Information Technology & Tourism, 2004, 7(2): 91 – 102.

[4] MARCHIORI, ELENA, LORENZO CANTONI. The role of prior experience in the perception of a tourism destination in user-generated content[J]. Journal of Destination Marketing & Management, 2015, 4(3): 194-201.

[5] JIN, SEUNGA VENUS, JOE PHUA. Making reservations online: The impact of consumer-written and system-aggregated user-generated content (UGC) in travel booking websites on consumers' behavioral intentionsp[J]. Journal of travel & tourism marketing, 2016, 33(1): 101-117.

[6] 张艳蓉,何小芊.基于百度指数的省域旅游形象口号网络关注度时空特征研究[J].江西科学,2019,37(2):214-220.

[7] 黄文胜.基于百度指数的广西旅游网络关注率矩阵及营销策略研究[J].地域研究与开发,2019,38(5):101-104.

[8] 丁鑫,汪京强,李勇泉.基于百度指数的旅游目的地网络关注度时空特征与影响因素研究——以厦门市为例[J].资源开发与市场,2018,34(5):709-714.

[9] 孙晓蓓,杨晓霞,张枫怡.基于百度指数的中国A级旅游洞穴景区网络关注度分布特征研究[J].西南师范大学学报(自然科学版),2018,43(4):81-88.

[10] 林志慧,马耀峰,刘宪锋,高楠.旅游景区网络关注度时空分布特征分析[J].资源科学,2012,34(12):2427-2433.

[11] 李经龙,代传苗.安徽省旅游景区网络关注度的时空特征——基于百度指数的分析[J].廊坊师范学院学报(自然科学版),2019,19(3):70-74.

[12] 张晓梅,程绍文,刘晓蕾,王琦,李照红.古城旅游地网络关注度时空特征及其影响因素——以平遥古城为例[J].经济地理,2016,36(7):196-202+207.

[13] 李会琴,董晓晴.世界遗产地丹霞山网络关注度分布特征研究[J].国土资源科技管理,2018,35(6):59-71.

[14] URTASUN A, GUTIÉRREZ I. Clustering benefits for upscale urban hotels[J]. International Journal of Contemporary Hospitality Management, 2017, 29(5): 1426-1446.

[15] 文吉.中国星级酒店空间布局研究[J].商业研究,2004(21):154-159.

[16] ADAM I, AMUQUANDOH F E. Dimensions of hotel location in the Kumasi Metropolis, Ghana[J]. Tourism Management Perspectives, 2013(8): 1-8.

[17] PUCIATO D. Attractiveness of municipalities in South-Western Poland as determinants for hotel chain investments[J]. Tourism Management, 2016(57): 245-255.

[18] LADO-SESTAYO R, VIVEL-BÚA M, OTERO-GONZÁLEZ L. Survival in the lodging sector: An analysis at the firm and location levels[J]. International Journal of Hospitality Management, 2016(59): 19-30.

[19] MARCO-LAJARA B, DEL CARMEN ZARAGOZA-SÁEZ P, CLAVER-CORTÉS E, et al. Tourist districts and internationalization of hotel firms[J]. Tourism Management, 2017(61): 451-464.

[20] 闫丽英,韩会然,陈婉婧,宋金平.北京市住宿业空间分布格局及影响因素研究[J].经济地理,2014,34(1):94-101.

[21] ADAM I, MENSAH E A. Perceived spatial agglomeration effects and hotel location choice[J]. Anatolia, 2014, 25(1): 49-60.

[22] 周美玲,刘春霞,李月臣.重庆主城区酒店业空间布局及影响因素研究[J].中国资源综合利用,2019,37(1):152-161.

[23] 刘宏盈,张娟.广西高星级酒店空间分布与优化研究[J].广西大学学报(哲学社会科学版),2015,37(2):51-56.

[24] PUCIATO D. Attractiveness of municipalities in South-Western Poland as determinants for hotel chain investments[J]. Tourism Management, 2016(57): 245-255.

点评

论文以西安市371家三星级以上酒店为对象,研究酒店网络关注热度时空特征和影响因素,指出西安市三星级以上酒店近三年来的网络关注数量总体呈先递增后下降、"大集聚、小分散"的趋势和格局,并分析了影响酒店网络关注热度空间分布的主要因素。论文选题得当,结构完整,语言表述清晰,对相关量化工具的运用合理有序,结论有一定的实践指导意义。建议增强文献回顾的广度和深度,深化研究的理论价值,主旨问题可进一步深化探讨,凸显研究的意义和创新之处。

On the Application and Translation Strategies of Economic and Trade Contract from the Perspective of Cooperative Principles

Tian Xiaosu[*]

Abstract: The paper tries to combine Grice's cooperative principle with economic and trade English contract. The purpose of the article is to yield insights into the translation of economic and trade contracts and it may also help to reduce the possible losses caused by the translation mistakes of contract. Grice's cooperative principle plays a guiding role in the translation of economic and trade contracts. Therefore, more attention should be paid to its application in business practice. Translators should fully grasp the stylistic characteristics of contracts and adopt the cooperative principles in translating contracts.

Keywords: Grice's cooperative principle; Economic and trade contracts; Stylistic features

Introduction

Background of the Study

Due to frequent foreign economic and trade activities, the translation of contracts is more important between Chinese and other countries. Once the contract comes into effect, the two parties of contracts will bear legal liability. So

---

[*] Tian Xiaosu: School of Foreign Languages, University of Shanghai for Science and Technology, master's degree candidate of the class of 2019.

the translation of contract is characterized by accuracy and rigorousness, setting strict requirements for the translation of the contract.

The cooperative principle is the guiding principles of human conversational activities based on the difference between formal logic and the logic of natural language. The cooperative principles consist of four principles, namely, quantity principle, quality principle, relevance principle and manner principle. The four principles have become the basis of pragmatics research. The translation of economic and trade contract concerns the interests of both parties of the contract. A few mistakes caused may make legal disputes between two parties of the contract and economic losses to both parties or one party. In view of this communicative function of contract style, the translator should abide by the four cooperative principles when translating the economic and English trade contracts.

Research Purpose and Significance

Grice believes that people's normal language communication is not a series of unrelated speech combinations, conversation is subject to certain conditions, and a successful conversation is the result of joint efforts of both parties. Both sides of the conversation often want to be able to cooperate together and abide by a cooperative principle in order to achieve a common goal. Many researchers have studied the application of the cooperative principle at home and abroad after the cooperative principle was put forward.

Now Chinese scholars have conducted in-depth research on the application of Grice's cooperative principle in various aspects including teaching, translation, writing, literature and other fields. However, there are relatively few systematic studies on the application of Grice's cooperative principle to economic and trade English contracts. The stylistic characteristics of contract text can reflect the influence of Grice's cooperative principle. This paper combines Grice's cooperative principle and economic and trade English contract and investigates the application of cooperative principle in economic and trade English contract. The conclusion drawn in this paper may give insights into the understanding of cooperative principle. We also hope that this paper can offer reference for translation of contracts.

1. Literature Review

1.1 Related Concepts

1.1.1 Concept of Contracts

A contract is between two parties and one party cannot make a promise to the other without evidence. Once a trade contract comes into effect, the parties shall bear legal liability and take on the obligations in the contract. The exporter must fulfill its obligation of delivery as agreed, otherwise it may claim compensation according to law (Qi, 2004).

A contract refers to an agreement establishing, modifying and terminating the civil rights and obligations between subject of equal footing, that is, between natural persons legal persons or other organization. (The PRC contract law, 1999)

A typical contract is between two parties. Usually one party's promise is always the reward promised to the other party, and the promise and the reward for the promise are exactly the expression of the will of both parties. Once a trade contract is effectively established, the parties are obliged to fulfill their obligations under the contract.

1.1.2 Textual Characteristics of Contracts

The following part will analyze the stylistic features of economic and trade English contracts from three aspects: lexical, syntactic and discourse features.

(1) Lexical Features of International Economic and Trade Contracts

Foreign trade English contract has the characteristics of formal writing, accurate words and strict structure. In order to understand and translate contracts correctly, we should master the lexical features of economic and trade contracts. The lexical features of foreign economic and trade contracts mainly include professional vocabulary, abbreviations, archaic words, overlapping synonyms, the use of "shall", time words and amount words. (Liu, 2006)

a. technical vocabulary

The technical vocabulary is a term used in a particular subject or field. They have a specific meaning. Such as: free on board, bill of lading, trade marks, general average, letter of credit, endorsement and so on. Except for the technical terms just mentioned, there are common words used as professional words in contract, which should be defined from a professional perspective rather than understood as common words, otherwise the meaning of the contract will be unclear. For instance, the words of "negotiation" and "collection" are used as professional terms, which are translated as "谈判" and "收取" respectively. However, two words should understand as "议付" and "托收" respectively.

b. Using acronyms

There are many abbreviations in English, such as clipped word, initialing, acronym, blend, etc. Such as: FOB (Free on board), FAS (Free alongside ship), CIF (Cost insurance and freight) and so on. In addition, some units and related words in economic and trade contract is usually take the form of truncated word, such as PC (piece), NO (number), V (vessel), M (meter), etc.

c. English archaic words

The compound words "here" "there" "where" and the prepositions "in" "under" "of" "to" "by" are archaic words that often used in English contracts. They are frequently used in business contracts. Such as hereafter "在下文"; hereinbefore "在上文"; hereto "对此/至此"; thereafter "以下/在下文"; wherein "在那方面"; whereby "据此"。

d. Overlap of synonyms

English contracts often come in pairs of synonyms with only slight differences in order to give the contract a rigorous and thorough characteristic in order to reduce or eliminate possible disputes. Such as: "Perform" and "fulfill" both mean "履行" in Chinese, but the former emphasizes subjective effort while the latter emphasizes objective results.

e. Time words and their translation

Because the payment and other clauses of contracts must have a clear time limit, so the provision of time in the translation must be consistent with the original. Such as:

Shipment: To be shipped on or before Feb.14, 2008.

This sentence selected from a clause on shipment. It could be translated into specialized translation as "装船：2008 年 2 月 14 日前(含 14 日)装船"。The parties attach special importance to the time of shipment in the contract.

f. Amount words and their translation

The sum of money indicated on the contract is of the greatest concern to the parties. In order to eliminate the loophole, when the contract amount is translated into English, the case must be used at the same time. Such as：

Total Price：RMB ￥5,200,000.00 (Say：RMB Five Million Two Hundred Thousand only)

g. use of "shall"

The modal verb "shall" is widely used in economic and trade contracts to express compulsory legal obligations. It refers to "必须" in Chinese. For example：If the cargo shipped are live animals, …, the freight for cargo shall be paid at the time of shipment.

In this sentence the "shall" means "必须" in Chinese. The sentence can be translated as："装运的货物如果是活动物，……其运费必须在装船时全部付清。"

(2) Syntactic Features of International Economic and Trade Contracts

In order to make the terms clear, the conditional sentences, declarative sentences and passive sentences with complex structures are often used. (Zhang, 2006)

a. Conditional sentence

Adverbial clauses of conditions are widely used in economic and trade contracts. For example：If the party who accepts the deposit defaults, he shall repay the deposit in double.

This sentence used conditional sentence to ask the duty of one party. Using this kind of sentence, the right and duty of contract will be clear and two parties can consider all kinds of conditions.

b. Declarative sentence

The basic sentence structure of economic and trade English contract is a statement structure, and there are no questions, exclamations and imperative sentences, and no general rhetorical devices. Such as：The Seller agrees to sell the goods on conditions stipulated below…

This sentence can be translated as "按照下列条款,卖方同意出售货物……" This declarative sentence can directly show meaning of contracts.

c. Passive sentence

Most of the clauses about payment, packing, shipment, insurance, inspection and dispute settlement in the economic and trade English contract adopt passive sentence structure. Such as: Insurance shall be covered by the Buyer against all risks, including war and strike risks, for 110% of the invoice value.

This passive sentence puts the word "insurance" in the first of sentence. In this way, wo can see it firstly. Wo could pay more attention to the specific insurances.

(3) Discourse Features of International Economic and Trade Contracts

The basic style of the economic and trade English contract is the program, terms and regulations, the structure of the economic and trade English contract has been basically fixed.

a. Parallel structure

The economic and trade English contract adopts the sub-clause and sub-clause. Besides, the structure of parallel clauses is frequently used. For example:

DOCUMENT: The Seller shall present the following documents to the paying bank for negotiation:

① One full set …;

② Invoice in quintuplicate …;

③ Packing list in quintuplicate;

b. Reuse of keywords

In business English contracts, the same word or phrase is usually used repeatedly in the cohesion of the text, and pronouns are rarely used. Such as: Party B shall arrange to … Party A within the time … Party B shall …, so that Party A may ….

1.1.3 Concept of Cooperative Principles

In order to cooperate effectively to complete the task of communication, Grice put forward the principle of cooperative. And then Grice argued that the cooperative principle in *Logic and Conversation* (1975). He thought that people followed in Conversation included four categories, and each category included a criterion and some sub-criteria, namely:

The first one is the maxim of quality which refers to the amount of information provided. That is, the words said should contain the information needed for the purpose of the conversation or the words said should not contain more information than is needed.

The second one is the maxim of quantity which requires that what you say true. That is, don't say what you think is untrue or don't say what you have not enough evidence for information.

The third one is the maxim of relevance which requires that content of the conversation should be related to the purpose of the conversation or be relevant.

The fourth one is the maxim of manner which refers to clear conversation, avoiding vague words and ambiguities, concise speech (be brief or avoid prolixity), and be orderly.

The first three of the four rules relate to what people say when they talk, and the fourth to how they say it. By following all four principles, our conversation will be clear and communication will be efficient.

1.2 Previous Research on Cooperative Principles

On the teaching, McCarthy (1987) used the cooperative principle to test the cooperative situation of students in writing, cell biology and poetry classes. Reed (1987) pointed out that Grice's cooperative principle to explain discourse in relation to context would help develop a sound literary theory and play a leading role in the study of texts, so he regarded it as a valuable "supreme principle".

In terms of verbal communication, Rundquist (1992) called Grice's cooperative principle as "social indirectness theory" and used it to counter the "common view that women are more indirect than men in conversations". Bethan (2007) pointed out that as a basic concept of pragmatics, Grice's cooperative principle is often misunderstood. These misunderstandings stem in part from a philosophical and linguistic reorientation of the cooperative principle.

Dou (2019) pointed out that Grice's cooperative principle regards interpersonal communication as a speech act that follows certain rules in a specific context, and explored the role of cooperative principle in English translation teaching practice. Fu (2017) used the conversational cooperative principle in pragmatics to analyze the deep meaning of the violation of cooperative principle by different advertising languages, which helped consumers understand advertising language. Zhang (2017) believed that when creating advertisements, we should pay attention to the cooperative principle of language and accurately express the characteristics of the product or service.

Gong (2020) studied interpretation in international business negotiations under the theoretical guidance of Grice's cooperative principle and analyzed that how to apply the conversational cooperative principles in interpreting international business negotiations according to the situation, so as to promote the success of negotiations.

1.3 Previous Research on Contract Translation

In terms of economic and trade contracts, foreign countries mainly focus on the application of cooperative principle in contracts. Kegan Paul studied the guiding principles of economic and trade contracts related to the sale of goods.

Hu (2018) pointed out the theory of functional equivalence is helpful for the accurate translation of various texts in business English. He believed that the target language and the source language could apply in the contract to discuss how to apply functional equivalence theory to contract translation. Li (2017) expounded the translation theory of functional equivalence, and then summarizes the methods of business English contract translation by analyzing the unique stylistic features of business English contracts. Hu (2019) considered that the effectiveness of contract translation should be guaranteed and the style and characteristics of English translation should be highlighted under the guidance of functional equivalence theory. Cong (2017) analyzed the translation of contracts with examples. He took the three principles of skopos theory as the guiding theory. He thought that at the level of vocabulary, the archaic words, professional words, synonyms and acronyms applied the fidelity principle. Chen (2015) adopted the skopos theory as the guiding theory to carry out the translation. She analyzed and summarized the examples of the contracts and the translation from the aspects of vocabulary and sentences.

In the term of adopting the systemic functional linguistics to the translation of

English contract. Rong (2017) adopted the systemic functional linguistics to analyzed the content of contract translation. Then he verified the feasibility and operability of the systemic functional linguistics which applied in the translation of business contracts. Yang (2005) attempted to analyze the translated text to help the translator to examine the translation problem. Then he tested the operability of this theory. At last, she concluded that the translation standard of business contract English is faithful, accurate and unified.

The above mainly reviewed the translation of contracts under the different theories such as: functional equivalence theory, skopos theory and systemic functional linguistics theory. Three theories have had guiding meaning for the translation of contracts. We can find that the research of translation of contract under cooperative principle is relatively few. So this paper mainly adopts the cooperative principle as a guiding theory. And mainly studies the application of the cooperative principle in business English contract and provides some suggestions to enterprise for cross-border trade.

2. Application of Grice's Cooperative Principle in Economic and Trade Contracts

This part is mainly based on the analysis of the characteristics of the contract text in economic and trade English, and studies the characteristics of the three major parts. Taking the Grice's cooperative principle as the starting point, this part analyzes the application of the quantity principle, the relevance principle, the manner principle and the quality principle in the contract. The cases in this paper are mainly from books and periodicals, including Duan Yunli's *Translation of Economic and Trade English*, Qi Yunfang's *Contract and Contract English* and Wu Min's *International Economic and Trade English Contract Writing*. After careful selection, this chapter mainly cites 19 cases which are selected from 20 economic and trade contracts.

2.1 Application of Quantity Principle in Economic and Trade Contracts

The quantity principle is to provide as much information as possible without providing too much information. Redundant information will bring misunderstanding in communication, however too little information cannot meet the expectation of the conversation. The following examples all reflect the quantity principle:

Example 1

Should the Force Majeure event last for more than 90 consecutive days...

Example 1 shows that the timing of the event is very accurate. The "consecutive days" in sentence especially refers to the continuous number of days. The parties of contract should understand accurately the time in the processing of trade exchange.

Example 2

Buyer is entitled to claim liquidated damages ... for each complete week of delay ...

In example 2, the time limitation for delayed delivery of goods is also very strict. It means more than a complete week, then the penalty for delivery, if it is 5 days, then it is not a complete week. Such a limit to the buyer and seller to treat the liquidated damages, it will be a clear indication. The strict limitation of time can reflect the quantity principle.

Example 3

The lay time allowed to Buyer ... shall be seventy-two (72) running hours after the arrival of the vessel at the discharge port including Sundays and holidays.

From example 3 we can see that the buyer is allowed to berth time for continuous uninterrupted, 72 hours, including Sundays and holidays. It suggests that contract strictly requires the time, especially using the "running hours" and "including Sundays and holidays" in order to define the time limitation and to avoid any misunderstanding on both sides. It is fully embodied the principle of quantity to provide the required information.

The above examples. We can see that in economic and trade contracts, the expression of time is strictly limited. The treatment of time words such as "hour, day, week" is quite different from other common problems. For example, "hours" is written as "running hours"(连续无间断小时), "week" as "complete week".

In other everyday styles, there are usually no such additional restrictions before nouns such as "week", "day", "hour", etc. Economic and trade English contracts prevent the two parties from making different interpretations of time by imposing additional restrictions on time words. Through these limitations, the quantity principle in Grice's cooperative principle is satisfied, and the information provided is up to the requirement of the amount of information needed for communication.

2.2 Application of Quality Principle in Economic and Trade Contracts

In other styles, the use of synonyms is often seen as redundant. In economic and trade contracts, in order to comply with the quality principle, usually using "and" or "or" to link two or more words with the same, similar, or related meanings side by side. In these structures, the two words are semantically similar or overlapping, which avoids misunderstanding and ensures the quality of the information conveyed.

Example 4

Any modification or alternation of the contract should be made by both Parties through negotiation.

In this example, the synonym "modification" and "alternation" were both used. The meanings of the words of "modification" and "alternation" are slightly different. So we should use specific words to impress in the contracts. The word of "modification" refers to the further improvement of the original contract. The word of "alternation" may refer to a material change to contract's content. Although the meaning is similar, but it will not appear cumbersome, so as to facilitate the contract parties to amend the contract clearly.

Example 5

Each party to this agreement shall perform and fulfill any of the obligation.

In this example, using the words "perform" and "fulfill" together. They are the synonyms. "Perform" and "fulfill" both refer to the meaning of "履行". Although their meanings are same, the "Perform" emphasizes subjective effort. The "fulfill" emphasizes objective results.

Example 6

The prices quoted above do not include any taxes, duties, impost and any other charges.

The example uses the words taxes, duties and impost to represent various "税费". Although the meanings of the three words are similar, in order to ensure that both parties have a clearer understanding of the information and provide quality information, the use of three synonyms in conjunction reflects the quality principle.

Similar to the above examples, the word of "破产" must write as "bankruptcy" or "insolvency". The word "费用" must write as "charges, fees, costs and expenses" in the economic and trade English contracts. This is because, as far as the four principles of Grice cooperative are concerned, the quality principle is the first to be followed. The use of synonyms in conjunction with this linguistic phenomenon, although contrary to the principle of quantity, provides the same redundant information. But it adheres to in order to meet the requirements of the quality principle.

2.3　Application of Relevance Principle in Economic and Trade Contracts

In business communication, both parties should focus on the topic and not say the wrong thing. In discourse communication, the discourse should be related to the current topic and relevant to the subject matter, which is to observe the relevance principle. In the economic and trade English contract, the adherence to the relevance principle is reflected in the use of the unique vocabulary and syntax of the economic and trade English contract.

Example 7

TERMS OF SHIPMENT：

① The Seller shall, at least 30 days before the date of shipment stipulated in the Contract ...

② Booking of shipping space shall be attended to by the buyer.

③ The Seller shall be liable for any dead freight or demurrage ...

The above clause consists of eight sentences, three of which are excerpted. Each sentence contains a modal verb "shall". "Shall" instead of "should", "have to" or "must", is used to express the responsibilities of both parties. This is because "shall" is a legal document term that emphasizes the legal responsibility of the parties to the contract. It cannot be replaced by "should" "have to" or "must". Therefore, this up-down response fully reflects the requirement of the relevance principle in the Grice cooperative principle. The vocabulary and syntax related to the economic and trade English contract should be used, and the words and syntax of general style should not be transferred to the legally binding economic and trade English contract.

Example 8

The agreement shall automatically terminate upon ...

The professional word "terminate" is used in example 8.

Example 9

Party A agree to assist Party B to install the equipment.

The professional word "assist" is used in example 9.

Analyzing the above examples, you can see that the formal verb is "terminate" instead of "end", although "terminate" and "end" have the same meaning. Again, "assist" is used instead of "help". Besides, we usually use the word "construe" instead of "explain" and "present" is used instead of "supply". In these examples, common words are replaced by formal written language. This is because professional legal vocabulary can better cover the meaning of the parties to the contract, and the concrete verbs can clarify the behavior of the parties.

Example 10

If, after 60 days from the date of commencement of friendly negotiations, the parties hereto fail to reach any agreement, either party hereto may submit the dispute, to arbitration for settlement.

Through the analysis of example 10, we can find that the word order is different from that of ordinary English. In ordinary English, adverbials are usually placed at the beginning of a sentence, separated from the main sentence by a comma, or at the end of a sentence. In example 10, the adverbial clause is placed after the conjunction "if" and before the subject of the clause. In example 10, the phrase "after 60 days from the date of commencement of friendly negotiation" is an adverbial modifier of "If the parties amicable fail to reach any agreement". It is placed after the "if" and separated by comma. In this way, the capacity of sentences is fully expanded. It is a major feature of the economic and trade English contract.

Example 11

The carrying vessel shall be arranged by the Seller, partial shipment and transshipment are allowed.

Example 12

L/C shall be opened within 30 days by the buyer before shipment, the Seller will remit the real value differences of buying and selling to the Buyer after shipment.

Example 11 is the terms of shipment and example 12 is the terms of payment. The passive voice was used in the example 11 and example 12 use, but active voice was not used. These examples show the characteristics of the economic and trade English contract. It uses the passive sentence structure in terms of payment, packing, shipment, insurance, inspection and dispute settlement to appear objective and fair. Meanwhile, declarative sentences are used in these examples, but not interrogative, exclamatory and imperative sentences. The above examples meet the stylistic requirements of economic and trade English contracts.

From the above several examples, we can see that in the economic and trade English contract using the formal written language and the preposition phrases "to" instead of simple common prepositions and conjunctions in informal style. Using the "If" guided virtual conditional sentence. Using the "If" in the beginning of the special sentence structure. Using statements and passive sentences both reflects the Grice relevance principles in the cooperative principle, namely only use the lexical and syntactic patterns associated with economic and trade English contract, and shall not apply to the general style of words or sentences.

2.4 Application of Manner Principle in Economic and Trade Contracts

2.4.1 Avoiding obscurity

The first requirement of the manner principle is to "avoid obscurity".

Example 13

Packing: To be packed in strong cartons, suitable for long distance parcel post/air freight transportation and charge of climates, well protected against moisture and shocks etc.

Example 14

Packed in wicker baskets of 50 kg each, lined with rush mat, covered with gunny cloth and secured with ropes.

In example 13 the words used in the contract are vague, the information is not fully expressed, and the necessary execution standards are not available. In contrast, example 14 is fully expressed, with clear provisions from the selection of packaging materials to the quantity and method of packaging, which meets the requirements of "avoiding obscurity".

2.4.2 Avoiding ambiguity

The second part of the manner principle requires "avoidance of ambiguity", and the second part of the manner principle is reflected in the economic and trade contracts.

Example 15

In case the Seller fails to ... in the Contract, the Buyer shall ... the Contract, and the Seller, ... the Buyer without delay.

In example 15, the key words are all nouns, such as "the Seller" "the Buyer" and "the Contract". Even if the contract party referred to appears again in the following text, "the Seller", "the Buyer" and "the Contract" are still referred to. The pronoun "I" is not used to refer to "the Seller", the pronoun "you" is not used to refer to "the Buyer", and the pronoun "it" is not used to refer to "the Contract". Using the same noun over and over again makes the sentence clear and clear. More importantly, it meets the requirement of avoiding ambiguity in Grice's cooperative principle.

Example 16

The Seller shall deliver the goods before August 20, 2004.

In this sentence, the word "before" is used. People in Britain and the United States usually explain that August 20th is not included in this sentence, while people in China usually think that the day of August 20th is included in this sentence. Usually using two participles before a time noun, such as "on or before" "on and after" "upon and from", thus achieving the starting and ending time including the date of the day. It meets the requirement of avoiding ambiguity in

Grice's cooperative principle.

2.4.3 Avoiding redundancy

The third requirement of manner principles is be brief (avoid redundancy). Many stylistic features of economic and trade contracts in English embody the requirements of the third criterion.

Example 17

Terms of Packing: Art.NO.8065 To be packed in cartons of 12 pcs each only.

Where "Art." is short for article (商品), "No." is short for Number (编号), and "PC" is short for piece (件、块). Economic and trade English contracts use acronyms to express information succinctly. It embodies the requirement of "be brief" in the Grice's principle of cooperative.

Example 18

Thereof … here to …

In sentence, "thereof" refers to "of the contract"; "hereto" refers to "to this contract". The use of an archaic word can instead express the meaning of several words. "Thereof" express the meaning of "of the contract", however uses "of the contracts", the sentence will use three words. But using the archaic word "thereof" can express the same meaning. In this way, the features of avoiding repetition and concise words reflect the manner principle.

2.4.4 being orderly

The fourth criterion of the manner principle requires "be orderly".

Example 19

(1) Advice of Shipment:

A: Immediately after loading the goods on board the ship, …

B: Should the Buyers be unable to cover insurance …

(2) Force Majeure:

The Sellers shall not be held responsible for late delivery …

From the perspective of the stylistic format of the body part of the economic and trade English contract, it is usually divided into several clauses or chapters according to the content nature. In the specific analysis of example 19, we can see that: From the perspective of terms, clause 1 and 2 are in parallel structure.

Within clause 1. Sub-clause A and sub-clause B are also in a parallel structure.

As far as the clauses are concerned, each term has a striking title. This title is named after the contents of the articles and numbered in order, which has a prominent guidance effect and makes the contents of the economic and trade English contract clear at a glance.

3. Translation Strategies from Perspective of Cooperative Principles

In the translation of the contract, the consideration should be given to the interrelation among textual features, lexical features, syntax and discourse to provide adequate and quality information. We must be accurate and precise in our translation. From the perspective of cooperative principle, this paper provides some suggestions on the translation of economic and trade contracts in the hope of greatly reducing the probability of trade disputes between the two parties.

3.1 Appropriately adding or subtracting words

Sometimes, for making the information clearer, we need to add words to impress more accurate meaning in the translation of contract.

Example 20

This year the export quantity of black tea increased by 20 percent, and jasmine tea by 30 percent.

In this sentence the verb "increase" is added. In this way, the increase in the export of scented tea is clearer, which also conforms to the indirect characteristics of English.

Example 21

Should the Force Majeure event last for more than 40 full days...

The duration of the force majeure event shall not exceed 40 days. For the time of 40 days, we add the adjective "full". In the context of the contract, the limit of 40 days shall be clear, so that both parties are clear of their responsibilities and avoid misunderstanding. Due to consideration of the quantity principle in the cooperative principle, words should be added and subtracted to provide appropriate information.

3.2 Accurately choosing words with clear meaning

Accurate translation means that the contract translation should be clear and precise in meaning. For example, sign the agreement is "made and entered into". Stressing that the contract is signed by the parties to the contract, to be used "by and between". "索赔" is "complaints and claims", "履行" is "fulfill" or "perform". If we choose the ordinary English vocabulary, may contract will produce misunderstanding, such contract text appears very unprofessional.

In addition, economic and trade contracts will also use a large number of specialized words, prepositional phrases, acronyms and modal verbs. With the continuous development of the economy, specialized vocabularies and some economic and trade terms emerge in an endless stream. For example, "bill of exchange" means "汇票", "acceptance" means "承兑", "sight of bill" means "即期汇票".

Example 22

The Buyers shall be filed the claim within 20 days after ... specified in the relative Bill of Lading ...

The sentence can translate as: "买方要在货到提单规定的目的地 20 天后, 进行索赔……" In example 22, "claim" means "索赔", and the phrase "Bill of Lading" means "提单". The terms "claim" and "bill of lading" are used here. In fact, the word "shall" is also a legal term to express a specific responsibility. The example 22 fully conform to the characteristics of the contract. It also reflects the relevance principle. And relevance principle requires the exclusive terms to economic and trade contracts.

3.3 Properly choosing proper syntax

As a legal style, once the contract comes into effect, the parties of contract will bear legal liability. When translating the economic and trade contracts, we should translate their specific stylistic features. In the contract, we often use "shall" and archaic words applied in the manner principle to express the obligations and responsibilities of the contractors.

Example 23

It shall be subject to ratification or acceptance by the signatory states.

The sentence is a very formal style and indicates that this convention is subject to ratification or acceptance by the signatory state. In addition, passive, declarative and conditional sentences should be used in the translation of the contract. The passive sentence is used in a series of clauses such as payment, mediation, dispute, etc. In order to make the clauses are clearly to the contract parties, the passive sentence should be used to put the important matters first. Declarative sentences are more formal, conditional sentences contain assumptions, in line with the language style of economic and trade contracts.

Example 24

If any of the joint ventures wish to assign its registered capital, it must obtain the consent of the other parties to the venture.

Example 24 uses a typical conditional clause to indicate that the registered capital of the parties to the venture must be agreed upon if it is to be transferred. It can be translated into Chinese as:"合营者的注册资本如果转让必须经合营各方同意。" The Chinese meaning changes the object of part of the original text into the subject. The subject in English should consider whether it can act as the executor of the action expressed by the verb, so we take "any of the joint ventures" as the subject in English. Such syntactic features reflect the characteristics of economic and trade contracts and apply the relevance principle in the principle of cooperative.

3.4 Correctly adopting similar structure of contract

The structure of economic and trade contract is compact and precise, the structure of the sentence is complete and rigorous to ensure to avoid ambiguity. As the fourth part of third chapter mentioned manner principles, including four requirements. "avoid ambiguity" and "to be clear", the criteria require that we must pay attention to when translating economic and trade contract sentence structural rigorous. It is because of this rigorous that we seldom see ellipsis in economic and trade contracts, and every sentence is related. For example, "about" seems to be an indeterminate word that rarely appears. When it does, it can be misunderstood by the parties for various reasons. Therefore, we should be precise in wording, and often use long sentences to convey the contract meaning in a more detailed and rigorous way.

Example 25

The prices stated are based on current freight rates, any increase or decrease in freight rates at time of shipment is to be the benefit of the buyer, with the seller assuming the payment of all transport at on charges to the point or place of delivery.

There are three contents. The calculation of the contract price, the buyer's responsibility for the freight and the seller's responsibility for the freight. The three meanings are closely connected, layer by layer. Under the guidance of the cooperative principle, we use the preposition "with" to connect clauses. The contract is more structured, the responsibilities of both parties are clear, and disputes are effectively avoided.

4. Conclusion

We can draw some conclusions such as: the lexical features of "time and the amount of the word is strictly limited" in the economic and trade English contract reflects the requirements of the quantity principle; Using "pairs of synonyms" in the English contracts reflects the requirements of the quality principle; the lexical features "using the modal verbs 'shall', written words and notional verbs" reflect the requirements of relevance principle; in the syntactic features "the use of conditional sentences", "the use of declarative sentences" and "the use of passive sentences" reflect the requirements of the relevance principle; in the discourse features, "continuous use of prepositions" and "repeated use of keywords" reflect the requirement of "avoidance of ambiguity" of the manner principle; in the lexical features, using the archaic words and abbreviations reflect the requirement of "avoid abundancy" of the manner principle; the similar and rigorous structure of the economic and trade contract reflects the requirement of "be orderly" of the manner principle.

After analyzing the application of the cooperative principles in economic and trade contracts, four suggestions are provided after the analysis. The first suggestion is appropriately adding or subtracting words to reached the required information; the second suggestion is accurately choosing words with clear meaning; the third suggestion is properly mastering the stylistic features of the contract and choosing proper syntax; the fourth suggestion is correctly adopting similar structure, words and words, sentences and sentences to have a sense of hierarchy.

It is concluded that Grice's cooperative principle is also of great significance to the translation of economic and trade contracts.

For translators, this study may help them to master cooperative principles, and choose more accurate language and clearer structure when translating contract text. When translating, the translators should meet the requirements of quantity principle to ensure that the transmitted information can be fully expressed.

To sum up, the Grice's cooperative principle plays an important role in the legal text of economic and trade English contract, and the Grice's cooperative principle theory can also serve as a guiding theory for the writing and translation of economic and trade English contract. However due to my experience is limited, the contract texts chosen are not enough so that the findings generated from this study need to be further investigated.

References

[1] BETHAN L. Grice's Cooperative Principle: Meaning and Rationality[J]. Journal of Pragmatics, 2007, 39(12): 19-23.

[2] GRICE H P. Logic and Conversation[M]//COLE P, MORGAN, J(eds). Syntactic Semantics, Vol.3: Speech Acts. New York: Academic Press, 1975: 42-58.

[3] MC CARTHY L. A Stranger in Stranger Lands: A College Student Writing across the Curriculum[J]. Research in the Teaching of English, 1987(21): 233-265.

[4] PAUL K. A Guide to Contracting for the Sale of Goods[M]. London: Bosten University Press, 1984.

[5] REED W. The Articulation of a New Rhetoric[J]. College Composition and Communication, 1987(38): 291-305.

[6] RUNDQUIST S. Indirectness: A Gender Study of Flouting Grice's Maxims[J]. Journal of Pragmatics, 1992(18): 431-432.

[7] 从琳. 目的论指导下的展会合同翻译报告[D]. 华北水利水电大学, 2017.

[8] 陈红. 目的论视角下商务合同的翻译报告[D]. 燕山大学, 2015.

[9] 窦璐. 合作原则对英语翻译教学实践的借鉴作用[J]. 读与写(教育教学刊), 2019(9): 04-16.
[10] 胡伟峰. 试论功能对等理论视角下的商务英语合同翻译[J]. 湖北开放职业学院学报, 2019(17): 180-181.
[11] 胡茜茜. 基于功能对等的商务英语翻译研究[J]. 安徽工程大学学报, 2018(6): 82-85.
[12] 李冰梅. 功能对等理论视角下的商务英语合同翻译[J]. 科技资讯, 2017(28): 218-219.
[13] 刘丽莹. 从合作原则看口译中的隐喻[J]. 内蒙古民族大学学报, 2016(3): 87-89.
[14] 戚云方. 合同与合同英语[M]. 杭州: 浙江大学出版社, 2004.
[15] 荣玉. 系统功能语言学理论指导下的商务合同翻译[J]. 海外英语, 2017(10): 195-198.
[16] 杨芳. 系统功能语言学理论指导下的商务合同翻译[J]. 中国科技翻译, 2005(1): 42-44.
[17] 张青松. 从会话合作原则看商务合同英语词汇的文体特征[J]. 徐州工程学院学报, 2006(11): 33-35.
[18] 张天心. 合作原则理论下中英广告语语用研究[J]. 科教文汇, 2017(2): 183-186.

点评

  论文探讨了格莱斯合作原则在经贸英语合同中的应用问题,分析了经贸英语合同词汇和语篇结构如何体现合作原则中数量原则、质量原则、关联原则和方式原则的要求,并指出了翻译经贸合同要以合作原则为指导,适当增减信息、调整结构、明确语义,以翻译出具有专业特色的目的语版本。论文结构较合理,语言较流畅,写作格式符合基本规范。建议增强理论视角创新,将参考文献与研究内容进一步密切结合。

《中国日报》和《纽约时报》态度资源运用对比研究

——以2020年意大利新冠肺炎疫情暴发后对政府行为的新闻报道为例

王慧敏[*]

摘要：研究以《中国日报》和《纽约时报》对2020年意大利新冠肺炎疫情大规模暴发后政府的处理方式的新闻报道为语料，以评价理论之态度系统中的裁决和鉴赏子系统为语义分析框架，采用定性和定量相结合的方法，对两者就同一国际问题报道中态度资源的运用进行对比研究，并从批判话语分析视角解读其异同。研究结果表明：两者裁决、鉴赏系统频次基本相同、比例差异较大。两者裁决、鉴赏子系统策略分布均力图塑造新闻话语表达的"客观性"，就态度系统运用而言，媒体报道的"客观性"只是话语建构的语言表象，态度系统所传达的态度极具意识形态色彩，并参与了意识形态话语建构。

关键词：评价理论；态度系统；批评话语分析（CDA）；新闻话语；对比分析

引言

中西媒体话语的比较研究是颇受关注的研究领域。现有中西媒体话语研究角度大致包括文体[1]、语类特征研究[2]、转述动词[3]与修辞等研究[4]等，对新闻话语的评价系统研究尚不多见。有学者探讨了新闻话语的评价系统框架，但相关实证研究尚显不足。王振华[5]结合语料分析了中英新闻评价系统，王欢、王国

---

[*] 王慧敏：上海大学外国语学院2019级硕士研究生。

凤[6]结合语料从语境入手分析了英语新闻语篇的评价策略,前者重在说明评价系统理论在新闻话语分析中的应用,后者重在解释语境与新闻评价策略的关系。这两个实证研究均未涉及新闻评价系统与意识形态建构之间的关系。新闻受各种价值因素操控[1],其意识形态与价值表达体现明显,新闻话语如何利用评价系统来建构意识形态值得关注。

研究以 Martin 评价理论中的态度系统为语义分析理论框架,以 *China Daily*(《中国日报》,下文简称《日报》)和 *New York Times*(《纽约时报》,下文简称《时报》)对意大利新冠肺炎暴发后政府行为的报道为语料,对两者就同一问题报道的态度资源运用进行对比研究,并从批判话语分析视角解读其异同,以求了解态度系统在新闻话语中的运用特征及其话语建构功能。

1. 态度系统:理论框架

评价理论是建构人际意义的语篇语义资源[7],关注语篇所协商的态度、所涉情感之强度以及表达价值的方式[8],是基于功能语言学人际意义研究发展而来的新词汇-语法框架[9]。评价下含三个子系统:态度(attitude)、介入(engagement)和级差(graduation)。本研究的试验研究(pilot study)发现《日报》与《时报》在介入、级差和态度系统中的情感系统资源上差异不大,在态度系统中的裁决子范畴和鉴赏子范畴则差异明显。这些差异值得深入剖析,故本研究从裁决子范畴和鉴赏子范畴入手对两者进行对比分析。下面对评价系统中的态度系统(Martin & White, 2005)作一概述。

态度是指语言所反映的对行为、道德、现象、语篇等的态度,包括情感(affect)、裁决(judgment)和鉴赏(appreciation)三个子系统,以下仅对本研究涉及的裁决、鉴赏两个系统进行介绍。

裁决系统根据相关规范、标准对行为进行判断,分为"社会评判"(social esteem)和"社会约束"(social sanction),有积极、消极之分。"社会评判"不受法律约束,倾向口语化,包括"行为规范"(normality)(典型词汇如 average、pitiful 等)、"做事才干"(capacity)(典型词汇如 powerful、insightful 等)和"坚忍程度"(tenacity)(典型词汇如 reliable、cowardly 等)。"社会约束"则与公约、法律等正式文本相关联,具有法律惩罚效力,与"真实可靠"(veracity)(典型词汇如 truthful、deceptive 等)、"是否得当"(propriety)(典型词汇如 moral、corrupt 等)

有关。

鉴赏是对文本、过程及现象等的评价,下含"反应"(reaction)、"构成"(composition)和"价值"(valuation),也有积极、消极之分。其中"反应"体现为"影响"(impact)(典型词汇如 captivating、dull)和"质量"(quality)(典型词汇如 welcome、revolting)。"构成"包括"平衡"(balance)(典型词汇如 balanced、discordant)和"细节"(complexity)(典型词汇如 precise、extravagant)。价值(valuation)通过社会标准来评价文本/过程的价值,(其典型词汇如 innovative、insignificant 等)。

基于以上态度系统理论框架,下文从词汇语义层面解读《日报》和《时报》对意大利新冠肺炎疫情大规模暴发后政府的处理方式的同期报道中态度资源的运用特征,并讨论其意识形态话语建构功能。

2. 研究方法

2.1 研究问题

本研究旨在回答:(1)《日报》和《时报》对意大利新冠肺炎疫情大规模暴发后政府的处理方式报道中的态度资源运用有何异同?(2)这些态度资源运用异同背后可能的原因是什么?

2.2 语料收集与分析

进行对比研究,语料对等是基础[10]。本研究语料来源中,《日报》是中国官方权威英文报纸,是国家重要外宣渠道;《时报》是美国权威英语报纸,倾向执政党的政治立场[11]。语料包括两家报纸网站在意大利新冠疫情确诊规模为全球最大时(2020年3月21日至3月27日)有关政府的处理方式的所有新闻报道(不含社论、特约评论等非新闻报道体裁),其中《日报》语料625词次,《时报》语料591词次。鉴于评价系统可通过"评价词汇"(evaluative lexis)传达意识形态[12],评价资源解读可基于词汇语义分析,两个目标语料规模相当,具有对等性。

笔者基于态度系统理论对语料从词汇语义层面进行编码、分类、定量统计,并对定量分析结果进行定性解读。定性解读侧重内容分析。笔者首先分析两者数量相当的态度资源之内容异同,以考察其态度资源运用目的是否一致,若其目的一致,其共同目的是什么,若其目的不同,其各自目的又分别是什么,以及这些异同体现出新闻报道什么样的话语特征,然后进行内容分析,以了解两者异同背后的态度立场差异及其新闻态度话语建构机制。

3.《中国日报》和《纽约时报》态度资源运用的对比分析

3.1 裁决系统

裁决系统的"社会评判"子范畴《日报》377 例,占 60%;《时报》353 例,占 59%。两者均以"做事才干"为最高,《日报》272 例,占 44%;《时报》250 例,占 42%。积极、消极情况详见表 1。举例如下:

(1) Cologna said there has been some enforcement [积极的做事才干] of the rules and each resident has been asked to carry a self-compiled notice, stating his or her purpose for going out.(March 21, 2020,《日报》)

(2) Italian authorities fumbled [消极的做事才干] many of those steps early in the contagion.(March 21,2020,《时报》)

两者"社会评判"系统内比例次高为"坚忍程度",《日报》105 例,占 17%;《时报》103 例,占 16%。积极、消极情况详见表 1。举例如下:

(3) "Every loss of life is a tragedy," Tedros said, calling it "motivation" [积极坚忍] to double down and do everything to stop transmission of the virus and save lives.(March 22,2020,《日报》)

(4) Some officials gave in [消极坚忍] to magical thinking, reluctant to [消极坚忍] make painful decisions sooner. All the while, the virus fed on that complacency.(March 22,2020,《时报》)

"社会评判"中"行为规范"在《日报》《时报》均未见相关实例。

"社会制约"子范畴中,"是否得当"在《日报》和《时报》中分别占 21%(129 例)、13%(76 例)。"是否真实"在《日报》中没有出现,《时报》中有 59 例,占 10%。举例如下:

(5) In the critical early days of the outbreak, Mr. Conte and other top officials sought to down play the threat, creating confusion and a false sense of security [行为不得当] that allowed the virus to spread.(March 23,2020,《时报》)

(6) Conte said that supermarkets and pharmacies would remain open, and banking and vital transport services would still be available, but that all non-

essential commercial activities would be prohibited[行为得当].(March 24,2020,《日报》)

(7) But tracing the record of their actions shows missed opportunities[非真实] and critical missteps[非真实].(March 25,2020,《时报》)

表1 裁决子系统使用频次和比例

《中国日报》	裁决(377)							
	社会评判 377(60%)				社会制约 353(59%)			
	做事才干		坚忍程度		是否真实		是否得当	
	积极	消极	积极	消极	积极	消极	积极	消极
频次	260	12	100	5	0	0	115	14
百分比	41%	3%	16%	1%	0	0	18%	3%
合计	272(44%)		105(17%)		0(0%)		129(21%)	
《纽约时报》	裁决(353)							
	社 会 评 判				社 会 制 约			
频次	12	238	21	82	15	44	13	63
百分比	2%	40%	4%	12%	3%	7%	2%	11%
合计	250(42%)		103(16%)		59(10%)		76(13%)	

3.2 鉴赏系统

《日报》鉴赏系统共69例(11%)。全部都是"质量",未见其他子范畴;《时报》鉴赏系统共162例(27%),只出现了两个子范畴,"构成"和"反应"。两个子范畴按频次从高到低为"构成"92例(16%)、"反应"70例(11%),举例如下。各子范畴的积极、消极频次及比例详见表2。

(8) Conte said he was speaking via social media because of a desire to "operate with complete transparency."[积极质量](March 26,2020,《日报》)

(9) Italy's piecemeal[消极构成] attempts to cut it off — isolating towns first, then regions, then shutting down the country in an intentionally porous[消

构成] lockdown — always lagged behind the virus's lethal trajectory[消极反应].(March 27, 2020,《时报》)

表2 鉴赏子系统使用频次和比例

《中国日报》	鉴赏(69)					
	质 量		构 成		反 应	
	积极	消极	积极	消极	积极	消极
频次	60	9	0	0	0	0
百分比	10%	1%	0	0	0	0
合 计	69(11%)		0(0%)		0(0%)	
《纽约时报》	鉴赏(162)					
频次	0	0	7	85	16	54
百分比	0	0	1%	15%	3%	8%
合 计	0(0%)		92(16%)		70(11%)	

根据以上定量分析,从词汇层面来看,《日报》和《时报》的裁决系统和鉴赏系统分布特征相反。下文讨论这些数据背后的具体态度表达。

4. 讨论

4.1 裁决

裁决系统在《日报》和《时报》中的频次及比例较为接近。两者均是"社会评判"高于"社会制约"。其他具体分析如下:

"社会评判":新闻报道面向大众读者"讲述事件",而不重"判定是非"。这可以解释为什么"社会评判"比"社会制约"比例高。《日报》积极"做事才干"高于"消极才干"比例,《时报》则相反;二者"做事才干"都与意大利政府对新冠肺炎暴发所做出的回应有关。如例(1),《日报》的积极"做事才干"烘托了意大利政府在要求民众隔离时坚定的态度和强硬的手段,这一点在民主国家本来是不太容易实现的;而例(2)中,《时报》对意大利政府开始没有采取积极措施,反而有所懈怠的消极一面进行了报道,侧面反映出现在疫情的大规模扩散和意大利政府办事不力有一定的关系。在这里可以看到,例(1)中,采用的词是"enforcement",是比较官方、权威的一个词。例(2)中,采用的是"fumble",是一个偏口语的贬义词,可以看出两家报纸在进行社会评判的时候各有偏重。通过对报道内容的选择和话语重复,《日报》建构出"支持意大利政府"的态度立场,表达了对意大利的鼓励。而《时报》对意大利政府采取的有效措施毫无提及。因此从《时报》和《日报》的"消极才干"在频次、比例上的差别就可以看出二者所传达的态度立场差异。

在"坚忍"范畴中,两者的"坚忍"资源都与疫情暴发初期意大利政府官员对待疫情的态度有关。《日报》更多见积极"坚忍",而《时报》的消极"坚忍"占据主导地位。《日报》的"坚忍"主要用来体现对意大利政府的信任态度,如例(3)所示,《日报》报道了意大利政府在对不幸在疫情中失去生命的公民的态度,其中,意大利政府把死亡的病人作为他们以后加强疫情防控管理和提升治疗手段的动力,化悲痛为力量,侧面肯定了意大利政府的毅力和决心,以及不被困难所打倒的勇气。《时报》的"坚忍"则很大程度上揭露了意大利政府官员表面下的虚伪和不作为,如例(4)所示,《时报》报道了意大利一些官员在疫情暴发初期沉迷于幻想,认为疫情并不严重,不太愿意"小题大做",尽早采取行动的现象。《日报》化消极为积极,而《时报》则倾向于犀利指出政府官员中一些消极被动的想法。可以从积极和消极"坚忍"资源的比例上看出二者对意大利当局政府内心活动的生动描写,并间接反映二者对意大利政府大相径庭的态度。

"社会制约":新闻报道基于已发生的事件、已发表的言论,不太需要突出强调内容的真实性,故两份报纸"是否真实"均低于"是否得当"。"是否得当"子系统中积极和消极资源比例在两份报纸中的大相径庭,体现出了二者不同的态度。《日报》中"行为得当"比例更大,而《时报》中"行为不得当"比例占主导地位,如例(5)和例(6)。例(5)出自《时报》,报道了意大利新冠疫情刚刚暴发的时候,高级政府官员们试图混淆视听,以期给大众营造一个"社会还是很安全"的印象,属于"不得当行为"。传播给大众一种意大利政府不负责任的形象。例(6)出自《日报》,报道了在意大利疫情发生后,政府已经勒令关掉了所有非必需的商业活动场所,属于"得当行为"。将意大利政府的正面形象传递给了读者。

4.2 鉴赏

《日报》和《时报》在鉴赏系统上差异较大,主要体现在"构成"、"反应"和"质量"上:

"构成":《日报》中未见"构成"类资源,《时报》中以消极"构成"类资源为主。消极"构成"着力体现意大利政府采取行动时懒散不力。如例(9)中,意大利政府对暴发的新冠疫情所采取的行动缓慢,本来疫情已经很严重了,意大利政府在防控的过程中,并没有做到"严防死守"。由此可见,《时报》表明了对意大利政府具体采取的步骤时,仍然是漏洞百出,行动不利的不支持和谴责,展示了自己的态度立场。

"反应":《日报》中未见"反应"类资源,《时报》中以消极比例高于积极比例。其中,消极"反应"类资源主要体现在意大利政府怠惰抗击疫情行为所产生的恶性后果,如例(9)中,由于意大利政府的怠慢行为,导致所采取的措施的防控能力远远赶不上病毒扩散的速度。层层递进,因果连环,表达了对意大利政府任由病毒肆虐的强烈不满。

"质量":《时报》中未见"质量"类资源,《日报》中以积极"质量"类资源为主。如例(8)中,《日报》报道了意大利政府对自己所采取措施的完全公开透明,目的是和民众建立信任感和纽带关系。从侧面反映出了《日报》对意大利政府拉近和公民关系的行为表示赞许和支持。

4.3 媒体话语中的态度系统与意识形态表达及建构

新闻话语要求"真实客观",但新闻又是新闻界与其他产业尤其是与政府和政治团体关系联盟的产物[13]。因此,意识形态的表达与建构是官方新闻话语的任务之一。评价系统中的态度系统在《日报》和《时报》中的运用充分体现出新闻话语的这一特点:一方面,两者的态度系统运用均力图塑造新闻话语的"真实客观性";另一方面,这一客观性所传达的两家媒体就同一重大国际问题的态度表述极具意识形态性,且两者运用"客观"语言所建构的态度存在差异。

汤普森和亨斯顿认为评价很难被挑战,因此可用评价来有效操纵读者。在快速新闻阅读中,读者不会细致入微地品读字句并决定是否同意其间蕴含的评价。相反,作者却假设读者是接受这些评价的,因此,评价在小句中的位置越不显眼,就越能成功地操纵读者[9],也越能成功地传达自己的态度。《日报》和《时报》作为中美权威报纸,运用态度系统建构"客观性"的同时,也通过态度系统与精选内容的嫁接,鲜明地传递了各自政府的态度与立场。

基于以上对比分析可以看出,新闻话语的"客观性"在很大程度上是话语建构的语言表象。其背后所传达的态度极具意识形态色彩,为各自所代表的机构、政党服务。

5. 结语

论文对《中国日报》和《纽约时报》有关意大利新冠肺炎疫情大规模暴发后政府的处理方式报道中的裁决、鉴赏两个态度子系统的使用特点进行了对比。研究结果表明:新闻话语中的态度系统运用参与了媒体的意识形态建构。笔者期望研究结果对读者解读新闻语篇的态度话语建构提供一定的参考价值。由于研究所采用的语料数量和来源均有限,只针对两个国家的两种报纸就一个主题的报道。研究结果尚需要在更广泛的语料中加以检验。

参考文献

[1] BELL A. The Language of News Media[M]. Oxford: Oxford University Press, 1991.

[2] 鞠玉梅.英语报刊体育新闻语体量化研究[J].外语研究,2004(2):23-27.

[3] MURATA K. Pro-and anti-whaling discourses in British and Japanese newspaper reports in comparison: a cross-cultural perspective. Discourse & Society[J], 2007, 18 (6): 741-764.

[4] 辛斌.《中国日报》和《纽约时报》中转述方式和消息来源的比较分析[J].外语与外语教学,2006(3):1-4.

[5] 王振华."硬新闻"的态度研究——"评价系统"应用研究之二[J].外语教学,2004(5):31-36.

[6] 王欢,王国凤.语言语境与新闻理解——英语硬新闻语篇评价策略解读[J].外语教学与研究,2012,44(5):671-681+799-800.

[7] MARTIN J R, WHITE P R R. The Language of Evaluation: Appraisal in English[M]. New York: Palgrave Macmillan, 2005.

[8] MARTIN J R, ROSE D. Working with Discourse: Meaning beyond the Clause[M]. London: Continuum, 2003.

[9] 李战子.评价理论:在话语分析中的应用和问题[J].外语研究,2004(5):1-6.

[10] 洪岗.跨文化语用学研究中的对等问题[J].外国语(上海外国语大学学报),2001

(2): 42-48.

[11] 沈国麟.《纽约时报》为什么支持奥巴马——美国大选中媒体和政党的关系[J].青年记者,2009(19): 78-80.

[12] 王振华.评价系统及其运作——系统功能语言学的新发展[J].外国语(上海外国语大学报),2001(6): 13-20.

[13] FOWLER R. Language in the New: Discourse and Ideology in the Press[M]. London: Routledge, 1991.

点评

论文以评价理论之态度系统中的裁决和鉴赏子系统为语义分析框架,聚焦2020年意大利新冠肺炎疫情大规模暴发后政府的处理方式的新闻报道,对比研究了《中国日报》和《纽约时报》就同一国际问题报道中态度资源的运用。论文选题新颖,观点鲜明,指出媒体报道的"客观性"只是话语建构的语言表象,态度系统所传达的态度极具意识形态色彩并参与了意识形态话语建构,结论具有一定的理论价值。建议扩大语料来源,增强结论的说服力。

问卷调查法在外语教育研究中的应用

王凯驰[*]

摘要：兹以 2015 年 1 月至 2020 年 5 月间发表在国内外 12 种外语类核心期刊的调查类文章为研究对象，采用内容分析法分析外语教学问卷调查研究的选题特点，问卷抽样方法的选择，信度效度评价以及问卷数据的描述。旨在通过以上这五方面来描述二语教学问卷调查研究的发展趋势并评价其中的研究方法质量。

关键词：二语教学研究；问卷；问卷调查发展趋势；研究方法质量

前言

近年来有关外语教学问卷调查法的研究综述有很多，例如郑新民和王玉山（2014）综述了 2008 年到 2013 年国内和国外的外语教学问卷调查研究文献，描述了近年来外语教学问卷调查研究的发展趋势。从 2015 年以来，调查类研究出现了哪些新趋势？外语教育研究者在做调查类的科研过程中都使用了什么样的抽样策略？问卷正式实施前是否有项目、信度、效度的评价？问卷数据的统计方法有哪些？通过检索中国知网，笔者发现有关上述问题的相关研究迄今还不多见。研究拟对 2015 年 1 月至 2020 年 5 月间国内外外语类核心期刊中发表的调查类文章进行分析，旨在了解当前我国外语教育研究中调查法使用的现状、趋势、存在的主要问题，并提出相应的对策和建议。以"外语教学"和"问卷"为主题词检索《外语教学》等国内外语类核心期刊，共得 30 篇文献。再以"second and foreign language teaching and learning"和"questionnaire"为主题词在综合类数据库 Web of Science 中检索 *The Modern Language Journal* 等国外外语类核心

---

[*] 王凯驰：上海大学外国语学院 2019 级硕士研究生。

期刊,共12篇文献。根据问卷研究话题、数据收集方法、数据统计方法以及信度、效度评价,将每篇研究报告进行对比分析。

首次文件检索后,笔者对收集到的6类外文期刊和6类中文期刊的摘要和方法部分进行了详细的分析,去掉了那些没有使用问卷作为数据收集方法之一的研究报告,留下了带有问卷的实证性外语研究;在第二轮数据审核中,笔者对手头的每一份数据进行了扫描,提取了问卷题目、数据收集方式等信息,并去掉带有言谈情境填充问卷的研究。此外,只注重收集研究对象的背景信息的问卷调查也需被移除,因为这类问卷不能表明问卷调查发展的趋势和选题。

通过以上两轮的数据审核,最终获得12篇外文文献和30篇中文文献。表1列出了各个期刊来源的研究论文数量。

表1 国内外12种外语类核心期刊近5年间发表的问卷调查研究论文

国内刊物名	论文数	国 外 刊 物 名	论文数
外语教学	7	The Modern Language Journal	1
外语学刊	7	TESOL Quarterly	3
外语电化教学	3	Studies in Second Language Acquisition	3
外语界	8	Language Learning	1
外语与外语教学	3	Applied Linguistics	2
外语教学与研究	2	Language Teaching Research	2

研究主要通过内容分析法,按照以下分析框架仔细阅读每篇论文的研究主题与研究方法部分:

① 外语教学问卷调查研究的选题特点:外语学习者(学习策略、学习归因研究等)、外语教师课堂教学(外语教师观念、教学知识的掌握以及应对教学难题时所持的教学态度等),以及教学评估等。

② 抽样方法的选择(有无抽样策略、抽样类型)。

③ 外语教学调查问卷的评价(有无项目、信度、效度分析以及操作过程是否严谨)。

④ 问卷数据的汇总和统计分析(描述性统计和推断性统计)。

1. 外语教学调查问卷适用范围

纵观国内外过去五年来的外语教学问卷调查研究,不难发现现有问卷所调查的对象和范围主要集中于外语学习者、外语教师课堂教学,以及教学评估等方面。其中用得最多的要数针对外语学习者的问卷。因此笔者将所收集到的文献按照以下选题进行分类[①]。

(1) 针对外语学习者的问卷

针对外语学习者的问卷着重于学习者个体差异或个人因素方面,学习者的认知、情感、能力和背景等内容。

在学习策略方面,边家胜和董玉琦(2018)研究了 CTCL 视阈下外语学习者的合作学习策略;秦利民与 Lawrence Zhang(2017)研究了多媒体环境下外语学习者的写作元认知策略。在外语者的学习动机、态度以及效能感方面,Courtney 等人(2017)研究了在早期二语学习阶段,学习动机以及对二语学习的态度对以法语为母语者的英语学习结果的影响。在外语交际意愿方面,Zhang 等人(2016)采用重复测量设计和一组中国大学生测试来研究英语课堂中外语交际意愿在一个学期内的波动情况和背后的原因。问卷还可以用来调查影响外语学习的因素(即学习归因研究)。Brunfaut 和 Révész(2015)调查了听力文本的语速、所用语言的复杂性、明确性等文本特征造成学习者听力理解困难的原因。由于无法排除学习者个人差异的影响,Brunfaut 和 Révész(2017)在前研究的基础上增加了用于调查学习者听力焦虑的问卷研究,使得研究结果更加具有说服力。

(2) 关于外语教师、外语教学现状和教学评估方面的问卷

外语教师观念、教学知识的掌握以及应对教学难题时所持的教学态度。比如,Indrarathne(2019)调查了教师对患有阅读障碍症的学生有多少了解,以及在教学实施中对患有该症状学生的教学态度。

(3) 二语学习者的文化身份研究和外语教学需求分析

外语教学研究常常包括文化身份与外语学习者语言能力的相关性研究,比如 Schroederet 等人(2017)发现了双语学习的几个方面包括二语习得年龄、二语熟练程度、二语口音、二语习得浸泡环境和当前语言接触环境对文化认同有预测

---

① 本研究综述文献较多,受篇幅限制恕未一一列出。

作用。

（4）外语反拨效应以及对外语教学理论的验证性研究

国内语言测试界对反拨效应研究的兴趣和重视程度与日俱增。蔡金亭等人（2018）对浙江省高考外语"一年两考"改革新模式的反拨效应进行了研究。

近年来外语教学理论验证性研究的文献数量大大减少，42篇文章中只有1篇文献属于对外语教学理论的验证性研究，即詹先君（2015）以中国大学生为研究对象，对二语自我中的核心因素、理想二语自我进行了多群组验证。

（5）翻译研究

文献分析还发现，近年来文献通过问卷进行翻译研究。调查译者的修辞认知对译文文学性的影响（冯全功，胡本真，2019）翻译标准理解上的一致性、译者对译文评价的一致性、译者对记忆与口译之间的关系的看法等。上述问卷研究的特点反映近年来我国外语界实证研究的一个重要趋势，同时也反映了当前外语教学的改革现状。

2. 抽样方法的选择

问卷调查研究中使用的抽样方法有很多，总的来讲有非概率抽样和概率抽样两大类。笔者按照有无抽样方法以及概率非概率抽样将收集到的文献分为三大类（如表2所示）。

表2 抽样类型统计

抽样类型	频率	百分比
未提到抽样	25	60%
概率抽样	10	24%
非概率抽样	7	16%
总计	42	100%

从表2可以看出，近5年外语教学领域问卷调查研究使用抽样方法偏少，抽样策略单调。无抽样的文章有26篇，占了63%，在使用了抽样的文章中，概率抽

样有9篇,而概率抽样有6篇,说明在调查类研究中,研究者更偏好概率抽样,少数进行质化研究或混合研究的研究者会使用非概率抽样。在42篇调查类研究论文中,有26篇文章未提到具体策略中的任何一种,也无法通过其文章来推断,由此推断,研究者对抽样策略的使用能力有待提高。在明确提到的抽样策略中,概率抽样使用最多的是随机抽样,有5篇;非概率抽样使用最多的是便利抽样,有3篇。在15篇提到抽样方法的文献中,只有一篇文献使用了3种及3种以上的抽样策略。

3. 外语教学调查问卷的评价

在完成问卷整理及数据准备工作后,还需进行问卷的评价。问卷的初步评价,包括问卷初稿完成后设计者的自我评价,专家或同行的评价,这些评价都是一些主观性的内容效度评价。除了主观性评价外,还需要根据问卷数据进行一些客观性评价,即问卷的项目分析、信度分析和结构效度分析。

3.1 问卷的项目分析

本研究讨论的项目分析仅限于定量分析的狭义的项目分析。通过项目分析可以排除答案变化太小的项目,确保问卷项目具有良好的区分度。常用的分析方法有极端分组法和内部一致性分析法。笔者根据有无项目分析以及两种项目分析方法将42篇文献分为三大类:

表3 项目分析统计

项目分析类型	频 率	百 分 比
无项目分析	13	31%
极端分组法	12	29%
内部一致性分析法	17	40%
总 计	42	100%

在42篇文献中,用来检验项目区分度的分析方法中使用频率最高的是用内部一致性分析法来检验项目内部的一致性,百分比为40%。除了上述方法以

外,问卷调查研究还利用独立样本 t 检验方法,比较高分组和低分组在每个项目上的差异,最后根据各变量的 t 值和 P 值来判断性显著性差异,该检验方法称为极端分组法。在进行项目分析的 29 篇文献中,有一篇文献同时使用了两种项目分析方法来检验项目区分度。

3.2 问卷的信度分析

信度也称可靠性,它是指测量结果的稳定程度或一致性程度。笔者根据有无信度分析以及外在信度和内在信度将所收集到的文献分为三大类:

表 4 信度分析统计

信度分析类型		频 率	百 分 比
外在信度	再测信度	4	10%
	复本信度	0	0%
	评分信度	3	7%
内在信度	折半信度	1	2%
	克朗巴哈系数法	26	62%
无信度分析		8	19%
总 计		42	100%

根据表 4 信度分析统计,在内在一致性检验中,最常用的信度系数为克朗巴哈系数,42 篇文献中就有 26 篇用到该方法。经文献分析发现,态度、意见式问卷的信度分析常用克朗巴哈系数法来测量问卷的信度。比如,在调查教师对患有阅读障碍症的学生的教学态度时,Indrarathne(2019)通过各调查项目相关系数的均值测量、关注问卷中每一个题目得分间的内在一致性。但是,笔者在文献分析时发现有些包括几个领域内容的问卷在估算克朗巴哈系数时,并没有将整体问卷分成几个维度来分别计算各个维度的内部一致性信度系数,而只是估算了整个问卷的信度系数,这将影响整个问卷的内部一致性,并且最终计算出来的信度系数较低。当然,信度分析最终得到的信度系数并不总是可以接受的,例如 Csizér 与 Kontra(2020)发现包含两个问项的用于调查社交学习策略问卷的克朗巴哈系数等于 0.50,因为该系数在 0.6 以下就要考虑重新编问卷,因

此两人决定将该问卷排除在数据分析步骤之外。

折半信度方适合于检验态度量表的内在一致性（Dörnyei & Taguchi，2015）。42篇文献中仅有1篇文献用到了该方法。该文献利用态度量表测量在早期二语学习阶段中二语学习的态度对以法语为母语者的英语学习结果的影响，并用折半信度法检验测量的内在一致性，通过在量表中增加一倍的测量项目，重复前半部分项目的测量内容，但在措辞上不同（Courtney等人，2017）。

在42篇文献中，未能发现汇报中使用了复本信度方法的问卷调查研究。笔者早已预料到这一统计结果，因为秦晓晴（2009）在《外语教学问卷调查法》一书中说明了应用语言学文献中倾向于再测信度而不是复本信度的原因在于复本信度需要设计两个版本的测量工具，需要耗费大量的时间，并且难度也很大。

3.3 问卷内容效度及其检验方法

检验问卷的内容效度主要是对问卷项目与研究目的之间的联系进行定性分析。笔者根据是否进行问卷内容效度检验将所收集到的文献分为以下两类：

表5　内容效度检验统计

内　容　效　度	频　　率	百　分　比
有内容效度	11	26%
无内容效度	31	74%
总　　计	42	100%

从统计结果可以看出，近5年外语教学领域问卷调查研究并不重视内容效度的检验，在所收集到的文献中仅有27%的文献进行了内容效度的检验，并且27%的文献中绝大多数使用内容效度的定性方法单一，不是只使用了专家评价或只通过试测让受访者进行效度检验。例如吴玉玲等人（2018）在问卷编制后进行了逻辑论证，邀请了3位专家和5位英语师范专业任课教师对问卷项目与测量结构的内容范围进行了对比、访谈、征求修改意见。

3.4 问卷结构效度及其检验方法

建立结构效度的方法主要是因子分析。因子分析有探索性因子分析和验证性因子分析之分。笔者根据有无结构效度检验方法以及因子分析的分类将42篇文献分为四类（如表6）：

表 6　结构效度检验统计

结构效度检验的类型	频　率	百 分 比
无结构效度检验	20	48%
探索性因子分析	11	25%
验证性因子分析	7	17%
探索性+验证性因子分析	4	10%
总　　计	42	100%

通过统计结果可以发现近 5 年外语教学领域问卷调查研究共有 22 篇文献用到了因子分析来检验问卷的结构效度。如果研究者主要依靠自己的探索性研究结果开发出问卷,而且事先对观测数据背后存在多少个基础变量(即因子)一无所知,就可用探索性因子分析方法以弄清所测结构的维度。例如 Saito 等人(2019)在调查受访者外语学习背景的问卷设计中(涵盖了 24 个背景变量),因为变量之间高度相关,导致多重共线性现象。因此他们使用探索性因子分析,采用方差最大化旋转法以获取 110 名受访者背景信息下的无法直接测量到的隐性变量。

4. 问卷数据的汇总和统计分析

问卷评价工作完成以后,就可转入正式的数据分析阶段。数据分析一般分为两个阶段:描述性统计和推断性统计。以下要讨论如何根据是非题、多项单选题、多项多选题、排序题、利克特量表等不同问题类型及编码结果进行数据描述。

(1) 单选题的数据描述

这里所讨论的单选题为是非题和多项单选题,在数据文件中这些问题变量均为定类数据。例如 Schroeder 等人(2017)为调查受访者外语文化活动的参与度的是非题"随着 X 语言能力的提高,你是否改变了参加与 X 文化相关的活动频率?"使用包含个案数和百分比的条形图形式进行数据描述。杨维东和赵娟(2016)用包含个案数和百分比的表格描述一个关于研究生经常阅读的课外英语读物,有 5 个选项的多项单选题,属定类变量。

(2) 多选题的数据描述

申云化等人(2016)调查不同英语课程的兴趣频率分布。共有英语口语、应用文写作、学术英语阅读、英汉翻译、学术英语写作以及英语听力六个选项。调查对象为来自理学、工学和人文3大学科的在校研究生。调查采用多重二分法录入问卷多选题数据,被选项定义为数值"1",未选项定义为数值"0",以此统计各选项的选择频次和百分比。并根据不同学科作聚类条形图,可以反映不同学科在英语课程兴趣方面的区别。

(3) 排序题的数据描述

例如在要求受访者对英语各项技能重要性进行排序,编码结果共有5个,每个变量有5个等级,每个变量都是定序变量,申云化等人(2016)使用包含频数、百分比的表格分别描述5种英语学习目的重要性的变化情况,从中可以看出对于每个受访者来说,不同的英语学习技能其重要性是不一样的。

(4) 多指标的数据描述

赵冠芳和吕云鹤(2019)使用的评估学术写作能力各因子重要性的克特量表中包括了17个项目,经过信度和效度分析后,将它们分为"语言能力""逻辑和分析论证""体裁知识"和"专业知识"4个方面。也就是说,根据原有的17个变量新生成了4个变量。对于这4个变量,赵和吕紧接着使用平均值、标准差、偏度和标准误进行数据描述。

5. 调查法使用存在的主要问题

通过分析调查类研究的研究主题、抽样方法、问卷评价和问卷数据的统计,我们发现在这些调查类研究中还存在着以下几大问题:

(1) 样本大小不合适

样本的大小取决于总体的分布区域。对42篇论文的分析显示,有14篇(33.3%)调查研究中样本的范围或大小不太合适。如有的研究者在文献标题前冠以"中国"等大概念,这属于全国性研究,平均样本数最好在1 500至2 500人之间(秦晓晴,2009),如要研究中国非英语专业研究生英语惯例语能力研究,我们要考虑到全国非英语专业研究生存在着地区差异、英语水平差异、性别差异等,但是该研究者只是从某城市的某高校中抽取了50名受试者,这显然不能代表全国大学的学生情况。

样本大小还取决于使用的统计分析方法。笔者发现42篇文献中使用方差分析的研究占到了定量研究的32%以上,但是有些研究却并没有满足使用方差分析所必备的条件,这些研究结果的效度也就可想而知了。这种问题在国内的学术期刊上也不是个别现象,如国内有人在研究基于微信的交互式翻译移动教学模式时采用了两组受试者进行对比,两组受试者人数均为26人,未提到各组数据是否呈正态分布,选用的分析方式是t检验。t检验是参数检验,它要求每组的人数最少不能低于30个,或者说要求各组数据呈正态分布。显然,该研究数据并未达到使用t检验的要求。当数据与分析方法不一致时,分析结果就可能是不可信的。

(2) 不重视问卷的项目区分度、信效度考证

一个调查问卷结果要令人信服,要让人相信问卷调查者确实调查到了想调查的东西,必须有信度和效度资料。从统计结果可以看出来,近5年外语教学领域问卷调查研究仍有许多研究并不重视问卷的信效度考证,在所收集到的42篇文献中13篇无项目分析;8篇文献无信度检验;有20篇文献无结构检验;31篇文献无内容效度检验,并且在有内容效度检验的文献中绝大多数使用的检验方法单一。任何不具备"全面性"的评估都不能获得令人信服的结论,这一点应该引起研究者的充分重视(Brown,2001)。

(3) 问卷效度评价的操作过程不严谨

在做因子分析之前,首先应检验数据是否适合因子分析。在22篇应用到了因子分析检验方法的文章中,有6篇文献并没有说明检验的数据是否符合因子分析的条件,这表明作者并没有按照严格的因子分析步骤进行效度检验,这显然是不合理的。判断数据是否适合因子分析可以通过主成分分析效度检验指标或巴特利特球形检验值来说明。例如戴朝晖和陈坚林(2016)在探索性因子分析前,首先查看问卷的KMO值为0.958,接近1.0,再进行巴特利特球形检验,分析发现所有题项达到极显著的水平,表明问卷比较适合做因子分析。

6. 结语

研究采用了内容分析法,通过对发表在国内外外语类核心期刊(2015年1月至2020年5月)上的42篇调查类文献进行文本分析。研究结果表明我国高校外语教育研究者在研究主题方面体现了多元化研究倾向,并且笔者在42篇文

献中未发现有文献使用了不合理的问卷数据统计方法,都满足了描述性以及推断性统计方法的使用条件。但研究也发现外语教育研究者在研究方法方面缺乏较系统的训练。笔者发现近5年外语教学领域问卷调查研究使用抽样方法偏少,抽样策略单调。在确定研究总体以及样本抽取时,存在样本总体范围过大而样本数过小、样本大小不符合数据统计分析的要求等问题。在研究方法质量方面,有不少研究者在问卷正式实施之前竟无任何考证资料来证实问卷的信度和效度。这一点与秦晓晴(2017)的研究结果相似。由于研究者缺乏较为系统和严格的方法论训练,在很大程度上影响了他们所撰写的研究论文的质量,间接导致论文成果的较低引用率。

参考文献

[1] 边家胜,董玉琦.CTCL视阈下外语学习者合作学习策略实证研究[J].外语电化教学,2018(6):16-23.

[2] 蔡金亭,陈艳君,胡利平.外语高考改革新模式的反拨效应研究[J].外语学刊,2018(1):79-85.

[3] 戴朝晖,陈坚林.基于慕课理念的大学英语翻转课堂影响因素研究[J].外语电化教学,2016(7).

[4] 冯全功,胡本真.译者的修辞认知对译文文学性影响的实证研究[J].外语学刊,2019(1):97-103.

[5] 高强,刘琳.大学英语教师听力教学信念及其与教学实践关系探究[J].外语界,2015(2):33-41.

[6] 秦利民,ZHANG L.多媒体环境下英语写作者元认知策略量表的研制与开发[J].外语电化教学,2017(3):28-36.

[7] 秦晓晴.外语教学问卷调查研究的发展趋势及选题特点[J].外语教学,2017(3):103.

[8] 秦晓晴.外语教学问卷调查法[M].北京:外语教学与研究出版社,2009:195.

[9] 申云化,ZHANG L J,潘海英.基于"输出驱动假设"的研究生英语学习需求调查[J].外语界,2016(5):44-51.

[10] 吴玉玲,邱思莲,李沐阳.英语师范生学科素养测量研究[J].外语教学,2018(5):61-65.

[11] 杨维东,赵娟.基于建构主义理论的"任务型、互动式"教学模式研究——以非英语专业硕士研究生英语课堂教学为例[J].外语教学,2016(5):56-60.

[12] 詹先君.中国情景中的理想二语自我多群组验证[J].外语教学与研究,2015(4): 573-584+641.

[13] 赵冠芳,吕云鹤.英语专业本科生对学术英语写作的构念认知[J].外语与外语教学,2019(6):69-79+147.

[14] 郑新民,王玉山.如何在外语教育研究中科学地使用调查法——基于我国外语类CSSCI期刊文章(2008-2013年度)的分析[J].外语电化教学,2014(4):8-13.

[15] BROWN J D. Using surveys in language programs[M]. UK: Cambridge University Press,2001:245-247.

[16] BRUNFAUT T, RÉVÉSZ A. The role of task and listener characteristics in second language listening[J]. TESOL Quarterly, 2015, 49:(1).

[17] COURTNEY L, GRAHAM S, TONKYN A, et al. Individual differences in early language learning: a study of English learners of French[J]. Applied Linguistics, 2017, 38(6): 824-847.

[18] CSIZÉR K, KONTRA E H. Foreign language learning characteristics of deaf and severely hard of hearing students[J]. The Modern Language Journal, 2020,104(1):233-249.

[19] DöRNYEI Z, TAGUCHI T. Questionnaires in second language research: construction, administration,and processing(2nd ed.)[M]. New York: Routledge, 2015.

[20] INDRARATHNE B. Accommodating learners with dyslexia in English language teaching in Sri Lanka: Teachers' knowledge, attitudes, and challenges[J]. TESOL Quarterly, 2019, 53(3).

[21] RÉVÉSZ A, BRUNFAUT T. Text characteristics of task input and difficulty in second language listening comprehension[J]. Studies in Second Language Acquisition, 2017, 35(1):31-65.

[22] SAITO K, TRAN M, SUZUKIDA Y, et al. How do second language listeners perceive the comprehensibility of foreign-accented speech? [J]. Studies in Second Language Acquisition, 2019,41(5):1133-1149.

[23] SCHROEDER S R, LAM T Q, MARIAN V. Linguistic Predictors of Cultural Identification in Bilinguals[J]. Applied Linguistics, 2017, 38(4):463-488.

[24] ZHANG J Y, BECKMANN N, BECKMANN, J F. One situation doesn't fit all: Variability and stability of state willingness to communicate in a Chinese ollege English classroom[J]. Language Teaching Research, 2019(4).

 点评

  论文研究了 2015 年 1 月至 2020 年 5 月发表在国内外 12 种外语类核心期刊的调查类文章,采用内容分析法分析外语教学问卷调查研究的选题特点、问卷抽样方法的选择、信度效度评价等,评测二语教学问卷调查研究的发展趋势和研究方法的使用质量。本文选题合理,主旨明确,分析较为合理,结论对于外语教学领域具有一定的理论和实践意义。

论萨拉·沃特斯《轻舔丝绒》中的女性亚文化风格[①]

魏韵玲[*]

摘要：《轻舔丝绒》是英国当代新锐小说家萨拉·沃特斯出版的第一部长篇小说。作者站在新历史背景下重构维多利亚时代女性的生活方式，真实地再现了当时女性的社会地位及女性亚文化的艰难发展。研究以《轻舔丝绒》这部小说为文本，基于伯明翰学派的亚文化理论，剖析维多利亚时代女性亚文化在社会生活中的体现，探究女性亚文化风格如何与男性主导的文化进行抵抗，以此对当下女性亚文化的发展及女性在社会中的地位提供反思和借鉴。

关键词：《轻舔丝绒》；萨拉·沃特斯；女性亚文化；亚文化风格；亚文化抵制

萨拉·沃特斯（Sarah Waters，1966—）是当今英国文坛最受瞩目的新锐女作家之一。她早期创作的三部长篇小说《轻舔丝绒》(Tipping the Velvet，1998)、《半身》(Affinity，1999)、《荆棘之城》(Fingersmith，2002)都是以19世纪英国维多利亚时代为创作背景，通过戏仿的形式展开历史和当代社会现实之间的对话，创作主题均围绕女性情感纠缠和女性婚姻等同性恋问题展开，以编撰历史的形式重构维多利亚时期被社会边缘化的女性生活状态，因此这三部作品也被称为"维多利亚三部曲"(the Victoria Trilogy)。三部曲出版后受到文学界的广泛关注和读者的追捧，媒体对她的评价是"笔触深邃、情节巧妙、人物刻画入微，充满了维多利亚时代特有的压抑情绪和蠢蠢欲动的禁忌氛围"。萨拉·沃特斯因独

---

[*] 魏韵玲：广州大学外国语学院2019级硕士研究生。
[①] 原载《安徽农业大学学报（社会科学版）》2021年第1期，本书收录时略有修改。

特的写作视角斩获多项文学殊荣,她被 Granta 杂志选为"20 位当代最好的英语作家"之一(2003),获得英国《星期日泰晤士报》的"年度青年作家奖"(2000)、"年度英语作家奖"(2003)、"CWA 历史犯罪小说匕首奖"(2002),入围"柑橘奖"(2002,2006)和"布克奖"(2002,2006,2009)等。

《轻舔丝绒》是萨拉·沃特斯出版的第一部小说,以牡蛎女孩南希(Nancy)的三段情感故事为主线。南希在游艺宫看表演时爱上了男装丽人演员姬蒂(Kitty),远离故土与姬蒂同去伦敦闯荡演出。南希在受到初恋姬蒂的情感背叛后离开姬蒂,成为贵妇戴安娜(Diana)的情人,过着纸醉金迷的生活。被戴安娜赶出门的南希投奔了曾有一面之交的朋友弗罗伦丝(Florence),最终两人成为共同为社会主义事业奋斗的恋人。

1. 女性亚文化的历史溯源

"亚文化"(Subculture)这一术语最早出现在 20 世纪 40 年代芝加哥学派的社会学研究中。1964 年,英国伯明翰文化研究(The Center for Contemporary Cultural Studies, CCCS)中心成立,云集了诸如斯图亚特·霍尔(Stuart Hall)、菲尔·科恩(Phil Cohen)、迪克·赫伯迪格(Dick Hebdige)等为代表的研究者。根据伯明翰学派的观点,由于社会、地区、阶级等方面的差异,出现了许多不同的文化群体。其中,在一个社会中占统治或主导地位的文化一般被称为"主流文化";而某一群体所持有的足以区别于他者的社会文化或行为特性则被称为"亚文化"[1]。"主流文化"体现的是社会主流的价值观,它所代表的是一个社会中占支配地位的阶级或群体的意志,而亚文化是社会中处于边缘地位的群体的文化表达,是从属、次要与支流的文化。在一定程度上,它的存在也是对主流文化的抵制和解构。伯明翰学派从文化的角度对亚文化进行界定:"正如前缀 sub 所示,亚文化是更为广泛的文化内种种富有意味而别具一格的协商(negotiations)。他们同身处社会与历史大结构中的某些社会群体所遭际的特殊地位、暧昧状态与具体矛盾相适应。"[2]这一定义指出亚文化抵抗性、风格化及边缘化的三个重要特征。然而,该学派对于"亚文化"的研究具有强烈的男性寓意,是对男性表达和男性风格的唯我独尊式的关注,女性群体很难成为被研究的主体,且受到长期忽视。20 世纪 60 年代由于受到第二次妇女解放运动及后现代主义思潮的影响,女性群体日益壮大,女性文化乃至女性亚文化在更包容多元的世界得以凸显。以安吉拉·麦克罗比(Angela McRobbie,1951—)为代表的妇女研究小组继承与批判伯明翰学派的亚文化理论基础,推动了女性亚文化(Female Subculture)的研究。麦克罗比认为女性在亚文化研究中并未缺席,而是亚文化特殊表现方式和社会特征使得女性"不露面或者是部分出场"[3]。她重点关注女性在亚文化中处于怎样的地位、扮演着怎样的角色以及通过何种方式建构了一个有别于男性的文化空间[4]。女性亚文化与男性亚文化的差异主要表现在"风格"与"文化空间"的不同。女性亚文化的形成经历了从第一个在亚文化中出场的女性群体"无赖女孩"(Teddy girls)到"慕嬉士女孩"的风格演变。文化空间主要集中在家庭、学校及俱乐部等。本研究以萨拉·沃特斯小说《轻舔丝绒》为文本,探究小说从哪些方面体现出维多利亚时期女性亚文化?维多利亚时期女性亚文化风格如何与主流文化进行"抵制与反抗"?维多利亚时期女性亚文化的研究又对当下思考女性亚文化发展及女性社会地位提供了怎样的思考和借鉴?

2.《轻舔丝绒》中的女性亚文化表现

萨拉·沃特斯在重构历史的过程中,极大地还原了维多利亚时期(Victorian era,1837—1901)真实的社会风貌。当时的英国在政治、经济、文化等各个领域都开创了一个崭新的时代,成为世界上最强大的"日不落"帝国。然而,工业革命迅速发展的同时也激发了一系列的社会矛盾。在这一时期英国社会的群体分化严重,社会阶层愈加复杂化,女性的生活状况也被卷入这场变化的洪流之中。工商业的发展培养了一批有闲阶层的女性。同时,社会化大生产将女性从琐碎的家务中解放出来,越来越多的女性不满足于成为男性的附庸,走出家庭谋求工作,从而也推动了妇女运动的发展。因此在这个时期女性亚文化显现在社会中的方方面面。沃特斯《轻舔丝绒》中女性亚文化主要表现在服饰、场景及语言三个方面。

首先是小说出现了大量维多利亚时期女性服饰的细致描述。罗兰·巴特(Roland Barthes,1915—1980)曾说过:"服饰可以被当作符号来对待,一面是样式、布料和颜色,另一面是场合、职业、状态、方式,或者我们可以进一步将其简化为一面是服装,另一面是世事。"[5]因此不同的服装特色体现不同女性的社会阶层。当时贵族女性的华美又多样化的服饰引领社会时尚,平民女性的服装是对上流社会的学习和模仿。维多利亚时代初期,复古风盛行,蕾丝被大量使用,配在衣服的领口、袖口、下摆等处。此外,还大量运用了荷叶边、蝴蝶结、包钮以及具有王室风格的高腰、公主袖等。维多利亚时期贵族还掀起了男女服饰元素混合的热潮。戴安娜让南希进行角色扮演,曾让她装扮成珀尔修斯、丘比特、亚马孙女战士、安提诺乌斯等人物,配上弯刀、翅膀、弓箭、古罗马宽袍及腰带等配饰。上流社会女性服饰元素成为平民女性争相模仿的对象。当南希还是牡蛎女孩的时候,在重要的场合穿上有绸缎腰带和蕾丝的晚装长裙、用中国丝绸做的低领短袖裙子。在音乐厅和剧场工作的女演员的服饰也出现了大量男性服饰特色。南希第一次见到台上的姬蒂时,她"穿着一套剪裁得体的男士西服,袖口和前襟镶着闪亮的丝绸。翻领上别着一朵玫瑰,前袋里插着一副淡紫色的手套。她背心下面穿的是雪白笔挺的衬衫,立领有两英寸高。她的领口系着一个白色蝴蝶结,头上戴着一顶礼帽。"[6]警察制服、禁卫军制服、法兰绒西裤等都是当时"男装丽人"非常热衷的装扮,系领结、穿裤子对于女演员们来说也很普遍。同时她们的装扮也会融入蕾丝、蝴蝶结手套、丝绸背心和长筒袜、天鹅绒等女性元素。南希和姬蒂成为双人组合登台表演之后,掀起了模仿热潮:"一对穿男装、戴礼帽、穿长靴的女孩比单独一个更令人激动,更有魅力,更有一种说不出的活泼俏皮……她穿着一英寸高的鞋子,我穿着女性化的平底鞋,那剪裁得当的西装凸显我苗条的身材和女性的曲线。"[7]后来南希和姬蒂一同在不列颠剧院演童话剧《灰姑娘》时,女演员的服装都非常精致美观,"简直是你这辈子见过的最好的演出服"[8],其中包括有金色的裤子、闪闪发亮的背心、马裤、薄纱、水手服等。女性和男性混合的服饰装扮形成了维多利亚时期独特的女性亚文化风景线。

第二个表现女性亚文化的是女性出现的场景。《轻舔丝绒》通过女主人公南希的个人成长缩影,折射出维多利亚时期女性逐渐挣脱家庭束缚,寻找社会位置的尝试。因此这个时期的女性有了更多在社会中活动的空间。南希最初是英国小镇惠特斯特布尔的"牡蛎女孩",在坎特伯雷游艺宫与姬蒂相识。姬蒂是女扮男装的"男装丽人",剪着帅气利落的短发,在舞台上歌唱舞蹈。由于南希对姬蒂的爱恋,她决定远离家乡,跟随姬蒂到伦敦,免不了家人的担忧:"她抱着我,哭着说放我走真是愚蠢。还有戴维,他荒谬地说,我现在去伦敦还太小了,一到伦敦就会被特拉法加广场的有轨电车撞倒。还有艾丽斯,听到这个消息她什么都没说,而是哭着跑出了厨房,谁也劝不动,直到午餐时间才出来干活。"[9]南希在离家之前,家人"哭",觉得南希"愚蠢","去伦敦还太小",姐姐"谁也劝不动"。家人的反应从侧面看出对于当时的女性,尤其是偏远小城镇的女性想要外出闯荡,是不被主流文化观念理解和接受的。

布利斯带领南希和姬蒂参观伦敦时,看见许多剧院和歌剧院,如瑞典著名女高音珍妮·林德(Jenny Lind,1820—1887)首场演出的女王剧院,还有克里剧院、帝国剧院、阿尔罕布拉剧院等等,众多女演员、女歌唱家都在这些地方成为明星,也吸引了不同阶层的女性观众如"从马车上下来的淑女"、"端着鲜花和水果的女孩"、"披着披肩的女人、系着领带的女人,还有穿着短裙,露出脚踝的女人"[10]前往剧场观看表演。然而,姬蒂并没有像他们预期的那样会大红大紫,因为"她的对手太多了,男装丽人太多了,这个行当原来和玩杂耍的一样具有专业性质,现在突然就成了个人满为患的行当。"[11]可见维多利亚时期演员成为女性在社会上谋生的重要职业选择之一,并且倾向于模仿男性的角色以获得更多关注。在沃尔特的鼓励之下,南希从原本姬蒂的服装师变成与姬蒂一同登台表演的演员:"双人组合!来个士兵,和他的伙伴!或者一个花花公子,和他的朋友!总之,两个可爱的女孩穿着裤子,比单个更强!你们什么时候看过这种演出?我们会引起轰动的!"[12]新颖的形式让她们的表演成为热门节目,大受欢迎,且掀起模仿热潮。南希和姬蒂放弃音乐厅生涯之后,选择到霍克思顿的不列颠剧院演童话剧《灰姑娘》的第一、第二男主角。有许多的女性都在剧院中谋生,如跳芭蕾舞的女孩、看管衣橱的女孩、饰演仙女和灰姑娘的女演员等均出现女性的身影。

正是因为女性在社会上有了更多的活动空间,女性群体的语言也体现出当时的时代特色。南希与弗罗伦丝重逢之后,由于弗罗伦丝参与到女性运动及慈善活动之中,因此她们与身边人的交流也常常涉及这些方面。弗罗伦丝家中经常有人来做客,常常涉及妇女自由联合会(Women's Liberal Federation)、妇女工会联盟(Women's Trade Union League)等与女性相关的组织。弗罗伦丝经常为改善底层妇女生活现状费尽心力:

> 另外,我并不觉得这件事没完没了。事情都是会变的。到处都有工会——有男人的工会,也有女人的工会。今天的女人做的事情,二十年前在她们的母亲看来就是笑话。她们甚至很快就要有选举权了!如果像我这样的人不去努力,那是因为他们把一切不公和肮脏都当作这个国家的堕落,并且习以为常。但是肮脏的土壤里会长出新的东西——新的工作制度,新的

人,新的活法,还有新的爱……[13]

弗罗伦丝的语言提到"女人的工会"、"选举权"、"新的工作制度"都是体现出当时小部分的女性群体努力争取女性权益,冲击男性主导的社会。女性之间的谈话不再仅仅停留在如何照顾好家庭成员,而是能寻找在社会中的位置。女性帮助残疾人、移民和孤女找工作、找房子等等,慈善组织进行家访、组织募捐。女性走出家庭聚集在一起,使社会意识到女性群体的需求。

女士俱乐部是当时女性休闲娱乐的隐蔽场所。弗罗伦丝称其为"享乐"。以下是弗罗伦丝第一次带南希到"船上的男孩"女士俱乐部的对话:

"那她们也像男人一样生活吗,这些女孩?"
"有些是吧,我想。大多数人想穿什么就穿什么,不在乎别人的眼光。
……
"如果我说我曾经以为自己是唯一一个这样的人,"我回答说,"你会不会觉得我很傻?"[14]

在维多利亚时期,女性群体处于社会边缘,受到社会的排斥。她们在繁华城市的隐蔽酒吧中汇集,享受属于她们的自由空间。她们可以随意地喝酒抽烟,拥抱情侣,穿上任何想穿的服装,不再生活在男性的目光和管控之中。南希"曾经以为自己是唯一一个这样的人",但是在此处寻找到了女性身份认同。

小说临近结尾处南希与拉夫尔共同完成的演讲将情节推向了高潮,还原了当时女性自行组织游行、演说活动的场景:

"我们想看到社会的大变革!我们想看到金钱被投入使用,而不是拿去产生利润!我们想看到工人的孩子们变得强壮,救济院被夷为平地,因为没有人再需要救济了!"
……
"你们必须行动。有工作的人——不论男女,都参加工会吧!有选举权的人,用上你们的选票!把你们自己的人选进议会。为女同胞们争取权利,为你们的姐妹、女儿和妻子——让她们拥有选票,来帮助你们!"[15]

拉尔夫在演讲中大胆地谈到了"社会的大变革"、"没有人再需要救济"的未来愿景,鼓励男女参加工会,有选举权的人"为女同胞们争取权利"。语言是社会文化现状的真实反映,维多利亚时期女性语言中出现诸多"社会主义"、"民主""集会""薪资"等词汇,正体现了女性群体在社会中现身与努力争取自己的权益的要求。女性积极投身慈善活动及女性运动是她们踏进社会十分重要的一步。她们逐渐涉足英国社会的各个方面,努力纠正社会弊病,在一定程度上缓和了维多利亚时期的社会矛盾。

3.《轻舔丝绒》中的女性亚文化风格"抵制与反抗"

亚文化是通过风格化的和另类的符号对主导文化进行挑战从而建立认同的附属性文化方式[16],如无赖青年(Teddy Boy)、嬉皮士(Hippie)、摩登派(Mods)、朋克(Punk)等。"风格"是亚文化最具有吸引力和可读性的特征,是亚文化的标志或符号[17]。根据菲尔·科恩(Phil Cohen)的概括,亚文化的风格主要由三种元素构成:形象、风度、行话。"形象"由服装以及发型、珠宝饰物和手工制品之类的配饰构成的外表;"风度"由表情、步法和身姿构成;"行话"是一套特殊的语汇以及它被传达的方式[18]。亚文化群体打破了日常符号系统的规则,以不同的文化作为原料,进行挪用、改换和拼贴,对主流文化进行解构,因而形成了具有独特风格的亚文化现象。在上一部分从服饰、场景及语言三大载体探讨了《轻舔丝绒》中女性亚文化的表现。女性亚文化在萌芽状态时是个人行为或狭小团体的自我愉悦和发泄,在社会上逐渐扩大规模并掠夺公众视线的过程中形成了女性亚文化风格,并对权威符码和社会制度带来一定的抵制与反抗。

首先就服饰而言,在维多利亚时期,衣服使个体变成了女人,在社会中看不到女性个体服装的真正自我,只能看到繁复、华丽、高度性别化的服饰。衣着不仅能够营造出一个性别化主体的假象,甚至能在身体上烙印上二元对立性别规范的痕迹[19]。英国主流社会女性服装的设计是创造完美的女性形象,大部分女性都会穿束腰胸衣(corset)、衬裙(petticoat)、裙撑(crinoline)等。这样的装扮也限制了女性的行动,身边需要男性的保护。《轻舔丝绒》中小部分的女性群体则尝试打破男性审美视角下女性服饰文化符号。南希和姬蒂能够穿戴男士服饰登台表演,演员女扮男装甚至成为维多利亚时期的热潮:"那些值得尊重的喜剧女演员都想改变戏路,穿上喇叭裤跳角笛舞"[20]。姬蒂在圣诞节赠送给南希深蓝色的晚装长裙,南希穿着却"眉头直皱",觉得是"一种伪装",像"一个穿着姐姐的舞会礼服耍戏的男孩"[21],但穿上禁卫军的制服感觉非常帅气。南希在弗罗伦丝家时"穿着裤子在家里做家务""穿着裤子走出了门"[22],被邻居们看到后也丝毫不介意。女士俱乐部中有很多女性都"穿着裤子和背心,剪了个像在监狱里一样短的头发"[23]。女性服饰随着女性在社会中的角色多样化而形成更加多元的女性亚文化服饰风格,颠覆原有的主流男性文化意义,形成女性自我的意指实践,冲破过去二元对立的服装性别差异。

其次是女性的活动场景也构成了独特的女性亚文化风格。维多利亚时代女性多被"囚禁"在社会权力之中。在那个时期家庭被赋予极高的象征意义和神圣地位,家庭生活的方方面面充斥着杂志、广告、手册和小说。"甜蜜的家"之观念的内涵中一个重要的观念是"家庭天使"(the angel in the house)观。"家庭天使"观认为女性应该柔弱、纯贞、善良、优雅,是家庭的天使[24]。因此"家庭天使"只能是装饰性的、被动的和依赖性的。《轻舔丝绒》中刻画了许多女性走出家庭束缚,以自己的方式建构起一种不同于传统的私人文化空间。南希"在十八岁以前,我从来没有怀疑过自己对牡蛎的感情,也从来没有离开父亲的厨房去寻找事业或者爱情。"[25]父母也是期盼她"嫁给一个惠特斯特布尔的男孩,就在他们身边成家"[26]但是南希后来为了追求爱情,勇敢摆脱家庭的安逸及束缚。南希在重返家庭之后与家人的各种矛盾正是体现了女性亚文化风格对传统家庭观念的抵抗。南希"觉得拘谨",闻到熟悉的鱼腥味却"吃了一惊"[27]。南希在为家人分发礼物时,父亲"笑声听起来却不那么自然",母亲"仿佛不敢去拿似的",屋里甚至"出现了一阵尴尬的踱步"[28]。姐姐甚至批评南希唱歌是"荡妇的生活"[19],并且评论姬蒂:"她做的事,没有一件是好的!她把你带走了,让你变得古怪了。我一点都不了解你了。我真希望你从来都没有跟她走,或者再也不要回来!"[30]探亲"开始就不顺利,随后也不太美妙","我越来越不明白自己为什么要回家了"[31]甚至在最后离开家的时候"母亲笑了笑,但是笑容生硬。艾丽斯到最后依然态度僵硬"[32]南希从开始哭泣想家到在家中一连串负面情绪的变化和不适应,可见女性从以家庭为主的活动场景挣脱出来,尝试对家庭权力关系进行解脱和违抗,走上独立和自由的道路,就难以融入原本传统的文化形态中。

相比起男性亚文化多出现在大街上,女性则多在私人领域中另辟文化空间,形成了独特的"卧室文化"及"俱乐部文化"的女性亚文化风格,对公众性的男性主导文化进行隐秘抵抗。"卧室文化"是女性在自己或朋友家的卧室里建构起来的、与女性伙伴分享生活体验的一种集体性文化。这种"女孩帮"式的集体性文化显示出安全、私密、排外等特征，散发着自我想象、彼此依赖的气息[33]。弗罗伦丝的家中经常有不同职业的女性聚集在一起，"她们经常来喝茶，带来书、小册子或者八卦"[34]，又或者是在客厅"召开紧急会议"，"进行无聊的辩论"[35]。工业化的快速发展拉大了社会贫富差距，许多底层平民失去了原本的住所，露宿街头。女性群体自发地成立民间慈善组织帮助有困难的群体，甚至在19世纪30—40年代形成了颇具影响的"家访运动"（Home Visiting Movement）[36]。"俱乐部文化"是女性在俱乐部休闲娱乐形成的女性亚文化风格，但是她们只能在城市的隐蔽空间中立足。卡文迪什女士俱乐部在"一栋狭窄的灰色建筑"中，楼梯很窄，名牌很小，门很窄，有"一位女士站在阴暗的门槛处"[37]。"船上的男孩"女士俱乐部在"路的尽头"，是个"低矮的建筑"[38]"从后面一个更小更黑的入口进去。一个坡度很陡的楼梯把我们带到地下"，[39]女性能够在其中谈论男性话题，找寻属于女性的自主意识。女孩们赢得了属于自己的时间和活动空间，建构起了不同于男孩的休闲和个人空间，也为她们提供了不同的"抗拒"自己处境的可能性。

最后是女性的语言也体现了女性亚文化风格。在男权秩序控制下的世界，无论是在政治、经济还是文化空间中，男性始终占有主导地位。19世纪末20世纪初的第一次女性主义政治运动在一定程度上解放了女性，为女性争取公民权、参政权等政治权利。女性书籍和杂志是女性得以发声的重要宣传途径，是女性亚文化风格抵抗男性统治阶级的力量。戴安娜为慈善机构捐钱出力，参与制作一本名为《箭矢》的女性参政杂志，其中内容涵盖了女性参政、女性教育等革新性观点，宣传英国女权运动。弗罗伦丝家中出现了杂志《正义》及书籍《走向民主》，文字颇具革命色彩。小说中引用了美国诗人沃尔特·惠特曼（Walt Whitman，1819—1892）《草叶集》（*Leaves of Grass*，1855）中的内容："忘掉差异吧！犯下的美德一样多的罪孽！让职业和性别平等！让所有达成一致！"[40]男性作家为女性发声，作家笔下的世界正是对真实社会现状的反映。惠特曼写到的"差异""罪孽"无不是对男女地位不平等的控诉，呼吁社会"平等"及"一致"。女性借助传播媒介在女性群体中迅速地传播、扩散，在消解和颠覆主流文化符号、抵抗主流意识形态。除了女性书籍和杂志之外，女性日常生活谈论的话题不再仅仅停留在家庭琐事，而是更多地加入了女性的个人想法，谈论社会问题、工作状况、未来愿景等等。相比于当时大部分底层女性对于是否参会抱有犹豫的态度,以丈夫的意见取代自己的想法:"我丈夫不想让我去,并非因为他自己不是工会成员,而是他觉得女人对这种事没有什么发言权。他觉得没必要。"[41]而弗罗伦丝对于自己所做的工作不论多么艰辛,始终都在坚持:"我怎么能休息呢,这个世界是如此残酷而艰难,却可以变得美好……我做的事情本身就是一种满足,不管能不能成功","想想这个世界会变成什么样!到时候就是一个新的世纪了。"[42]弗罗伦丝和南希以她们特有的方式表达女性在男性主导社会下的艰辛和危机,是对社会女性现状进行批判和抵抗的一种文化类型。

因此,女性亚文化风格的形成不是空穴来风,而是对现有的物品、服饰、音乐、语言等文化符号进行拼贴、挪用后形成的新的意义。迪克·赫伯迪格的著作《亚文化:风格的意义》(*Subculture: The Meaning of Style*, 1979)一书正是对不同群体亚文化风格抵抗的研究。亚文化的"抵抗"采取的不是激烈和极端的方式,而是较为温和的"协商",最后都无法摆脱被收编的命运。从对抗到缓和,从抵抗到收编,这样的过程构成了每一个接踵而来的亚文化的周期[43]。亚文化被整合到占统治地位的社会秩序中去主要靠两种途径。第一种途径是通过"亚文化符号(服饰、音乐等)转化为大量生产的物品"的商品形式来实现整合;第二种途径则是由"统治集团"(如警察、媒介、司法系统)对越轨行为进行"贴标签"和"重新界定",从而实现意识形态的整合过程[44]。女性亚文化风格在主流文化的收编过程中以新的形式保留下来,使得第二次女性主义政治运动从最初以亚文化形式出现,到后来这种文化价值观则被主流文化认同和吸纳。

4. 结语

20世纪70—80年代,西方文学界尤其是英国涌现了一大批以维多利亚时期为背景的小说,这些小说被统称为"新维多利亚小说"(neo-Victorian novels)。目前学界一般认为"新维多利亚小说"始于20世纪60年代简·里斯(Jean Rhys, 1890—1979)的《藻海无边》(*Wide Sargasso Sea*, 1996)和约翰·罗伯特·福尔斯(John Robert Fowles, 1926—2005)的《法国中尉的女人》(*The French Lieutenant's Woman*, 1969)两部作品。萨拉·沃特斯也是其中重要代表之一。沃特斯将历史与虚构、真实与想象糅合在一起,呈现维多利亚文学史中被边缘化的女性,比如女同性恋者、女囚犯、女欺诈犯、女变装演员等。通过当代女性知识分子的视角对维多利亚时代的历史进行重构,颠覆了那个时代女性娇弱、拘谨、压抑的刻板形象,消解了由男性话语所建构的所谓历史"真相"。

然而,受维多利亚时代大环境的影响,女性生存空间毕竟有限,社会主流文化对于女性自我身份的建构依旧是以男性为标准。西蒙娜·德·波伏娃(Simone de Beauvoir,1908—1986)的著作《第二性》(The Second Sex,1949)中曾提道:"定义和区分女人的参照物是男人,而定义和区分男人的参照物却不是女人。她是附属的人,是同主要者(the essential)相对立的次要者(the inessential)。他是主体(the Subject),是绝对(the Absolute),而她则是他者(the Other)。"[45]因而在沃特斯"维多利亚三部曲"的结局中,女性经历了觉醒之后,尝试冲破身份禁锢,但最终还是被安排回归到边缘化的地位。《轻舔丝绒》中南希和弗罗伦丝只能在工人阶级女同性恋群体内部得到认同;《半身》中多丝和薇格离开伦敦,远走他乡,而拜尔只能投入滚滚的泰晤士河结束自己的生命;《荆棘之城》中苏珊和莫德远离尘世,隐居荆棘山庄。这些带着逃离意味的结局,既是维多利亚时代处于边缘的女性群体在追求自我的残酷现实之间所做的妥协,也是作者在现代和历史之间所做的平衡。因此,女性亚文化在不断融入社会主流文化的过程中受到重重阻隔。伯明翰学派对于女性主义的进入所抱有的始终是"不合作"的态度。主要代表人物斯图亚特·霍尔回顾伯明翰文化研究历程时还是对女性主义介入文化研究持相当大的敌视态度:"它就像一个贼在夜晚破门而入,扰乱安宁,制造了不适宜的噪声,伺机在文化研究的桌上胡闹。"[46]女性亚文化在历史进程中发展曲折,但其在社会生活发挥的积极和消极作用也是一体两面的存在,是解构和适应男性主流文化的一把双刃剑。在一个动态的、变迁的社会中,主文化与亚文化之间可能会相互转化[47]。女性亚文化是人类社会文化结构中不可或缺的组成部分,与处于社会主导地位的文化形态共存于同一个文化体系中。主流文化是对整个社会价值系统的集聚,因而也对女性亚文化因素加以吸纳。与此同时,女性亚文化在保持了自身的特殊性的基础上,又在补充了主流文化的建构。在各种各样的亚文化形态中,虽然存在着消极的甚至危险的文化成分,但同时也存在着积极的、富有创造性的文化成分,正是后者会成为一股驱使主导文化不断调整自身、改变自身的力量,是一股优化社会总体文化结构的力量。因此女性亚文化研究对于父权制为主导的文化研究具有极大的补充和深刻的启发意义。

实际上,如何看待亚文化在社会中的地位和作用,与一个社会的包容度有很大的关系。一个宽容的社会把亚文化看作是社会的"选择性文化"(alternative culture),纳入社会的多样选择中[48]。丰富多样的亚文化在冲击既定文化的一元格局、调整价值系统和推动文化的总体变迁上具有重要的意义。研究女性亚文化的发展,正是为了能更加关注当代女性群体的生活状态,更加关注女性亚文化对主流文化的补充及影响。维多利亚时代女性亚文化处在被男权社会审查、监视的位置,女性冲破牢笼的行为显示出女性在这样一个传统道德与现代文明相交织的时代的反抗力量,因此这一时代是维多利亚女性向现代女性迈进的曙光。

新维多利亚小说并不是怀旧或者是倒退的,它们是一场过去、现在与未来的对话,有选择性地构建了被遗忘和忽略的那部分历史及群体。曾被边缘化的女性角色有了自己的"声音",她们在逆境中掌握自己的命运。作者以当代的理论认识为基础对历史进行再现,从而赋予了作品鲜明的时代意义。重返过去是为了反思现在,明白当下女性建构自我认同及在社会中不断受到重视所经历的曲折,女性在未来也将继续为个人价值及社会定位不断做出新的努力。

参考文献

[1] CHUDACOFF, HOWARD P. The Age of the Bachelor: Creating an American Subculture [M]. Princeton: Princeton University Press, 1999.

[2] 约翰·费斯克,等.关键概念:传播与文化研究辞典[M].第二版.李彬,译.北京:新华出版社,2003.

[3] 安吉拉·默克罗比.女性主义与青年文化[M].张岩冰,彭薇,译.郑州:河南大学出版社,2011.

[4] 石丽薇.安吉拉·麦克罗比的"女性亚文化思想"研究[D].河北大学,2015.

[5] 罗兰·巴特.流行体系——符号学与服饰符码[M].敖军,译.上海:上海世纪出版集团,2000.

[6] 萨拉·沃特斯.轻舔丝绒[M].陈萱,译.上海:上海人民出版社,2017.

[7] 胡疆锋.伯明翰学派青年亚文化理论的生成语境[J].青年研究,2007(12):14-20.

[8] 和磊.伯明翰学派——文化研究的源流与方法[M].北京:北京大学出版社,2016.

[9] 迈克尔·布雷克.青年文化比较:青年文化社会学及美国、英国和加拿大的青年亚文化[M].孟登迎,宓瑞新,译.北京:中国青年出版社,2017.

[10] 孙梦天.萨拉·沃特斯的《灵契》和《轻舔丝绒》中的性别表演[J].广西师范大学学报(哲

学社会科学版),2017,53(2):102-108.

[11] 李宝芳.维多利亚时期英国中产阶级婚姻家庭生活研究[M].北京:社会科学文献出版社,2015.

[12] 郝明然.维多利亚时期英国慈善组织的特征[J].内蒙古农业大学学报(社会科学版),2009,11(2):331-333.

[13] 迪克·赫伯迪格.亚文化:风格的意义[M].陆道夫,胡疆锋,译.北京:北京大学出版社.2009.

[14] 西蒙娜·德·波伏娃.第二性[M].陶铁柱,译,北京:中国书籍出版社,1998.

[15] HALL STUART. Critical Dialogues in Cultural Studies[M]//Brunsdon, Charlotte, A Thief in The Night Stories in the Feminism in the 1970s at CCCS. London:Routledge, 1996.

[16] 黄瑞玲.当代西方亚文化的基本特征和发展趋势[J].理论视野,2014(8):49-55.

点评

论文基于伯明翰学派的亚文化理论,以小说《轻舔丝绒》为文本,基于当代的理论认识再现历史,分析维多利亚时代女性亚文化在社会生活中的体现,关注女性亚文化对主流文化的补充及影响。研究认为丰富多样的亚文化在冲击既定文化的一元格局、调整价值系统和推动文化的总体变迁方面具有重要的意义。论文主题明确,结构合理,行文格式基本规范。建议将结论进一步与现实社会结合,增强理论和现实意义。

山本鼎的"自由画"美术教育运动及其儿童个性观[①]

邢广伟[*]

摘要：在日本美术教育中，促进学生自我表现是一个重要内容，20世纪之前，日本的美术教育是以临画为主的教学模式，限制了学生个性的发展。在20世纪初山本鼎为此提出了自由画运动，该运动为当时的美术教育提出新的观点，使日本美术教育观发生转向。研究以山本鼎的个性观念为中心，分析当时日本美术教育儿童个性观的形成过程。

关键字：山本鼎；自由画；创造；个性

山本鼎（1882—1946，图1 山本鼎自画像）是日本大正年间最重要的美术教育家，他提倡的自由画运动扭转了日本美术教育的动向，为日本美术教育界注入了新教育思想，使教育者及教育界开始注重学生个性的发展。自由画运动彻底批判了过去以"临画"为中心的图画教育，提倡重视儿童个性的图画教育，这是日本美术教育史上第一次尝试以儿童为中心的教育视角。从大正七八年（1918—1919）时期的教育背景思考图画教育受到"新教育"[②]的影响，以儿童为中心的图画教育通过"自由画"的形式受到了教育现场老师们的认可。之前的图画教育是正

图1 山本鼎自画像

---

[*] 邢广伟：杭州师范大学美术学院2018级硕士研究生。
[①] 原载《当代美术家》2020年第4期，本书收录时略有修改。
[②] 新教育注重儿童自发性的自我活动和与社会相协的实践教育。

确的临摹、作画能力和美感的培养,尤其注重临摹和作画的能力,这是与日本富国强兵的近代教育政策相联系的,所以教师注重培养学生对实际生活有用的画法。山本提倡的自由画运动,主要内容是通过写生的教育方式,培养学生对事物的认识,让学生可以自由地进行创造。这种教育方式有益于学生个性的发展,因此成为反对"临画"教育的有力手段。自由画教育看似只是图画教育方法的改变,其实质是日本美术教育观念的改变,尤其是让教育者认识到学生个性发展的重要性。为此,笔者将从以下几个方面论述自由画运动,分析该运动背后个性观念的形成过程。

1. 自由画运动概述

大正时期(1912—1926),随着第一次世界大战后世界范围内的民主运动的高涨,从欧美输入的推崇个性和创造性的以儿童为中心的自由教育思想,自然给日本教育界很大的震动,出现了稻毛金七的《创造教育论》、手塚岸卫的《自由教育论》以及片上伸的《文艺教育论》等教育著作[1]。这些学者都很重视培养儿童的个性和陶冶情操的艺术教育。在这样的历史背景下,日本掀起了改造教育运动,并由此引发了自由画教育运动。

在自由画运动开始以前,《新定画帖》等教科书已经出版,该教材在课程中已适当地安排了写生画、记忆画和艺术创作等不同绘画形式,实际上图画教育仍然是临摹画谱的模式,距离"培养审美感受"的大纲要求有一定的差距,因此,自由画运动从一开始就反对使用教科书《新定画帖》的图画教育。自由画教育运动的领导者——山本鼎,在东京美术学校的西洋画科毕业后,明治四十五年(1912)五月去往法国留学,大正五年(1916)六月途经莫斯科回国时,他被当地苏联农民和儿童美术展览所吸引。回到日本后,就发起了农民美术运动,担任生产与艺术相结合的工艺美术指导者,并乘势开始着手改革因临画教育而畸形的儿童画创作。大正七年(1918)十二月他在长野县的神川小学发表以《自由画的奖励》为题的演讲,翌年四月在该校举办了第一届"儿童自由画展览会",引起了全国性的反响[2]。同年八月以这个运动为中心设立了"日本儿童自由画协会",创立协会的有山本鼎、片上伸、岸边福雄、长原孝太郎等8名成员。翌年协会更名为"日本自由协会",成员增加(北原白秋、弘田龙太郎、足立源一郎、山崎省三、北原铁雄等)到18名。大正十年(1921)一月开始,由"日本自由协会"创办的《艺术自由教育》期刊发布，这本期刊成为连接自由画运动指导者与现场教学的桥梁，但因资金困难，第10期停刊。

随着自由画运动的发展，许多人对山本鼎的自由画教育论提出了反对意见。虽然自由画协会的成员较多，但面对反对之声，几乎无人回应，只有山本鼎对这些反对意见作出回应。山本倾尽全力推动运动的发展，但该运动并未出现继承人，于是山本在昭和三年（1928）宣布终止自由画运动。虽然自由画运动结束，但是以学生为中心，注重学生个性发展的教育却已悄然生根。

以上内容概述了自由画运动的过程，该运动主要是对"临画"教学模式的批判。山本从法国回国时途经莫斯科，被当地举办的"儿童创造展览会"①所吸引，通过此展览山本坚定了对日本美术教育改革的信念。加上当时"新教育"的影响，加快了山本改革美术教育的步伐。随着运动的发展，山本鼎的美术教育观念开始传播，对诸多美术教育者产生影响，从而推动了日本美术教育理念的发展。

2. 自由画的要点——个性

由于山本受到新教育思想的影响，他对当时的图画教育进行反思，并提出了若干问题，例如：如何教、教的内容以及如何指导学生等，其根本目的还是为了改变当时图画教育模式限制学生个性发展的问题。为此山本提出自由画运动，以相对自由的"写生"绘画形式，解除临本对学生的限制，从而促进了学生个性的发展。

首先，笔者从自由画不言而喻的关键词"自由"来看山本对"个性"的定位。关于"自由"一词，山本的著作《自由画教育》中有以下记述：

"自由画という言葉を選んだのは、不自由画の存在に対照しての事である。云ふまでもなく不自由画とは、模写を成績とする画の事であって、臨本——扮本——師伝等によって個性の表現が塞がれてしまふ其不自由さを救はうとして案ぜられたものである。"[2]

---

① "儿童创造展览会"是山本鼎对莫斯科儿童画展览的称谓，从展览的名称可知：重视儿童创造表现，山本同样也是通过创造的形式彰显学生个性，这表明山本受到此展的影响。此展览可能受到"巡回展览画派"的"将艺术带给所有人"的影响，让乡间的人们有机会看到俄罗斯艺术的成就，教百姓如何欣赏艺术，从小就培养儿童艺术的表现。

山本在此所论的"自由"是个性表现的自由。笔者以图示(图2)的方式对此进行分析。山本之所以选用"自由"一词,是对当时图画教学环境不自由实况的反映,导致不自由的原因主要是《新定画帖》的使用,《新定画帖》是以临画为主的图画教育范本,教师进行图画教学时主要以此书的内容为范例,这就使图画教育过于死板、教学空间缩小,因此学生无法进行主观创造。山本鼎为改变此种状况,选择"自由"一词显得更加适切,山本所言的自由就是以自然为师进行自主性的创造,即写生。山本言明:"自然是独一无二的范本。"[2]学生通过自主性的选择,描绘真实所见之物,表现出学生各自的自然观。山本就是通过这种方式,逐步解除限制学生个性发展的不利因素。自由代替不自由,创造代替摹写时"自由"背后的隐性关键词"个性"才得以显示。对于山本而言,"自由"是"从","个性"是"主",个性依附自由创造的方式突显而出。

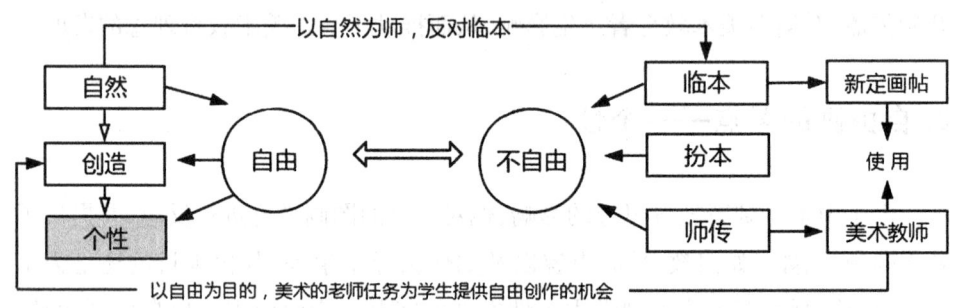

图2　山本鼎论自由画教育

其次,笔者从通过发挥个性的绘画方式——写生,来考察山本是如何引导学生自由创造的,即如何引导学生彰显个性。笔者通过对山本鼎所著的《自由画教育》总结得出(如图3):进行图画教育是为了让学生个性得到发展,其主要方式就是自由的创造。"写生"作为自由画教育的主要形式,被诸多教师运用到图画教育中,通过"写生"的形式鼓励学生勇敢的创作,实则是为培养学生在创作中各抒己见,彰显自己的个性。山本所言的写生画同时包含记忆、想象画——即儿童不依靠临本而直接表现的自由画[2]。学生通过自主性选择,积极调动自己的感官获取所要描绘的形象,自然而然地流露出真情实感,与临画相比较,这是写生画最大的优势,能改变临画教育造就的千篇一律。从山本教授的一个自由画案例来看,学生想绘出餐桌上的茶碗却无从下笔,山本启发学生就依你所见进行描画,并提示学生注重浓淡的变化。山本给予学生极大的自由空间,表现的内容、表现的主体都是自由的。在这个意义上,自由画并不只是表现形式,也是表现精神的东西,即使同一表现内容,自由之人的感受不同表现也就不同。山本又说"图画教育的使命必须有鉴赏教育"[2],所以通过写生知其物,也就同时进行了鉴赏,使创造力、个性表现与鉴赏三位一体,描绘的美同时也有潜移默化的作用。自由画教育用简洁语言概括为:"不以模写为成绩而以创造为成绩。"[2]自由画之前的教授方式,老师通过学生临摹作品的像与不像给予评定,而山本提倡的自由画是集智慧、知识、经验、印象与感觉为一体的创造性绘画,极有利于学生个性的发展,能全方位的评价学生。

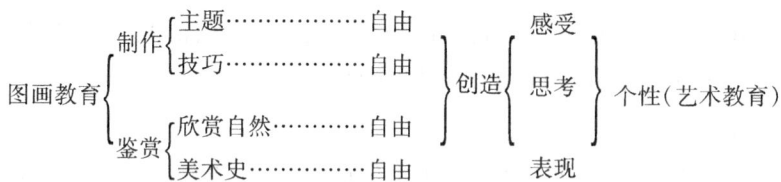

图3 山本鼎论图画教育的使命

最后,山本所提倡的"个性"具体是指什么呢?笔者虽阅读了山本多处以"个性"为中心的论述,令人意外的是直接触及个性具体形象的言论少之又少,从中读取"个性"的定义也不明确。但笔者还是通过山本鼎关于"个性"相关的几处言论"……全国数百万儿童的,有魅力的创造力"[2]"对太阳下的现象、空气、各种不同的物象、形态的个性等的表现欲……"[3]判断提取出一个观点:山本所言的个性不仅包括人文属性,还具有某种"神秘色彩"。山本认为个性具有普遍性,是全国数百万儿童都具有的品质,在普遍性中"个性"也有差异性——每个人对同一事物的认识有所不同。所以在图画教育中教师的任务更多的是为学生提供自由创造的机会,培养学生创造的精神。同时山本受到19世纪末西方印象派画家的影响:个性地描摹自然,以真实感受为主导,合理的纯粹的方式画出形与色。山本认为这是发挥个性的有效途径,合理的、纯粹的(儿童自己的表现手法)表现方式更加突出儿童绘画的稚朴,这种稚朴便是儿童绘画最有魅力的表现方式,也是山本个性观念的"神秘色彩"。

综上所述,笔者认为山本鼎通过自由画运动,提出了注重儿童"个性"发展的观念。虽然山本没有直接言明个性的含义,但不难看出山本将"个性"注入自由画教育中,这也就表明自由画不只是作为反对"临画"教育的绘画形式,而且也将自由画作为绘画的精神来提倡。以自由为名,培养学生创造的精神,引导学生个性的发展,这使得日本美术教育风向发生转变,从教师本位逐渐转为学生本位。

3. 个性观念的延续

"自由画"不只局限于绘画实践、造型表现的部分,同时也贯彻了美术教育的精神,写生画和记忆画都只不过是其中的一种绘画形式。因此,不应该只从单方面理解"自由画",而应从整体上分析自由画运动,为此,笔者有必要分析众多教师的自由画教育实践,还应分析自由画反对者和参加者的意见,正确的统筹关于自由画教育的意见,从不同角度解读"个性"观念。

3.1 自由画运动的参与者

自由画运动,始于大正八年(1919),不足10年,山本鼎就宣布自由画运动破产。在此期间,美术教育界受到山本鼎教育思想的影响,不少教育者投身于自由画教育的实践中去。自由画运动开始的第二年(1920),自由画教育的实践者堀孝雄撰写了《儿童自由画及其处理》一书,从堀氏对自由画的观点及著书时间来看,堀氏对自由画教育的思想非常接近山本。堀氏认为自由画运动是促进教育改革的一大警钟,是对计划性、机械性、形式性、灌输式教育弊端的改革。他宣称自由画是"儿童通过自身观察、记忆、想象,不拘泥于大人所教授形式,赤裸裸地按自己意愿将形状和颜色描绘出来的绘画"[4],又言"自由画是图画科的一部分,那并不是全部"[4]。堀氏认为自由画教育与全体教育有关,是以儿童为中心的新图画教育,与山本的教育思想非常接近。堀氏对自由画运动给予肯定,并积极实践,该书也刊登了他指导的儿童绘画作品。从照片看,和山本《自由画教育》登载的作品并无太多不同,只是,从作品过于整齐来看,具有指导的成分。这表明堀氏进行自由画实践时,缺少引导的成分,不过也逐渐脱离了之前的图画教育模式。

随着运动的开展,丸山克彦可谓是山本自由画学说的忠实信徒。丸山通过实践指出自由画教育中存在的问题,于昭和四年(1929)在《信浓教育》发表《自由画指导的反省》。山本虽然在自由学园中轻松地教授学生(图4),但是未将自由画指导具体化,所以令其教育现场混乱,对学生的指导全凭教师现场摸索,为此丸山提出:"为了正确的指导自由画,必须让儿童凝视自然、读取自然,即不仅

图 4　图画课堂

是让儿童自然地去面对眼前物体,而且还必须指导儿童'解体''构成'对象。另外,必须注意自然界中的'永久性法则'即'本来的美'。"[5]山本提出的自由画是儿童按照自己的意愿、表现形式进行写生,并无太多指导。但是,仅仅只让儿童面对静物或是风景,不给予指导,是无法正确引导学生的,站在教育的角度,必须让学生一步一步地走向较高水平。从主张向自然学习的自由画教育的观点来看,笔者认为丸山对于自由画教育的反省是正确的,必须让学生正确地认识自然,且给予学生相应的指导,丸山也为解决自由画无具体指导法做出了贡献。这也进一步证明学习指导纲领存在的正确性,同时也反映出山本未将自由画指导法成文,这也成为加速自由画运动破产的影响因素之一。

与承认自由画教育并积极实践的教育家相比,未进行自由画实践的木村庄八关于个性的观点与山本的观点有相同之处,但未着重强调学生个性的发展。木村庄八与山本鼎同为春阳会①的成员,木村在《艺术自由教育》期刊上刊登了《关于少年的教育》,其论述显示了与山本思想的不同之处。"其实我不认可孩子的'个性',即使承认也不认为是第一要义""我认为发挥个性的教

---

①　春阳会:与院展的日本画部对立,以西洋画为中心,作品具有东洋画风的手法和构思,没有特定的主张,多为前卫作品。

育不适合一般的教育。"[6]在此可以看出木村对"个性"的态度,木村勉强承认个性的观念,但他认为在图画教育中最重要的不是培养学生个性,而是培养学生的实用能力。注重学生个性的教育并不适用于普通教育,以木村的角度并无任何错误,因山本并未将自由画指导法具体化,对自由画具体的指导都需依靠现场教师的摸索,这对于学校教育而言确实不适合。但这两点都可表明木村思想的局限性,所持的"个性"观念不够彻底,只是就当前教育局面小心翼翼地向前摸索。

自由画运动的参与者,并不只有以上论述的几位,该运动影响范围广泛,积极参与该运动的教育人员极多,总体而言,他们都持有尊重儿童个性发展的观点,对之前"临画"教育模式有所反思,希望通过自由画教育运动转变教育模式。山本为美术教育界注入了新的教育思想,其"个性"观念的提出推动了日本美术教育的发展,但是也有些教育人员反对自由画运动,笔者接下来将对自由画运动的反对者进行论述。

3.2　自由画运动的反对者

《自由画教育》中有一个论题为《反对者》,是山本反驳反对自由画教育的论述。下面引用对白浜徵的反驳:

> 白浜先生,我对你所言的"儿童从不受其他的束缚,天真烂漫地画就是发挥个性,是一件很了不起的事情"感到异样。要说为何,因我感觉你是一个既需临本也需范画,束缚学生个性表现的人。儿童个性的成长更需要自由还是规范呢?[2]

山本反驳白浜的要点在于:规范会限制个性的成长。自由画运动的出发点是废除临本,即对《新定画帖》的废除。《新定画帖》自1910年开始发行,直至1932年发行《小学图画》为止,大约持续了22年,山本鼎开始提倡自由画教育运动是在1919年,是该教科书出版的第9年,《新定画帖》是由正木直彦、小山正太郎、白浜徵、阿部七五三吉等5人编著而成。因为这一缘故,山本鼎才将白浜徵视为束缚学生个性表现的教育者。当时白浜徵考察欧美图画教育后,将其与日本的图画教育相较后称:"当然,外国图画教授时也在使用范本,但那只是作为参考,其实际上描绘的是所见之物"[7],这一点表明,白浜先生在接受欧美图画教育的基础上也相对赞成以范本为辅助的写生画教育,尽管如此,当时在日本,把《新定画帖》当作临本的教师占很大比例,所以《新定画帖》也就成为限制学生个性发展的范本。因此,山本将《新定画帖》等同于规范,这也表明自由画运动的缺陷,只提出废除表面性的规范,并未进一步深入追究导致规范产生的原因是什么。

另一位在《反对者》中被山本指名的石川寅治言:"必须广泛研究艺术画作、诸大家的画风,但不能无视自己的个性,也能在其中不断成长,大放光彩。"[2]石川虽主张向范画学习,但没有否定自身的个性。山本对此认为这是培养专业美术家的教育,并不适合普通小学的图画教育,这表明山本的观点具有远瞻性,这种问题在现代美术教育中依然存在。另外,还有未对山本本人提出反对意见,但对自由画教育持批判态度的仲川明认为,应该尊重儿童的个性、自发性,就教材选择而言不能自由(对教材的使用有一定的执念)[8]。

笔者从两个维度剖析了山本所提倡的"个性"观念。参与自由画运动和与山本观点相似的教育家非常注重学生个性的发展,无论是在理论,还是实践中都积极探索自由画教育如何更好为学生服务。最大的问题是教师在自由画实践时,因无具体的指导法,花费太多时间摸索,成效不显著,反而限制了自由画运动的发展,不过好在山本的个性观念被延续。而对自由画持反对观点的教育家,也有不少不否定个性价值的论述,但是反对者的个性观念对山本起了负面影响,这种含糊不清的承认个性观念,导致了山本对自己提倡的个性观念产生动摇,不过可以明显地表明注重学生个性发展的观点已经被时代所承认。

综上所述,山本顺应时代的发展发起自由画运动,把个性的培养带入美术教育的领域,以自由画的形式反对临画的教授法,将矛头直接指向限制个性发展的主要问题,在当时教育史上这可谓有力的举措。同时也影响了其他美术教育者,例如横井曹一就是受到自由画运动的影响,确立了自己的图画教育理论;还有创造美育协会也受到了山本民主主义思想的影响。另外,箕田源二郎虽然对创造美育协会提出批判,但他却极其注重对学生个性的培养。从而可以看出培养学生个性表现在美术教育领域中已经得到认可,也为后来的美术教育打下根基,这不仅仅是美术教育界的转变,整个教育界也已悄然发生转变。

4. 总结

笔者通过对自由画运动的论述,以探讨日本美术教育儿童个性观的形成过程。在山本提出自由画运动之前，日本教育界已有论述个性的苗头，加之山本留学时所受到的影响，这促使山本进行了图画教育的改革，以"自由画"的形式，将"个性"观念渗入图画教育。随着自由画运动的普及，既有积极的参与者也有反对者，但是两者都承认"个性"本身的价值，其中，有些反对者只认为自由画是一种绘画形式，不承认自由画运动的精神，出现这种观点是因为反对者未能对自由画运动进行全面的理解。山本将美术教育的精神寄托在"自由画"上，希望通过这种形式改变当时的图画教育，并且折射到大的教育环境中。该运动最大的功绩就是使图画教育不再是单纯学习绘画技术的过程，而是将图画教育重新定位为美术表现活动，使注重个性发展的观念在美术教育中生根。教育模式改变的同时，儿童绘画作品的地位也发生了改变，之前作为"未开化"人的绘画，只因是单纯的模仿，所以被断定为无价值而被忽视，现在作为独立的儿童绘画作品，赋予了儿童自身的个性而得到了关注。因为自由画运动，日本美术教育才有了转向，并且越来越注重儿童个性的教育。

参考文献

[1] 张小鹭.现代美术教育理论与教学法——中日美术教学方法的综合比较[M].厦门：厦门大学出版社,1996：109.

[2] 山本鼎.自由画教育[M].名古屋：黎明书房,1982：161.

[3] 山本鼎.农民美术と私[J].中央公论,1920(8)：46－63.

[4] 堀孝雄.儿童の自由画と其取扱[M].东京：目黑书店,1920：8.

[5] 丸山克彦.自由画指导の反省[J].信浓教育,1929(511)：7－15.

[6] 木村庄八.少年の教育に就て[J].艺术自由教育,1921(4)：11.

[7] 白浜徵.新定画帖解说[M].东京：大日本图书,1916：46.

[8] 仲川明.自由画の教育の价值[J].教育时论,1920(1279)：12.

点评

论文通过对自由画运动的论述探讨日本美术教育儿童个性观的形成过程，认为自由画运动最大的功绩是使图画教育不再单纯聚焦绘画技术，而是将图画教育重新定位为美术表现活动,注重美术教育中的个性发展,指出虽然自由画运动已经终止,但注重儿童个性的教育越来越重要。论文视角新颖,观点清晰,写作层次分明,语言流畅,格式基本符合规范。研究结论有一定的实践价值,可以为今后教育的发展提供新的思考。